University of Hertfordshire

Learning and Information Services
Watford Campus Learning Resources Centre
Aldenham Watford Herts WD2 8AT
Renewals: Tel 01707 284673 Mon-Fri 12 noon-8pm only

This book is in heavy demand and is due back strictly by the last date stamped below. A fine will be charged for the late return of items.

ONE WEEK LOAN

This volume deals with the crisis in the representation of the monarchy that was provoked by the execution of Charles I, the three hundred and fiftieth anniversary of which falls in 1999. It looks at both sympathetic and hostile representations of Charles I, and addresses not only the period of mid-century crisis but also the earlier years of his reign and the afterlife of his royal image. Besides courtly and popular literary representations, it examines Charles's visual image in paintings, sculpture, engravings and coins, and considers the role of the King's Music in projecting a positive view of the monarch. The volume will appeal not only to literary scholars but also to historians, art historians and musicologists.

The

Royal Image

Representations of
Charles I

The

Royal Image

Representations of
Charles I

edited by

Thomas N. Corns

Department of English
University of Wales, Bangor

CAMBRIDGE
UNIVERSITY PRESS

PUBLISHED BY THE PRESS SYNDICATE OF THE UNIVERSITY OF CAMBRIDGE

The Pitt Building, Trumpington Street, Cambridge CB2 1RP, United Kingdom

CAMBRIDGE UNIVERSITY PRESS

The Edinburgh Building, Cambridge CB2 2RU, UK http://www.cup.cam.ac.uk
40 West 20th Street, New York, NY 10011–4211, USA http://www.cup.org
10 Stamford Road, Oakleigh, Melbourne 3166, Australia

First published 1999

Printed in the United Kingdom at the University Press, Cambridge

Typeset in Dante (MT) 11.75/14.5pt, in QuarkXPress™ [SE]

A catalogue record for this book is available from the British Library

Library of Congress cataloguing in publication data

The royal image: representations of Charles I / edited by
Thomas N. Corns.
p.   cm.
Includes index.
1. Great Britain – history – Charles I, 1625–1649 – historiography.
2. English literature – early modern, 1500–1700 – history and
criticism.   3. Monarchy – Great Britain – history – Seventeenth century –
historiography.   4. Monarchy – Great Britain – public opinion –
history – Seventeenth century.   5. Charles I, King of England, 1600–1649 –
public opinion.   6. Charles I, King of England, 1600–1649 – in
literature.   7. Charles I, King of England, 1600–1649 – in art.
8. Kings and rulers in literature.   9. Kings and rulers in art.
I. Corns, Thomas N.
DA395.R69   1999   941.06′2–dc21   98-38093   CIP

ISBN 0 521 59047 7 hardback

Contents

List of illustrations [ix]   List of contributors [xii]   Preface [xv]

I
Duke, prince and king
THOMAS N. CORNS
[1]

2
'A ball of strife': Caroline poetry and royal marriage
ANN BAYNES COIRO
[26]

3
Popular representations of Charles I
JOAD RAYMOND
[47]

4
'Incendiaries of the state': Charles I and tyranny
MARTIN DZELZAINIS
[74]

5
The king among the radicals
DAVID LOEWENSTEIN
[96]

6
Eikon Basilike and the rhetoric of self-representation
ELIZABETH SKERPAN WHEELER
[122]

vii

7

Milton and King Charles

SHARON ACHINSTEIN

[141]

8

The King's Music

JONATHAN P. WAINWRIGHT

[162]

9

The visual image of Charles I

JOHN PEACOCK

[176]

10

The royal martyr in the Restoration

LOIS POTTER

[240]

11

Reviving the martyr king: Charles I as Jacobite icon

LAURA LUNGER KNOPPERS

[263]

12

The royal image: an afterword

KEVIN SHARPE

[288]

Index [310]

Illustrations

6.1 William Marshall, frontispiece to *Eikon Basilike*, 1649 (c59a24). By permission of the British Library [123]

9.1 Nicolas Briot, silver crown of Charles I, 1631–1632. By permission of the National Museum of Wales [181]

9.2 Shrewsbury mint, silver twenty shillings of Charles I, 1642. By permission of the National Museum of Wales [184]

9.3 Bristol mint, gold twenty shillings of Charles I, 1645. By permission of the National Museum of Wales [185]

9.4 Thomas Simon (attributed), crown of Charles I, *c.* 1646. Copyright British Museum [186]

9.5 Marriage of Charles I and Henrietta Maria medal, 1625. Copyright British Museum [189]

9.6 Medal to commemorate the meeting of the King and Queen at Kineton, 1643. Copyright British Museum [190]

9.7 Nicolas Briot, Dominion of the Seas medal, 1630. Copyright British Museum [191]

9.8 Nicolas Briot, Return to London medal, 1633. Copyright British Museum [193]

9.9 Thomas Rawlins, Declaration of Parliament medal, 1642. Copyright British Museum [194]

9.10 Thomas Rawlins (attributed), Battle of Edgehill military badge, 1642. Copyright British Museum [196]

9.11 After Anthony van Dyck, *Charles I wearing the Garter Star, c.* 1632. Copyright Victoria and Albert Museum [197]

9.12 Heinrich Reitz the younger, Charles I memorial medal, 1649. Copyright British Museum [199]

9.13 Renold Elstrack, *Charles I on Horseback*, engraving, third state. Copyright British Museum [201]

9.14 Gerrit Mountin, *James I and his Descendants*, engraving, *c.* 1634–1635. Copyright British Museum [203]

9.15 Cornelis van Dalen, *Charles I Crowned King of Scots*, engraving, 1633. Copyright British Museum   [205]

9.16 William Marshall, engraved title page to Xenophon, *Cyropaedia*, trans. Philemon Holland, 1632. Copyright British Library   [207]

9.17 Wenceslas Hollar, *Charles I*, etching, 1649. Copyright British Museum   [210]

9.18 George Lid, *Charles I*, etched frontispiece to Thomas May, *A Continuation of Lucan*, 1630. Copyright British Library   [211]

9.19 Hubert le Sueur, Charles I, marble, [1631.], Victoria and Albert Museum. Copyright Victoria and Albert Museum   [213]

9.20 Hubert le Sueur, Charles I, bronze, 1635, Bodleian Library. Copyright Bodleian Library, University of Oxford   [214]

9.21 Hubert le Sueur, Charles I in antique military costume, gilt-bronze, *c.* 1638, Stourhead. Copyright National Trust   [217]

9.22 Inigo Jones, choir screen of Winchester Cathedral, 1637–1638. Copyright Royal Institute of British Architects   [219]

9.23 Daniel Mytens, *Charles I as Prince of Wales*, *c.* 1623. Copyright the Royal Collection, Her Majesty the Queen   [223]

9.24 Daniel Mytens, *Charles I*, 1628. Copyright the Royal Collection, Her Majesty the Queen   [224]

9.25 Daniel Mytens and a later hand, *Charles I and Henrietta Maria*, *c.* 1630–1632, Hampton Court Palace. Copyright the Royal Collection, Her Majesty the Queen   [227]

9.26 Robert van Voerst after Van Dyck, *Charles I and Henrietta Maria*, engraving, 1634. Copyright British Museum   [227]

9.27 Anthony van Dyck and a later hand, *Charles I on Horseback*, *c.* 1633–1640, Petworth House. Copyright National Trust   [229]

9.28 Inigo Jones, ancient hero for *Coelum Britannicum*, 1634, Devonshire Collection, Chatsworth. By permission of the Trustees of the Chatsworth Settlement   [233]

10.1 Design for statue of Charles I. Proposed monument to Charles I by Christopher Wren, *c.* 1678. By permission of the Codrington Library, All Souls' College, Oxford   [253]

10.2 Design for rotunda. Proposed monument to Charles I by Christopher Wren, *c.* 1678. By permission of the Codrington Library, All Souls' College, Oxford   [255]

10.3 *Basilika*, engraved title page with portrait of Charles I, 1662. By permission of the Folger Shakespeare Library   [256]

10.4 Frontispiece. James II's *Imago Regis*, 1692. By permission of the University Library, University of Durham   [258]

11.1 Engraving of Charles the martyr king, n.d. By permission of the Ashmolean Museum, Oxford   [265]

11.2 *The Black Memorial*. Broadsheet on the execution of Charles I, 1710. By permission of the Ashmolean Museum, Oxford   [271]

11.3   *The True Portraicture of ye Royall Martyr Charles 1st, King of England.*
        Published by John Faber, 1713. By permission of the Ashmolean
        Museum, Oxford   [272]

11.4   Engraving of the Stuart Royal Oak, July 1715. By permission of the
        Ashmolean Museum, Oxford   [276]

11.5   Engraving of Charles Edward Stuart, 'the Pretender', 1745.
        By permission of The Huntington Library, San Marino,
        California   [283]

Contributors

SHARON ACHINSTEIN is an associate professor of English at the University of Maryland. Her *Milton and the Revolutionary Reader* (1994) won the James Holly Hanford Award of the Milton Society of America. She is currently completing a book on post-Restoration politics and aesthetics entitled *The Dissenting Muse: Milton to Defoe*.

ANN BAYNES COIRO is an associate professor at Rutgers University. She has published on Herrick, Lanyer, Jonson, Shakespeare, Donne, Marvell, and Milton. She is currently completing a study called *Repetition and Parody: Authority and Form in the Seventeenth Century*.

THOMAS N. CORNS is Professor of English and Head of the School of English and Linguistics at the University of Wales, Bangor. His publications include *The Development of Milton's Prose Style* (1982), *Milton's Language* (1990), *Uncloistered Virtue: English Political Literature, 1640–1660* (1992), *Regaining 'Paradise Lost'* (1994), and *John Milton: The Prose Works* (1998). He edited *The Cambridge Companion to English Poetry, Donne to Marvell* (1993). With David Loewenstein and Ann Hughes, he is editing the complete works of Gerrard Winstanley.

MARTIN DZELZAINIS is a senior lecturer in English at Royal Holloway, University of London. He has edited John Milton's *Political Writings* for Cambridge Texts in the History of Political Thought (1991) and (with Warren Chernaik) a collection of essays on *Marvell and Liberty* (1999). He is currently editing *The Rehearsal Transpos'd* for the forthcoming Yale edition of Andrew Marvell's prose.

LAURA LUNGER KNOPPERS is an associate professor of English at the Pennsylvania State University. Her publications include articles on Milton's poetry and prose, on Shakespeare, and on Cromwellian portraiture. Her book, *Historicizing Milton: Spectacle, Power, and Poetry in Restoration England*, appeared in 1994. She has recently completed a book-length study of seventeenth-century representations of Oliver Cromwell.

DAVID LOEWENSTEIN is Professor of English at the University of Wisconsin, Madison. He is the author of *Milton and the Drama of History: Historical Vision, Iconoclasm, and the Literary Imagination* (1990). He has also co-edited *Poetics, Politics, and Hermeneutics in Milton's Prose* (1990) and *The Emergence of Quaker Writing* (1995; with Thomas N. Corns). With Ann Hughes and Thomas N. Corns, he is editing the complete works of Gerrard Winstanley. He is also the co-editor of *The Cambridge History of Early Modern English Literature: Writing in Britain from the Reformation to the Restoration* (in progress).

JOHN PEACOCK is a senior lecturer in English at Southampton University. His research has focused on English art of the sixteenth and seventeenth centuries, and its relations with the continent; his book *The Stage Designs of Inigo Jones: The European Context* came out in 1995. He is now writing on the portraits of Van Dyck.

LOIS POTTER, Ned B. Allen Professor of English at the University of Delaware, is the author of *A Preface to Milton* (1971), *Twelfth Night: Text and Performance* (1986), and *Secret Rites and Secret Writing: Royalist Literature, 1641–1660* (1989); she edited book III of *Paradise Lost* for the *Cambridge Milton* (1976), volumes I and IV of *The Revels History of Drama in English*, to which she also contributed (1984, 1981), the Arden edition of *The Two Noble Kinsmen* by John Fletcher and William Shakespeare (1997) and *Playing Robin Hood: The Legend as Performance in Five Centuries* (1998). She has also published many articles on theatre history and the relation of seventeenth-century literature and politics, as well as theatre reviews.

JOAD RAYMOND is a lecturer in English at the University of Aberdeen. He is editor of *Making the News: An Anthology of the Newsbooks of Revolutionary England, 1641–1660* (1993), the author of *The Invention of the Newspaper: English Newsbooks, 1641–1649* (1996), and of articles on literature and politics in the mid-seventeenth century. He is presently working on studies of Milton and of the pamphlet between 1588 and 1688.

KEVIN SHARPE is Professor of History in the School of Research at the University of Southampton. His books include *Criticism and Compliment: The Politics of Literature in the England of Charles I* (1987), *Politics and Ideas* (1989), and *The Personal Rule of Charles I* (1992). He has co-edited, with

Steven Zwicker, *The Politics of Discourse* (1987) and *Refiguring Revolutions: Aesthetics and Politics from the English Revolution to the Romantic Revolution* (1998). He has recently completed *Reading Revolutions*, has forthcoming *Remapping Early Modern England* (1999), and is now writing a study of representations of authority and images of power, 1500 to 1700.

JONATHAN WAINWRIGHT is a lecturer in music at the University of York and Assistant Choir Trainer at York Minster. His research interests concern sixteenth- and seventeenth-century English and Italian music and his book *Musical Patronage in Seventeenth-Century England: Christopher, First Baron Hatton (1605–1670)* was published in 1997. Dr Wainwright is editor of the Royal Musical Association's *Research Chronicle* and is also director of Concertare, who have recently released their first CD: *Queen of Heavenly Virtue – Sacred Music for Queen Henrietta Maria*.

ELIZABETH SKERPAN WHEELER is Professor of English at Southwest Texas State University, where she teaches courses on Milton, seventeenth-century literature, and rhetoric. The author of *The Rhetoric of Politics in the English Revolution* (1992), she is currently working on a study of historical rhetorical theory and Milton's late poems, and a CD-ROM edition of *Eikon Basilike*.

Preface

This volume claims a twofold timeliness. The imminence of the millennium stimulates a fresh awareness of centenaries: the year 1999 marks the three hundred and fiftieth anniversary of Charles I's execution; the year 2000, the four hundredth anniversary of his birth. But the book has another kind of timeliness too, for it appears as crises have developed in the United Kingdom and the United States in the representation of the royal family and the presidency, crises which, like those which figure centrally in this volume, originate in part in profound uncertainties about the exposure of what is private and intimate to the searching view of the public domain, uncertainties which find a parallel in some aspects of the Caroline royal image.

A metaphor of refraction recurs throughout this volume. Influenced in part by the splendour of Hapsburg and Bourbon precedents, Charles promoted and stimulated a court culture that projected regal splendour with a refulgence unmatched in English history. Painting and sculpture, among the finest in western Europe, music, masque, poetry and song proclaimed his pre-eminence among men and celebrated the affection and fertility of the royal couple; court ritual and a new disciplined decorum hedged round his dignity. That positive image was partially grounded in an unusual concern with the public display of his private life and with his and Henrietta Maria's advancement as paradigmatic wedded lovers. Yet Charles was the only English monarch to be tried by his subjects or to be executed publicly, and his reign terminated in the establishment of England's only republican government. Political discourses deeply sceptical of the assumptions of Stuart monarchism developed in the later years of the reign of James I, and offered, both in the parliamentary opposition of the late 1620s and in the 1640s, a destabilizing critique of Charles and a profoundly altered version of the royal image. Amid the mid-century crises, other ideologies emerged, refracting that image not through the medium of constitutionalism but through the prism of more radical critiques of the old order. Attempts to control and manage the perception of Charles by a larger public occurred from his earliest state appearances, but such manipulation became difficult amid the widening public interest in the affairs of state in the 1620s, and utterly impossible amid the conflicts of the 1640s.

Nor did the royal image of Charles expire at the regicide. His representation as model and martyr dominated many aspects of royalist political writing from his death into the Restoration, and it remained a desperately contested site of ideological struggle for Jacobites, Williamites and Hanoverians in subsequent decades.

Historically informed literary critics predominate within this volume, though art history and musicology are significant components and the concluding chapter falls to a political historian. The volume is organized on roughly chronological principles, though two contributions which have a larger role require a particular word of preface. My opening chapter aims both to trace the construction of the image of Charles I from his earliest appearances as Duke of York to the early 1630s and to set a context within that framework for the developments traced by some of the following chapters. Similarly, Kevin Sharpe's concluding chapter functions as a reflection on the whole volume and the larger arguments that emerge from it.

I am grateful to several libraries, museums and art collections for supplying illustrations and for their permissions to print them here. I should like to thank contributors for their attempts to observe a strict schedule of deadlines amid that welter of competing obligations that characterizes higher education in the English-speaking world, and I am especially grateful to those contributors who actually succeeded in those attempts. I should like to thank Josie Dixon of Cambridge University Press for her patience and her encouragement, and the anonymous readers for the Press, not least for their valuable insistence that the collection should mesh into something greater than the sum of its parts. Not for the first time, my greatest debt is to Linda Jones, research administrator of the Bangor English department, who has worked so hard to turn the diverse contributions into the fair copy of a book.

THOMAS N. CORNS

Duke, prince and king

Thomas N. Corns

I

The representation of the future Charles I long preceded his accession in 1625. His princely persona, as Duke of York and later as Prince of Wales, was carefully figured in court masque and commemorated in court portraits, and, as we shall see, in those roles, he fitted perfectly within a mature royal ideology, in ways which permitted an accomplished negotiation of the death of Prince Henry, his elder brother. However, in the 1620s the developing crises in Stuart foreign policy and in the relationship between the crown and parliaments radically destabilized the image of James I and rendered Charles's own intentions and values quite enigmatic to large sections of the political nation. His marriage and accession were overshadowed by anti-Catholic sentiment and anxiety. Though the almost immediate reformation of those aspects of the conduct of the king's court which fell within his control certainly addressed some aspects of public perception, uncertainties about his objectives and values were exacerbated in the late 1620s, the years of the Forced Loan and of sometimes bewildering foreign policy decisions, and control of the most formal aspects of the royal image remained insecure probably until 1630, while alternative, negative constructions lurked beneath the public surface of the political consciousness throughout the period of the Personal Rule, returning like the repressed in the late 1630s.

II

But it had begun well. As part of the elaborate celebration of Prince Henry's investiture as Prince of Wales, Charles had taken a leading role in

the court masque *Tethys' Festival*, performed on 5 June 1610, probably in
the second Banqueting House in Whitehall (the immediate precursor to
Inigo Jones's extant masterpiece).[1] His mother, Anne of Denmark, took
the principal role, and his sister, Princess Elizabeth, the future wife of the
Elector Palatine, masked too. Surprisingly perhaps, the masque, written
by Samuel Daniel, a protégé of the queen, and designed by Inigo Jones,
deflected some attention away from Henry and James, and towards Anne
and her other children. It depicted a process by which Tethys, through the
agency of Zephyrus, presented to Oceanus-James a triton, symbolic of his
rule over the ocean (and perhaps also an allusion to his rule over the three
kingdoms) and to Henry a sword, reputedly worth £500.[2] As David
Lindley has observed, Tethys, as mother of 3,000 rivers, represented a
species of fertility, and as such offered an appropriate role in which Anne
could mask with two of her children before her eldest child and their
father.[3] The primary message of the masque confirmed the argument of
Ben Jonson's text for *Prince Henry's Barriers*, performed five months earlier
to commemorate Henry's 'first bearing of arms': indeed, the age of
Elizabethan chivalric militarism *could* be revived in Henry, but it has to be
restrained by the wiser policy of his irenic father. The description of the
sword carried the thesis in *Tethys' Festival*:

> [Tethys-Anne] wills [Zephyrus-Charles] greet the lord
> And Prince of th'isles, the hope and the delight
> Of all the northern nations, with this sword,
> Which she unto Astraea sacred found,
> And not to be unsheathed but on just ground.
> . . .
> For there will be within the large extent
> Of these my waves and wat'ry government,
> More treasure and more certain riches got
> Then all the Indies to Iberus brought:
> For Nereus will by industry unfold
> A chemic secret, and turn fish to gold.[4]

Astraea, goddess of justice but frequently a mythological attribute of
Elizabeth I, is a pleasingly complimentary inclusion. Old Protestant acti-
vists from the age of Elizabeth looked to Henry to reanimate the confessional dimension in English politics.[5] The sword he takes up is one
associated with Astraea's rule, which fits nicely with another concern of
the masque, the establishment of continuities between the Tudor and
Stuart dynasties: the setting is Milford Haven, 'The happy port of union,
which gave way / To that great hero Henry [VII] and his fleet', when he

returned to displace Richard III.[6] But the text explicitly warns against a western design, to match Spanish and Portuguese imperialism with an English one. In place of such adventurism, it seems to suggest, Prince Henry should look to the British fishing industry to generate wealth, thus turning 'fish to gold'.

The issue of Jacobean foreign policy and the framework it set for James's sons is one to which we shall return. But we should note, too, the vividly realized image of the young Charles. At a purely technical level, the part he played indicates a considerable assurance and competence for a child less than ten years old. Moreover, he is represented as a glittering embodiment of power, fertility and affection, in ways that curiously anticipate the court celebrations of the 1630s. He appears,

> in a short robe of green satin embroidered with golden flowers, and a round wing made of lawns on wires, and hung down in labels. Behind his shoulders two silver wings. On his head a garland of flowers consisting of all colours, and on one arm, which was out bare, he wore a bracelet of gold set with rich stones. Eight little ladies near of his stature represented the naiads, and were attired in light robes adorned with flowers, their hair hanging down and waving, with garlands of water ornaments on their heads.[7]

The first song celebrates Zephyrus-Charles as a figure of fertility, a bringer of a new spring:

> Youth of the spring . . . mild Zephyrus blow fair,
> And breathe the joyful air
> . . .
> Breathe out new flowers which yet were never known
> Unto the spring, nor blown
> Before this time, to beautify the earth,
> And as this day gives birth
> Unto new types of state,
> So let it bliss create.[8]

Part of the appeal of the succession of James I to the English political nation had rested in his proven fertility – he already had two sons, and the dynastic uncertainties that had characterized the later years of Elizabeth I's reign were unlikely to arise at the close of his.[9] In the context of a period in which life-threatening epidemics could touch even the wealthiest and in which political assassination attempts were not infrequent, there were advantages in having a reserve for the dangerously ebullient Prince Henry.

As Ann Coiro vividly demonstrates in chapter 2 below, a near-obsession with the fertility of the royal couple characterizes royal panegyric of the 1630s. But we should recognize that this component of the royal image was already well established in the earlier representation of Charles. The young Zephyrus of *Tethys' Festival* is father to the man whom Ben Jonson, in a fragment of an entertainment of uncertain date, greets thus:

> Fresh as the Day, and new as are the Howers,
> Our first of fruits, that is the prime of flowers
> Bred by your breath, on this low bancke of ours;
> Now, in a garland by the graces knit:
> Upon this obeliske, advanc'd for it,
> We offer as a Circle the most fit
> To Crowne the years, which you begin, great king,
> And you, with them, as Father of our spring.[10]

The same myth underlies Jonson's figuring of Henrietta Maria as Chloris, the nymph pursued and 'breathed on' by Zephyrus to become Flora, the goddess of flowers, in the masque *Chloridia: Rites to Chloris and Her Nymphs* (1631), though in a genteel variation Zephyrus is played, not by Charles, but by 'a plump boy' in 'a bright cloud'.[11]

Of course, the cultural and political Primavera associated with Prince Henry was curtailed by his death in 1612. His legacy to Charles remains somewhat uncertain. He had established himself as patron of a formidable literary circle, and writers plainly looked to him for protection and advancement. In contrast, probably only in his final and most unhappy years did the literary text (as opposed to the performance of play, masque or song) assume a central role in Charles's cultural life.[12] At no time was his library extensive, and most of it would seem to have been inherited from Henry.[13] In contrast, though, his enthusiasm for music was reflected in the considerable ensemble he retained in his princely court.[14] It is unsurprising that his court as king found its most abiding cultural expression in musical forms, in the song of Henry Lawes, the instrumental music of William, and in that consummate synthesis of words, design and music, the masques of the 1630s, as Jonathan Wainwright explores in chapter 8 below.

Charles was created Prince of Wales in 1616, and in 1618 he presented to his father a masque, *Pleasure Reconciled to Virtue*, which neatly differentiated his priorities from those of his late brother; the title could serve as epigraph to the cultural agenda of the Caroline court. Formally, the masque resembles quite closely *Oberon, the Fairy Prince*, Prince Henry's

Christmas masque of 1611. In that, however, a chivalric – indeed, Arthurian – aesthetic obtains, as the martially accoutred masquers proceed from a cleft in a rock to pay homage to James.[15] A similar epiphany occurs in *Pleasure Reconciled to Virtue*, though here, as the rock gives forth the masquers, led by Charles, the disappearing antimasque depicts, not innocent satyrs, but 'the voluptuous Comus, god of cheer', whose transient regime as lord of misrule gives way to a new era in which 'Pleasure [is] the servant, Virtue looking on'. Ben Jonson's text stresses the role of discipline and education as well as innate goodness, nurture as well as nature, in founding this new golden age. As Mount Atlas opens to disclose the masquers, a song declares,

> Ope agèd Atlas, open then thy lap,
> And from thy beamy bosom strike a light,
> That men may read in thy mysterious map
> All lines
> And signs
> Of Royal education and the right.
> See how they come and show,
> That are but born to know.
> Descend,
> Descend,
> Though pleasure lead,
> Fear not to follow:
> They who are bred
> Within the hill
> Of skill
> May safely tread
> What path they will,
> No ground of good is hollow.[16]

The Arthurianism of *Oberon* gives way to a decidedly Horatian aesthetic, which relegates martial nature to civilizing nurture.

Unusually, the masque was restaged six weeks later, with a new antimasque of stage Welshmen, as *For the Honour of Wales*, a celebration of the prince's relationship to the principality. The refashioned version suggested something of the facility with which the early Stuarts represented their sovereignty over all the nations of the British Isles. But the Welsh context supported a flirtation with Arthurianism, as when Evan notes that James I's full name is an anagram:

> *Jenkin.* Aye, that is *Claims Arthur's Seat*, which is as much as to say your madesty sould be the first king of Great Pritain, and sit in *cadair Arthur,*

which is Arthur's chair, as by God's blessing you do. And then your son
Master Sharles his, how do you call him? is Charles Stuart, *Calls True
Hearts*, that is us, the Welse nation, to be ever at your service . . .[17]

But here the Arthurian gestures are confined to the antimasque, and find
expression in the (presumably amusing) broken English and fragmentary
Welsh of characters whose inarticulate expression offers a view of the
monarch and his son, as if from the margins of his realm. They are displaced by the same manifestation of cultured virtue that dismissed the
bellygod.

III

Court masque was among the most controllable of cultural forms. It was
collaborative, and so its contents were open to pre-performance scrutiny.
It was expensive to produce, and so intricately tied into the most elevated
levels of the patronage system. It actively involved participants of the
highest rank, usually including members of the royal family, so the
unmanaged and unsanctioned introduction of critical material was
improbable. Its audience came by invitation, and was narrowly circumscribed to include a section of the court and appropriate ambassadorial
representatives, and so counter-cultural audience response was scarcely
possible. That is not to say that masque necessarily reflected a simple
image of the royal family as all-powerful and all-virtuous. Kevin Sharpe, in
a study that gave a new depth to the critique of the cultural ideology in the
Caroline court, has demonstrated that the masques of the 1630s echo
alternative voices in ruling circles and reflect concerns and anxieties that
run counter to the remote and over-confident perspective sometimes
attributed to them.[18] But latterly closer consideration of the inner governmental circles of early Stuart England has disclosed a much more fissured
system in which both the objectives of policy and its implementation were
debated and disputed. The apparent monolith of royal rule admitted – and
perhaps required – internal debates of considerable intensity, sometimes
reflective of radically different political, religious and cultural ideologies,
while the clash of interests in the pursuit of office and patronage generated savage political infighting.[19]

The literary culture of the court was more permissive than it
superficially seems, but the alternative voices it entertained were required
at last to accept the finality of the official position. Prince Henry may
indeed have offered a vision of a restored Elizabethan militancy, but it had

to submit to the irenic wisdom of James, just as the Jonsonian antimasque, representing satyrs, witches, bumpkins and citizens, was controlled and expelled by the mere disclosure of the masquers. Expelled, but not finally beaten, for the struggle of sovereignty is an unending one.

The early masques of Charles, Prince of Wales, while celebrating monarchy agonistes as well as triumphans, nevertheless defined his image with clarity and precision. At the same time, the martial aspect of royalty was being established and developed, though in a different context. Charles had been a sickly child, and at sixteen in the tilt to commemorate his creation as Prince of Wales he 'was not strong enough to put on an impressive display, so his opponents had to hold back lest they outshone' him.[20] At barriers, at the same age, Henry had performed 'with wonderous skill, and courage, to the great joy and admiration of all the beholders'.[21] But princes could be assiduously fashioned. Quite simply, Charles trained hard, and by 1620 he appeared to acclaim in great tilts. Whereas masques offered a wholly closed and narrowly select audience, tilts functioned instead as a significant interface between the court and the city. The tilting yard roughly ran along what is now Whitehall. While within the precincts of the palace of Whitehall and overlooked from royal buildings, it afforded spectacle to both the court and invited ambassadors and to a wider section of the populations of London and Westminster. Thus, on the most memorable occasion, Charles 'mounted on a powerful white horse, decked in splendid plumes, and wearing a suit of the finest armour inlaid with gold and silver', tilted with sundry aristocrats, and, according to a contemporary account, 'distinguished himself to the great joy of the people'.[22]

No doubt some of the success in image building in the late 1610s and early 1620s depended on James's favourite, the future Duke of Buckingham. Charles and he had masked together in *Pleasure Reconciled to Virtue*. In a frequently cited passage, the chaplain to the Venetian Embassy, who was present, described how Buckingham 'danced a number of high and very tiny capers . . . that made everyone admire him' (especially the king), whereas Charles's style was marked by the quality of his bows, 'being very formal', and the precision of his footwork ('nor was he seen to dance once out of step').[23] In the masques that followed, Charles danced with 'several lords', and Buckingham more often than not is named among them. It was the public and formal recognition of a new political configuration within the ruling circle, and in the 1620s James, Buckingham and Charles formed a sort of troika, though one which, at critical periods, evidently did not pull together. But the higher political profile of the prince and his association with Buckingham, a figure of labile public standing, fractured the elegant simplicity of representation which had been arrived at by 1620; we have the beginnings of that diversifying of perception and representation which most of the chapters in this volume engage with.

IV

Foreign policy and its intersection with fiscal concerns and domestic attitudes to Catholicism strained the royal image of James as well as Charles to breaking point and, it is often remarked, rendered Buckingham the most hated man in England. Frederick, the Elector Palatine, had married Charles's sister Elizabeth in 1613, amid elaborate and extended public celebration. *The Lords' Masque*, scripted and orchestrated by Thomas Campion, had anticipated their fertility and happiness:

> Live you long to see your joys
> In fair nymphs and princely boys,
> Breeding like the garden flowers,
> Which kind heav'n draws with her warm showers.[24]

Perhaps more significantly in terms of its abiding significance for the political nation, the Middle Temple and Lincoln's Inn, in one of those occasional demonstrations of wealth and latent power which characterized the Inns of Court's relationship with the crown, processed to Whitehall to masque, with 'such a glittering shew that all the King and all the companie were excedingly pleased', as a contemporary observed.[25] In a script by George Chapman, amid similar anticipations of 'fruitage' and much talk of Honour, Love, Virtue, and Beauty, a religious theme is intermittently heard, as pagan sun worshippers, 'Virginian princes', recognize the power of James and celebrate him as a monarch spreading Protestant light:

> Virginian princes, you must now renounce
> Your superstitious worship of these suns,
> Subject to cloudy dark'nings and descents;
> And of your fit devotions turn the events
> To this our Briton Phoebus, whose bright sky
> (Enlightened with a Christian piety)
> Is never subject to black Error's night . . .[26]

James brings the true light of Christian piety, dismissing 'superstitious worship', which in the lexicon of contemporary politics and religion most

Protestant Englishmen would have decoded as allusion to Catholic practices. The Inns gave the hymeneal celebration a distinctly denominational
feel, in ways curiously prophetic of Frederick's emergence, in the 1620s, as
Protestant icon.

In November 1619 Frederick accepted the crown of Bohemia, thus
involving the Palatinate in a major way in the developing continental
conflict which was to be known as the Thirty Years' War. In its earliest
phase, it had the characteristics of a war of religion, between the
Protestant states of northern Germany and the Catholic states of Austria
and southern Germany. Such a conflict would in any case have excited and
interested the partisanship of the English political nation, which was traditionally fiercely anti-Catholic, but Frederick's actions, which amounted
to assuming the leadership of the emerging Protestant alliance, established his status as Protestant hero (and, quite soon afterwards, Protestant
martyr), aroused an abiding sympathy for the Palatinate and its people,
and stimulated an unprecedented interest in news. Appropriately, Joseph
Frank begins his standard history of early English newspapers at 1620. As
Frank observes, the earliest newspapers in English were conspicuous in
their avoidance of 'any news having to do with England', reflecting at
once a concern to negotiate a *modus vivendi* with the English authorities
and an awareness of their readers' appetites for continental news.[27]
Control and monitoring of the circulation of news were recurrent concerns of government in the 1620s and 1630s.

But early corantos were just one of several mechanisms for the distribution of news, and the factors of news, characteristically London-based,
kept provincial England informed through the dispatch of manuscript
newsletters. *News from the New World Discovered in the Moon*, scripted by
Jonson and presented by Charles and Buckingham as the prince's Twelfth
Night masque of 1620, reflected something of the official edginess about
popular interest in the *arcana imperii*. The masque begins with discussion
among two heralds (as we are later told, 'the muses' heralds'[28]), a factor, a
printer and a chronicler. The exchange anatomizes the problem for
government: a plurality of voices produces a plurality of versions of
events, and the authoritative statements of heralds, proclaiming the
official version, are no longer privileged. Jonson satirically suggests the
simultaneously mercenary and tendentious nature of unofficial versions.
His factor confesses, 'I do write my thousand letters a week ordinary,
sometimes twelve hundred, and maintain the business at some charge . . . I
have friends of all ranks and of all religions, for which I keep an answering

catalogue of dispatch wherein I have my Puritan news, my Protestant news and my Pontifical news.'[29] The masque acts out a royal fantasy in which a unity of perspective replaces such a divisive and intrusive plurality, as an antimasque of flying creatures is dismissed and the masquers descend. The second song, separating the opening dance from the main dance and revels, explains that the masquers reflect the values of the monarch, that there is complete concord between them, and that the living discourse of monarchy is uniquely privileged once more:

> Now look and see in yonder throne
> How all those beams are cast from one.
> This is that orb so bright
> Has kept your wonder so awake,
> Whence you as from a mirror take
> The sun's reflected light.
> Read him as you would do the book
> Of all perfection, and but look
> What his proportions be;
> No measure that is thence contrived,
> Or any motion thence derived,
> But is pure harmony.[30]

The masque ends with the figure of Fame, celebrating James as 'The knowing king', and with the two heralds who began the masque acknowledging that Fame, which is truth-telling, has displaced alternative constructs:

> 1ST HERALD   See, what is that this music brings,
>   And is so carried in the air about?
> 2ND HERALD   Fame, that doth nourish the renown of kings,
>   And keeps that fair which envy would blot out.[31]

In this agreeable fantasy, Charles and Buckingham danced discourse back into unity; James saw clear advantages in a legislative framework of control.[32] But the problem could not be thus negotiated. From the early 1620s onwards, two tendencies developed in step. As Joad Raymond demonstrates in chapter 3 below, populist versions of the royal image had wide currency in media that, by their nature, escaped from the management of the government. Again, the English obsession with contemporary continental conflict set a framework for the interpretation and evaluation of government policy which profoundly influenced English politics through the 1620s and 1630s and into the Civil War and Interregnum. In chapter 7 Sharon Achinstein explores the role of English anxieties about international 'Popish Plots' in shaping the political consciousness of John Milton and in informing his multifaceted critique of kings and kingship.

Late Jacobean foreign policy sat awkwardly amid the rubble of Europe and posed problems in presentation that were never satisfactorily resolved. James entertained conflicting objectives – support for his daughter and son-in-law (necessary to appease both popular Protestantism and familial honour) and avoidance of involvement in a continental war which would have required parliamentary grants of supply (and thus would have rendered the crown dependent on frequent parliaments enjoying unusual degrees of power). James sought a resolution to the impasse in close association with Spain or with France, European superpowers in the early 1620s who were still relatively aloof from the conflict. The developing strategy impacted profoundly on the perception and representation of Prince Charles in that his intended role was that of partner in a marriage alliance with a Spanish or French princess. Crucially, either match was blighted by populist hostility to Catholicism, for of course both Spanish and French royal families were devoutly Catholic.

The first recourse was to a Spanish match, which Charles and Buckingham abortively pursued by an initially incognito mission to Spain in February 1623; Charles's return, in the October of that year, occasioned rejoicing on a scale more appropriate to royal wedding – indeed, with a kind of popular acclaim singularly absent from his proxy wedding, in 1625, to a French princess. Of modern accounts, Thomas Cogswell's is the most vivid synthesis of contemporary materials. Bells were rung, ordnance discharged, bonfires lit; 'in all the "universall joy", the main attraction remained Charles'. As he passed in London through spontaneous demonstrations of loyalty, the crowds cried out, 'We have him . . . We have our prince again.' As Cogswell observes, 'Unprompted and rapturous acclaim for a member of the royal family was a phenomenon with which the early Stuarts had not regularly dealt . . . Nothing [Charles] had ever done had produced such unmistakable satisfaction.'[33]

Through the months following the return, the formerly Hispanophile Buckingham was at the centre of a radical realignment of Jacobean foreign policy that saw both the replacement of the Spanish Match with an active pursuit of a French match and the preparation for war with Spain. Such a volte-face was premised on the euphoria which greeted the return, and found its most abiding literary commemoration in Thomas Middleton's remarkable play of mid 1624, *A Game at Chess*, which is extraordinary in the explicitness of its engagement with government politics and in its depiction, in the allegory of a game of chess, of Charles and Buckingham as White Knight and White Duke. The denouement depicts the two heroes' checkmate of the scheming Black King (that is, the King of Spain) with that classiest of endgame manoeuvres, checkmate by discovery:

> BLACK KNIGHT   Now you're brother to us; what we have done
>   Has been dissemblance ever.
> WHITE KNIGHT   There you lie then
>   And the game's ours – we give thee checkmate by
>   Discovery, King, the noblest mate of all!
>   *A great shout and flourish.*
> BLACK KING I'm lost, I'm taken!
>   . . .
>
> WHITE KING O let me bless mine arms with this dear treasure,
>   Truth's glorious masterpiece![34]

Only the brassiest countenance could represent the Spanish debacle as a glorious masterpiece, and Truth has little to do with Middleton's account. But Cogswell rightly grasps its real significance, which lay in its stunning reception: 'since 3,000 people a day reportedly saw the play, slightly less than 30,000 people, almost one-tenth of London's total population, saw *A Game at Chess*'.[35]

Charles's image had been taken from the controlled environment of the masquing hall and made public property in the most conspicuous of ways. But the perception of him – and of Buckingham – as Protestant heroes established paradigms and expectations that conflicted bewilderingly with their apparent objectives and palpable failures through the rest of the 1620s. Uninvited, a far wider section of the population had begun to evaluate government policy, and the unrivalled and in some ways unlooked-for public relations triumphs of 1623–4 soon assumed a poignancy.

V

The responses to the abandonment of the Spanish Match both reflected and provoked anti-Catholic sentiment and a popular commitment to the Protestant cause on the continent. As Thomas Cogswell concludes, by the early 1620s 'there was widespread interest in the European war and considerable enthusiasm for English intervention'.[36] A successful prosecution of an effective and perhaps even lucrative war would have substantiated the martial expectations aroused around Charles in the weeks after his return from Spain. In the event, the war with Spain petered out after the utterly inept expedition to Cadiz. The Spanish Match was replaced by betrothal to and then proxy marriage with a French princess, despite which war followed with France, primarily in defence of French Huguenot Protestants against threats to their stronghold of La Rochelle by Louis XIII. Again, a successful outcome could have substantiated the rather atavistic Elizabethan aspirations surrounding the adventure; instead, two expeditions – one led by Buckingham in person to the Ile de Ré – cost money and lives and ended in humiliation.

The war policy had two principal concomitants. It necessitated a protracted engagement between government and parliaments, seven of which were called in the 1620s, and it left the crown open to popular resentments in ways which severely degraded its opportunities to project a positive royal image through state ceremonial.

The political conflict between parliament and crown, its fiscal implications, and the larger ideological issues it raised have latterly received a great deal of investigation.[37] Its compound impact by 1629 was considerable. As Charles asserted his rights to govern – and to raise the funds necessary for the process in time of war – the nature of his claim to divine sanction was explored with a new explicitness on both sides. The issue had a complexity sometimes ignored by those – particularly cultural historians and critics – who represent Caroline culture as an assertion of a new absolutism in face of a progressive constitutionalism. As Sommerville observes, 'Some modern commentators have concluded that [many writers] endorsed the theory of the Divine Right of Kings. This does not follow. The important questions were: did royal power come *directly* from God or from the people, and was it circumscribed by ancient custom?'[38] Divine sanction, once problematized within a parliamentary context and subject to debate at both a practical and a theoretical level, inevitably emerged as a weakened concept. Moreover, as the controversy between parliamentarians and the crown proceeded through the mid and late 1620s, the inadequacy of Charles at engaging with his opponents within the appropriate discourses of the ancient constitution and the common law became apparent. As Burgess puts it, 'Charles came across as an absolutist (whatever his intentions) because he insisted on ignoring the rules for the usage of languages of divine right and absolute prerogative . . . Charles's statements sounded foreign to his subjects.'[39]

How subjects perceived their place within the structure of government radically fashioned their perception of the head of the government. The

Forced Loan of 1626, for example, eroded the notions that government protected their property and that the local hierarchies within county gentries represented the monarch's will at local level because they were all part of the same governmental process. The impact of the loan was to shape individuals' perceptions of monarchical government and their place in it, and, as Cust observes and as others have noted, 'many of those who came to the fore as loan resisters also . . . actively supported Parliament during the Civil War'.[40]

Anxieties about the sincerity of Charles's anti-Catholicism rumbled through parliamentary debate and popular opinion in the mid to late 1620s. But religious issues confused the royal image in another way. Charles's own predilections were certainly Protestant, but he was drawn to and supported the Arminian tendency which, in its deviation from Calvinist theories of salvation, in its priestliness, and in its concern for religious ceremonialism, seemed in the popular regard very similar to Catholicism.[41] Consideration of the early modern perception and representation of kingship, in the chapters that follow and elsewhere, generally focus on ceremonial, on high culture, on written texts. But the widest image of kingship in England, apart from the king's head on coins, and the one most insistently made available to the very poorest and illiterate, was the image of the monarch as head of the Church of England. Every edition of The Book of Common Prayer asserted the liturgical requirement that the congregation should pray for the monarch as head of state, godly ruler and God's minister as a necessary component of the ministration of Holy Communion, and in other orders. The weekly liturgical transaction asserted and confirmed all the congregation in their status as subjects, and figured the king primarily as godly minister within an established church. Erosion of his reputation as protector of a Protestant faith was potentially deeply problematic within a far wider community than gentry-class parliamentarians. The pursuit of a religious aesthetic so tractable to misperception and misrepresentation proved hazardous. The beauty of holiness was expensive in political as well as material terms.

Combinations of circumstances further maimed those rites of state in which the monarch represented himself to a broader gaze. The fact of Henrietta Maria's Catholicism and French insistence on a wider degree of toleration than any English parliament would have accepted both protracted negotiations and occasioned delays in opening the parliament of

1625.[42] The marriage was effected by proxy, which was perhaps as well, though the entry of Charles and Henrietta Maria into London was effected in some state. His coronation was postponed until 1626, in part because of an outbreak of plague. In the event, the queen declined to attend on the grounds that she wanted to be crowned by her own confessor; Buckingham turned the procession to Westminster Abbey into the occasion for factional feuding; the high profile given to the Arminian Laud in the proceedings ensured that the ceremony itself was an example of division within the Church rather than a manifestation of confessional unity; and civic celebrations were cancelled because of fear of plague.[43] The last great state occasion of the 1620s, the funeral of Buckingham, was set against such deep and widespread animosity to the late duke that the course of the procession was drastically curtailed amid fears that the body would be stolen by demonstrators.[44]

Charles is sometimes represented as a monarch whose wish for privacy disinclined him from participation in state ceremonial of a kind which proved effective for his immediate predecessors. Perhaps it did, and the outcome suited his temperament, though we should note that he participated in elaborate public ceremonial during his Scottish coronation, that he took a leading part in the greatest of all Jacobean occasions, the funeral of Prince Henry, and, as we have seen, was active in the rites of the tilt yard. The curtailment of the state occasions of the mid and late 1620s was not elective but a result of combinations of adverse circumstances, and no doubt his inability to show himself at best advantage to his subjects – at least to the citizens of London – depleted the potency of the royal image in the popular context.

VI

Cadiz, the Ile de Ré, a French Catholic match in place of a Spanish one, and with it what Milton would later call 'tolerated Popery', no effective relief for the Elector Palatine, parliamentary opposition of a new intensity, explicitness and confidence, and the political survival of Buckingham in face of disasters seemingly of his own making, followed by his evidently popular assassination: it is unsurprising that the royal image was at best somewhat blurred in those years of transition around Charles's marriage and his succession.

Certainly, though, Charles swiftly and effectively controlled those aspects of the public (and indeed private) conduct of his court which lay within his will. As Sharpe has demonstrated, 'Charles's impact upon the style of the court had been felt within days of his succession.' He quotes the report of the Venetian ambassador in April 1625:

> the king observes a rule of great decorum. The nobles do not enter his apartments in confusion as heretofore, but each rank has its appointed place . . . The king has also drawn up rules for himself, dividing the day from his very early rising, for prayers, exercises, audiences, business, eating and sleeping. It is said that he will set apart a day for public audience and he does not wish anyone to be introduced to him unless sent for.[45]

Charles insisted on sexual probity from the courtiers around him; the scandalous were dismissed; swearing and impiety were not tolerated; and access to the royal presence was carefully and precisely controlled. The contrast with the style of his father's court was immediate and profound, and the codes of conduct were refined and enhanced in the years that followed. In place of the sometimes outrageous, sometimes profane, sometimes inebriated, and always open court of James, came an obsessive decorum, an obvious piety, a scrupulous sexual morality, and a new fascination with court ritual. These reforms had significant impact on the wider perception of the monarch, in part because the more public operations of the court constituted an important interface between Charles and his subjects, and in part because of the sheer scale of the royal household itself. On Carlton's calculation, the royal household employed a workforce which, together with its dependents, constituted a population about the size of Exeter or Norwich and which was, in effect, the 'seventh or eighth largest community in the realm'.[46] Its conduct could effectively reflect the values and assumptions of its head, and Charles's changes certainly defined some aspects of his public image. In a frequently cited commendation from an unlikely source, Lucy Hutchinson, fiercely puritanical wife of a parliamentary colonel and regicide, summarized the transformation thus: 'The face of the court was much changed in the king, for King Charles was temperate, chaste and serious, so that the fools, and bawds, mimics and catamites of the former Court grew out of fashion.'[47]

Moreover, as the cultural retinue of his princely court amalgamated with the one he inherited from James's and as he added new talents to it, Charles rapidly assembled around him the most glittering array of creative and imaginative ability in the history of the English monarchy. In later chapters, Jonathan Wainwright considers the musical achievement of the Caroline court as reflection of the royal patron, John Peacock writes on the presentation of Charles in the visual arts, and Ann Coiro analyses literary modes of royal panegyric. Charles inherited in Ben Jonson a massively able laureate talent, eager to effect the vital transition from the patronage of James to that of the new king, and in Inigo Jones a peerless celebrant of kingship in masque design and architecture. Charles's own large musical ensemble, combined with many of James's retainers, included not only the ablest performers but also the most significant composers of the early Stuart period. His interests in the visual arts, hugely stimulated by his experience of the Hapsburg court culture of Madrid, prompted him to commission new works glorifying the royal image as well as to collect masterworks on a scale unprecedented in England. Poets of extraordinary accomplishment (within their limitations), such as Aurelian Townshend, Edmund Waller, William Davenant, and perhaps pre-eminently Thomas Carew, eventually refracted a brilliant image of Charles and his queen in poems of compliment, in song and in masque. But till the early 1630s, the message of court poetry emerged very indistinctly.

And why would it not? The return from Madrid had offered to a credulous public the spectacle of Charles as Protestant hero; but how could that view be sustained in the face of the military failures of the 1620s and the inglorious peace treaties with Spain and France? Checkmate by discovery of the Spanish king was followed, arguably, by fool's mate at the hands of the French. Again, the prince 'bred up' in the parliaments of the early 1620s lost the dialogue he needed with later parliaments, indeed, on Burgess's account, lost the language of constitutional discourse completely.

Comparisons between coronation odes for Charles I and those for his father and his elder son are profoundly instructive. The principal aspirations for the English political nation on the accession of James I related to his Protestantism, his survival skills (he had escaped numerous botched coups as king of Scotland), and his fertility – all of which promised religious and dynastic stability. Thus Henry Petowe's ode, 'His Maiesties Most Royal Coronation', celebrated in these terms a monarch whose personal image appeared clear and unequivocal:

> *Haile Caesar* with a shrill toung'd streyne:
> *Caesar* the princely Author of their peace,

> Whose very name pierc't through the liver veyne
> Of hot *Rebellion*
>
> . . .
>
>   the name of King
> Made forward Insurrection start and die.
> Oh wholesome *North* from forth whose wombe did spring,
> The blessed Sunne of our felicitie.[48]

Coronation odes and related panegyrics for Charles II far outnumber those for James I or Charles I, but despite the number (and the diversity of the authors' experiences of the Interregnum), the poems showed a surprising uniformity of theme, ideology and strategy, and a general agreement about how the new king was to be represented. None ignored the interruption to his rule, and all represent him as stronger because of his suffering. Thomas Jordan's 'On the Day' is wholly representative:

> He who liv'd a life like *Job*
> Shall now with Crown, Scepter, and Globe,
> With peaceful seed ascend his Throne,
> And every man shall have his own:
> The *Juncto*, *Oliver*, and *Rump*
> That turn'd up all the *Knaves* for *Trump*,
> Are totally dissolv'd, and we
> Are *Subjects* to true *Majesty*.[49]

But the odes for the 1626 coronation are much less certain of the terms in which to celebrate the new king. By his death, and indeed for many years before, James had been represented as Solomonic and as a peacemaker, the words *Beati pacifici* frequently serving as epigraph to his reign. But does Charles I bring peace or war? Stability or adventurism? Defence of the faith or liaison with Catholicism? An evasive emptiness characterizes his coronation odes, as in Sir John Beaumont's 'Panegyrick at the Coronation of our Soveraigne Lord King Charles':

> Shine forth great *Charles*, accept our loyall words,
> Throw from your pleasing eies those conqu'ring swords,
> That when upon your Name our voyces call,
> The Birds may feele our thund'ring noise, and fall . . .

The poem continues with wishes that he may enjoy 'Large Honour, happy Conquest, boundless Wealth / Long Life, sweete Children, unafflicted Health', which may seem to cover all the bases, but which also discloses uncertainties about the direction of the new regime: in the English context, conquest and wealth were usually regarded as alternatives.[50]

In the 1630s, as Coiro's account in this volume demonstrates, the royal image reflected in the literary culture of the court is focused on the celebration of the halcyon days of England's peace and, to an almost morbid degree, the fertility embodied in the royal partners, the Carlomaria figure of Caroline masque. Charles's coronation as king of Scotland was deferred until 1633.[51] Sir Henry Wotton's ode in celebration, in its lucid rehearsal of the agreed message, could not contrast more sharply with the floundering odes of 1626:

> Long may He [Charles] round about him see
> His Roses and his Lilies bloom:
> Long may His Only Dear [Henrietta Maria], and Hee
> Joy in *Ideas* of their own,
> And *Kingdomes Hopes* so timely sown.
> Long may They Both contend to prove,
> That best of Crowns is such a *Love*.[52]

Wotton, former diplomat, royal pensionary, and, through the patronage of Buckingham, Provost of Eton, reflects with precision the brand new image of Charles as lover (sanctified by wedlock) and father. Indeed, the ritual of his return emphasized the significance of the relationship with the queen as a defining element in his regime. She had not accompanied him to Scotland, but advanced to Stratford to welcome him home, with the infant Prince Charles, who, on a contemporary account, welcomed him back 'with the prettiest innocent mirth that can be imagined'.[53] Surely, within the English context, the court finally got the symbolism clear. While Charles's coronation as king of England had been frustrated by the queen's refusal to be anointed by a Protestant bishop, in the 1633 version, Charles exits and returns like a conqueror, though, crucially, as one whose victories are achieved through love and peace, not war. As Abraham Cowley observed,

> Welcome Great Sir, and with all the joy that's due
> To the return of Peace and You
> . . .
> Others by War their conquests gain,
> You like a God your ends obtain.[54]

But whereas the issues and priorities in courtly representation were resolved in the early 1630s, the best disposed of poets found themselves sometimes wrong-footed earlier in the reign. As late as 1630, Sir William Davenant was hailing Charles in terms which anticipated renewed dealings with parliament, though with parliamentarians more compliant than in the session dismissed in the previous year:

> A Session . . . of such who can obey,
> As they were gather'd to consult, not sway:
> Who not rebell, in hope to git
> Some office to reclaime their wit;
> Let this yeare bring
> To *Charles* our King:
> To *Charles*; who is th'example and the Law,
> By whom the good are taught, not kept in awe.[55]

Perhaps not a picture of the king that Sir John Eliot, in his cell in the Tower, would have recognized; nor is it one, though, that implies a very clear notion on Davenant's part of how Charles's political persona should be represented at the start of the Personal Rule. One could multiply examples. Waller's poem 'Of His Majesties receiving the newes of the Duke of Buckinghams death' evades the larger problems of how the duke's unpopularity tainted the king by deflecting attention from the victim to the mourner, and to his enigmatically stoical response. Even so, Waller's depiction of Charles functions largely by stating what his conduct was not like – not like Hector's for Patroclus, or Apollo's for Hyacinthus, or David's for Absalom.[56]

It is surely with the possibilities made available by the birth of Charles in 1630 and the developing love story surrounding the royal couple that court poets find clear themes through which to represent the monarchy. A sequence of poems by Ben Jonson illustrates the point well. His 'Epigram. To our great and good K. Charles On his Anniversary Day', written for 27 March 1629, begins unpromisingly:

> How happy were the Subject, if he knew,
> Most pious King, but his owne good in you!
> How many times, Live long, CHARLES, would he say,
> If he but weigh'd the blessings of this day?[57]

The poem implies a public relations disaster: the subject would speak well of the king, if he were properly informed, if he shared the right conceptual framework – with the obvious implications that most subjects did not. But the 'Epigram on the Princes birth', from May 1630, shows a poet suddenly on message: 'Blest be thy birth, / That so hath crown' our hopes, our spring, and earth, / The bed of the chast *Lilly*, and the *Rose*!'[58] Jonson returned to the old masque fixation with royal fertility and added new aspects, in the celebration of Charles and Henrietta Maria as a couple and in the obsession with married chastity, of sexuality rendered chaste by the marriage sacrament. The issues are central to Jonson's final court masque, the queen's Shrovetide masque of 1631, *Chloridia: Rites to Chloris and Her Nymphs*, which concludes by hailing Henrietta Maria as

> Chloris the queen of flowers,
> The sweetness of all showers,
> The ornament of bowers,
> The top of paramours![59]

The next Jonson poem in the sequence, 'An Epigram to the Queene, then lying in' (that is, after the birth of Prince Charles), flirted with a Catholic inflection, greeting her with 'Haile *Mary*, full of honours',[60] which was followed by 'An Ode, or Song, by all the Muses. In celebration of her Majesties birth-day' (November 1630 – she was twenty-one), which pondered further the courtly stud-farm:

> Sweet! happy *Mary!* All
> The People her doe call.
>   And this the wombe divine,
> So fruitfull, and so faire,
> Hath brought the Land an Heire!
>   And CHARLES a *Caroline!*[61]

'All The People'? Scarcely that. But from the birth of Prince Charles onward, at least within the discourse of the court, the royal image took a settled and confident form. The court panegyrists and masque writers perceived clearly what the objectives of government were, and strove to project them. Of course, within the ruling elite there were still major issues of debate and disagreement, and these, too, find expression in the most courtly of literary forms.[62] Moreover, as Coiro demonstrates, the focus on royal sexuality proved more disturbing, more disruptive to the principal messages of Caroline ideology, than at first it seemed. But English anti-Catholic sentiment remained a powerful component in the political consciousness of the nation and always ensured the cult of Henrietta Maria achieved very limited popular celebration. At the same time, the seemingly confident image of the royal pair in their halcyon days rested uncomfortably against a continental Europe engaged in a confessional war, while the discourse of the ancient constitution, of parliament's role in the governance of England, while subdued, retained a currency; the political categories current in the early 1640s had been established in the 1620s. The royal love story would be available as a poignant element in the cult of Charles as royal martyr, explored by Elizabeth Skerpan Wheeler in chapter 6 and Laura Knoppers in chapter 11 of this volume, just as surely as popular dislike of the papist queen gave added potency to *The Kings Cabinet Opened* (London, 1645), perhaps the most effective and influential parliamentary pamphlet of the 1640s, considered by Loewenstein in chapter 5 below.

But at least the distinctions from the Jacobean royal image were clear enough, inscribed in court ritual and custom as surely as in cultural discourses. At or near the start of the Personal Rule, Charles and his court had effected a considerable transformation within those ideological domains they could control. But ideological apparatuses outside the court could not so easily be mastered, a distressing plurality of alternative images remained available, and, as the next chapter shows, the eroticized vision of majesty played uncertainly on sensibilities unaccustomed to the idiom of the court.

Notes

1 On the festivities surrounding the investiture, see Roy Strong, *Henry Prince of Wales and England's Lost Renaissance* (London: Thames and Hudson, 1986), 152–60. All references to early Stuart masques are to the text printed in Stephen Orgel and Roy Strong, *Inigo Jones. The Theatre of the Stuart Court*, 2 vols. (London: Sotheby Parke Bernet; Berkeley and Los Angeles: University of California Press, 1973), I, 192–6.

2 Orgel and Strong, *Inigo Jones*, I, 191.

3 David Lindley, ed., *Court Masques: Jacobean and Caroline Entertainments 1605–1640* (Oxford and New York: Oxford University Press, 1995), 231–4.

4 Lines 136–40, 150–5.

5 Strong, *Henry*, 70–9.

6 Lines 127–8.

7 Lines 52–60.

8 Lines 70–1, 77–82.

9 See James I's coronation odes, considered below, and Ann Coiro's chapter, which follows.

10 *Ben Jonson*, ed. C. H. Herford and Percy and Evelyn Simpson, 11 vols. (Oxford: Clarendon Press, 1925–63), VIII, 416 (all subsequent references are to this edition); on the uncertainties of the dating, see *Ben Jonson*, ed. Ian Donaldson (Oxford and New York: Oxford University Press, 1985), 727. For a good account of the larger significance of the masque in the representation of Prince Henry, see John Pitcher, '"In those figures which they seeme": Samuel Daniel's *Tethys' Festival*', in *The Court Masque*, ed. David Lindley (Manchester University Press, 1984), 33–46. See also Graham Parry, *The Golden Age Restor'd: The Culture of the Stuart Court, 1603–42* (New York: St Martin's Press, 1981), 74–5.

11   Orgel and Strong, *Inigo Jones*, II, 420.

12   Charles Carlton, *Charles I: The Personal Monarch*, 2nd edn (London and New York: Routledge, 1995), 12–13, compares the rate of literary dedications to Henry and Charles.

13   On Henry's role in establishing the Royal Library, see Strong, *Henry*, 199–211.

14   Peter Holman, *Four and Twenty Fiddlers: The Violin at the English Court, 1540–1690* (Oxford: Clarendon Press, 1993), especially chapters 9 and 10.

15   Orgel and Strong, *Inigo Jones*, I, 204–28.

16   Ibid., I, 276–88, lines 210–27.

17   Ibid., I, 288–93, lines 367–73.

18   Kevin Sharpe, *Criticism and Compliment: The Politics of Literature in the England of Charles I* (Cambridge University Press, 1987), *passim*.

19   Kevin Sharpe, *The Personal Rule of Charles I* (New Haven and London: Yale University Press, 1992), *passim*. On ideological distinctions among courtiers, see Sharpe, *Criticism and Compliment*, 21–2.

20   Carlton, *Charles I*, 17.

21   Contemporary opinion, quoted by Orgel and Strong, *Inigo Jones*, I, 159.

22   Carlton, *Charles I*, 16, 26–7.

23   Orgel and Strong, *Inigo Jones*, I, 283.

24   Ibid., I, 243–6, lines 429–32.

25   Ibid., I, 255.

26   Ibid., I, 253–64, lines 595–601.

27   Joseph Frank, *The Beginnings of the English Newspaper, 1620–1660* (Cambridge, MA: Harvard University Press, 1961), 5.

28   Orgel and Strong, *Inigo Jones*, I, 306–12, line 293. The ideological implications of the masque are well discussed in Sara Pearl, 'Something to Present Occasions: Jonson's masques of 1620–5', in Lindley, ed., *Court Masques*, 60–77.

29   Orgel and Strong, *Inigo Jones*, I, 306–12, lines 34–41.

30   Ibid., lines 328–39.

31   Ibid., lines 373–6.

32   Frank, *Beginnings of the English Newspaper*, 6.

33   Thomas Cogswell, *The Blessed Revolution: English Politics and the Coming of War, 1621–1624* (Cambridge University Press, 1989), 6–12.

34   Thomas Middleton, *A Game at Chess*, ed. T. H. Howard-Hill (Manchester University Press, 1993), v.iii. 157–68.

35   Cogswell, *Blessed Revolution*, 303.

36   Ibid., 309.

37   See, especially, Conrad Russell, *Parliaments and English Politics, 1621–1629* (Oxford: Clarendon Press, 1979); Cogswell, *Blessed Revolution*; Roger Lockyer, *Buckingham: The Life and Political Career of George Villiers, First Duke of Buckingham, 1592–1628* (London and New York: Longman, 1981); Richard Cust, *The Forced Loan and English Politics, 1626–1628* (Oxford: Clarendon Press, 1987); L. J. Reeve, *Charles I and the Road to Personal Rule* (Cambridge University Press, 1989); Kevin Sharpe, ed., *Faction and Parliament: Essays on Early Stuart History* (Oxford: Clarendon Press, 1978); Richard Cust and Ann Hughes, eds., *Conflict in Early Stuart England: Studies in Religion and Politics, 1603–1642* (London: Longman, 1989); J. F. Merritt, ed., *The Political World of Thomas Wentworth, Earl of*

Strafford, 1621–1641 (Cambridge University Press, 1996); J. P. Sommerville, *Politics and Ideology in England, 1603–1640* (London and New York: Longman, 1986); Glenn Burgess, *The Politics of the Ancient Constitution: An Introduction to English Political Thought, 1603–1642* (Basingstoke: Macmillan, 1992) and *Absolute Monarchy and the Stuart Constitution* (New Haven: Yale University Press, 1996).

38 Sommerville, *Politics and Ideology*, 232.

39 Burgess, *Ancient Constitution*, 200–1.

40 Cust, *Forced Loan*, 334.

41 On the (disputed) role of Arminianism in the Caroline church and on its significance in the origins of the civil war conflict, see Nicholas Tyacke, *Anti-Calvinists: The Rise of English Arminianism, c. 1590–1640* (Oxford: Clarendon Press, 1987); Sharpe, *Personal Rule*; Julian Davies, *The Caroline Captivity of the Church: Charles I and the Remoulding of Anglicanism, 1625–1641* (Oxford: Clarendon Press, 1992); and Kenneth Fincham, ed., *The Early Stuart Church, 1603–1642* (Basingstoke: Macmillan, 1993).

42 Russell, *Parliaments and English Politics*, 204.

43 Carlton, *Charles I*, 76–8; Lockyer, *Buckingham*, 308.

44 Carlton, *Charles I*, 109. The coffin in the funeral procession was empty; the body had been buried the night before, out of concern that the mob would seize and desecrate it.

45 Sharpe, *Personal Rule*, 210–11.

46 Carlton, *Charles I*, 124.

47 From her *Memoirs of the Life of Colonel Hutchinson*, quoted in Sharpe, *Personal Rule*, 212. David Loewenstein discusses the passage in chapter 5 below.

48 Henry Petowe, 'His Maiesties Most Royal Coronation', *Englands Caesar. His Maiesties most Royall Coronation. Together with the manner of the solemne shewes prepared for the honour of his entry into the Cittie of London* (London, 1603).

49 Thomas Jordan, *A nursery of novelties in Variety of Poetry* (London, n.d.).

50 Sir John Beaumont, 'A Panegyrick at the Coronation of our Soveraigne Lord King Charles', *Bosworth-field: With a Taste of the Variety of Other Poems* (London, 1629).

51 For an account, see Carlton, *Charles I*, 184–8.

52 Sir Henry Wotton, 'An Ode to the King, At his returning from Scotland to the Queen: after his Coronation there', *Reliquiae Wottonianae. Or a collection of lives, letters, poems* (London, 1651), 521.

53 Sir Francis Windebank, quoted in Carlton, *Charles I*, 187.

54 Quoted ibid., 188.

55 Sir William Davenant, 'To the King on New-yeares day 1630. Ode', lines 17–24, in *The Shorter Poems, and Songs from the Plays and Masques*, ed. A. M. Gibbs (Oxford: Clarendon Press, 1972), 31.

56 Edmund Waller, 'Of His Majesties receiving the newes of the Duke of Buckinghams death', *Poems &c.* (London, 1645), 1–2. Waller wrote against the background of widespread anti-Buckingham literary activity, in part expressed in popular verse. See Gerrald Hammond, *Fleeting Things: English Poets and Poems, 1616–1660* (Cambridge, MA and London: Harvard University Press, 1990), 49–66.

57 'An Epigram. To our great and good K. Charles On his Anniversary Day', lines 1–4, *Ben Jonson*, VIII, 236.

58 'An Epigram on the Princes birth', lines 1–3, *Ben Jonson*, VIII, 237.

59 Orgel and Strong, *Inigo Jones*, II, 420–2, lines 269–72.

60 'An Epigram to the Queene, then lying in', line 5, *Ben Jonson*, VIII, 238. Coiro, in chapter 2 below, offers a more detailed reading of this sequence.

61 'An Ode, or Song, by all the Muses. In celebration of her Majesties birth-day', lines 49–54, *Ben Jonson*, VIII, 240.

62 For a fuller development of this notion, see Thomas N. Corns, 'The Poetry of the Caroline Court', *Proceedings of the British Academy*, 97 (1998).

2

'A ball of strife': Caroline poetry and royal marriage

Ann Baynes Coiro

I

Charles's royal image was profoundly collaborative. It was his loving and remarkably prolific marriage with Henrietta Maria that was the public projection by which Charles defined himself as king and by which he meant to be understood and obeyed by his subjects. As Roy Strong and Dolores Palomo have argued, imagery of war joined to peace and of a halcyon moment of national calm was crucial to the Caroline vocabulary, but this imagery was created out of the potent, overarching symbolism of royal marriage.[1] Charles was Mars and Henrietta Maria was Venus; the halcyon brooding quietly on the still waters evoked the queen endlessly pregnant and maternal. The importance of the cult of neoplatonic love which Henrietta Maria imported from France and imposed as a style on the English court has been a single note played, perhaps, too loudly in our understanding of the Caroline reign.[2] For at the same time that Henrietta Maria was ruling over and play-acting in this chaste and stringent love regime, she was almost constantly gravid or recovering from childbirth. The dissonance is palpable and recorded in Caroline poetry.

II

It was literally only a generation before Charles took the throne that England lived through an extremely worrying and edgily prolonged shift in power from the Tudor to the Stuart dynasty. A new, multinational identity, British, began its long, violent birth. In the sixteenth century, Englishmen had spent several decades speculating about and trying to control the sexual life of their queen, but by the end of the century the Tudor line was over. In *The Faerie Queene*, for example, we can read the propaganda value *and* the barely hidden criticism of the idea of the Tudor virgin queen, the poem's chief reader and ostensible subject. The one social formation that is insistently promulgated in the poem is marriage. It is the fulfilment, the great destiny, the national duty of the major characters. Indeed, throughout his career as England's Protestant poet, Spenser presents marriage as the ideal human bond.

Yet we can also see in Spenser's poem an argument for a strong masculine force as the ultimately proper form of government: the divine-right patriarch certainly informs, prophetically, the nationalist epic. James I fulfilled that role, after a fashion. His position as father was multiple. He brought with him to England an heir, a back-up heir and a marriageable princess. He wrote and published a letter of fatherly and kingly advice to a son, *Basilike Doran*. He styled himself publicly and explicitly as the father and husband of his people. He also introduced a disturbingly erotic valence to the notion of fatherhood. He and his wife, Anne of Denmark, maintained, very expensively, separate households. His succession of favourites were sons and lovers. He fussed over them, married them off. Buckingham, his last and dearest favourite, was urged upon the king by his wife. James called Buckingham his son, his sweetheart, his wife, and Buckingham called the king dad. By the time Elizabeth and James had finished playing with the categories of virgin, queen/king, and father, the sexual vocabulary of the English court had been heavily deployed and imaginatively expanded.

Nevertheless, in a country that had not seen a functional royal marriage for generations and that had lived through the dire consequences, the idea of a fertile marriage and the stable dynasty it could produce must have seemed enormously desirable. In Charles I and Henrietta Maria, the British finally got, quite splendidly and successfully, that wish fulfilled. In the cultural praise celebrating them, however, there is also unease. The poetry produced during the Caroline years is largely concerned with the relationships of men and women. Even the war poetry of Lovelace and Suckling (and the anti-war poetry of Carew) frame masculine concerns and relations in tension with the lures and demands of women. This chapter will concern itself with the ways in which the paradigm at the centre of Caroline culture – highly sexual, prolific marriage – pervades and worries its poetry.[3] I will focus on a range of poets, some usually considered cavalier (such as Lovelace, Carew, Davenant and Herrick) and some who are rarely thought of as Caroline artists (such as Milton, Marvell, Jonson and Crashaw).

The year 1629 is remarkable in the reign of Charles I as the year he dissolved Parliament and began eleven years of personal rule. Arguably, it is equally remarkable that in 1629 Henrietta Maria began producing children. A son, Charles, died at birth in May of 1629. Another Charles was born a year later, in May of 1630. Year after year, more children would appear – over the course of fifteen years, four sons and five daughters (born in 1629, 1630, 1631, 1633, 1636, 1637, 1639, 1640, and 1644). The unusual four-year hiatus between children, in the 1640s, was due, presumably, only to the separations necessitated by the war; the last child was dramatically delivered on the southern shores of England and left behind as Henrietta Maria fled from pursuing parliamentary forces. The burgeoning royal family is especially striking since, by the mid-seventeenth century, the birth of any child to a reigning English monarch was remarkable. Anne of Denmark had borne a daughter, Mary, in 1605, who died a toddler, and Sophia in 1606, who lived only a few hours, but before that the last royal birth was that of Edward to Henry VIII and Jane Seymour in 1537.

The implications of a king's children, of a royal childbed, for the cultural imagination were at once joyous and threatening, an analogical fulfilment of a wished-for dream that had overtones of sexual-political nightmare. On an immediate, literal level, until Charles produced heirs, the next in line for succession to the throne was his sister, the Protestant heroine Elizabeth of Bohemia, so that the birth of a child to Charles's French Catholic queen meant the end of a genealogical hope for militant Protestant English.[4] But the fecund rule of Charles I was a dream and a nightmare in ways less concrete than simply the spectacle of cosy domestic bliss while the king ruled alone, patriarch without parliament, or the loss of a firm Protestant line. Since kingship was a political and social analogy, Charles's reign introduced the analogical possibilities of overwhelming dynasty, on the one hand, and of a feminized king dominated by a woman, notably a papist woman, on the other.

The idea of genealogy, of momentous family history, lies at the centre of the seventeenth-century imagination. Family connections were, of course, terribly important politically, as they had been for many generations, since wealth and power rested largely in the hands of the nobility. As Michael McKeon has demonstrated, however, by the seventeenth century England was experiencing a crisis in the hegemony of aristocratic ideology.[5] The assumptions that in high birth resided intrinsic honour and that power and wealth were locked in a system of genealogical transference were being eroded by rational questioning and by such pragmatic facts as the sale of titles and the growing power of capital.[6] It is not surprising then that propagation and lineage are the subjects of intense interest to the late Renaissance, since, as McKeon articulates it, 'in those moments when the delicate workings of intellectual and institutional convention, strained to their limits, seem all at once to proclaim what they would enjoin, we see the mechanisms of historical change laid bare'.[7] The symptom of that attention in seventeenth-century poetry and drama is striking and raw. The nationalist focus on genealogy gives way increasingly and disturbingly to a focus on the sexual act itself.

Political and social relationships were understood by organic correspondence in the sixteenth and early seventeenth centuries. The state was conceived of as a human body, for example, the king, the body's head. Or the state was understood as a family, the king, its father and its husband. Such biological, physical analogies were enormously powerful, embracing and reciprocal. If the state was a family, then the family was a state. If the state was a body, then each body was a state. There were always potential instabilities inherent in such thinking, for the separate body and the individual family could be vastly graced by these analogies, empowered rather than disempowered by being set in analogical play with monarchy.

There were also innumerable inconsistencies generated by analogical political thought and in order for it to work it needed to absorb contradiction, even direct contradiction, into itself; so that Elizabeth, for example, could be a husband to the state even though she had a woman's body. In exploring the ways in which the crown was gendered as both male and female during the Renaissance, Stephen Orgel reminds us that the Renaissance 'interpretive technique in which anything can also be its opposite (as well as any number of other things) is so common as to constitute a critical topos in the age'.[8] But ages end, and as they do their topoi become inexplicable rather than explanatory, evidence of power's lack rather than power's pervasive sway. And in the seventeenth century there was an increasing unease with the capacity of images to mean almost anything. Francis Bacon wanted a stable language, stripped of confusing play. Jonson argued that his words should have controlling power over Jones's images. Donne examined with meticulous logic the literal implications of images, pushing the play in the image out into the open. So also, long-accepted images of society were open to logical conclusions, to literal extrapolation. The results of such attention would prove disastrous for British kingship.

England had just had a strong queen, Elizabeth, and a strong king, James. Charles's mother, Anne, had been a visible queen, fond of progresses and masques and head of an important household, but it was clear that the influential role of consort belonged truly to James's favourites. The importance of Henrietta Maria as queen consort was, therefore, a surprise and not a pleasant one. It is true that Henrietta Maria was a welcome substitute for the hated possibility of the Infanta, but her attractiveness was, to the English people, relative and limited. She had begun her marriage scorned by her husband and inept at negotiating the political and religious shoals of the English court. She quickly became the absolute imaginary centre of the Caroline reign, the romantic heroine to Charles's hero, the mythological embodiment of the peace Charles came to espouse (for reasons both psychologically needful and economically practical). At this moment when the theoretical role of kingship had been pushed into strained visibility, when notions of divine-right kingship or of organic correspondence throughout nature – the great chain of being – had begun to seem artistic rather than natural, to be insisted upon rather than formulated without a thought, the analogical meanings of this foreign, Catholic queen were only alarming.

On 1 April 1627, for example, John Donne preached a sermon before Charles on the text: 'Take heed what you heare.' Donne was apparently trying to defend the Church and the king against criticism, and yet the sermon caused the king serious displeasure. Donne had stumbled over analogical rupture; he had pushed a long-standing metaphor too far into reality:

> The Church is the spouse of Christ; Noble husbands do not easily admit defamations of their wives. Very religious Kings may have had wives, that may have retained some tincture, some impressions of errour, which they may have sucked in their infancy, from another Church, and yet would be loth, those wives should be publikely traduced to be Heretiques, or passionately proclaimed to be Idolaters for all that. A Church may lacke something of exact perfection and yet that church should not be said to be a supporter of Antichrist, or a limme of the beast, or a thirster after the cup of *Babylon*, for all that. From extream to extream, from east to west, the *Angels* themselves cannot come, but by passing the middle way between; from that extream impurity, in which Antichrist had damped the Church of God, to that intemperate purity, in which Christ had constituted his Church, the most Angelicall Reformers cannot come, but by touching, yea, and stepping upon some things, in the way.[9]

Rather than feeling vindicated by this ameliorative argument for the middle way, Charles felt criticized and threatened. Implying a comparison between his actual wife and his analogical wife, Henrietta Maria and the Anglican Church, exposed both relationships to danger. When analogy is taken too literally, its ideological magic is lost, and its machinery is dangerously, even ridiculously, visible. A king with a sexy, flirtatious, foreign and prolific queen was vulnerable to unfriendly readings that troped precisely upon his own state vocabulary. Applied too closely, allegory becomes an obvious script, or game, and in England in the seventeenth century the allegory of kingship, the idea that the king is the nation's head (or husband, soul, or father) began to seem a metaphysical conceit that could be appreciated, perhaps, for its wit but not for its truth.

We can see in poems that take Charles and Henrietta Maria as their direct or indirect subject the workings and the dysfunctions of the heavily iconographic and allegorical Caroline court culture. Certainly in the masques performed before and by the king and queen, the centrality of marriage symbolism is striking and, while Caroline masques have recently received strong critical attention, the gendered politics of these masques would generously repay more attention still. But the conventional-bordering-on-parodic language of the poetry written in the second quarter of the seventeenth century is inestimably important to an understanding of Caroline England. Its littleness, formal perfection and conventionality have, however, been barriers to cultural analysis. It is its very formality which makes it a resistant discourse, one which resists its rulers and rules even as it parodies neatly itself, the artful objects that we think of as cavalier, or royalist poetry.

In the poetic effusions prompted by the birth of the royal children to Charles and Henrietta Maria, for example, we can see characteristics of and fault lines in Caroline monarchical imagery. Although birthday poems and poems on royal recoveries from sickness can seem like greetings card verse, such occasional poetry and the complex advice, criticism and reservations that can be decoded from it are integral and meaningful in a patronage society.[10]

Probably in his role as poet laureate, Jonson wrote several poems to the king and queen in 1629 and 1630. They seem strange gifts to give at the time, and in 1640, published by Sir Kenelm Digby as a sequence in *Underwood*, they signal at once a harsh warning and a bizarre familiarity. The first poem is an 'Epigram Consolatorie' to the king and queen for the loss of their first-born son. It lectures sternly, 'Who dares denie, that all first-fruits are due / To God, denies the God-head to be true', making a harshly self-referential gesture to his poem on the loss of his own first son and namesake.[11] If Charles and Henrietta Maria do not 'grutch', God will repay this investment of a dead child with 'large int'rest' (a usurious metaphor which appears repeatedly in the university volumes on this sad occasion but also in later years as the infant interest rate increased impressively).

Placed between the epigram consolatory and a congratulatory epigram on the birth of the second son, Charles, is an anniversary epigram for Charles's 1629 ascension day. As Thomas Corns notes in chapter 1 above, its topic is the nation's uneasiness with the king. Great Britain is a woman who is 'barren growne of love' (line 15) and cannot be filled with gratitude. It is a frank and surprising choice for a purported compliment on an ascension anniversary, for the king's failures are seen in the light of abortive sexual failure on the part of Charles as husband of his people.

Jonson's next epigram on the birth of an heir plays with the unusual appearance of the heavens at his birth, as most poems written to celebrate the birth of Prince Charles did, a sign that poets tried hard to read as propitious but that could easily be seen as ominous to an early modern observer. But instead of troping, as did most other poets celebrating that day, on the fact that the evening star appeared at noon on the day of Prince Charles's birth, Jonson ends his poem by poetic reference to a much more sinister astronomic omen. Two days after the prince's birth there was an eclipse of the sun. The poet invokes the 'envious' moon to haste 'and interpose thy selfe, ("care not how soone.) / And threat" the great Eclipse. Two houres but runne, / *Sol* will re-shine. If not, CHARLES hath a Sonne' (lines 9–12). Again, an ostensible compliment is jagged edged. To conjure a world of darkness at the birth of this child is to conjure the deepest human fears. In this brief poem, Jonson includes as well another unsurprising cliché, given the child's natal month. He styles newborn Charles as the 'Prince of flowers', who has sprung from 'The bed of the chast *Lilly*, and the *Rose*'. The conceit of a flower-bed barely conceals the sexual, marital bed.

The sexual bed of the king is made completely explicit and then dangerously complicated in the following epigram 'to the Queene, then Lying In', which begins 'Haile *Mary*, full of grace'. Most of the poem is concerned with its own blasphemy. After all, the angel-poet says boldly,

> When was there seene
> (Except the joy that the first *Mary* brought,
> Whereby the safetie of Man-kind was wrought)
> So generall a gladnesse to an Isle,
> To make the hearts of a whole Nation smile,
> As in this Prince?   (lines 6–11)

The idea of Mary (it was common practice to anglicize Henrietta Maria's name) as the Virgin Mother is dangerous and seems to be deliberately challenging. It suggests, for one thing, her Catholicism (and Jonson's). While it ostensibly suggests that Charles is God's representative on earth ('Let it be lawfull, so / To compare small with great' (lines 11–12)), it also suggests that Henrietta Maria lies in this bed still a virgin. The poem's transgression is capped by its ending, where the queen becomes mediatrix, 'Then, Haile to *Mary*! spring / Of so much safetie to the Realme, and King' (lines 13–14). While the anniversary poem marked the king's unhappy position in March of 1630, now in May his saviour has arrived in the form of a child and his mother Mary. Charles's implied position as impotent and as weak, fallen man requiring rescue, is not enviable.

The next poem in the sequence celebrates an event of a few months later, Henrietta Maria's twenty-second birthday in November of 1630. Instead of an epigram, Jonson writes an ode with stanzas sung by each of the muses. Again, this birthday compliment is freighted with anxiety, warning, and a weird intimacy. Jonson's choice of message from each muse is carefully tailored. Clio, the muse of history, begins by exhorting some kind of 'publike joy' even – ominously – 'though the Parish-steeple / Be silent' (lines 1, 4–5). Melpomene, the muse of tragedy, harps again on the silence of the Tower's bells and guns, guessing them

> As fearfull to awake
> This Citie, or to shake
>   Their guarded gates asunder?   (lines 10–12)

But the muses of comedy and lyric poetry, Thalia and Euterpe, gaily call on court trumpets, strings and song in lieu of public rejoicing. Terpsichore imagines the queen invested with the pomp and glory of France, 'the royall *Mary*, / The Daughter of great *Harry*! / And Sister to just *Lewis*!' (lines 25–7) and Erato, love poetry, sees her reigning as Venus in England.

By the end of the poem, however, the ominous quality of these fairy-godmothers returns to haunt the feast. Calliope, the muse of epic poetry, summons an astonishingly graphic jousting pun:

> See, see our active *King*
> Hath taken twice the Ring
>   Upon his pointed Lance:
> Whilst all the ravish'd rout
> Doe mingle in a shout,
>   Hay! for the flowre of *France*!   (lines 37–42)

We are asked to look at the king and queen's sexual acts in our mind's eye. And even as we do so, we hear the shouts of 'the ravish'd rout'. Calliope is the mother of Orpheus, and the presence at this marriage of a dionysian crowd, willing to rip a man to shreds for sexual failures, is extremely troubling. Polyhymnia, sacred music, concludes

> Sweet! happy *Mary!* All
> The People her doe call.
>   And this the wombe divine,
> So fruitfull, and so faire,
>   Hath brought the Land an Heire!
>   And CHARLES a *Caroline!*   (lines 49–54)

The rhyme divine / Caroline is at once easy and distasteful. Elizabeth had deftly mantled herself with the old charm of the Virgin, but a Catholic queen dressed poetically as the Mother Mary is a clumsy appropriation, dangerously Duessa-like, dangerously provocative. After all, though, Jonson was old, sick and disgruntled. (The next poem in *Underwood* blames Charles's household for denying Jonson his entitlement to a vat of wine. The hostile joke with which the poem ends, however, ''T were better spare a Butt, then spill his *Muse*' (line 12), is aimed as much at Charles as it is his servants.) The lavish, almost sacrilegious praise barbed with unease evident in the laureate's poems may simply be attributable to his unhappy place in Caroline society. Other poems on the princes' births can serve as controls.

III

In 1630 Robert Herrick was about to assume the vicarage of Dean Prior, patronage that was also a kind of exile. Before he left the court he wrote a 'Pastorall upon the birth of Prince Charles', which was set to music by Nicholas Lanier and performed before the king. A shepherdess, Amarillis, and two shepherds lie happily talking of the birth of a babe to 'The Court'.[12] Here the omen of the evening star's appearance is given a spin so heavy-handedly positive as to roll on into the desecratory:

> And that his birth sho'd be more singular,
> At Noone of Day, was seene a silver Star,
> Bright as the Wise-mens Torch, which guided them
> To Gods sweet Babe, when borne at *Bethlehem*;
> While Golden Angels (some have told to me)
> Sung out his Birth with Heav'nly Minstralsie.   (lines 19–24)

And so the three shepherds decide to go visit the child, bearing country gifts, 'To have his little King-ship know, / As he is Prince, he's Shepherd too' (lines 43–4). The poem's jolly blasphemy is knotted up jauntily by its ending couplet: 'And when before him we have laid our treasures, / We'll bless the Babe, Then back to Countrie pleasures' (lines 47–8). Again, as in Jonson's poems, we see an abrading degree of sacrilege which takes the form of evoking the Virgin Mary and Christ.

Herrick's pretty Amarillis and his linking of Christ–king–shepherd strike a tiny, tinkling note before the sonorous beauty of Milton's 'Lycidas', written seven years later. It seems blasphemy even to whisper a common vocabulary.[13] But Milton did himself write a natal poem at precisely the moment when court and university poets were mourning and rejoicing the death and birth of heirs. In 1629 Milton was a student at Cambridge and (like Henrietta Maria) twenty-one years old. Oxford University would produce *Britanniae natalis* in 1630, celebrating the birth of one Charles and noting the loss of another, but Cambridge University was markedly remiss on the occasion of this truly noteworthy court event. It was not until 1631 that Cambridge would produce a volume of natal verse, *Genethliacum Illustrissimorum Principium Caroli & Mariae*, and by then there was already a princess to celebrate as well. In Milton's Christmas poem, it can be argued, however, Cambridge paid its required tax on time.

In significant ways Milton's 'On the Morning of Christ's Nativity' is concerned with Caroline state imagery. Written on the Christmas day that fell between the birth of the first two sons to England's king and the queen called Mary, the poem is at once a repudiation and a celebration of the sexual vocabulary of queenship and kingship. That Milton's first great poem would be inspired by Christmas is in itself significant, for Christmas was a holiday objectionable to puritans, who saw it as pagan and superstitious and who were particularly uneasy with the drunken sexual roistering that accompanied its celebration.[14] Christmas was ceremonial, papist and decadent, associated with the Stuart court, which had long upheld the practice of festival, and associated, inevitably, with the Virgin Mother and thus with Catholicism.[15]

Milton was working in a long tradition of nativity poems, ranging from popular vernacular ballads and carols to late classical and neo-Latin poetry, a tradition which flourished in the seventeenth century.[16] But writing a Christmas poem was not simply a traditional exercise for Milton in 1629; it was a political act, and one thickly embedded in the tensions of Caroline culture.

In the Nativity Ode itself, as many critics have noted, there is a conspic-uous absence of the bodily. There is a great deal of music and starlight, of silence and ancient mythologies, but a jarring absence of the mother and baby in the manger surrounded by animals. The sexual sweetness and taboo of Christmas is present, however, in the poem's frame. The poem begins:

> This is the month, and this the happy morn
> Wherein the Son of heav'n's eternal King,
> Of wedded maid, and virgin mother born,
> Our great redemption from above did bring;
> For so the holy sages once did sing,
> That he our deadly forfeit should release,
> And with his Father work us a perpetual peace.[17]

The paradox of 'wedded maid' and 'virgin mother' and the incestuous suggestion of the unnamed maid as the consort of her own Father and the mother of her Father's Son is touched on immediately, but then the poem seems to recoil from the crèche and the act of childbirth that is going on in the suspended moment of the poem's time. Throughout the body of the poem, however, the act of birth is present in its deliberate absence. The 'Hymn' begins by telling the story of its first stanza again, but in a conflicted past tense:

> It was the winter wild,
> While the heaven-born child,
>   All meanly wrapt in the rude manger lies;
> Nature in awe to him
> Had doffed her gaudy trim,
>   With her great master so to sympathize:
> It was no season then for her
> To wanton with the sun her lusty paramour.   (lines 29–36)

Personified Nature, the ur-mother to the virgin mother, consort to the Heavenly Father, cloaks herself in snow to cover her 'naked shame', 'Confounded, that her maker's eyes / Should look so near upon her foul deformities' (lines 43–4). This rather shocking reference to female geni-talia brings the poem back to the crèche and the divine birth, asking us to look at the sexual woman even as she hides from the gaze of 'her maker's eyes', and daring us, even taunting us, not to hear the old pun on the homonym sun and son which, heard, opens the madonna and child to the sexual speculation that the poem seems to be trying to hold at bay with the light.

The third stanza of Milton's poem is markedly Caroline. To comfort

Nature in her sexual shame, God sends a powerful personification, one who can suspend sound and time, war and unrest:

> But he her fears to cease,
> Sent down the meek-eyed Peace,
>   She crownd with olive green, came softly sliding
> Down through the turning sphere
> His ready harbinger,
>   With turtle wing the amorous clouds dividing,
> And waving wide her myrtle wand,
> She strikes a universal peace through sea and land.   (lines 45–52)

Sweet amorous peace is the state imagery used for Henrietta Maria for years after this, in the paintings of Van Dyck, for example, and in the court masques.[18] When this personification descends, 'No war, or battle's sound / Was heard the world around . . . The Trumpet spake not to the armed throng' (lines 53–8). With eerie precision, Milton's poem evokes what is to become the quintessential Caroline imagery, the halcyon moment. The night is peaceful 'Wherein the Prince of Light / His reign of peace upon the earth began', the ocean still 'While birds of calm sit brooding on the charmed wave' (lines 62–8). The central conceit of the poem, the halting of time and light, the poem's power to dwell in the split second of the baby's world-changing arrival, is literally enacted by the stars, which do not yield their place to Lucifer, the harbinger of morning.

Milton is writing this poem five years into Charles's reign, as the potent imagery of kingship begins to mantle him after the death of Buckingham and the *rapprochement* with his wife. The poem's vocabulary is clearly evocative of imagery we bracket off as cavalier (and sycophantic). Just as Herrick's poem 'Rex Tragicus' describes uncannily the crucifixion of Christ in terms that seem to be a description of Charles's execution, but months before it happened, so Milton's 'On the Morning of Christ's Nativity' seems to conjure the ideograms that become the constantly reiterated symbolism of Caroline culture after the birth of Prince Charles, an event which happened months after Milton wrote his poem. Indeed, Christ's nativity was to be the reigning metaphor used by court poets for the birth of an heir to Charles and Henrietta Maria. Even the aberrant behaviour of the morning star and the suspended moment of darkness at a prince's birth are going to be repeated at Charles's birth and then repeatedly troped upon by Caroline poets. A perverse argument can be made that the pre-eminent poet of Charles I is not poor old Ben in his grumpy time-serving, nor Herbert in his cloistered parish, nor Carew, fanciful and brilliantly sarcastic, nor Lovelace and his dashing bravado, nor Donne preaching his last sermons, nor

Herrick far away miniaturizing the court in charming talismans, but that the pre-eminent poet of Charles I is John Milton.[19] No one else took him quite so seriously; no one else paid tributes – albeit elliptically – quite so touching in their vision of what might have been.

But Milton understood the treacherous as well as the beguiling nature of images. 'On the Morning of Christ's Nativity' is also a warning of the dangers inherent in the mythology of Christmas, dangers that curse those who attempt to assume the nativity aura as their own. The vivified world of ancient religion is drained of its tutelary presences – the oracles banished, the geniuses and nymphs, ancestral spirits and spirits of the dead sent weeping away, and

> In urns, and altars round,
> A drear and dying sound
>   Affrights the flamens at their service quaint;
> And the chill marble seems to sweat,
> While each peculiar power forgoes his wonted seat.   (lines 192–6)

Milton's contemporary implications are clear – a true celebration of the birth of Christ will banish the false worship of contaminated church ceremonialism. As Milton strips myth after myth of its power to charm, he comes right up flush with the Mother Mary when he scorns 'mooned Astaroth, / Heaven's Queen and mother both' who 'Now sits not girt with tapers' holy shine' (lines 200–2). The danger and much of the power of the poem's subject has been, all along, the mother at its heart, heaven's queen. And yet, in the final stanza, when Milton rounds again to the manger he asks us to look once more at the centre of the universal spectacle he has been summoning and ignoring: 'But see the virgin blest, / Hath laid her babe to rest.' Marked in the poem is a demonic Christmas, a pagan mother whom Milton desperately needs to put aside so that we can 'see' the 'virgin blest' uncontaminated by sexual and idolatrous myths and their appropriation. 'Upon the Morning of Christ's Nativity' is very much a poem of its historical moment and part of its haunting effect is the overlay of negative and positive images of an embodied and bodiless Christ and Mary during the breathless moment of this brilliant early Caroline poem.

IV

If we look to the other end of the central Caroline decade and to young poets who came of age artistically during the symbolic reign of royal marriage, we see the divine, sexual bodies of the queen and king troped upon still, but with increased self-consciousness and unease. Marvell, who rivals Carew as the most perceptive literary critic of the seventeenth century, wrote, early in his career, a kind of companion poem to his great 1674 commentary 'On Mr Milton's *Paradise Lost*'. In addressing Richard Lovelace on the occasion of his 1648 *Lucasta*, Marvell laments the loss of 'That candid Age' of a few years before which 'no other way could tell / To be ingenious, but by speaking well. / Who best could prayse, had then the greatest prayse'.[20] In fact, Lovelace's body of praise extends prettily to women, the only public poem a rather tortured celebration/elegy for the Oxford volume commemorating the one-day life of Princess Catherine. Marvell's poem to Lovelace is thus slyly funny; it ends, for example, with the spectacle of women in dishabille sallying forth to do battle with Parliament in defence of their valiant poet. Marvell does mean to praise Lovelace, but in such a way that simultaneously enacts the very critical tendency Marvell professes to abhor: 'He highest builds, who with most Art destroys'. The object of Marvell's ostensible regret is 'the Civicke crowne' of unbounded praise, but the mocking praise of this poem identifies that crown with a feminized kingdom.

And yet, Marvell's first published poem was an Horatian ode on the birth of Princess Anne in the Cambridge volume on that occasion, Συνωδια *sive Musarum Cantabrigiensium Concentus et Congratulatio* (1637), written when Marvell was fifteen.[21] Marvell entitles his poem a parody, that is a formal imitation, in this case of an ode by Horace which describes the horrors of civil war and begs Caesar to save the state.[22] The poem offers critical difficulties. It could be argued, for example, that it is simply a schoolboy exercise, an excellent imitation of a poem chosen as a model compliment. Almost all such university poems are marked as academic exercises, which does not obviate, and perhaps underscores, their political valence. What Marvell intends in imitating this poem, written on the eve of the end of the Republic and indeed inviting its end and the rise to total power of Caesar Augustus, is impossible to say.[23] Within the context of its volume, however, the poem is richly revealing of Caroline culture. The horror that Marvell's poem summons (on what would seem to be a happy occasion) is present to varying degrees in all four university volumes on the princesses, and is even more strongly marked in the two volumes commemorating the birth of Henry, Duke of Gloucester in 1640.

Marvell repeats exactly Horace's question: 'Quem vocet divum populus ruentis / Imperi rebus?' (What god shall the people invoke when the state collapses?). For Roman images of civil war, Marvell substitutes the plague and structures his poem much more strongly than Horace around the recurring notion of father. It is the father who has sent this punishment on his people. But, at the same time, it is parents who are its cause:

> Audiit mortes vitio parentum
> > Rara juventus.
> Quem vocet divum populus ruentis
> Imperi rebus?   (lines 23–6)

> They have heard of the deaths caused by their fathers' vices.
> What god shall the people invoke when the state collapses?[24]

The speaker pleads with the national parents, Charles and Mary, who can expiate for the past sins of the fathers, 'neglectum genus et nepotes / Auxeris' (aid your forgotten people). Marvell wrote this poem during Henrietta Maria's pregnancy, so the sense of dread and wished-for salvation is tied to the unknown outcome. A child, boy or girl, born alive will repair the damage the plague has visited upon the nation:

> Hic ames dici pater atque princeps,
> Et nova mortes reparare prole
> > Te patre, Caesar.   (lines 50–2)

> Here may you delight to be called prince and father,
> and with new birth make good our losses, Caesar.

The poem's closing word underscores its intense ambiguity. Charles's clear association here with Caesar Augustus will be repeated with equal opacity of political valuation in Marvell's later Horatian ode when 'restless Cromwell could not cease / In the inglorious arts of peace' (lines 9–10) but

> > Caesar's head at last
> > Did through his laurels blast.
> 'Tis madness to resist or blame
> The force of angry heaven's flame.   (lines 23–6)

The Latin ode's title, 'Ad Regem Carolum Parodia', does, however, offer a teasing clue. All through these middle years of the seventeenth century the slippage between Latin and English is electric and culturally central. Most poets wrote in both languages and were able to play elegant games with words caught between the ossified and evolving languages. *Parodia* is a neutral, descriptive word meaning a close imitation, but *parody* had already mutated in its transition to English into mockery and burlesque. Marvell's parodia is astonishingly exact *except* in the three verses on

Henrietta Maria, Charles, and their children. Where Horace talks of a terrible war-weariness, Marvell talks of the queen's fecundity as the antidote to death, the birth of a royal baby balancing the subjects' death, and where Horace addresses 'te duce, Caesar', Marvell salutes 'Te patre, Caesar'. Marvell's Horatian ode seems, at least retrospectively, to balance somewhere between a counter-turn and a parody – written on the eve of civil war rather than its ending, and addressing a king who is already the volatile father that Horace wishes to propitiate.

Richard Crashaw has been regarded as an aberration from English seventeenth-century poetry because of his extravagant, grossly bodily, flamboyantly sexual poetics. Rather, he is a master of the central early modern discourse we have been considering. Crashaw, who contributed steadily to university volumes, including the one in which Marvell's ode appeared, does what scores of other poets of this period attempt to do: he moves with brilliant bilingual fluidity from Latin to English and back again; he pushes cliché into the range of explicitness and discomfort so that it becomes metaphor charged with a stunning strength; he creates an intimate closeness with the Virgin Mother and the body of Christ that challenges gender and hierarchy.

It is not surprising, then, that Crashaw is the most truly passionate Caroline poet – and the object of his fascination is, significantly, not Charles, but the queen. (And Henrietta Maria would remain central to his life. He joined her in exile in Paris, and she wrote to the Pope to recommend Crashaw's services to the Catholic Church.) After matriculating at Cambridge in 1632, he wrote eight poems for six royal commemorative volumes, three of these poems appearing in Cambridge's rather desperate outpouring of 1640, *Voces votivae*.[25] It is perhaps fitting to end a consideration of Charles's eleven years of personal rule with Crashaw's 1640 poem on the occasion of the birth of another son, a poem which was enlarged and retitled in the 1648 *Delights of the Muses*, 'To the Queen, Upon her numerous Progenie.'[26] The poem repeats the Christic nativity imagery and incorporated pagan mythology characteristic of Caroline poetry, but here the birth of children is explicitly marked as an enormous, even perhaps unbearable stress on Britain. 'Thou art opprest / With thine owne Gloryes' (lines 3–4)

> for lo! the Gods, the Gods
> Come fast upon thee, and those glorious ods,
> Swell thy full gloryes to a pitch so high,
> As sits above thy best capacitye.   (lines 5–8)

The marriage of Charles and Henrietta Maria was richly symbolic, trapped with divinity. But the erotic and the sacred were a volatile mix in a country increasingly sensitive to Catholic influences, to anything that could be regarded as superstition. More than that, the very nature of symbolism was being effected by the shift from ceremonial and analogical thinking to a much more literal form of understanding.

During the central Caroline years the notion that the body of Christ was still present in the world – the notion celebrated most fully in the ceremony of the Eucharist – was still being embodied by artists in the idea of the king (and even more so in the idea of his children and their mother Mary). Oxford's 1641 volume celebrating the return of Charles from Scotland is entitled, for example, *Eucharistica*.[27] But the capacity for kingship to carry divinity had been radically diminished in a linguistically rich, densely developed Protestant humanist culture, which had reached a crescendo and was now at a loss. Mikhail Bakhtin posits a critical moment when 'linguistic consciousness – parodying the direct word, direct style, exploring its limits, its absurd sides, the face specific to an era – constituted itself *outside* this direct word and outside all graphic and expressive means of representation . . . the creating artist began to look at language from the outside, with another's eyes, from the point of view of a potentially different language and style', and I am proposing that the Caroline period is exactly such a moment of dawning parodic consciousness.[28] The vocabulary of queen as Mother Mary and of an uxorious king is clearly a provocation to puritans, but it is linguistically provocative as well: highly stylized and elegant, decorative and self-involved, it loses its potency in its refinement. Instead, its potent energy moves into self-consciousness. The Caroline period is the cusp of the great age of translation and mockery.

The king's body had for centuries a numinous power which extended to – even rested in – his personal, bodily intimacies.[29] And yet, at the same time that Charles rested his sense of rule on divine right, an emerging sense that the divine rested in the individual – a sense intrinsic to Protestantism – was inexorably reshaping power and gender relations.[30] Charles himself had a fastidious sense of privacy, insisting on elaborate procedural rules to hedge his body and his private chambers from unwanted contact.[31] And he and Henrietta Maria enjoyed an unusually close relationship, which entailed a retreat into privacy which was remarkable given their rank. Court poetry had come, therefore, to inhabit a space that was suddenly liable to embarrassment and even furtive amusement.

Jonson's jousting Charles thrusting his spear through Henrietta Maria's ring is in many ways more disturbing than the detailed eroticism of Carew's 'Rapture'.

We began by thinking about the ways in which the Elizabethan poet Spenser had promulgated marriage as a political act. But, at the same time, *The Faerie Queen* is livid with fear of women. No female allegorical figure is more dangerous than Duessa, who in the poem bears an extraordinary range of meanings, from the abstract to the historical (when she means Mary, Queen of Scots, Charles's Catholic grandmother). The tension of Book I is in the ever-present fear that the Red Cross Knight will succumb to this monstrous, papist shape-changer. Finally, he does take off his armour, lies down under a tree, and falls into her power; epic victory cannot be achieved until he casts off Duessa and her minions. Charles I prized and fostered the symbolism of the Order of the Garter; on the reverse of his cross of St George, which he wore constantly, was a picture of his wife.[32] He took it, in part, as an emblem of his romantic marriage. But clearly the lady in the icon could be read as Duessa, seducing the king into a pastoral shade and holding him and the English people in thrall to a lurking papist giant. Charles wore on his person a nuanced and sophisticated cultural reference that was liable to collapse into a strong (and damning) statement.

V

In *Eikonoklastes*, Milton's legalistic dismemberment of *Eikon Basilike*, he dismisses out of hand Charles's horror at the way his 'Protestant subjects'[33] have treated his wife: 'what concerns it us to hear a Husband divulge his Household privacies, extolling to others the virtues of his Wife; an infirmity not seldom incident to those who have least cause'.[34] In order to demystify the aura of kingship, Milton argues that the family is a private affair. In the moment, he did not succeed, and in some ways *Eikon Basilike* controls the king's imagery to this day. But in Milton's epic, *Paradise Lost*, he succeeds. Eve brings down Adam, as the queen brings down the king, because of the irresistibly sexual nature of their relationship. Milton understood royal symbolism as a metaphoric system that was already shifting to the individual. Even a generation earlier Donne had played teasing games (of serious import in an analogical world) with monarchical roles and sexual privacy:

> She'is all States, and all Princes, I,
>   Nothing else is.
> Princes doe but play us, compar'd to this,
>   All honor's mimique.[35]

Charles I delighted in the idea of such an analogical marriage as well. He thought, however, that his private world should be the only public world. It was his downfall.

Notes

1 See Roy Strong, *Van Dyck: Charles I on Horseback* (London: Allen Lane, 1972) and Dolores Palomo, 'The Halcyon Moment of Stillness in Royalist Poetry', *Huntington Library Quarterly*, 44 (1981): 205–21.
2 See Erica Veevers's fine study, *Images of Love and Religion: Queen Henrietta Maria and Court Entertainments* (Cambridge University Press, 1989).
3 Very oddly, Heather Dubrow's excellent study of the Stuart epithalamium, *A Happier Eden: The Politics of Marriage in the Stuart Epithalamium* (Ithaca, NY: Cornell University Press, 1990) makes no mention of the marriage at the centre of Caroline culture.
4 As Malcolm Smuts points out, reports were made that 'Puritans' refused to join in the celebration for the birth of the Prince of Wales, 'saying God had already provided for the succession in the family of the Elector Palatine, the German Calvinist married to Charles's sister'. See 'The Political Failure of Stuart Cultural Patronage', in *Patronage in the Renaissance*, ed. Guy Fitch Lytle and Stephen Orgel (Princeton University Press, 1981), 182.
5 See Michael McKeon, *The Origins of the English Novel, 1600–1740* (Baltimore: Johns Hopkins University Press, 1987), 150–9.
6 Mark Kishlansky has pointed out that
> in 1603 . . . James I created more knights in four months than Elizabeth I had in forty-four years . . . The precision of these distinctions was significant, for it created the impression of stability which was otherwise constantly belied . . . The Stuarts continued the pattern with a vengeance, nearly tripling the size of the titular aristocracy both by selling titles in the second quarter of the seventeenth century and by rewarding office-holders in the later decades.

See *A Monarchy Transformed: Britain, 1603–1714* (London: Allen Lane, 1996), 24.
7 McKeon, *Origins of the English Novel*, 151.
8 Stephen Orgel, 'Gendering the Crown', in *Subject and Object in Renaissance Culture*, ed. Margreta de Grazia, Maureen Quilligan and Peter Stallybrass (Cambridge University Press, 1996), 136.
9 John Donne, *The Sermons*, ed. Evelyn M. Simpson and George R. Potter, 10 vols. (Berkeley: University of California Press, 1962), VII, 409.
10 See Thomas N. Corns, *Uncloistered Virtue: English Political Literature, 1640–1660* (Oxford: Clarendon Press, 1992); M. L. Donnelly, 'Caroline Royalist Panegyric: The Disintegration of a Symbolic Mode', in *'The Muses Common-weale': Poetry and Politics in the Seventeenth Century*, ed. Claude J. Summers and Ted-Larry Pebworth (Columbia: University of Missouri Press, 1988), 163–76; Annabel Patterson, *Censorship and Interpretation: The Conditions of Writing and Reading in Early Modern England* (Madison:

University of Wisconsin Press, 1984); and Kevin Sharpe, *Criticism and Compliment: The Politics of Literature in the England of Charles I* (Cambridge University Press, 1987).

11 *Ben Jonson*, ed. C. H. Herford and Percy and Evelyn Simpson, 11 vols. (Oxford: Clarendon Press, 1925–63), VIII, 235–6, lines 1–2. All further references to Jonson will be to this edition; line references will be given within the main text.

12 Robert Herrick, *The Poetical Works*, ed. L. C. Martin (Oxford: Clarendon Press, 1956), 86. All subsequent references to Herrick will be to this edition and will be given within the main text.

13 On Milton's early poetry in its contemporary context see Richard Helgerson, *Self-Crowned Laureates: Spenser, Jonson, Milton and the Literary System* (Berkeley: University of California Press, 1983), 185–282.

14 See Chris Durston, 'Lords of Misrule: The Puritan War on Christmas, 1642–60', *History Today*, 35 (December 1985): 7–14. See also David Cressy, *Bonfires and Bells: National Memory and the Protestant Calendar in Elizabethan and Stuart England* (London: Weidenfeld & Nicolson, 1989); Ronald Hutton, *The Rise and Fall of Merry England* (Oxford: Clarendon Press, 1994); and David Underdown, *Revel, Riot and Rebellion: Popular Politics and Culture in England, 1603–1660* (Oxford: Clarendon Press, 1985), 256–70.

15 See Leah S. Marcus, *The Politics of Mirth: Jonson, Herrick, Milton, Marvell, and the Defense of Old Holiday Pastimes* (University of Chicago Press, 1986).

16 See J. B. Broadbent, 'The Nativity Ode', in *The Living Milton*, ed. Frank Kermode (London: Routledge and Kegan Paul, 1960), 12–31; and Rosemond Tuve, *Images and Themes in Five Poems by Milton* (Cambridge, MA: Harvard University Press, 1957), 37–72.

17 *The Poems of John Milton*, ed. John Carey and Alastair Fowler (London and Harlow: Longman, 1968), 101, lines 1–7. All subsequent references to Milton will be to this edition and will be given within the main text.

18 Helgerson points out how masque-like this description is in *Self-Crowned Laureates*, 265.

19 See Malcolm McKenzie Ross, *Milton's Royalism: A Study of the Conflict of Symbol and Idea* (Ithaca, NY: Cornell University Press, 1943).

20 *The Poems and Letters of Andrew Marvell*, ed. H. M. Margoliouth, rev. Pierre Legouis with E. E. Duncan-Jones, 2 vols. (Oxford: Clarendon Press, 1971), I, 3.

21 Marvell also wrote a Greek poem for the occasion, which plays upon the number five, since Anne was the fifth surviving child of Charles and Henrietta Maria. Much more attention should be paid to the body of academic verse produced for occasions deemed significant by Oxford and Cambridge, and this is especially true for the Caroline years, when the practice reached its apex of activity. During the reigns of James I and Charles I, Oxford University produced twenty-four volumes of commemorative poetry (STC 19019–19039; Wing O883, O941, and O903). Cambridge produced fifteen (STC 4475, 4477, 4479, 4480, 4481, 4483, 4484, 4486, 4487, 4489, 4491, 4492, 4493, 4495, and Wing C340). See Raymond Anselment, 'The Oxford University Poets and Caroline Panegyric', *John Donne Journal*, 3 (1984): 181–201 and J. C. T. Oates, 'Cambridge Books of Congratulatory Verse, 1603–1640', *Transactions of the Cambridge Bibliographical Society*, 1 (1953): 395–421.

22 Book 1 Ode 2. References to Horace's text will be to *The Odes and Epodes*, trans. C. E. Bennett, rev. edn (Cambridge, MA: Harvard University Press; London: Heinemann, 1927), 6–11.

23 As Malcolm Smuts argues, much of court culture was a recall of Augustan Rome and its age of peace. There is deep tension, however, between the ideological use of

Augustan Rome and the ideological use of the birth of Christ in Stuart culture, since they represent historically concurrent but potentially competing world views. See 'Political Failure of Stuart Cultural Patronage'.

24 The translation is from Andrew Marvell, *Complete Poems*, ed. Elizabeth Story Donno (Harmondsworth: Penguin, 1972).

25 This volume commemorated the birth of Henry, Prince of Gloucester.

26 In 1640 the poem was entitled 'Upon the Duke of Yorke his Birth'. Crashaw got his dukes confused, of course. James, Duke of York had been born in 1633. It was Henry, Duke of Gloucester who was born in 1640. The text cited is from Richard Crashaw, *The Poems English, Latin and Greek*, ed. L. C. Martin, 2nd edn (Oxford: Clarendon Press, 1957), 176.

27 The polyglossia of this moment is largely lost to us, but the play and danger possible as words crossed the boundary line from one language to another is one of the most teasing aspects of Caroline poetry. In Latin *eucharistica* simply means thanksgiving, but there was nothing simple about its use in 1641 as the title of this volume.

28 Mikhail Bakhtin, 'From the Prehistory of Novelistic Discourse', in *The Dialogic Imagination*, ed. Michael Holquist, trans. Caryl Emerson and Michael Holquist (Austin: University of Texas Press, 1981), 60. Bakhtin is referring to classical Roman literature.

29 See David Starkey, 'Representation Through Intimacy: A Study in the Symbolism of Monarchy and Court Office in Early-Modern England', in *Symbols and Sentiments: Cross-Cultural Studies in Symbolism*, ed. Joan Lewis (London: Academic Press, 1977), 187–224.

30 See Michael McKeon, 'Historicizing Patriarchy: The Emergence of Gender Difference in England, 1660–1760', *Eighteenth-Century Studies*, 28 (1995): 295–322.

31 See Kevin Sharpe, *The Personal Rule of Charles I* (New Haven and London: Yale University Press, 1992), especially 209–22.

32 On the Order of the Garter, see ibid., 219–22. For an important argument about the importance of chivalry and romance outside the king's circle, see William Hunt, 'Civic Chivalry and the English Civil War', in *The Transmission of Culture in Early Modern Europe*, ed. Anthony Grafton and Ann Blair (Philadelphia: University of Pennsylvania Press, 1990), 204–37.

33 *Eikon Basilike*, ed. Philip Knachel, 30.

34 *Complete Prose Works of John Milton*, ed. Don M. Wolfe, 8 vols. (New Haven: Yale University Press, 1953–82), III, 419.

35 John Donne, 'The Sunne Rising', *The Complete English Poems*, ed. C. A. Patrides (New York: Alfred A.Knopf, 1985), 5, lines 21–4.

3

Popular representations of Charles I

Joad Raymond

I have in my time seen certain *Pictures* with two *faces*. Beheld one way, they have presented the *shape* and *figure* of a *Man*. Beheld another, they have presented the *shape* and *figure* of a *Serpent*. Me thinks, Sir, for some years, whatever *Letters* the *King* wrote either to the *Queene*, or his *friends*, or what ever *Declarations* he publisht in the defence of his *Rights* and *Cause*, had the ill fortune to undergoe the fate of such a *Picture*. To us who read them impartially, by their own true, genuine *light*, they appeared so many cleare, transparent *Copies* of a sincere and Gallant *Mind*. Look't on by the People, (of whom you know who said, *populus iste vult decipi, decipiatur*) through the *Answers* and *Observations*, and venomous *Comments*, which some men made upon them, a *fallacy* in *judgement* followed very like the *fallacy* of the *sight*; where an *Object* beheld through a false deceitfull *medium*, partakes of the *cosenage* of the *conveyance*, and *way*, and puts on a false *Resemblance*. As *square*, *bright*, *angular* things through a mist show *darke* and *round*; and *straight* things seen through water show *broken* and *distorted*.[1]

I

Jasper Mayne's simile is a key to the king's celebrity. Charles I was the first ruler of England, Wales, Scotland or Ireland to be represented by a popular press beyond his control. Competing images, both verbal and visual, endure to this day, leaving their residue in conflicting interpretations of Charles's reign.[2] The growth in popular representations stemmed from several related factors: the expansion of interest in politics in the early seventeenth century; the rapid development of journalism in the popular press; the political divisions nurtured by Charles's rule. The resulting *exposure* of the king's person, a theme which countless writers harped upon, was one of the great ideological tremors of the 1640s.

Through this desacralizing and demystifying exposure at the hands of a commercial printing trade, Charles's political career frequently appears as a series of vignettes, decisive or symbolic moments in his personal fortune and in the history of his times. These are precisely those which were colourfully depicted in the popular media: the failed Spanish match; the assassination of Buckingham; Charles's return from Scotland in December 1641; the assault on the five members on 4 January 1642; the publication of his private letters in 1645; his disguised flight from Oxford in April 1646; his imprisonment at Holmby and Carisbrooke castles; his wilful defence at his trial and his execution. These events were the rudiments of the contemporary popular image of the king, the collective memory on which pamphleteers freely drew; but they proceeded to permeate subsequent histories of the war by Rushworth, Clarendon, Hobbes and many others.[3]

While I shall acknowledge the place of popular perceptions and interpretations, I am concerned here with the depictions themselves. This is to draw a distinction between production and reception. Too often the two have been conflated, and mass representations used as unmediated evidence of popular opinion, on the grounds that authors were greedily pandering to their readers' tastes and prejudices, and were capable of gauging their market precisely.[4] Studies of popular culture and of the history of reading suggest that the hermeneutic path is not so direct, and that consumption frequently transforms the texts and images consumed.[5] Hence popular representations are here defined as accessible and inexpensive images and texts: broadsides, quartos, octavos, and duodecimos, containing one or two sheets of paper, and thus costing no more than a penny or two. These texts were plentifully dispersed across the country, into the purview of many of the middling sort.[6] The oral circulation of ballads and libels suggests that their representations had a special currency among their audience, and that they offer more accurate insights into popular perceptions.

It is also possible to identify a popular publication, to some extent, by the content; though this must be done with caution. Complex classical references, Latin quotations, and the assumption of detailed legal or historical knowledge suggest strict limits on the possible audiences of a text. Manifestly populist and widely read texts, nonetheless, might contain dense levels of allusion: though the ability of readers to decode these doubtless varied. Humble readers, versed in the Bible, could respond to

complex texts involving allegorical modes; the rhetoric of chivalry seems
to have been widely disseminated; some pamphlets use the simpler elements of the pastoral genre, perhaps drawing upon popular reserves of
anti-court sentiment; some libels draw on the conventions of revenge
tragedies.[7] Many of those who set out to read these pamphlets were possessed of nimble interpretative skills, and some were well-informed on
contemporary events through the perusal of the newsbooks. Yet because
any attempt to move from aspects of style to assumptions about consumers' identities are at best tenuous, for the purposes of this chapter I
will examine the full range of inexpensive vernacular publications, rather
than restrict myself to the proportion that now seem easier to read and
therefore potentially more demotic.

John Selden's assessment of the informative value of ephemera is well
known:

> Though some make slight of libels, yet you may see by them how the
> wind sits: as take a straw and throw it up into the air, you shall see by
> that which way the wind is, which you shall not do by casting up a stone.
> More solid things do not show the complexion of the times so well, as
> ballads and libels.[8]

Many of the items explored below may seem less representative of
popular culture than the most insubstantial, ephemeral texts. Some were
certainly written by 'elite' authors. While the most widely disseminated
image of the king and his authority was presumably that on small denomination coins, these convey less information than more restrictive, though
nonetheless widespread representations. The same can be said of many
chapbooks and ballads, which tend to be sluggishly generic and hence
information-cold. A satiric pamphlet, or something more information-
hot, by virtue of its greater complexity, may impress in greater detail the
contemporary currency of the images it carries. Such sources reveal that
popular perceptions of the king were fed upon texts that were far from
merely conservative or traditionalist. As this chapter suggests, popular
culture, and its representative images, were not wholly embodied in the
slow-moving substratum of commonplace and proverbial wisdom, the
'*longue durée*' as one historian of popular culture has suggested, but also in
swifter moving currents, responding to topical events, elastic and capable
of radical reformulations in comparatively short cycles of time.[9] Pictures
of the same king, variously refracted, could seem radically altered, and
even popular representations participated in different rhythms of change.

II

Charles's reign began with a chorus decrying corruption, ill counsel and sodomy, and ended with a plainchant for a martyr. In 1623, two years before his accession, doubtful glances were cast at the prospect of a Spanish match, when the prince travelled to Madrid with George Villiers, Duke of Buckingham, his father's former lover and current favourite. These were countered by considerable popular celebration at his safe return without a popish bride.[10]

Widely circulating manuscript verses on the Spanish expedition cast aspersions upon the duke, and in doing so reflected badly on the future king. Buckingham's reputation as the most unpopular man in England and Wales and probably Scotland was secured when he performed the marvellous acrobatic of becoming the son's favourite upon the death of the father, and when he led the disastrous expedition to the Ile de Ré in 1627. Copious verse libels against the duke, both before and after his death in August 1628, comment on his relationship with the king.[11] The most sympathetic verses defended the king's innocence. Most, however, left an uneasy silence around him or even criticized by implication. One asked of the duke: 'O who shall then the sceptre sway / And kingdomes rule, when thou art gone away?' In another: 'Hee shall be king there, sitt in the kings throne, / Or els commaund the king, and that's all one.' Another charged that: 'God's deafe to kings that will not heare the cries / Of their oppressed subjects' injuries.'[12] And another, employing the metaphor of a game of cards: 'The King winnes from the loosing commonweale, / The Duke keep's stakes . . .'[13] An epitaph on the duke went as far as saying that he had 'brought downe / The glorie of the English crowne.' Though most libels blame the duke as a libidinous, avaricious and megalomaniac ill-counsellor, the effect is often to portray Charles as hapless, passive and ill-judging. The verses praising the duke's murderer, John Felton, generally did not reflect upon the king; though the praise of him as another Brutus hardly commends Charles. In one verse Charles is said to be honoured to be the king of such a subject.[14]

Some did not hesitate to impugn the king. In 1628 a Somerset man was arrested for allegedly saying 'that the King was as unfit to rule as his shepherd, being an innocent'. Milton's tutor, Alexander Gill, was charged with proposing a toast to Felton and with saying: 'We have a fine wise king', who was 'Fitter to stand in a Cheapside shop with an apron before him, and say *What do you lack?* than to govern a kingdome'. In 1644 a London woman, nettled by the government of 'His Majestye . . . a stuttering foole', invoked his spirit, asking: 'Is there never a Felton yett living? If I were a man, as I am a woman, I would helpe to pull him to pieces.' These more aggressive comments easily develop from the suggestion that the king was the passive victim of poor advice. Felton was the subject of toasts among the 'base multitude' and even gratified those of 'better degree'. John Rous transcribed numerous verse libels against the duke into his diary, commenting after the return from Ile de Ré: 'this I knowe, that those which are in esteeme and greatest favor with princes are most subjecte to slander of tongues, the vulgar delighting herein, who judge of all things by events, not by discretion'. After the duke's murder he added: 'Hence maye be seene how that the greatest are subject to the scorne of witte. Light scoffing wittes, not apte to deeper reache, can rime upon any the most vulgar surmises, and will not faile to shewe themselves, though charity and true wisdome forbidde.' Rous's comments suggest that the slanders were intended transparently to reflect upon the king. A similar ambiguity coloured the attacks on the king's evil counsellors in the 1640s. The Earl of Strafford's offences, like Buckingham's, were said to have 'indanger'd a general insurrection against Majesty itself'.[15] In these cases it is not always clear whether the author attacks the counsellor because s/he does not wish to speak ill of the king; or whether s/he attacks the counsellor as a means of criticizing the king.

III

After the relative quiet of the 1630s, the representations of 1641 seem explosive. This fact has been interpreted both as evidence of silenced discontent and of peaceful contentment over the preceding decade.[16] The first half of the seventeenth century witnessed the changing winds of consensus and conflict, but overall there was a decline in the majesty of kingship.[17] This decline was facilitated by expanding modes of publicity, founded on the growth of popular awareness and expanding mechanisms of print and distribution.

It is an overstatement to suggest that, notwithstanding his awareness of popular expectations, 'between 1625 and 1640 Charles systematically distanced himself from his subjects'. Nevertheless Charles's inclination to privacy, his aloofness, affected his appearance in the popular eye. He generally shied from the festive celebrations, entries and pageants, with which Elizabeth had courted her subjects; his entertainments became focused on the court. In 1626 the king requested that the mayor and aldermen of London remove their preparations for a coronation pageant, on the grounds that it was both costly and an obstruction to traffic.[18]

The main popular entertainment in Charles's reign greeted his coronation trip to Edinburgh in 1633.[19] Though he journeyed to Edinburgh 'priuily', on the day of the coronation a dramatic pageant was performed; advising, amongst other things, against raising new taxes. As the king left the stage, gold and silver commemorative coins were flung among the people; coins with 'ye kings face one ye one syde, in his Coronatione Robes . . . and one ye reversse a Thissell'. Perhaps attempting to seem like a man of the people, Charles even attended a football match, though one played by 'Barrons & Gent of Qualitie'.[20] The planned reception of the king on his return to London was apparently cancelled after delays (a smaller salutation was held at Stratford); and subsequent processions in 1637 and 1639, when popular support was surely crucial, did not offer pageant dramas.[21]

The calling of the Long Parliament in November 1640 led to a resurgence in praise of the king; and though no pageant adorned the 1641 trip to Scotland, Londoners welcomed his return with joy and acclamations. The king seems to have been concerned to carry the people's support.[22] The praise of the king was fulsome, and subsequent news pamphlets commemorated the event with the familiar trope, not limited to courtly verse, of the king as sun:

> These clouds of darknesse, whose resistlesse might
> In the Suns absence, turn'd the day to night:
> Shall by his presence, vanish, swiftly flie
> Like foggy exhalations of the skie,
> His glorious rayes of Majestie shall shine
> In spight of envy, glorious and divine.

John Bond echoed the sentiment:

> Welcome thou Son of glory, whose bright beames
> Doe so illuminate those obscure dreames
> Of adverse Fortune, unto which we were
> Late incident, by our quotidian feare.

A broadside ballad by John Cragge foretold:

> You and your blood the Crown shall ever weare,
> So long as you for Christ the Scepter beare . . .

A prose pamphlet described the entry as a Roman triumph, and effused, 'now the Joyful, happy, and comfortable return of the *Sun* into our *Horizon*, hath restored our hearts and revived us . . . By this little (though much more might be said) it may be hoped, that the Mouths of all *Pasquillers* might be stopped.' Even the praise here has an admonitory edge. Cragge's qualification seems prophetic. The authors are conscious of the inclement conditions, and see storm clouds they hope to dispel. The 'full and pleasing Harmony' anticipated from 'The joyfull Acclamations of your People, upon the sight of your Royal Person', emerges out of discord. Charles's participation in the popular celebration did not long silence the dissonance. By December 1641, the Grand Remonstrance had already been published, fear of popery and of sectarianism had begun to rise, and popular hostility to the bishops spilled on to the streets.[23]

Charles's failure to exploit public appearances as a means of generating support during his reign adversely affected popular representations and perceptions of him.[24] He was in the early years of his reign less than enthusiastic to touch for King's Evil, or scrofula, and a royal proclamation informed those who would flock to see him that 'Hee is contented to dispence with those publike shewes of their zeale, chearefulnes, and alacritie.'[25] Perhaps Charles sought to enhance the mystery and majesty of kingship by distance and inaccessibility. If so, his efforts failed. For the 1630s, he might be described as an *impersonal* monarch.

IV

Responding to the Mayor of London's address in December 1641, the king expressed contentment at finding that the former tumults arose only 'from the meaner sort of People: and that the affections of the better and main part of the *City*, have ever been *Loyal* and affectionate to my *person*, and *Government*'. Charles's suspicion of his people, and the resentment of the people for him, were continuing themes through his reign. In his 1628 parliamentary speech to the king, Buckingham had said: '*Opinion* that your People loved you not, had almost lost you in the Opinion of the World.' Though spoken to qualify praise, this is a telling admission. Subsequent royalist propaganda promoted the view that the king's only committed enemies were the ignorant and vulgar. These were not just the brewers, draymen and ironmongers who led the assault on his authority, but the nameless multitude conjured up by the commonplaces of rhetoric. One 1649 ballad on the regicide, supposed to have been written by Charles himself, succinctly commented: 'So doth the dust destroy the Diamond.'[26]

This contempt for the vulgar was mirrored by the admission, even in some royalist propaganda, that the king was the object of popular dislike. The 'clamorous people' who hated him were 'barking dogs'. 'Dark jealousies' were spread to engender 'popular hatred'; 'the ignorant and seduced vulgar . . . reviling and laughing to scorn their publick Father'.[27] This suspicion of his subjects' allegiance and contempt for the integrity of the poor was a symptom both of the king's own attitude and of the political polarization of the years 1640–2. As the stereotypes of cavalier and roundhead emerged in an unlicensed press that explored the polemical potential of the brief, vernacular pamphlet, so propagandists tried to exploit perceived differences in social status between the king's courtly followers and those clamouring for ecclesiastical reform. While parliamentary propagandists escalated their uncompromising accusations against evil counsellors, Charles's supporters underscored his legitimacy in terms stronger than those hitherto employed. 'He cannot be a Royall King, that lets a Subject rule him. His royalty consisteth in your obedience, or in suppressing your disobedience: in which the King still appears Royall, and the Subject disloyall', wrote one propagandist. A ballad writer expostulated:

> How with unhallowed hands you strive to strike
> Him whom you should your Loyalty afford
> (Great *CHARLES*) the blest anoynted of the Lord . . .[28]

Notwithstanding the concessions made to parliamentary limitations upon the king's prerogative in the answer to the Nineteen Propositions, propagandists increasingly employed the commonplaces of absolutism, referring to the 'anoynted King', and 'his Sacred Person'; he was 'God's vicegerent'. Though familiar, this language grated in the tense political climate. It reinforced the fears of creeping absolutism. Parliamentary propagandists, inspired by constitutional debate, and disinclined to make rhetorical concessions, challenged the king's authority in sharpening, radical terms.[29] Even in the cheap and accessible pamphlets of St Paul's booksellers, political polarization and radicalization took place.

The king was accused of pursuing an absolute prerogative. While he was implicitly compared to King David, he also found himself juxtaposed with Richard II, and, later, Edward II, Richard III and even Nero.[30] In a remarkable printed petition of the spring of 1643, which claimed that a million subjects would be prepared to sign it, Charles was asked: 'Have not your eyes seen it, and your Eares heard the Groanes of the Wounded, gasping for Life? Is all this nothing in your Eyes? . . . What if you were to part with something of your Right, yet should not your Majestie do it to save the Life of your People, from whom, and for whose Good, you first received it?' The pamphlet blamed evil counsel: 'Its true, we are forced to take *Antidotum contra Cæsarem*; or rather to save our Throats from the Violence of desperat Persons about You; but we beseech You call not this bearing Arms against You.' The petition uses a simple discourse and form while taking a hard-nosed attitude to the king that it would not have a year previously. It even raised the future issue of blood guilt.[31]

The blaming of evil counsel could operate either as a means of restraining criticism by making it anodyne, or as a platform for expressing it. The topic was prominent in popular print culture as well as in official declarations and more abstract political thought. A flurry of pamphlets in 1641–2 identified Laud and Strafford as guilty of leading the king astray since the death of Buckingham and during the intermission of parliament that followed the death of Buckingham. After the impeachment of these two, the identification of 'the predominance of evill Counsells imposed upon us', as a printed petition from Nottingham put it, was much more widespread.[32] Charles was 'seduced by wicked Counsell'. In the most favourable reading he was either sufficiently willing, unconscientious, or naive to find himself seduced.[33] More critical pamphlets spread the shot wider, and in doing so wounded his majesty: 'If ought then hath appeared in the shape of Disobedience, it hath been when your Majesties commands have differed from the Royall stamp, as mens discourse in sleep from what is waking; they want their Councell: For if the bare motion of the Royall lippe give absolute authority unto the word, then may your Dreames be powerfull as lawfull Pattents.' One writer offered a framework for reading between the lines of the charges of ill-counsel: 'It was the saying of Malignant *Machiavell*, That Princes should exercise their cruelty, not by themselves, but by their Ministers, so they might save themselves and their dignities by sacrificing whomsoever they would. But surely that prince puts off man, and goes into a beast, that is so cruell.' Reminding the reader that '*A good King is a public servant*', the author dispelled the coy defensiveness of much parliamentary propaganda, even suggesting that the king endorsed this parliamentary pretence as a Machiavellian strategy to limit censure. The author sternly argued that 'when the great day of

Account comes, which neither Magistrate not *Prince* can shun; There will be required of them a Reckoning for those whom they have trusted, as for themselves, which they must provide.' Others warned that kings were exposed to God's judgement, even when their subjects dare not reach so high. By 1643, Samuel Butler was complaining: 'we will no longer wrong our King secretly, through the Sides of His evill *Counsellors*, or *Cavaliers*, but charge him *directly*, and *poynt blanke*'.[34]

These and like recriminations in common circulation reveal little about the king's character or personal appearance. The same is true of royalist writing of the early and mid 1640s. This circumstance owes much to the logic of the political exchanges of the first Civil War. Parliamentarian writers denied that they were attacking the king: they were attacking counsellors responsible for an encroachment upon parliamentary prerogatives and the liberty and property of the subject. Royalist writers defended regal power rather than the king. Hence the king's personal qualities were *explicitly* not at stake, and praise of them could little hope to succeed in debate.[35] In the early 1640s accusations of tyranny were rare, so those pamphlets which repudiated the charge seem provocatively and suspiciously over-defensive.[36] Expressions of popular royalism in the early 1640s are more frequently attacks on parliament and its representatives, and on puritans and 'Brownists'.[37] Representations of the king's virtue, including those in ballads, are often bland and formulaic: 'Piety and Clemencie, Prudence, Justice, Fortitude, and Temperance . . . a Pattern to other Potentates, and a President to succeeding Monarchs.'[38] Most descriptions which delineate any detail are, naturally, epideictic: 'His owne uncruell, and un-Tyrant Spirit, and disposition, will Conquer him; So farre from thirst of Bloud, and severity of vengeance, that Justice may rather seeme to complaine of being cloyed with so great a Sweetnesse.'[39] This beatific image accords with the stately and aloof profile of the woodcuts and engravings of the king first encountered by the popular reader in the pamphlets and newsbooks of the 1640s. There seem to have been no satiric visual images of the king during this period. The woodcut portraits of him remain unpersonalized or merely cloying until after the regicide, when the martyrological imagery became dominant.[40]

V

The king was 'seduced by wicked Counsell', and the carnal metaphor was richly grounded in the religious, political and sexual culture of the period.

The courtly images of the royal couple in the 1630s imagined a royal love story; many 1640s representations subverted this narrative.[41] The very striking radical pamphlet *Vox Populi: Or the Peoples Humble Discovery* (1642) complained of the king's choice of a Catholic 'to be the Consort of your Royall bed'. Sex and Catholicism were easily linked. The confessional difference of the royal couple meant that Henrietta Maria was frequently associated with fears of a popish plot and plans to reintroduce Catholicism by gradual counter-reform.[42] These fears became especially pronounced when a cabinet containing the king's correspondence was captured at Naseby in June 1645. The documents therein purported to show serious flaws in the king's character: his passion for authority; his propensity for dissimulation and duplicity; and his unnatural and unmanly submission to the orders and desires of a popish wife.[43] The parliament decided to exploit the propaganda value of the letters, and ensured their wide distribution. The incident helped crystallize popular opposition to the king and infused the exchange of rhetoric with even greater bitterness.

The annotations accompanying the published letters in *The Kings Cabinet Opened*, probably by Henry Parker, Thomas May and John Sadler,[44] were mild by Civil War standards. They were not animadversions but consisted only of a brief preface and a conclusion. Marchamont Nedham, editor of the parliamentary newsbook *Mercurius Britanicus*, evidently thought these bland annotations needed supplement. He reproduced excerpts from the letters in *Britanicus*, accompanied by caustic marginal elucidations. Nedham violated both decorum and his licenser's instructions with a Hue and Cry alluding to the king's person: '*If any man can bring any tale or tiding of a wilfull King, which hath gone astray these foure yeares from his Parliament, with a guilty Conscience, bloody Hands, a Heart full of broken Vowes and Protestations: If these marks be not sufficient, there is another in the mouth; for bid him speak, and you will soon know him.*'[45]

Nedham's abuse was only icing on an already rich cake. *The Kings Cabinet Opened* was so effective not least because it purported to allow the king to condemn himself in his own words: 'the King himselfe . . . is presented upon the stage'. The letters were publicly read to London citizens gathered at Guildhall on 3 July. One of the official speakers, Mr Brown, piously advised: 'it much concerns us all, that we may pray for, and pitty our King, and to learn us to look to our selves'. The meeting drew:

> a great confluence of some thousands of Citizens of all sorts . . . who at the reading of the Letters, by their shouts and exhibilations declared their dislike and disapprobation of the Kings and Queens expressions in

> them; and on the contrary, their approbation of the *Parliaments* pro-
> ceedings, by their unanimous acclamations upon the observations
> made upon the said Letters by the Members of the House of Commons,
> manifesting their resolutions of adhering to the *Parliament*, and their
> detestation of the hypocrisie and dissimulation of the other Party, and
> of their evident intentions to introduce Popery & Tyranny.[46]

There is some evidence that the strategy was convincing.[47] The annotators claimed that malignants would either deny that the letters were in the
king's hand or would have to admit that their constructions were just. The
Earl of Northumberland suggested that the letters should be put on
display so that they could be consulted, so 'none might pretend and give
out (as the Malignants are ready to do) that they were not reall'. It was an
insightful proposal: a Spittlefield turner, as late as March 1647, was charged
with claiming that the king's letters were counterfeit. *Mercurius Anti-
Pragmaticus* commented: 'The Kings Letters and other Papers taken at
Naseby are ordered to be kept safely amongst other Records: it were a pity
but the ensuing Ages should read the plots and juglings that were practised by a Popish party, to advance their Italian Lord.'[48]

Most interpretations of the letters avoided explicit personal censure,
but there was no pretence that they were not critical of the king. The
annotators carefully played on gender anxieties, suggesting that the king
failed the demands of masculinity, and was governed by a woman: 'It is
plaine, here, first, that the Kings Counsels are wholly managed by the
Queen; though she be of the weaker sexe, borne an Alien, bred up in a
contrary Religion, yet nothing great or small is transacted without her
privity & consent.' Sexual transgression is aligned with religious deviance.
The queen encourages the king to overcome his inhibitions to fulfil his
dark ambitions: 'The King doth yet in many things surpasse the Queene
for acts of hostility, and covering them over with deeper and darker
secrecy.' A comparison to Richard III follows this passage; though
Macbeth seems an equally plausible analogue. The evasion of blaming evil
counsel is now redundant. The king is a malignant. The offensive language he bestows on his parliament and people 'comes from a Prince
seduced out of his proper sphear'.[49]

Royalist defences ingeniously suggested an alternative reading: that the
letters reflected the king's literary abilities. Any decoding of political deviance was purely malicious, as a 'Spyder sucks a poysonous juice out of the
same flower a Bee doth Hony'. So elegant a writer must be virtuous. As
propaganda, these suggestions are fairly lame, but they did precipitate a

crystallization of the king's character in the popular pamphlet culture. The letters were 'the truest Mirour of the King's mind; Here you may say He was not drawne, but He shewed himselfe to the life.' Another Oxford pamphlet affirmed:

> the King a Prince of very choice endowments; and I judge him so by his letters, which wise men have oft told me give the best Characters of their Authors. I finde his stile masculine, his Counsells sharpe and rationall, his expressions full of judicious fancy, he digests businesses thoroughly, and makes it all his owne . . . he that writes thus deserves to governe, and my thoughts tell me, that this is the very man I should elect to a Throne were I to choose a King by Epistles.

A Satyr, Occasioned by the Author's Survey of a Scandalous Pamphlet praised:

> Lines of so *cleare*, yet so *Majestick* straine,
> A most *Transparent*, yet a *close-wove* Veine.
> Which when we reach its *Sense*, we may discrie
> We see more by *its Light*, then *our owne* Eye.

Another lamented: 'The *cabinet* hath imparted to you, so perfect an *Image* of the Kings very *Thoughts* . . . See, but what an even *spirit* of *Elegancy* runnes through every line; which beates and leaps, as much, in the description of His *saddest* condition, as of his *serenest* Fortune; in so much, that, posterity will a little, *love* His *Misery*, for her very *cloathing*.'[50]

Most horror was voiced at the way the king had been exposed.[51] It was an unprecedented event. Some of the letters between the king and queen were indeed intimate in tone; the reader was invited to remember at every line that the implied reader was a Roman Catholic. The publishing formula seems to have worked, and a number of other pamphlets based on intercepted letters followed.[52] Even more provocative, however, was Nedham's overbearing Hue and Cry, alluding to the king's speech impediment. Nedham was long reviled, along with the parliament's leniency.[53]

Thereafter the speech impediment was less infrequently broached. Nedham was required to publish an apology in which he disavowed his unpremeditated and unseemly foolishness, and professed: 'That I have mentioned any thing to disgrace the *King* in his naturall infirmity, (as some conceive) I utterly deny.' After years of silence, or the repetition of mere formulae, the characterization offers a refreshing insight into the king's presence. The blemish was mentioned more by the king's defenders than by his accusers. One admitted: 'though he hath some imperfection in his speech, yet he meanes speedily with his pen, or at leastwise, he can answer all their Propositions'. Lilly wrote in 1651: 'He has a natural imperfection in his speech; at some times he could hardly get-out a word, yet at other times he would speak freely and articulately; as at the first time of his coming before the *High Court of Justice*, where casually I heard him: there he stammered nothing at all, but spoke very distinctly, with much courage and magnanimity.' A 1660 panegyrist described the king's words, 'The Images of mens souls, their very issues, he was rather Slow then Fluent (as well by Grace as a Natural imperfection).'[54]

VI

The polarization of opinion meant that *The Kings Cabinet Opened*, as some royalists predicted, backfired. The hardening of opinion among the army and London Independents met with a corresponding softening of opinion elsewhere. The shift towards blaming the king directly, and to accusing him of blood guilt, was paralleled by an increasing focus on his personal circumstances and virtues. The critical year was probably 1647, when victory and peace divided the parliament, and the army elected to use threats to coerce its resolutions.[55] While many royalist pamphlets and newsbooks continued to express their views negatively and satirically, by attacking heresy, greed and ambition in the parliament and army, a developing strain of writing discussed the king himself. Imprisoned, he becomes naked and helpless. Two years before the execution, the image of the royal martyr shifts into the foreground.

The Scots helped by selling the king to the English in January 1647. A ballad entitled *Judas Justified by his Brother Scots* proclaimed: '*Judas* before a Traytor *Scot* shall weare / A Saintly Rubrick in Times Calendar.' The Scots as a canny Judas, profiting rather more by their enterprise, became a commonplace in pamphlets. Charles thus became a type of Christ.[56] A 1647 broadside ballad compared Nedham to the Scots, and in turn to Judas, as they would all sell their king for silver. In 1649 a broadsheet poem addressed parliament: 'Is this your *Glorious King?* . . . / The *Ax* design'd, you might have spar'd the *Kiss*.' Picking up the same theme, a broadside verse dialogue distinguished between the executioner Richard Brandon and Judas: 'And yet no *Judas*; in Records 'tis found, / *Judas* had thirty pence, he thirty pound.'[57]

Increasingly, Charles became presented as a lonely victim. *Mercurius Melancholicus* wrote: 'Wee are the execrable thing, and the Curse of God is upon us all: Our King is curs'd, being as yet thrust out of his Throne, and made as poor as *Job*, as low as *Telegon*, so that his people cannot enjoy him, nor he enjoy his people.' A later broadside poem, in the voice of the king and once thought to have been written by him, exclaimed: 'Yet I am level-l'd with the Life of JOB.' The king became a fugitive prey:

> Much like a Partidge the King they did chase
> from mountain to mountain they did him pursue . . . [58]

In November 1647 *Mercurius Pragmaticus* reported the Independent chaplain Hugh Peters as saying:

> that his Soveraigne *Oliver* is content (he sayes) poore *Charles* should live still at *Hampton*, upon condition he will be quiet, that is, never seeke to be restored again, and have the *patience* to bee hunted once a weeke with this, that, and 'tother unreasonable *Demand*, when *King Nol*, and his *Spaniels* go a *Hawking* with their *Propositions*, to catch the *Royall Assent*.

Charles was a victim, dragged from place to place, ever in danger of his life from rebels of low birth. Suddenly his deprivation was a concern:

> We cannot but much bewaile his Majesties present condition, when we see his Court so peopl'd, and not so much as any Signe of its former beauty or civility left; tag, rag and long-tayle admitted to his Majesties *Person*, that any being there, and looking in many of their faces, might have just occasion to think, His Majesty in apparent danger of his life; for truly, they look more like a people for an Hospitall, then attendants for a Princes Court.

A report on the king at Hirst Castle in December 1648 lamented: 'his condition there is most sad and dismall, being kept close prisoner, and not having any, either of his own Servants or acquaintance about him'. The king lived on alms; he was sent begging to his subjects; he was deprived of the right materials for dressing meat.[59] The path was prepared for *Eikon Basilike*.

Some pamphlets suggest the increasing accessibility of the king at Hampton Court: 'there is great resort of all sorts of people to him, but not so many Cavaliers as is reported, it is confessed, no Gentleman is debarred the liberty of kissing the Kings hand, yet no stranger stayes long'. We hear not only of the subjects' joy at the sight of their king, but the surprised king's gratification by this joy.[60] Other pamphlets and news-books realized this renewed sense of the king's personal touch by describing his mood or his health. His cheerfulness, sometimes 'indifferent', became a commonplace. *The Mad Dog Rebellion worm'd and muzzl'd* barked: 'surely it is not impertinent, or much out of the way of Loyalty to ask or be a little inquisitive whether the King be in health or sick, or alive or dead . . . it is too well knowne that he hath not one friend to attend him, nor any one that loves him can be suffered to come nere him'.[61]

Most strikingly, portraits of Charles's deprivations increasingly focused on his separation from his family. Sympathizers cunningly appropriated the gender anxieties circulating around the perverse influence of a Catholic queen, and drew attention to his unnatural separation from a loving wife, and the infrequent access to children: 'It is Ordered that the Earle of Northumberland shal have liberty to let his *Majesty* see his *Children* now and then. So that you see the fighting for the *liberty of the Subject*, was to this end, that the *King* should have no more *Liberty*, then what they please to allow him.' The royal love story of the 1630s was restored, before a greater audience, and with added pathos. 'His greatest delight is in his Children', reported one newsbook. In *His Majesties Complaint*, a 1647 pamphlet poem modelled on George Herbert's 'The Sacrifice' which thus introduces a martyrological theme, Charles is made to exclaim: 'Our Wif's debar'd us, Our deare Children too.' Broadside poems and ballads attended to this detail, one echoing *Mercurius Pragmaticus*:

> His Freedome is, to have but what's his owne;
> His Libertie, his Kingdomes, Crowne, and Throne,
> His Wife, his Children . . . [62]

One ballad-monger spared a thought for the queen: 'Who in France like a Turtle forsaken doth moan.' Reports of the king's final days seized upon the details of his last meetings with his children, their farewell words, his prayers and advice. After his death these were reprinted severally, one edition an inexpensive octavo.[63] Such products tapped into the market for *Eikon Basilike*. Though perhaps accidental, the triumph of this representational shift was to change Charles from a brow-beaten husband into a family man, from a ruler deprived of his rights into a human deprived of affection and compassion, with whom the common reader could identify.

VII

Others asked: 'Is not his condition too good for him, considering so many thousands and ten thousands honest people that have been seduced and destroyed by his obstinat tyrannous disposition.' While impeaching him with blood guilt, and thus brushing away the remnants of his sacred authority, depictions of his person became more particular and evocative.[64] The representations frequently worked by metonymy, substituting a singular activity or trait for the whole of his character.

One such activity was his interest in games and sports. A 1620s verse libel against Buckingham alleges that Charles's favourite game was the duke; a news report from 1628 mentions the two men playing bowls together. Another opines: 'The State's a game at cards', adding that the people lose out in it. The king was discovered playing 'trictrac' with Hamilton by the Scots at Berwick, when he was supposed to be taking counsel; his response to the news of the Irish Rebellion was to play golf.[65] *News from Yorke*, a satirical broadside newsletter of April 1642, depicts him frivolously hawking. Lilly reported the king's interest in a game called 'pigeon-holes'. In April 1647, when the king was at Holmby, Cleveland commented facetiously on the propensity of newsbooks (at least those written by John Dillingham) to associate the king with games. During his subsequent imprisonment at Hampton Court, news pamphlets reported the king hunting. When Charles was engaged upon the personal treaty at the Isle of Wight, newsbooks reported him playing bowls.[66] Not all were hostile, but the persistence of the image suggests that it was being used politically, in order to evoke the king's interest in frivolous pursuits, particularly late in his reign, as if he were bowling while kingdoms burnt. Perhaps some of these images were intended to recall the second Book of Sports of 1633, and protests against it.[67]

Notwithstanding the widespread hostility to the Scots south of the Tweed, particularly after the second Civil War, few writers mentioned the king's national origins, even when he was sold by his own countrymen. Those writers who did were more likely to be Scottish themselves.[68] By the English, he was perceived as an adopted Englishman, though also, by those both sympathetic and hostile, as the king of three kingdoms.[69] After his death and the abolition of monarchy, however, his Scottishness was emphasized along with the turbulent history of Scottish kings. Lilly suggested that Charles's ability to dissemble was inherited 'partly from his Father, and partly the *Climate* he was born in, *viz. Scotland*'.[70]

Another leitmotif that developed in popular representations late in the reign was the king's interest in literary culture. He was shown to be a considerable man of letters. One ballad reported: 'Every one doth think / That great *Cæsars* Inke, / Never wrot better.'[71] Detractors turned this into an unnatural concern with high art to the exclusion of his real responsibilities. *The None-Such Charles* (attributed to Charles's former agent, Balthasar Gerbier) claimed 'this said mans soule, was more fixt on *Bens* verses, and other Romances, during the time of his imprisonment, then on those holy Writs, wherein salvation is to be sought for the soul, as well as for the body'. The issue arose in the dispute over Pamela's prayer, plagiarized from Sidney's *Arcadia* and inserted in *Eikon Basilike*. John Milton, who exposed the theft in *Eikonoklastes*, argued it was to the disgrace of the king and his clergy that they were forced to borrow from a romance 'a Prayer stol'n word for word from the mouth of a Heathen fiction praying to a heathen God; & that in no serious Book, but the vain amatorious Poem of Sʳ *Philip Sidneys Arcadia*'. This accusation was deployed in the legal case prepared by John Cook, who turned the king's interest in literature into a psychological disturbance: 'He was no more affected with a List that was brought in to *Oxford* of Five or six thousand slain at *Edgehill*, than to read one of *Ben Johnson's* Tragedies.' Even as the court of justice was being set up, popular pamphlets warned that justice was providential, and that the king would soon be judged by a king above him.[72] Yet the initiative in exemplifying the king's character was soon, and definitively, snatched from his detractor's hands.

VIII

The image of Charles as a sun was abundant in popular representations. His return dispelled clouds; his brightness illuminated his subjects. One sympathetic writer in 1642 blamed clouds, which interposed themselves between the sun and the people, for the obfuscation of the king's rays.[73] Others less sympathetic seized on the popularity of astronomical/astrological metaphors (as testified by allusions to Charles's Wain, or the Great Bear), and claimed that the evil bodies around him had caused an eclipse.[74] One commented: 'the King being in full conjunction with the Popish Planet the Queen, he was totally eclipsed by her counsell'. The image of a sunset was an obvious one for hack poets to reach for upon his death.[75]

'Ile die a *Martyr*, or Ile live a *King*' announced some broadside verses, supposedly composed by the king at the Isle of Wight. Charles's martyrdom, even in popular writings, was a long time in the making. The comparison of the Scots to Judas had been an important stage in the process. As Charles had been persecuted and slandered by his own people (Scots and English), so Christ had been crowned with thorns by the Jews. In November 1648 it was reported that the king said he was prepared to 'with Christ suffer any thing that can befall him'. Brian Duppa's sermons prepared him for the martyrdom.[76] The triumph of the image was guaranteed by the phenomenal publishing success of *Eikon Basilike. The Pourtraicture of His Sacred Majestie in His Solitudes and Sufferings* (1649), with its famous engraved frontispiece depicting Charles grasping a crown of thorns, his eyes fixed on a heavenly crown. No longer could a royalist accuse the king's enemies of 'making a Mountain of every Mole-hill of his imperfections'; for suddenly he had none.[77]

Not least through the commercial success of *Eikon Basilike*, his 'speaking Ghost, the Echo of his Life and Death', Charles rapidly became 'A Butcher'd Martyr King', with little respect paid to the blasphemies that might entail. The term infected ballads and pamphlets, and the king was presented as a saint who had taken no pleasure in his earthly crown, who had been too good for this world.[78] He was 'The Glory of all Martyrologies'. His life was paralleled with that of Jesus. He was, according to *A Hand-Kirchife for Loyall Mourners*, 'A Martyr both of the State and the Church, for the liberties of his Subjects.' One encomium even suggested a degree of self-conscious emulation:

> 'Twas a far more glorious thing
> To dye a Martyr, than to live a King.
> When he had copy'd out in every line,
> Our Saviour's Passion (bating the Divine) . . . [79]

After the Restoration he was effectively canonized when 30 January was made a day of thanksgiving. By coincidence, the Book of Common Prayer prescribed for this date Matthew 27, on the crucifixion of Christ. For generations – until 1859 – churchgoers heard sermons on the royal martyr. Presenting an anodyne image of the king, they usually served, at least until 1688, as a lesson in politics. By 1694, J. G. G. could admit that 'the fact was an horrid Murther', but nonetheless complain: 'we are not satisfied to make him a Saint, but a Martyr too, for that is now the Name given him, *the Martyr*, by Excellency: I confess here I am somewhat at a Stand, to see such a Name so much misapplied . . . I declare I charitably believe God shewed him Mercy, but withal it is not the Manner, but the Cause of Death makes one a Martyr.'[80]

Even at the moment of his death, Charles had been transformed. The king himself had become an image. In this respect he was much more effective dead than alive. He had resumed touching for scrofula when imprisoned; and those who had 'blasphemed' (*sic*) the king died by sudden accident. On his death the miracles intensified: it was foretold that 'though *Charles* might not speak, his *Bloud* will crie'. It soon did, when a teenage girl near Deptford was cured of the King's Evil by a handkerchief dipped in the martyr's blood. The royal blood cured scrofula and blindness, even producing sympathetic stigmata.[81]

More striking than this, through draining the memory of the king of depth and nuance, Charles became an emblem of tragic kingship. This is shown in the illustrations of the beatific corpse accompanying broadside elegies:

> Whose true Effigies drane by just desert,
> Causeth him live in each true Subjects heart:
> Living he dy'd, and dying life he gain'd,
> Death conquer'd him, his foes with shame he stain'd.

Entirely dehumanized, he regained his mystique: 'Behold the Mirror of a Prince pourtraid! / The living Emblem of a glorious shade . . .' He was 'The Quintessence of MAJESTIE; / Which being Set, more Glorious shines.' Once again the dominant popular representation had laterally shifted, and Charles, no longer seduced by popery, had become an icon of virtue. As a text, his body no longer had a literal signification, but defied interpretation:

> No strain'd *Hyperboles* adorne thy *Herse*,
> Thy SELF art both a *Monument* and *Verse*.[82]

Notes

1 Jasper Mayne, *OXΛO–MAXIA. Or The Peoples War* (1647), 1. For seventeenth-century items the place of publication is London unless otherwise stated. My thanks to Sarah Pennell and Tom Corns for their comments on this chapter; and to Diane Purkiss for an interesting discussion.

2 Kevin Sharpe, *The Personal Rule of Charles I* (New Haven and London: Yale University Press, 1992), chapter 17; Ann Hughes, *The Causes of the English Civil War* (Basingstoke: Macmillan, 1991); Richard Cust and Ann Hughes, eds., *Conflict in Early Stuart England: Studies in Religion and Politics, 1603–1642* (London: Longman, 1989); Richard Cust, 'News and Politics in Early Seventeenth-Century England', *Past and Present*, 112 (1986): 60–90; Thomas Cogswell, 'The Politics of Propaganda: Charles I and the People in the 1620s', *Journal of British Studies*, 29 (1990): 187–215; Joad Raymond, *The Invention of the Newspaper: English Newsbooks, 1641–1649* (Oxford: Clarendon Press, 1996), 87–100.

3 For example John Vicars, *A Sight of yᵉ Transactions* (1646); Raymond, *Invention of the Newspaper*, chapter 6.

4 Joseph Frank, *The Beginnings of the English Newspaper, 1620–1660* (Cambridge, MA: Harvard University Press, 1961), *passim*; Joyce Lee Malcolm, *Caesar's Due: Loyalty and King Charles, 1642–1646* (London: Royal Historical Society, 1983), 152–63; David Underdown, *A Freeborn People: Politics and the Nation in Seventeenth-Century England*

(Oxford: Clarendon Press, 1996), chapter 5; Raymond, *Invention of the Newspaper*, chapter 5.

5 There is proliferating literature on this subject; see, for example, Peter Burke, 'Popular Culture in Seventeenth-Century London', in *Popular Culture in Seventeenth-Century England*, ed. Barry Reay (1985; London: Routledge, 1988), 31–58; Lisa Jardine and Anthony Grafton, '"Studied for Action": How Gabriel Harvey Read his Livy', *Past and Present*, 129 (1990): 30–78; Roger Chartier, *Forms and Meanings: Texts, Performances, and Audiences from Codex to Computer* (Philadelphia: University of Pennsylvania Press, 1995); James Raven, Helen Small and Naomi Tadmor, eds., *The Practice and Representation of Reading in England* (Cambridge University Press, 1996); Anthony Grafton, 'Is the History of Reading a Marginal Enterprise? Guillaume Budé and His Books', *Papers of the Bibliographical Society of America*, 91 (1997): 139–57.

6 For popular access to pamphlets and ballads, see Tessa Watt, *Cheap Print and Popular Piety, 1550–1640* (Cambridge University Press, 1993); Margaret Spufford, *Small Books and Pleasant Histories: Popular Fiction and its Readership in Seventeenth-Century England* (London: Methuen, 1981); Bernard Capp, 'Popular Literature', in *Popular Culture*, ed. Reay, 198–243; Raymond, *Invention of the Newspaper*, chapter 5; Dagmar Freist, *Governed by Opinion: Politics, Religion and the Dynamics of Communication in Stuart London, 1637–1645* (London and New York: Tauris Academic Studies, 1997).

7 Alastair Bellany, '"Rayling Rymes and Vaunting Verse": Libellous Politics in Early Stuart England, 1603–1628', in *Culture and Politics in Early Stuart England*, ed. Kevin Sharpe and Peter Lake (London: Macmillan, 1994), 290; J. S. A. Adamson, 'Chivalry and Political Culture in Caroline England', in *Culture and Politics*, ed. Sharpe and Lake, 161–97; *The Pentitant Traytor* (1647); *Calver's Royall Vision* (1648); James Holstun, '"God Bless thee, Little David!": John Felton and His Allies', *ELR*, 59 (1992): 539; more generally Nigel Smith, *Literature and Revolution in England, 1640–1660* (New Haven and London: Yale University Press, 1994).

8 John Selden, *The Table Talk of John Selden* (Chiswick: C. Whittingham, 1818), 87. By libels Selden means abrasive pamphlets rather than legally libellous publications.

9 Ibid., 143; Barry Reay, 'Introduction: Popular Culture in Early Modern England', in *Popular Culture*, ed. Reay, 24.

10 *A Relation of the departure* (1623), in *Somers Tracts*, 16 vols. (1748–52), v, 242; *Calendar of State Papers: Domestic, 1623–1625*, ed. Mary Anne Everett Green (London: Longman, 1859), 93–4 (hereafter *CSPD*); Thomas Cogswell, *The Blessed Revolution: English Politics and the Coming of War, 1621–1624* (Cambridge University Press, 1989), 6–12.

11 Bodleian Library (hereafter Bod.) MS Rawlinson D. 1048, fols. 50v, 76; MS Rawl. D. 398, fos. 188r-v, 229r-v; National Library of Scotland (hereafter NLS), MS Adv. 33.1.7 (Denmilne MSS v.24), items 19, 21, 43, 44; Arthur F. Marotti, *Manuscript, Print, and the English Renaissance Lyric* (Ithaca, NY: Cornell University Press, 1995), 107–10; Cogswell, *Blessed Revolution*, 46–8. Pauline Croft describes the libels against Robert Cecil as 'spontaneous expressions of popular culture' generated by 'public interest in current affairs' ('The Reputation of Robert Cecil: Libels, Political Opinion and Popular Awareness in the Early Seventeenth Century', *Transactions of the Royal Historical Society*, 6th series, 1 (1991): 43–69, at 62–3. For other studies of libels which suggest their validity as evidence of popular political culture, see Martin Ingram, 'Ridings, Rough Music and Mocking Rhymes in Early Modern England', in *Popular Culture*, ed. Reay, 166–97; Capp, 'Popular Literature', 227; Bellany, 'Libellous Politics'; Bellany, 'Mistress

Turner's Deadly Sins: Sartorial Transgression, Court Scandal, and Politics in Early Stuart England', *Huntington Library Quarterly*, 58 (1996): 179–210; Thomas Cogswell, 'Underground Verse and the Transformation of Early Stuart Political Culture', in *Political Culture and Cultural Politics in Early Modern Europe*, ed. Susan Amussen and Mark Kishlansky (Manchester University Press, 1995), 277–300; Holstun, 'John Felton and His Allies'.

12   'A Satyr' (49–50) and 'A Charitable Censure' (50–1); for the critical views see 'Upon the Dukes' (9–10); 'Upon the D. of B.' (35); 'A Dialogue' (62); 'The Duke Return'd' (21), in *Poems and Songs Relating to George Villiers, Duke of Buckingham*, ed. Frederick W. Fairholt (London: Percy Society, 1850).

13   Bod. MS Tanner 465, fo. 100.

14   Jo. Heape, 'Prosopopeia on the D.' (51–2), 'On the Murder' (5) and 'To Charles' (73), in *Poems and Songs*, ed. Fairholt.

15   George Roberts, ed., *Diary of Walter Yonge*, Camden Society, 41 (London, 1848), 114; David Masson, *The Life of John Milton*, vol. I (London: Macmillan, 1881), 208; *Middlesex County Records*, vol. III, ed. John Cordy Jeaffreson (Middlesex County Records Society, 1888), 93; *CSPD, 1628–1629*, ed. John Bruce (London: Longman, 1859), 268, 271; *Diary of John Rous*, ed. Mary Anne Everett Green, Camden Society, 66 (London, 1856), 22, 30; on Strafford see *The Downfall of Greatnesse* (1641), 7.

16   See the writings of Christopher Hill; Sheila Lambert, 'Richard Montagu, Arminianism and Censorship', *Past and Present*, 124 (1989): 36–68; A. N. B. Worden, 'Literature and Political Censorship in Early Modern England', in *Too Mighty to be Free: Censorship and the Press in Britain and the Netherlands*, ed. A. C. Duke and C. A. Tamse (Zutphen: De Walburg Pers, 1987), 45–62; Kevin Sharpe, *Criticism and Compliment: The Politics of Literature in the England of Charles I* (Cambridge University Press, 1987); Sharpe, *Personal Rule*, chapter 6.

17   Cogswell, 'The Politics of Propaganda', 214; Bellany, 'Mistress Turner's Deadly Sins', *passim*.

18   Judith Richards, '"His Nowe Majestie" and the English Monarchy: The Kingship of Charles I before 1640', *Past and Present*, 113 (1986): 94, 78. The money for the pageant had already been disbursed; David M. Bergeron, *English Civic Pageantry, 1558–1642* (London: Edward Arnold, 1971), 105–9. Also Margot Heinemann, *Puritanism and Theatre: Thomas Middleton and Opposition Drama Under the Early Stuarts* (Cambridge University Press, 1980), 131–2.

19   Bergeron, *English Civic Pageantry*, 110–15.

20   NLS, MS Adv. 33.2.26, fols. 36–42v; Bod., MS Rawl. D. 49, fo. 5.

21   Bergeron, *English Civic Pageantry*, 117–18; Richards, 'Kingship of Charles I', 83–4; Sharpe, *Personal Rule*, 630–1, 702.

22   Bergeron, *English Civic Pageantry*, 118; report by Giovanni Giustinian, in *Calendar of State Papers: Venetian*, XXV, 1640–1642, ed. Allen B. Hinds (London, HMSO, 1924), 254–5; *A Relation of the Kings Entertainment* (1641); Martin Parker, *An Exact Description* (1640), in *Cavalier and Puritan: Ballads and Broadsides . . . 1640–1660*, ed. Hyder E. Rollins (New York University Press, 1923), 78–83.

23   *King Charles His Entertainment* (1641), 5–6; see also Cleveland, 'Upon the Kings return from Scotland', *The Poems of John Cleveland*, ed. Brian Morris and Eleanor Withington (Oxford: Clarendon Press, 1967), 2–3; Bond, *King Charles his Welcome Home* (1641), 1; Cragge, *Englands Congratulatorie Entertainment* ([1641]); the pamphlet is *Ovatio Carolina*,

in *Somers Tracts*, IV, 151, 156; also John Taylor, *Englands Comfort and Londons Joy* (1641); on discord and the Grand Remonstrance see *CSPD, 1641–1643*, ed. William Douglas Hamilton (London: Longman, 1887), 188; Anthony Fletcher, *The Outbreak of the English Civil War* (1981; London: Edward Arnold, 1985), chapter 5; Raymond, *Invention of the Newspaper*, 111–25.

24 See Corns's introduction to this volume for a different emphasis.

25 R. Malcolm Smuts, 'Public Ceremony and Royal Charisma: The English Royal Entry in London, 1485–1642', in *The First Modern Society: Essays in English History in Honour of Lawrence Stone*, ed. A. L. Beier, David Cannadine and James M. Rosenheim (Cambridge University Press, 1989), 65–93; Richards, 'Kingship of Charles I', 74–5, 77–8, 86–92; Sharpe, *Personal Rule*, 630–1, 642, 782; James F. Larkin, ed., *Stuart Royal Proclamations*, II, *Royal Proclamations of King Charles I, 1625–1646* (Oxford: Clarendon Press, 1983), 34–7.

26 *Ovatio Carolina*, 156; on suspicion, Buckingham and royalist propaganda see Malcolm, *Caesar's Due*, 157–8; Lois Potter, *Secret Rites and Secret Writing: Royalist Literature, 1641–1660* (Cambridge University Press, 1989), 26–30; P. W. Thomas, *Sir John Berkenhead, 1617–1679: A Royalist Career in Politics and Polemics* (Oxford: Clarendon Press, 1969), 77, 120–5; the ballad is 'Majesty in Misery', in *The Roxburghe Ballads*, VII, ed. J. Woodfall Ebsworth (Hertford: Ballad Society, 1893), 620.

27 *King Charles His Defence* ([1642]), 2; Mayne, *OXΛO–MAXIA*, 4; Edward Symmons, *A Vindication of King Charles* (1648), 9 and also 165.

28 Thomas Jordan, *Rules to Know a Royall King* (1642), 2; *The City* (1643; 669f.8 (5)).

29 For absolutist language see *King Charles His Defence*, 2; A. A. *No Peace* (1645), 2; [Samuel Butler] *A Letter from Mercurius Civicus* (1643) in *Somers Tracts*, V, 417; J. L., *A Just Apologie* (1642); John Taylor, *A Plea for Prerogative* (1642), 4, 6; *A Remonstrance for the Republique* (1643), sig. A4; *Christus Dei, or the Lords Annoynted* (Oxford, 1643); Bond, *King Charles his Welcome; King Charles His Royall Welcome* (1647); T[homas] S[wadlin], *The Souldiers Catechisme* (Oxford, 1645). For the Nineteen Propositions and the radicalization of parliamentary propaganda see David Wootton, 'From Rebellion to Revolution: The Crisis of the Winter of 1642/3 and the Origins of Civil War Radicalism', *English Historical Review*, 105 (1990): 654–9; Michael Mendle, *Dangerous Positions: Mixed Government, the Estates of the Realm, and the Making of the Answer to the XIX Propositions* (University: University of Alabama Press, 1985), and *Henry Parker and the English Civil War: The Political Thought of the Public's 'Privado'* (Cambridge University Press, 1995), chapters 5 and 6.

30 *An Item* (1642[3]); *Mercurius Davidicus* (Oxford, 1643); also C[harles] G[randison?], *The Modest Cavalieres Advice* (1647), 7; for negative analogies see *The Life and Death of King Richard the Second* (1642); *A mis-led King* (1642[3]); *The People Informed of their Oppressors* (1648); *The Kings Cabinet Opened* (1645), 48; see also Symmons, *Vindication*, 38, 41; *A Petition to His Maiesty; of the three revolting Counties* (1645), 5.

31 *England's Petition to their King* (1643), in *Somers Tracts*, XIII, 160–1, 162.

32 The quote is from *To the Kings Most Excellent Majesty A Petition presented to the Kings Majesty at York, the first of April* (1642); see also *Vox Populi* (1642); *The Second Part of Vox Populi* (1642); *The Parliaments Love and Loyalty* (1642); T. B., *Observations Upon Prince Ruperts White Dog* (1643); *Remonstrance for the Republique; A mis-led King; A Key to the Kings Cabinet-Counsell* (1644); *The Great Eclipse of the Sun* (1644); Thomas Ellyson, *The Shepheards Letters* (1646). Defending the charge, see *King Charles His Defence*, 2; *Christus*

Dei. For Laud and Strafford see Martin Butler, *Theatre and Crisis, 1632–1642* (Cambridge University Press, 1984), 236–46; Heinemann, *Puritanism and Theatre*, chapter 13; Terence Kilburn and Anthony Milton, 'The Public Context of the Trial and Execution of Strafford', in *The Political World of Thomas Wentworth, Earl of Strafford, 1621–1641*, ed. J. F. Merritt (Cambridge University Press, 1996), 230–51.

33 *A Parallel Betweene the late troubles in Scotland* (1642), 5–6; [William Prynne], *Newes from Ipswich* (1636; 1641), imputed to the king culpability for tolerating the reforms introduced by the Bishops.

34 *Second Part of Vox Populi*, sig. A3; *Observations concerning the Late Treaty* (1645), 3–5; other warnings appear in *Englands Petition to their Soveraigne King* (1646), 5–6; *The Remonstrance of the Generall Assembly* (1645); [Butler] *Letter from Mercurius Civicus*, in *Somers Tracts*, v, 417.

35 For example *Christus Dei*; Thomas Browne, *A Key to the Kings Cabinet* (Oxford, 1645); *King Charles Vindicated* (1648).

36 *King Charles His Defence*, 2; John Morrill, 'Charles I, Tyranny and the English Civil War', in *The Nature of the English Revolution* (London: Longman, 1993), 285–306.

37 'Rupert's March' (7), 'The Cavaliers' Muster' (12–13), 'Wigan's Retreat' (19–21), 'The Sally from Coventry' (24–6), 'The Three Scars' (32–3), in *Songs of the Cavaliers and Roundheads, Jacobite Ballads, &c.*, ed. George W. Thornbury (London: Hurst and Blackett, 1857); Keith Lindley, *Popular Politics and Religion in Civil War London* (Aldershot: Scolar Press, 1997), 255.

38 J. L., *A Just Apologie*, sig. A2 quoted; see also John Taylor, *The Kings Most Excellent Majesties Wellcome* (1647); *A Letter in Which the Arguments of the Annotator*, 2nd edn (Oxford, 1645: Wing L1558). For ballads see Bod. Wood 401; *Roxburghe Ballads*, VII; Thornbury, ed., *Songs of the Cavaliers*; Rollins, ed., *Cavalier and Puritan*; Charles Mackay, ed., *The Songs and Ballads of the Cavaliers* (London: Charles Griffin, 1864).

39 A. A., *No Peace*, 5.

40 Contrast, for example, the numerous chivalric and heroic engravings of Essex, Hotham and Fairfax in the Thomason Collection in the early and mid 1640s; they seem to have made more plausible pin-ups than the king.

41 See Thomas Corns's introduction to this volume and Ann Coiro's chapter above.

42 *Vox Populi*, 3; also *The Sussex Picture* (1644); Caroline Hibbard, *Charles I and the Popish Plot* (Chapel Hill: University of North Carolina Press, 1983), 198–9, 214, 221–2, 228.

43 *Kings Cabinet opened*, especially 11, 17–18, 28, 30–1, 34–6; *Mercurius Civicus*, III (3–10 July 1645), 983–4.

44 Mendle, *Henry Parker*, 25–6, 193.

45 *Mercurius Britanicus*, 92 (28 July – 4 August 1645), in *Making the News: An Anthology of the Newsbooks of Revolutionary England, 1641–1660*, ed. Joad Raymond (Moreton-in-Marsh: Windrush Press, 1993), 348–9; Raymond, *Invention of the Newspaper*, 43 and n. 101.

46 *Kings Cabinet Opened*, sig. A4v; *Three Speeches Spoken at a Common-Hall* (1645), 19; on the meeting see *Kingdomes Weekly Intelligencer*, 107 (1–8 July 1645), 849–50, quoted; also *The True Informer*, 11 (30 June – 5 July), 87–8; on the controversy, see Potter, *Secret Rites and Secret Writing*, 59–64.

47 *A Petition to his Majesty*, 2; *The Moderate Intelligencer*, 19 (3–10 July 1645), 146.

48 *Kings Cabinet opened*, sig. A3v; *A Diary*, 60 (3–10 July 1645), sig. Kkkk2; *Middlesex County Records*, 3:99, 184; *Anti-Pragmaticus*, 4 (4–11 November 1647), 7.

49 *Kings Cabinet opened*, 43, 44, especially 28 and sig. A3; also Francis Freeman, *VIII Problems*

Compounded (1646); the same offensive language, calling parliament 'rebels' and Fairfax 'brutish', was noted by William Lilly, *Several Observations on the Life and Death of King Charles I* (1651), in *Select Tracts Relating to the Civil Wars in England, In the Reign of King Charles the First*, 2 vols., ed. Francis Maseres (London: R. Bickerstaff, 1815), I, 142.

50 *Some Observations Upon Occasion of the Publishing their Majesties Letters* (Oxford, 1645), 2; *A Letter in Which the Arguments of the Annotator*, 2–3; [Martin Llewellyn], *A Satyr* (Oxford, 1645), 10; Browne, *Key to the Kings Cabinet*, 51–2.

51 *A new Ballad, called a review of Rebellion* (1647); Browne, *Key to the Kings Cabinet*, 53; Symmons, *Vindication*, passim; Mayne, *ΟΧΛΟ–ΜΑΧΙΑ*, 35.

52 *The Kings Packet of Letters* (1645); *The Lord George Digby's Cabinet* (1646); *The Irish Cabinet* (20 January 1645[6]); S. E., *A Briefe Abstract of the Kings Letters* (1648).

53 *Queres to be considered* (1647); G[randison?], *Modest Cavalieres Advice*, 4; *Welcome, most welcome News. Mercurius Retrogradus* (1647), 3; *Mercurius Pragmaticus*, 9 (9–16 November 1647), 65, 70; Cleveland, 'The Kings Disguise', in *Poems*, 9; see Joad Raymond, 'The Daily Muse; Or, Seventeenth-Century Poets Read the News', *The Seventeenth Century*, 11 (1995): 193–7. And following the escape from Hampton Court: Symmons, *Vindication*, 9–10; *The Scotch Souldiers Speech* (1647), 5.

54 *Mercurius Britanicus, His Apologie to All Well-Affected People* (1645), 3–4; G[randison?], *Modest Cavalieres Advice*, 6; Lilly, *Several Observations*, in *Select Tracts*, ed. Maseres, I, 141; *The Faithful, yet Imperfect, Character of a Glorious King* (1660), 50.

55 Mark Kishlansky, 'The Emergence of Adversary Politics in the Long Parliament', *Journal of Modern History*, 49 (1977): 617–40; Robert Ashton, *Counter-Revolution: The Second Civil War and its Origins, 1646–1648* (New Haven: Yale University Press, 1994), chapter 6; see also the chapters by Dzelzainis and Loewenstein in this volume.

56 *Judas Justified* (1647) quoted; I[ohn] L[ilburne], *Plaine Truth* (1647), 5; *Mercurius Pragmaticus*, 7 (26 October – 2 November 1647), 49; *A Faithful Subjects Sigh* (1649), 5; *The Scotch Souldiers Lamentation* (1649), 1; *Loyalties Tears* (1649); *Iter Carolinum* (1660), in *Somers Tracts*, X, 299; John Arnwey, *The Tablet. Or Moderation of Charles the I. Martyr* (1649), 10; Lilly, *Several Observations*, in *Select Tracts*, ed. Maseres, I, 177; *An Elegy, Sacred to the Memory* ([1649]; Wing E447); Symmons, *Vindication*, 206.

57 *The poore Committee-mans Accompt* (1647); [Francis Gregory?], *An Elegie upon the Death of Our Dread Soveraign Lord King Charls* (1649); *A Dialogue. Or, A Dispute* (1649); see also Henry Leslie, *The Martyrdome of King Charles* (The Hague, 1649).

58 *Mercurius Melancholicus*, 6 (2–9 October 1647), 33; the broadside poem is 'Majesty in Misery', in *Roxburghe Ballads*, VII, 619; see also Gilbert Burnet, *The Memoires of the Lives and Actions of James and William Dukes of Hamilton and Castleherald* (1677), 381–3; the partridge analogy in 'A Loyal Subjects Admonition', verso of *The Worlds Wonder! Or, The Prophetical Fish* ([?1666]).

59 *Mercurius Pragmaticus*, 8 (2–9 November 1647), 58; for peregrination, *The Case of the King Stated* (1647); *Turn apace, Turn apace* (1648); *Great Britans Vote* (1648); for deprivation, *Vox Civitatis* (1647), 6; for imprisonment, *A true and certaine Relation* (1648), 8; *Mercurius Pragmaticus*, 4 (5–12 October 1647), verses; for alms, etc., *Mercurius Pragmaticus*, 5 (12–19 October 1647), 39; *Mercurius Melancholicus*, 2 (18–25 September 1647), 22.

60 *A Letter Sent from Colonel Whaley* (1648), 5, quoted; *Gallant Newes for London* (1647), sig. A3; see also *Kingdomes Weekly Intelligencer*, 215 (22–29 June 1647), 579; contrast *The Royall Entertainment* (1645), 4.

61 *A Letter from the Kings Majesties Court* (1647), 6; *The Cavaliers Diurnall* (1647), 2; *Anti-*

Pragmaticus, 2 (21–28 October 1647), 6; *The Kings Majesties Most Gratious Message* (1647), 1; *The Kings Majesties Speech* (1648; Wing C2779), 5; *A Declaration of the Proceedings of the Kings Majesty at Carisbrooke* (1648), 6; *Moderate Intelligencer*, 197 (21–28 December 1648), 1801; *The Mad Dog Rebellion* (1648), 7.

62 *Mercurius Pragmaticus*, 7 (26 October – 2 November 1647), 51; on his children, *Kingdomes Weekly Intelligencer*, 230 (12–19 October 1647), 693; see also *A Letter from the Kings Majesties Court* (1647), 6; John Taylor, *The Kings Most Excellent Majesties Wellcome* (1647), 2–3. *His Majesties Complaint* (1647), 1; for the verses see *Seven yeares expired* (1647). See also John Hammond, *A Harmony of Healths* (1647), in *Cavalier and Puritan*, ed. Rollins, 188–94; *The Old Protestants Litany* (1647), in *Songs*, ed. Mackay, 23–7; *A Word in the Kings Eare* (1647); *The Monument of Charles the First* (1649); *The Kings Last Speech*, in *Roxburghe Ballads*, vii, 625–6; *The Manner of the Kings Trial* ([?1649]).

63 *The true Protestants humble Desires* (1647); see also *The Weeping Widdow* (1649), in *Cavalier and Puritan*, ed. Rollins, 238–40; *His Majesties Prayers* (1649); also *Monumentum Regale* (1649).

64 *Englands Troublers Troubled* (1648), 11; Patricia Crawford, '"Charles Stuart, That Man of Blood"', *Journal of British Studies*, 16 (1977): 41–61; for popular ultra-hostility see, for example, the newsbook *Mercurius Militaris* in October / November 1648; John Redingstone, *Plain English to the Parliament and Army* (1649).

65 'To the Duke of Buckingham', in *Poems and Songs*, v, ed. Fairholt; Bod., MS Rawl. D. 859, fo. 132; see also MS Rawl. D. 49, fo. 5; *CSPD*, 1628–1629, 4; *Diary of John Rous*, 17; Bod. MS Tanner 465, fo. 100; for Berwick Conrad Russell, *The Fall of the British Monarchies, 1637–1642* (Oxford: Clarendon Press, 1991), 91, 329; see also *Perfect Occurrences*, 25 (12–19 June 1646), 33; *A Continuation of Papers from the Scots Quarters*, 3 (5 November 1646), 5.

66 T. K., *News from Yorke* (1642); see also *Diurnal out of the North* (18 July 1642), 7; Raymond, *Invention of the Newspaper*, 133; Lilly, *Several Observations*, in *Select Tracts*, ed. Maseres, i, 159; [Cleveland], *Character of a Moderate Intelligencer* (1647), 1–2; on Hampton, see *Letter Sent from Colonel Whaley*, 5; on the Isle of Wight, see *Moderate Intelligencer*, 127 (26 August 1647), 1235; *Mercurius Britanicus Alive Again* 1 (16 May 1648), 7; *Kingdomes Weekly Intelligencer*, 260 (16 May 1648), [944]; *Mercurius Aulicus Again*, 15 (18 May, 1648), sig. Ov. See also S. R. Gardiner, *History of the Great Civil War*, 4 vols. (Moreton-in-Marsh: Windrush Press, 1986 / 7), iii, 269; Joseph Frank, *The Beginnings of the English Newspaper, 1620–1660* (Cambridge, MA: Harvard University Press, 1961), 129.

67 Also *Mercurius Politicus*, 14 (5–12 September 1650); Raymond, ed., *Making the News*, 181; on the *Books of Sports* see David Underdown, *Revel, Riot and Rebellion: Popular Politics and Culture in England, 1603–1660*, 2nd edn (1985; Oxford University Press, 1987), 66–8, 95, 130, 177; Leah S. Marcus, *The Politics of Mirth: Jonson, Herrick, Milton, Marvell, and the Defense of Old Holiday Pastimes* (University of Chicago Press, 1986); and Thomas N. Corns, *Uncloistered Virtue: English Political Literature, 1640–1660* (Oxford: Clarendon Press, 1992), 102–14.

68 *The Scotch Souldiers Speech*, 3; 'Ane Epitaph', NLS, MS Adv., 23.3.24, fo. 92.

69 [Gregory?], *Elegie Upon the Death*; A. B., *An Epitaph* ([1649]); W. F., *An Elegie* ([1649]); *King Charles His Speech* (1649), in *Cavalier and Puritan*, ed. Rollins, 233.

70 Lilly, *Several Observations*, in *Select Tracts*, ed. Maseres, i, 139; see also 177.

71 G[randison?], *Modest Cavaliers Advice*, 6; *The Parliaments New and Perfect Catechisme* (1647); C. R., *In a Cloud* (1647).

72 [Balthasar Gerbier? or Silas Taylor?], *The None-Such Charles* (1649), 170; John Milton, *Complete Prose Works*, III, ed. Merritt Y. Hughes (New Haven: Yale University Press, 1962), 362; Cook, *King Charles his Case* (1649), in *Somers Tracts*, IV, 171; for pamphlet warnings see *The Remonstrance of the Generall Assembly*, sig. A4v; *Englands Petition to their Soveraigne King*, 5; *Englands Petition to their King* (1643), in *Somers Tracts*, XIII, 162; *Observations Concerning the Late Treaty* (1645), 5.

73 *King Charles his Entertainment*; Bond, *King Charles his Welcome*, sig. A2; *King Charles His Royall Welcome*, 1, 5; *Gallant Newes*, sig. A3; *Ovatio Carolina*, 4:151; also *A Relation* (1623), in *Somers Tracts*, V, 242; [Llewellyn], *A Satyr*, 10; *A Word in the Kings Eare*; *Mercurius Elencticus*, 6 (29 December – 5 January 1647/8), 43–44; the sympathetic writer is J. L., *A Just Apologie for His Sacred Majestie* (1642), sig. A3.

74 Bod., MS Rawl. D. 1048, fo. 50v (verse on the Spanish Match); *Downfall of Greatnesse*, 6; *Calver's Royall Vision*, 5; *The Great Eclipse of the Sun, Or, Charles His Waine* (1644); Ann Geneva, *Astrology and the Seventeenth-Century Mind: William Lilly and the Language of the Stars* (Manchester University Press, 1995), especially 81–3, 206–7, 267.

75 S. E., *Briefe Abstract*, 5; *A Sigh for an Afflicted Soveraigne* (1649), 1.

76 *A Copie of verses* (1648) quoted; *The Insecuritie of Princes* (1648[9]); Symmons, *Vindication*, 241–51; *Mercurius Pragmaticus*, 9 (9–16 November 1648), E414(15), 65; *The City*; A. N. B. Cotton, 'London Newsbooks in the Civil War: Their Political Attitudes and Sources of Information', Ph.D. thesis (University of Oxford, 1971), 198; for the quote and Duppa see *Moderate Intelligencer*, 193 (23–30 November 1648); *Packets of Letters*, 35 (7–14 November 1648); Raymond, ed., *Making the News*, 207–8.

77 *King Charles His Royall Welcome*, 2; see Skerpan Wheeler's chapter in this volume.

78 *Faithful, yet Imperfect, Character*, 17, quoted; *Monument of Charles the First*, quoted; Leslie, *Martyrdome of King Charles*; with irony, *The Assenters Sayings* (1681); *The Kings Last Farewell* (1648[9]); for the language of martyrdom see *A Crowne, A Crime* (1648[9]); A. B., *An Epitaph; An Elegie* ([1649]); W. F., *An Elegy* ([1649]); 'To the Eternall Memory . . .', Bod., MS Rawl. D. 737, fo. 16v; *Two Elegies* (1649); [Butler?], *King Charles' Case Truly Stated*, in *Somers Tracts*, IV, 198–210; H. Ferne, *A Sermon Preached* (1649), sig. A2v.

79 D. H. K., *A Deepe Groane* (1649), 6; for the Jesus parallel see *The Life and Death of King Charles the Martyr* (1649); Symmons, *Vindication*, 241–51; *A Hand-Kirchife for Loyall Mourners* (1649), 5; 'To the Eternall Memory of Charles the First', Bod., MS Rawl. D. 737, fo. 16v.

80 J. G. G., *Some Observations* (1694), in *Somers Tracts*, III, 173; Helen W. Randall, 'The Rise and Fall of a Martyrology: Sermons on Charles I', *Huntington Library Quarterly*, 10 (1946/7): 135–67; see also the chapter by Lois Potter in this volume.

81 *The Visible Vengeance* (1648); *Loyalties Tears*, 6; for the Deptford case see *A Miracle of Miracles* (1649); see also Bod., MS Rawl. D. 737, fo. 16v; for other miracles 'Miranda', Bod., MS Ash. 826, fo. 125.

82 *The Monument of Charles the First; A Crowne, A Crime*; A. B., *An Epitaph; An Elegy, Sacred to the Memory*.

4

'Incendiaries of the state':
Charles I and tyranny

Martin Dzelzainis

I

Today the equestrian statue of Charles I by Hubert Le Sueur stands at Charing Cross, as it has done for over three centuries, gazing down Whitehall towards the site of the king's execution on 30 January 1649. Ultimately descended from the equestrian monument to the Emperor Marcus Aurelius in Rome, via Giambologna's statue of Cosimo I de' Medici in Florence and Tacca's of Henri IV in Paris, the so-called 'CAROLUS MAGNUS' was commissioned in 1630 by Charles's Lord Treasurer, Richard Weston, who wanted it for the gardens at Mortlake Park, his Roehampton estate.[1] In many ways, however, the *fortuna* of the statue is more significant than the object itself. Although Le Sueur finished casting it in Covent Garden in 1633 (two years before Weston's death), it was not to go on public view for another forty-three years. Still in Covent Garden after the regicide, hidden in a crypt, it was finally tracked down during the Protectorate and sold on as scrap to a brazier in Holborn, John Rivett. But instead of breaking the statue up, so the story goes, Rivett buried it in his garden and started a trade selling brass-handled knives, and other paraphernalia supposed to be made from it, as relics (or souvenirs, depending on the purchaser). At the Restoration, Weston's son, the Second Earl of Portland, claimed ownership, but he died shortly after-wards, and it was his widow who later offered to sell it to Charles II. By the time the sale was completed in May 1675, plans to erect it at Charing Cross were already in hand, overseen by the Earl of Danby. Sir Christopher Wren was instructed to draw up plans for the plinth, to be executed by Joshua Marshall, the king's master-mason. Work began in July 1675, broke off for the winter, and was completed late in 1676, when the statue was finally displayed, ensconced behind iron railings.[2]

What is striking is how closely the saga of the statue, the 'royal image' as Waller dubbed it in a commemorative poem, had shadowed the *fortuna* of its original, the king himself, over the years.[3] From ostentation to occlusion to ignominy to rehabilitation, the two marched in step. The ideological significance of erecting *this* statue on *this* site was moreover unmistakable, for Charing Cross was where many of the regicides had been executed. In effect, one cult, that of Charles the martyr, was being deployed to drive out another, that of the martyrs to the Good Old Cause.[4] Although republican satirists responded by comparing the statue's rider to Nero rather than Marcus Aurelius, Waller's likening of the erection of the 'sacred brass' to the Resurrection proved more representative of the sentiments which accrued to the site.[5] Royal proclamations were read out at Charing Cross until the death of Queen Victoria, and it was only in 1912 that the Office of Works finally reached an accommodation with the Jacobites, who sought to lay wreaths there unofficially on each anniversary of the regicide.[6]

My concern here is only with the early phase of the narrative; that is, with the reduction of Charles I, so to speak, from 'CAROLUS MAGNUS' to under-the-counter sets of commemorative cutlery. That a fall of this severity should have happened at all is in many ways remarkable. European monarchs had been deposed or assassinated before, and monarchy itself abjured in the Dutch Revolt, but the public trial and execution of a ruler regarded by most of his subjects as the Lord's anointed was altogether unprecedented. Recently, however, historians have converged on the view that he had only himself to blame for his troubles. L. J. Reeve, for example, charting the road to Personal Rule, finds that 'Charles was an excellent connoisseur of the visual arts, but as a reigning monarch he was woefully inadequate.'[7] Conrad Russell, narrating the fall of the British monarchies, concludes that while Charles was 'not, in fact, nearly as duplicitous as he is sometimes taken to be', he nevertheless bears 'a very heavy responsibility' for alienating his subjects.[8] Examining the causes of the English Civil War, Russell's verdict is that Charles 'was unfit to be a king' and that he was indeed 'a necessary condition' of that war.[9] And, concluding a litany of the mistakes made by Charles in the Bishops' Wars, Mark Charles Fissel roundly declares that he 'bears responsibility for his own fate and the sufferings of the realm', and even that he 'fell from the throne; he was not pushed'.[10]

The bleakness of these judgements can be seen as the function of a larger argument. For the more the crimes and misdemeanours of Charles

I as a ruler are emphasized, the more they throw into relief the stability and even inertia of those he ruled, especially in England. Only a society which was not riven by any fundamental ideological divisions, so the argument goes, could have remained quiescent for so long in the face of so many provocations – and would have done so for even longer had it not been for the vexed issue of religion. Ironically, 'revisionist' historians turn out to have as much invested in Charles I's delinquencies as the 'Whiggish' practitioners against whom they reacted, though to a different end; not by way of explaining why it became necessary for his subjects to assert their civil liberties, but for the purpose of demonstrating how little they were animated by such abstractions.[11]

This thesis has been pushed to its limits in a recent volume by John Morrill, who is if anything even more scathing about 'the incompetence and authoritarianism' of the king.[12] Adopting early modern definitions of tyranny as a yardstick, he selects five examples of Charles's behaviour from 1626 to 1629 alone which 'surely constituted a formidable *prima facie* case of legal tyranny'. Indeed, by August 1642 the 'evidence for labelling Charles I a tyrant was very palpable'. Having wound matters up to this pitch, Morrill then points to the fact that the charge of tyranny was not actually levelled against the king at the time, even though to do so 'would have unlocked the principal arguments for resistance in early modern Europe'. Moreover, the fact that 'the constitutional case for Parliament was muddled and avoided the most obvious and potent traditions of argument' left the two Houses themselves 'vulnerable to having [Charles] pin the label of tyranny on them'. The conclusion we are bound to draw from this, he suggests, is that it must have been 'a religious case for resistance, not the case from secular tyranny, which mobilized men against Charles I'.[13] The proposition is thus that 'it was religious arguments which proved to be the solvents of resistance to resistance theory'. More broadly, Morrill cleaves to the view that 'what England suffered in the 1640s was its delayed, or deferred wars of religion'.[14]

Some of these contentions are less plausible than others. It seems counterintuitive to append the Civil War to the religious conflicts of the sixteenth century by way of seeking to eliminate 'secular tyranny' from the equation, given that it was those religious conflicts which gave birth to a secularized theory of revolution in the first place.[15] Morrill, like some others, has also arguably misconstrued the role of resistance theory in the 1640s. But rather than pursue these objections, my main aim is to sketch an alternative account of how Charles managed to evade the charge of tyranny before the outbreak of the Civil War; more specifically, an account which registers the fact that parliamentary apologists remained sharply aware at all times of the arguments which had been used to sustain the legal tyranny of the 1630s. Only then can we begin to consider why he was finally unable to evade the charge. What this should reveal in turn is that, however inflexible Charles may have been personally, his image as monarch – tyrant, defender of the ancient constitution, 'man of blood' – proved remarkably malleable in the hands of his supporters no less than those of his opponents. Even in a period noted for its abstract political theory, controlling the royal image remained vital in ideological terms.

II

Few could be as well placed as John Selden was to comment on the way the English monarchy was defined and redefined over two decades. Not only was he one of the first victims of Personal Rule, imprisoned for his part in the Commons' disturbances at the end of the 1629 session, but, by virtue of publishing *Mare Clausum* in 1635, he was also implicated in the Ship Money project, which symbolized the whole Caroline enterprise. When speaking of these events, however, he cast his net rather wider than modern historians:

> Fancy to yourself a man sets the city on fire at Cripplegate, and that fire continues, by means of others, till it comes to White Friars, and then he that begun it would fain quench it; does not he deserve to be punished most that first set the city on fire? So 'tis with the incendiaries of the state: they that first set it on fire (by monopolizing, forest business, imprisoning parliament men *tertio Caroli, &c.*) are now become regenerate, and would fain quench the fire; certainly they deserved most to be punished for being the first cause of our distractions.[16]

Selden's failure to mention Ship Money is unlikely to have stemmed from any personal embarrassment. This is because he was reflecting not so much on what the 'incendiaries of the state' had done in the 1630s as on how they dealt with the legacy of their actions. What Selden apparently could not stomach was the hypocrisy of those who were now 'become regenerate'; converts to the path of righteousness, the 'incendiaries' had consigned their former selves to oblivion, and expected everyone else to do likewise. Selden's remark appears to have been made in the early 1640s, since it captures so precisely aspects of the ideological repositioning which went on in these years, a good deal of which revolved around arguments in the Ship Money Case and, above all, those to do with the doctrine of necessity.

As S. R. Gardiner argued long ago, Ship Money had its origins in the *rapprochement* with Spain in the early 1630s.[17] This was not a policy which could be avowed, and the first Ship Money writ of October 1634 accordingly cited threats to trade from pirates and Turks before invoking the 'dangers . . . which, on every side, in these times of war do hang over our heads, [so] that it behoveth us and our subjects to hasten the defence of the realm with all expedition'. Virtually the same form of words was used the following year.[18] Indeed, by the time a test case came to court in November 1637, there had been four such writs. No emergency obviously requiring 'expedition' having manifested itself in the meantime, the pretext had become threadbare. In February 1637, before the case could be heard (the scheduled defendant at this point was Viscount Saye and Sele), Charles therefore asked the judges to sanction his view of the prerogative.[19] The questions were so framed that to answer them in the affirmative (as they did) would underwrite not only Ship Money but also, in principle, any other initiative of this kind, since it left 'the king sole judge, both of the danger, and when and how the same is to be prevented and avoided' (col. 844). In effect, the judges had given 'legal shape to the king's absolute prerogative'.[20]

When the hearing began, the reality of the dangers mentioned in the Ship Money writs was no longer an issue, firstly because the judges could be expected to affirm that this was solely for the king to determine, and secondly because the defendant – now John Hampden – had demurred as to matters of fact alleged by the Crown (a precondition of the case being allowed to proceed). Despite this, Hampden's counsel, Oliver St John and Robert Holborne, found ways to engage in an examination of the doctrines of necessity and *salus populi* which, together with the counter-statements it provoked, amounted to a comprehensive – and conspicuously public – airing of these topics.

St John's aim was to reduce the extra-legal prerogative to vanishing point. He began by itemizing the ordinary means available to the king for defence: the military service due from various feudal tenures, prerogative rights such as wardship, and revenues such as tonnage and poundage (cols. 864–77). The crucial question for him, as for the judges in February, was what would happen when these ordinary means had been exhausted; whether 'his majesty, without consent in Parliament, may in this case of extraordinary Defence, alter the Property of the Subjects Goods' (col. 881).

His response was to concede that there were circumstances in which this could happen, but these were defined in such a way as to render void the idea of its being done by virtue of the prerogative:

> for Property being both introduced and maintained by human laws, all things by the law of nature being common, there are therefore some times, like the Philistines being upon Samson, wherein these cords are too weak to hold, 'Necessitas enim' (as Cicero saith) 'magnum humanae imbecillitas patrocinium omnem legem frangit [Necessity, the great resource of human weakness, breaks every law];' at such times all property ceaseth, and all things are again resolved into the common principles of nature. (cols. 903–4)[21]

In such an emergency, property did cease, but this was because the legal structures which created and upheld it had gone into abeyance – the point being that the prerogative lapsed along with these structures. Any emergency in which the right to property could be annulled was, *ipso facto*, one in which there would no longer be any authority capable of effecting the annulment. It followed that the only meaningful question to ask about the prerogative in relation to defence was what it could do by way of altering the subject's property 'in time of peace' (col. 905) – in which case the usual battery of common-law arguments came into play, in turn allowing St John to maintain that the subject's property was beyond the king's reach.

St John's argument is less exotic than it seems. The Latin maxim about necessity derives not from Cicero but Seneca's *Controversiae*, and can be found, in the form cited by St John, embedded in a passage in *De Iure Belli ac Pacis* where Grotius analyses the proposition 'That in case of necessity men have the right to use things which have become the property of another, and whence this right comes.'[22] For Grotius, property was originally a right common to all to use the things of this world, while private property was an arrangement which gradually evolved through agreement. At no stage, however, would it have been rational for such agreements to exclude the possibility of the common right to use being revived in necessity. This is recognizably St John's theory of property, the difference being that St John had generalized it, whereas Grotius (at least in this section of *De Iure Belli*) was thinking exclusively in terms of individuals.

These Grotian materials were also exploited by Holborne. When faced by 'instant and apparent danger', it was clear that 'particular property must yield much to necessity'. But this would leave the king no better placed to act than anyone else, since it was 'not only in the power of the king, but a subject may do as much'. In fact, Holborne took the argument to its logical conclusion: that the king was as liable to *suffer* as anyone else, since, 'in that case, the subject may prejudice the king himself in point of property' (col. 975; see col. 1012). This (unacknowledged) use of Grotius made Hampden's counsel his spokesmen in what was effectively an intellectual exchange by proxy. Selden himself did not attend the trial but, in English legal circles at least, his *Mare Clausum* was widely held to have seen off Grotius's *Mare Liberum*. Throughout the Ship Money Case, *Mare Clausum* was cited as definitive on the sovereignty of the sea. As we shall see, however, while Selden disagreed with Grotius on the revival of a common right to use *in extremis*, his view on pleas of necessity in general was very close indeed to that of St John and Holborne.[23]

St John's argument was still too exotic for Sir Edward Littleton who, replying for the Crown, refused to entertain his hypothesis of a total dissolution. On the contrary, Littleton's argument stemmed from assuming the perdurability of civil society. For while it was true to say that 'positive laws are abrogated, when the safety of the kingdom and people are in danger', the point of doing this (as opposed to its being something which just happened) was to avoid a general collapse, so ensuring that 'we have a kingdom to use them'. All 'formalities' were dispensable 'when the keeping of the laws would end the commonwealth'. This stance left Littleton free to articulate the familiar maxims: that 'whatsoever is done for the public safety is best'; that 'other laws are tributary, and must give way to the law of necessity'; and that 'things are lawful by necessity, which otherwise are not'. It also unlocked a set of doctrines to do with the public good – in particular, the maxim that 'the commonwealth is to be preferred before all private estates'. The implicit accusation was that Hampden, in standing on his rights, was guilty of preferring these to the public good. What individual property owners should consider, Littleton argued, was that the 'public and the private are so nearly connext that they can hardly be separated: the public loss falls immediately, and by consequence upon particular persons'. The lesson to be drawn from this was both that 'Private interests must give place to the public good' and that it was nevertheless in the individual's self-interest that this should be so, because it 'is impossible to save private fortunes if the public be lost' (cols. 926–8).

Others dismissed St John's argument out of hand. Thus the Attorney-General, Sir John Bankes, derided it as something 'made by the people, or

to please the people', which would result in 'the introducing of a demo-
cratical government' (col. 1060), while Judge Berkeley found it 'a dangerous tenet, and kind of judaizing opinion', which would leave the country
as defenceless as the Jews 'upon their Sabbath' (cols. 1097–8). And it is
significant that it was not taken up by the two judges who found for
Hampden most decisively, Sir George Croke and Sir Richard Hutton. But
several judges did echo the terms of Littleton's reply: for example, Sir
George Vernon (see col. 1127), Sir John Bramston (see col. 1248), and, most
fully, Sir John Finch. He too declared that 'all private property must give
way to the public', maintaining nevertheless that individuals should not
think of this only in terms of personal loss:

> as every one hath a particular property in his own goods, so every one
> hath a property in general in another man's goods, for the common
> good. For the commonwealth hath a property in every man's goods, not
> only in time of war, but also in time of necessity in time of peace. (col.
> 1225)

In countering one Grotian line of argument, however, Finch like Littleton
had effectively invoked the no less Grotian concept of eminent domain –
an underlying continuity between the two sides' arguments which makes
later developments easier to explain.[24]

Although Ship Money was debated in the Short Parliament (where the
king offered to relinquish it in return for twelve subsidies) and was finally
abolished by the Long Parliament after being condemned on all sides, the
arguments in the case went on being exploited throughout, often in unexpected ways. For example, the General Council meeting of 16 August 1640
discussed raising forces for a second campaign against the Scots which,
like the first, had not been sanctioned by parliament. Finch, now Lord
Keeper, argued that the 'whole kingdom is bound in person and estate to
serve: *This, Hatton* [sic] *and Croke, in case of invasion'*.[25] When delivering his
Ship Money verdict, Finch had largely ignored the arguments of
Hampden's counsel and turned his fire instead on his two fellow judges.
He now pounced on their admission that, 'in case of necessity and
danger', the king could 'command his subjects, without parliament, to
defend the kingdom' (col. 1134; see col 1199). While this alone does not
make Finch one of the 'regenerate', it is significant that his private counsel
eventually made its way into the public arena. The royal proclamation of
20 June 1642 defended Commissions of Array by pointing out that they
were 'agreed to be legall even by the two learned Judges, Sir George
Crook, and Sir Richard Hutton (amongst all the rest) in their Arguments

which concluded on the Subjects part in Our Exchequer-Chamber in Master Hampdens Case'.[26] Moreover, this concern with legal propriety was placed in sharp contrast to the conduct of the two Houses in passing the Militia Ordinance 'under pretence of imminent danger, and urgent and inevitable necessity of putting Our Subjects into a posture of Defence'.[27] What this example encapsulates, in fact, is the reversal of roles which took place between 1640 and 1642, a process which reached its culmination when (to borrow Michael Mendle's pungent phrase) 'Charles became Hampden'.[28]

A corresponding shift on the other side was initiated by Henry Parker in *The Case of Shipmony* (1640). Parker began by rehearsing the 'variety and contrariety of opinion amongst the greatest Sages of our Law' to make the point that nothing could be hoped for from that quarter. Having dismissed the cacophany of views, he nevertheless proceeded to endorse much of what had been said about necessity during the trial:

> the supreame of all humane lawes is *salus populi*. To this law all lawes almost stoope, God dispences with many of his lawes, rather than *Salus populi* shall bee endangered, and that iron law which wee call necessity it selfe, is but subservient to this law; for rather than a Nation shall perish, any thing shall be held necessary, and legall by necessity.[29]

This is far closer to Littleton than it is to St John. Parker was not interested in what a total dissolution would be like because his concern was with *institutions* which were fit to be entrusted with the public safety. For him, *salus populi* literally was *suprema lex*: even 'that iron law which we call necessity' was subordinate to it. What he meant by this was that only a body which could be relied upon unfailingly to place the public safety above all else could be trusted to do whatever was dictated by necessity, and the only body which met this criterion was parliament. Neither the king nor the judges had been able to reconcile the demands of law, policy and conscience, but in parliament, Parker claimed, 'Justice and Policie kisse and embrace'.[30]

Although Parker's response to Ship Money was highly untypical in 1640, there were members of the parliamentary leadership sympathetic to this kind of thinking. One was Parker's uncle, Lord Say.[31] Another was John Pym, reported as arguing in February 1641 that 'in case of necessitie and in pursuance of that truste that is imposed [*sic*] in us for the safety of the commonwealth wee may assume a Legislative power to compell suche as bee noted riche men to lend ther moneyes'.[32] But these remained isolated usages until the two Houses began to organize themselves militarily in

1642, when safety and necessity became part of the idiom of an emerging parliamentary absolutism.[33]

However, those who drafted parliament's offical remonstrances mostly showed themselves unwilling to follow Parker's lead in abandoning constitutionalism. This can be seen in their contrasting responses to what became a central theme of the king's propaganda, and crucial to his image as a reformed constitutional monarch; that his rights were essentially no different from those of his subjects. Early in May 1642 the king asserted his proprietorial right to Hull (site of the most important magazine in the north): 'we would fain be answered what Title any Subject of our Kingdom hath to his House or Land, that we have not to the town of Hull? Or what right hath he to his Money, Plate, or Jewels that we have not to our Magazine or Munition there?'[34] The parliamentary *Remonstrance* of 26 May dismissed the attempt to link the two rights; for, its authors asked, 'if the King had a Property in all his Towns, what would become of the Subjects Propriety in their Houses therein?' What the king enjoyed was at most a fiduciary interest, and they accordingly interpreted his claim to Hull as a sinister assault on the subject's property:

> This erroneous Maxim being infused into Princes, That their Kingdoms are their own, and that they may do with them what they will, (as if their Kingdoms were for them, and not they for their Kingdoms) is the Root of all the Subjects Misery, and of all the invading of their just Rights and Liberties.[35]

In construing the threat as they did, and in responding to it with an unyielding defence of private property, they thus reaffirmed the most familiar and long-standing constitutionalist objection to tyranny.

By contrast, Parker, at ease with the language of absolutism, responded more innovatively. In *Some Few Observations upon His Majesties Late Answer* (May 1642) he addressed the argument that 'by the same power' by which the two Houses 'make Ordinances for the *Militia*', they 'may disseise both the King and Subiects from their estates'. The force of this, he recognized, rested on the claim that the king had 'an interest in the *Militia* as legall and proper as ours are, in our Lands or Tenements'. Unlike his fellow parliamentarians, Parker simply conceded the point. But, he then cautioned,

> we must avoyde mistakes herein; for in our goods and inheritances we have not so pure and unconditionall a right, but that it is inconsistant with the common right, and in this respect the Kings possessions are not privileged more than a subiect, for the States proprietie cannot be excluded out of eyther.[36]

The king's attempt to argue that he had the same property in the militia (or in Hull) that his subjects had in their houses was mistaken, not because, as the *Remonstrance* argued, the subject alone could have a right of property, but because *neither* of them had a 'pure and unconditionall' right to the exclusion of 'the States proprietie'.

Although this line of argument went against the constitutionalist grain, it was rapidly adopted by other apologists like John Marsh, Chancellor of Lincoln's Inn.[37] By December 1642 a royal *Declaration* on the Assessment Ordinance needed to consist of little more than a *summa* of alleged parliamentary illegalities. It first reminded its readers of the admission in parliament's *Remonstrance* of 26 May 'that if they were found guilty of that charge of destroying the Title and Interest of Our Subjects to their Lands and Goods, it were indeed a very great crime'. This being the case, it was difficult to believe that in

> the same Parliament, a Law should be made to declare the proceedings and judgement upon Ship-money to be illegal and voyd, and during that Parliament, that an order of both Houses shall, upon pretence of Necessity, inable foure men to take away the twentieth part of their Estates from all their Neighbours.

While the parliamentarians would 'say they cannot manage their great undertakings without such extraordinary wayes', this only proved that they had 'undertaken somewhat they ought not to undertake, not that it is lawfull for them to do anything that is convenient for those ends'. Their ordinance was not only illegal but also self-contradictory, since it imposed taxes 'by such rules of unlimited Arbitrary power, as are inconsistent with the least pretence or shadow of that Property it would seem to defend'.[38]

The ease with which the *Declaration* mined the seam of differences between official and unofficial versions of the parliamentary case helps to explain how the royalists could plausibly pass themselves off as 'regenerate'. Selden, for one, was not impressed by this posturing, particularly since he thought that the king's Commissions of Array were manifestly illegal. But he was also unhappy with attempts to justify the Militia Ordinance by the plea of necessity, to which he objected in exactly the same way that Hampden's counsel had to the Ship Money writs:

> whereas necessity is pretended to be a ground of this ordinance, that can be no true ground of it, for in that case where there is a true and an apparent necessity every man hath as great a liberty to provide for his own safety as the two Houses of Parliament; neither can any civil court pretend to do anything out of necessity which they cannot do by the

ordinary rules of law and justice, so when such a real necessity comes there must be a stop of the courts of justice.[39]

In terms of Selden's analogy, the Houses' willingness to embrace the tyrannical doctrines of the 1630s, exposing themselves in the process to the corresponding counter-arguments, was how the fire had spread through the city. But he did not forget who had started the fire in the first place, and there is no reason to suppose that others did either. Even so, it had become increasingly difficult, arguably unnecessary, and possibly counter-productive to bring the charge of tyranny against Charles-as-Hampden. This was, in effect, the price the Houses paid for creating the military organization which allowed them actually, and not only theoretically, to resist the king.

III

The work which did most to lock the two sides into their respective positions was *His Majesties Answer to the XIX Propositions*. Drafted by Lord Falkland and Sir John Culpepper and published in June 1642, this sought to counter the two Houses' arrogation of the functions of the state by redefining the role within it of the monarch. That is to say, the *Answer* simultaneously identified the king's cause with that of the ancient constitution and recast that constitution in terms of mixed monarchy:

> There being three kinds of government among men, absolute monarchy, aristocracy and democracy, and all these having their particular conveniences and inconveniences, the experience and wisdom of your ancestors hath so moulded this out of a mixture of these as to give to this kingdom (as far as human prudence can provide) the conveniences of all three, without the inconveniences of any one, as long as the balance hangs even between the three estates.[40]

Some royalists were dismayed by a reduction of the king *to* one of the three estates from being king *of* them (i.e., lords spiritual, lords temporal, and commons), since it seemed to reduce him to little more than a Venetian doge.[41] Anglicans like Edward Hyde were no less alarmed by the apparent abandonment of the bishops. But the *Answer* was designed above all to appeal to those who might regard 'the King as a lesser danger to legality than the [parliamentary] Junto', and to set out a programme around which a royalist party could coalesce.[42]

Thomas Hobbes, who thought that 'gentle answers, and reasonable declarations' served only to undermine morale when the king's cause would have been better served by a naked call to arms, later poured scorn on this *démarche*:

> those men, whose pens the King most used in these controversies of law and politics, were such (if I have not been misinformed) as having been members of this Parliament, had declaimed against ship-money and other extra-parliamentary taxes, as much as any; but when they saw the Parliament grow higher in their demands than they thought they would have done, went over to the King's party.[43]

While Selden's remarks were aimed at the architects of the Personal Rule, who then allowed the edifice to be dismantled, Hobbes had uppermost in his mind figures like Falkland and Hyde, who had urged on the dismantling and then sought to stop the process in its tracks. But the way in which these defectors did most harm to the king's cause, Hobbes thought, was by being 'in love with *mixarchy* which they used to praise by the name of mixed monarchy, though it were indeed nothing else but pure anarchy'. A 'fault' which had been 'generally in the whole nation' thus finally penetrated even the king's innermost counsels. And the fatal consequence of this, Hobbes suggested, was that it 'weakened their endeavour to procure him an absolute victory in the war', since this would inevitably spell the end of the mixed monarchy.[44]

Hobbes's insight into how the idea might affect the war aims of its exponents arguably has more purchase on the parliamentary side. As Richard Tuck has recently pointed out, the notion of a limited or balanced monarchy was no less useful 'to those opponents of the Crown's policies who wished to maintain a constitutionalist position, and who in particular were committed to working inside a *monarchical* structure'.[45] Presbyterians north and south of the border had a long tradition of thinking about church organization in terms of the three estates and, especially in the case of the Scots, this dovetailed with their other ideological commitments. The fact that the Calvinist theory of resistance assigned a crucial role to the magistracy was precisely why many of its classic texts, such as Hotman's *Francogallia*, scrutinized the topic of the estates so intensively.[46] Moreover, as Tuck suggests, 'what Calvinists all over Europe in the late sixteenth and early seventeenth centuries wished to do was to *capture* their monarchs and use their power to establish a Presbyterian system of Church Government'.[47] It followed that an absolute victory for the parliamentary side would not have served the Presbyterians' interests if it led straightforwardly to the establishment of a republic, especially given that the army was dominated by Independents averse to any attempt to impose religious uniformity. The Presbyterians remained open to the prospect of reaching an accommodation with Charles to the end, just as Charles, after he surrendered to the Scots in 1646, came under sustained pressure from the exiled court in Paris to reach a settlement at the expense of the Church of England.

There was therefore every chance that the monarchy, having redefined itself before hostilities commenced, might yet survive the war, if reconstructed along lines acceptable to Presbyterians (especially once the king had rejected the army's peace terms in the *Heads of the Proposals*). In explaining why this did not happen, historians have once again stressed the role of religious beliefs. During the course of the war, they point out, the accusation of tyranny against the king began to be supplemented and even superseded by one that he was, simply, a man of blood who should be brought to justice on that account alone. This accusation was grounded upon divine positive law. Texts such as Genesis 9:6 and Numbers 35:33 laid down that the shedding of blood must not go unpunished, and that until it was the land would be defiled. What was important about these imperatives of blood guilt and retribution, as Patricia Crawford has argued, was that they operated 'on another level from rational political argument'. To talk in this fashion 'avoided awkward constitutional issues', and offered a way of breaking the stranglehold exerted by the doctrine of mixed monarchy. More importantly still, it served to destroy 'Charles's sacredness' as king.[48] In a final, decisive transformation, King Charles I became merely Charles Stuart, the accused.

This nexus of ideas can be seen at work in *Phinehas's Zeal in Execution of Ivdgement. Or, a Divine Remedy for England's Misery*, a fast sermon preached before the House of Lords in October 1644 by Edmund Staunton – one of several sermons aimed at expediting proceedings against Archbishop Laud. Staunton's text was Psalm 106:30: 'Then stood up Phinehas, and executed judgment: and *so* the plague was stayed.' It is true that Staunton begins cautiously, noting that Phinehas 'was *privatus, e plebe unus*, a private man, one among the people, so that this act of his might seem not to be *zeal*, but *murther*'. One way of removing this doubt would be to argue that Phinehas 'did it by *speciall instinct*, and by a *motion extraordinary*' from God, but Staunton thinks this 'no constant rule for us to walke by'. Fortunately, verse 31 of the Psalm makes it 'cleare that this act of *Phineas was counted unto him for righteousnesse*, to wit, as a *righteous act* unto all generations'. Staunton can now deliver his brutally direct equations: the 'removall of the Cause takes away the effect also, execution of judgement removes the sinne or the sinner, and therefore takes away Gods wrath and judgement'. Laud's blood would thus help *'quench'* the *'fire of civill war kindled in England'.*[49] Some of the Lords may have been inspired by the image of themselves as *'Phinehas* with zeale in his heart and a javelin in his hand', since they agreed to the Act of Attainder in January 1645, swiftly followed by Laud's execution.[50] The crucial point, however, is that Laud, imprisoned in the Tower since December 1640, had not even played a part in the first two years of warfare. Charles, who had personally appeared in the field, was therefore *a fortiori* vulnerable to this kind of attack. Office had proved no obstacle where Laud was concerned, and neither would it in the case of a king who had been delegitimized and desacralized.

The decisive step was Charles's decision to go to war again, having subscribed an 'Engagement' with the Scots in December 1647. As the Scots mobilized and skirmishes broke out in Wales, the army leadership concluded a three-day prayer meeting at Windsor Castle late in April 1648 by accepting that it was their duty 'to call Charles Stuart, that man of blood, to an account for that blood he had shed, and mischief he had done'.[51] Many see this as the moment which sealed the king's fate. Thus David Underdown refers to the 'scripture-laden hysteria' of the meeting, and concludes that the 'Army was now out of hand; Cromwell and Ireton could no longer control it even if they wished'.[52] Ian Gentles sees it as an 'emotional catharsis'; henceforth 'propelled' by the conviction that Charles was a man of blood, the army 'rode rough-shod over the will of the people, to bring the King to his public trial and execution'.[53] David Smith concurs that nothing 'could cut through' ingrained mental habits of obedience and deference but 'another, deeper, religious imperative – the need to expiate the king's "blood guilt"'; ideas such as these, he adds, 'unleashed savage, elemental forces'.[54] The execution of the king, in the view of Morrill, was therefore 'a violent act carried out by a fairly isolated band of well-placed soldiers and civilians, mainly driven by religious fanaticism (the regicides) which gave rise to a political programme supported by a wider and more pragmatic group (the republicans)'.[55]

There seems little doubt that holding these beliefs about blood guilt and retribution constituted a powerful motive for the army to intervene, as it eventually did in December 1648. But this is to tread a thin line between explaining events and explaining them away, for the implication is that the regicide was an aberration, resulting from an upsurge of religious mania among an unrepresentative band of fanatics before wiser counsels prevailed. This comes close to endorsing Hobbes's view of the regicide (arrived at after scrutinizing the case of Phinehas in the 'Review and Conclusion' appended to *Leviathan*) as 'a conjunction of Ignorance and Passion'.[56] Just as the secular case for tyranny was held insufficient when seeking to account for the outbreak of the war, so it would appear that the regicide could not have been brought to pass in consequence of rationally pursuing political objectives.

While the army's deliberations were often marked by an intense scripturalism and seeking after God's purposes, these were routine aspects of the early modern attitude to resistance and tyrannicide. And although the Scriptures were uniquely authoritative in these matters, they were hardly univocal. Writing to Lord Wharton in January 1650, for example, Cromwell sought to assuage his doubts about the regicide. 'Perhaps', Cromwell suggested, 'no other way was left. What if God accepted the zeal, as He did that of Phineas, whose reason might have called for a jury?'[57] By contrast, when Colonel Thomas Harrison announced to a meeting of officers on 11 November 1647 that one of the 'thinges that lay uppon his spirrit' was that 'the Kinge was a Man of Bloud', Cromwell responded by 'putting severall cases in which merther was not to bee punished'. In particular, he cited that 'of David upon Joab's killing of Abner [2 Samuel 3], that hee spar'd him upon two prudentiall grounds; one that hee would nott hazard the spilling of more blood in regard the sons of Zeroiah were too hard for him'.[58] To those well versed in the Scriptures, counter-examples were always to hand, and hence an element of choice about *which* biblical imperative to follow.

Individual examples could also be interpreted divergently, even by those within the same political grouping. Inevitably, the story of Phinehas came in for scrutiny at the time of the regicide. John Price simply followed the Marian exile John Ponet in maintaining that Phinehas had acted upon '*some speciall inward commandment, or surely approved motion of God*', with the implication that the army had done likewise.[59] John Goodwin, however, maintained that Phinehas's act could be 'imputed' only to 'his zeal for God', and not to 'any extraordinary *afflatus*, or revelation from heaven'.[60] The Baptist Samuel Richardson pointed out that Phinehas was 'no Magistrate' and was therefore 'not cloathed with any Authority from God or man to doe it', and flatly denied that he had 'any express Command from God'. He had acted solely out of his zeal for the Lord, and 'what the Army hath done' could be 'justified upon the same ground'.[61]

A good deal hung on these interpretations since in January 1649 the Presbyterians had invoked the Calvinist theory of resistance in a last-ditch *defence* of the king.[62] Forty-seven London ministers issued a *Representation* reminding the army leaders that 'in reference to the Power of Magistracie' they were 'but private persons'. Although 'the Lawes of God, Nature, and Nations, together with the dictates of Reason' had allowed the two Houses 'to take up Armes for their owne Defence', they did not allow the same to 'a multitude of Private Persons'.[63] In purging parliament and in placing the king on trial, the army had manifestly usurped the role of the inferior magistrates. Anyone claiming to act on the authority of those Scriptures which appeared to sanction individual political initiatives therefore faced a dilemma. To argue, as Goodwin and Richardson did, that there was nothing extraordinary about Phinehas, so making him available as a precedent, left them entangled in the distinction between private persons and inferior magistrates. But to argue, as the less cautious Price did, that Phinehas was divinely inspired meant that those modelling their actions on his instantly identified themselves as antinomians, thereby confirming the accusations levelled against the army by Presbyterians throughout the later 1640s.

That the army leadership was aware of these difficulties is apparent from what has been described as 'the nearest thing we have to a manifesto of the revolution': the *Remonstrance* drafted by Henry Ireton, finally accepted by the General Council on 18 November 1648, and read out to the Commons two days later.[64] This formally adopted, for the first time, the demand for 'capital punishment upon the principal author and prime instrument of our late wars, and thereby the blood thereof expiated'.[65] Strikingly, however, this was buttressed by none of the standard scriptural citations; indeed, the *Remonstrance* was an austere, severely abstract document.

It was only several weeks later, on 27 December, that Fairfax and the General Council authorized publication of *An Abridgment of the late Remonstrance of the Army. With some Marginall Attestations, both for the better Understanding, Remembrance, and Judgment of the People.* As the title page made clear, this was intended '*to undeceive the Kingdome as to the false Glosses by some put upon the said Remonstrance*'. Possibly the work of Hugh Peter, it supplied the full array of scriptural materials absent from the original about the punishment of murder, and rehearsed a range of examples of individual resistance to the oppressors of Israel.[66] While these glosses suggest the extent to which the army's thinking could be recast in scriptural terms, the supplementary nature of the *Abridgment* nevertheless serves to highlight the originally free-standing nature of the political programme it summarized. In some respects, it even improved upon Ireton's text.

Condensing material spread over three pages in the original resulted in perhaps the clearest formulation of the army's programme prior to the trial and execution of the king:

> The summe of publique interest of a Nation in relation to common right, and in opposition to tyrrany [sic] of Kings or others, is, that for all matters concerning the whole they have a Parliament consisting of Deputyes or Represeners freely chosen and with as much equality as may be, And that the power of making or altering Lawes and of finall judgement be in them, and that it may not be left in the will of the King, or any other particular persons to make voyd their determinations.[67]

Self-determination and the elimination of discretionary power were to be the defining characteristics of a form of government free from the tyranny of a Charles or a Long Parliament.[68]

But the *Abridgment*, drawn up after the Purge, also excised the pages Ireton devoted to justifying the intervention. These consisted of a remarkable meditation on the doctrines of *salus populi* and necessity in which Ireton showed himself at least as sophisticated an exponent of these ideas as St John, Holborne or Parker. When faced with assertions during the Putney debates in 1647 that there was a natural right to vote, Ireton had repeatedly deployed the Grotian argument about the revival of the common right to use *in extremis*, which, he maintained, was almost the *only* natural right to which men could lay claim.[69] The imminent restoration of the king as a result of the Newport treaty in the autumn of 1648 led him to reconsider the case for a general version of these arguments, although aware of their troubled history:

> We are not ignorant that that rule of *Salus populi suprema lex* is of all others most apt to be abused or misapplied, and yet none more surely true. It is too ordinary (especially of late times) for men who, either from intentions of evil or inordinate temper of spirit, would break those bonds of law and magistracy which they find to restrain them, to frame pretences of public danger and extremity.[70]

Notwithstanding this, the doctrines were available to any 'that engageth upon such pretences really for public ends, and but upon public necessity or extremity, and with a sober spirit', provided that all other means were tried first, and only on condition that, as soon as these 'public ends' were 'secured', there would be a 'return to magistracy and order'. Admitting that it was 'a desperate cure in a desperate case', he committed the army to act unless parliament renounced the treaty with the king.[71] In the end, it was necessity – the 'tyrant's plea' – that brought down the tyranny of Charles I.[72]

Notes

A version of this chapter was presented to the Early Modern Group at the University of Durham. I am indebted to the audience for their comments, and especially to Christopher Brooks.

1 See C. Avery, 'Hubert Le Sueur, the "Unworthy Praxiteles" of King Charles I', *Walpole Society*, 48 (1980–2): 140, 146–7, 201 (document 51); Margaret Whinney and Oliver Millar, *English Art, 1625–1714* (Oxford: Clarendon Press, 1957), 115–18.

2 See D. G. Denoon, 'The Statue of King Charles I at Charing Cross', *Transactions of the London and Middlesex Archaeological Society*, new series 6 (1933): 460–86; K. A. Esdaile, 'The Busts and Statues of Charles I', *Burlington Magazine*, 91 (1949): 10.

3 Edmund Waller, 'On the Statue of King Charles I at Charing Cross' (line 11), in *The Poems of Edmund Waller*, ed. G. Thorn Drury (London, 1893), 203.

4 On Danby's programme 'of doing all possible honours to the memory of king Charles the First', of which the Charing Cross project formed part, see Gilbert Burnet, *History of His Own Time* (London, 1875), 248; Mark Goldie, 'Danby, the Bishops and the Whigs', in *The Politics of Religion in Restoration England*, ed. Tim Harris, Paul Seaward and Mark Goldie (Oxford: Basil Blackwell, 1990), 81–2. For the regicides, see Laura Lunger Knoppers, *Historicizing Milton: Spectacle, Power, and Poetry in Restoration England* (Athens and London: University of Georgia Press, 1994), 43–51.

5 See 'A Dialogue Between the Two Horses' (line 134), in *The Poems and Letters of Andrew Marvell*, ed. H. M. Margoliouth, rev. Pierre Legouis with E. E. Duncan-Jones, 2 vols. (Oxford: Clarendon Press, 1971), I, 212; Waller, 'On the Statue' (line 4).

6 See Denoon, 'The Statue of King Charles', 482–3.

7 L. J. Reeve, *Charles I and the Road to Personal Rule* (Cambridge University Press, 1989), 3.

8 Conrad Russell, *The Fall of the British Monarchies, 1637–1642* (Oxford: Clarendon Press, 1991), 530.

9 Conrad Russell, *The Causes of the English Civil War* (Oxford: Clarendon Press, 1990), 207, 208.

10 Mark Charles Fissel, *The Bishops' Wars: Charles I's Campaign Against Scotland, 1638–1640* (Cambridge University Press, 1994), 297, 298.

11 A significant exception is Kevin Sharpe who, in *The Personal Rule of Charles I* (New Haven and London: Yale University Press, 1992), highlights the social and political stability of the 1630s *without* feeling obliged by the same token to present Charles as anything other than a man 'of profound conscience and deep principle' (954).

12 John Morrill, *The Nature of the English Revolution* (London: Longman, 1993), 6.

13 Ibid., 291, 292, 293, 295, 303, 304.

14 Ibid., 36, 43.

15 See Quentin Skinner, *The Foundations of Modern Political Thought*, 2 vols. (Cambridge University Press, 1978), II, 338–9.

16 *The Table-Talk of John Selden* (London, 1800), 51 (s.v. 'Incendiaries').

17 See S. R. Gardiner, *History of England from the Accession of James I to the Outbreak of the Civil War, 1603–1642*, 10 vols. (London, 1883–4), VII, 368–72; Simon Adams, 'Spain or the Netherlands?: The Dilemmas of Early Stuart Foreign Policy', in *Before the English Civil War: Essays on Early Stuart Politics and Government*, ed. Howard Tomlinson (London: Macmillan, 1983), 82–5; A. J. Loomie, 'The Spanish Faction at the Court of Charles I,

1630–38', *Bulletin of the Institute of Historical Research*, 59 (1986): 40–2; Sharpe, *Personal Rule*, 545–53.

18 S. R. Gardiner, ed., *The Constitutional Documents of the Puritan Revolution 1625–1660*, 3rd edn (Oxford: Clarendon Press, 1979), 105–6. For the 1635 writ, see W. Cobbett, T. B. Howells, *et al.*, eds., *A Complete Collection of State Trials*, 34 vols. (London, 1809–28), III, col. 845. This is the volume of *State Trials* used throughout, and referred to in the main text and notes by column number only.

19 See N. P. Bard, 'The Ship Money Case and William Fiennes, Viscount Saye and Sele', *Bulletin of the Institute of Historical Research*, 50 (1977): 177–84.

20 Glenn Burgess, *The Politics of the Ancient Constitution: An Introduction to English Political Thought, 1603–1642* (Basingstoke: Macmillan, 1992), 209.

21 The translation of the Latin is taken from Hugo Grotius, *De Jure Belli ac Pacis Libri Tres*, trans. F. W. Kelsey, 3 vols. (reprinted New York: Oceana Publications, 1964), II, 193–4 (II.II.VI.4).

22 Ibid., III, 193. For the quotation from Seneca, see A. Kiessling, ed., *Annaei Senecae Oratorvm et rhetorvm sententiae divisiones colores* (Stuttgart: B. G. Teubner, 1967), 421 (IX.iv.5 [IV.xxvii]). The substitution of Cicero for the elder Seneca in this passage is not as egregious as it seems, since Cicero was regarded as an unimpeachable spokesman for the claims of necessity; see Peter Miller, *Defining the Common Good: Empire, Religion and Philosophy in Eighteenth-Century Britain* (Cambridge University Press, 1994), 22–4, 28–9, 51–9.

23 See cols. 928, 934, 1023, 1210, 1226, 1247; Richard Tuck, *Natural Rights Theories: Their Origin and Development* (Cambridge University Press, 1979), 97.

24 For Grotius on *dominium eminens*, see *De Iure Belli*, II.III.XIX.2, II.XIV.VII, III.XIX.VII, III.XX.VII.1.

25 Philip Yorke, Second Earl of Hardwicke, ed., *Miscellaneous State Papers* [*Hardwicke Papers*], 2 vols. (London, 1778), II, 147.

26 James F. Larkin, ed., *Stuart Royal Proclamations, Vol. II, Royal Proclamations of King Charles I, 1525–1646* (Oxford: Clarendon Press, 1983), 779.

27 Ibid., 778.

28 Michael Mendle, 'The Ship Money Case, *The Case of Shipmony*, and the Development of Henry Parker's Parliamentary Absolutism', *Historical Journal*, 32 (1989): 532.

29 [Henry Parker], *The Case of Shipmony, briefly discoursed, according to the Grounds of Law, Policy and Conscience* (n.p., 1640), 2, 7.

30 Ibid., 38.

31 For Say, see Michael Mendle, *Henry Parker and the English Civil War: The Political Thought of the Public's 'Privado'* (Cambridge University Press, 1995), 12–13; Richard Tuck, *Philosophy and Government, 1572–1651* (Cambridge University Press, 1993), 118.

32 Wallace Notestein, ed., *The Journal of Sir Symonds D'Ewes* (New Haven: Yale University Press, 1923), 382n.

33 See Russell, *British Monarchies*, 481, 484.

34 John Rushworth, ed., *Historical Collections* (London, 1721), IV, 572. See Robert Ashton, 'From Cavalier to Roundhead Tyranny, 1642–1649', in *Reactions to the English Civil War 1642–1649*, ed. John Morrill (London: Macmillan, 1982), 185–207.

35 Rushworth, *Historical Collections*, IV, 579.

36 [Henry Parker], *Some Few Observations upon His Majesties Late Answer* ([London, 1642]), 7, 8.

37 See John Marsh, *An Argument or, Debate in Law* (London, 1642), 7–9, 32–3.

38 *The Ordinance and Declaration of the Lords and Commons for the Assessing all such who have not contributed sufficiently for raising of Money, Plate, & c. With His MAJESTIES Declaration to all His loving Subjects upon occasion thereof* (Oxford, 1642), 1, 2, 5, 6.

39 Richard Tuck, '"The Ancient Law of Freedom": John Selden and the Civil War', in *Reactions*, ed. Morrill, 149.

40 J. P. Kenyon, ed., *The Stuart Constitution, 1603–1688* (Cambridge University Press, 1966), 21.

41 See J. G. A. Pocock and Gordon J. Schochet, 'Interregnum and Restoration', in *The Varieties of British Political Thought, 1500–1800*, ed. J. G. A. Pocock, Gordon J. Schochet and Lois G. Schwoerer (Cambridge University Press, 1996), 149–50.

42 David L. Smith, *Constitutional Royalism and the Search for Settlement, c. 1640–1649* (Cambridge University Press, 1994), 91.

43 Thomas Hobbes, *Behemoth, or The Long Parliament*, ed. F. Tönnies, introduction Stephen Holmes (University of Chicago Press, 1990), 117.

44 Ibid., 114–15, 116–17.

45 Tuck, *Philosophy and Government*, 233.

46 See Michael Mendle, *Dangerous Positions. Mixed Government, the Estates of the Realm, and the Making of the Answer to the XIX Propositions* (University, AL: University of Alabama Press, 1985), 63–96, 114–28.

47 Tuck, *Philosophy and Government*, 203.

48 Patricia Crawford, '"Charles Stuart, That Man of Blood"', *Journal of British Studies*, 16 (1977): 42, 45, 51. See further David Loewenstein's chapter in this volume, pp. 103–8.

49 Edmund Staunton, *Phinehas's Zeal in Execution of Ivdgement. Or, a Divine Remedy for England's Misery. A Sermon Preached before the Right Honourable House of Lords in the Abbey of Westminster, at their late Solemne monethly Fast, October 30. 1644* (London, 1645), 5–6, 10, 24.

50 Ibid., 9.

51 Ian Gentles, *The New Model Army in England, Ireland and Scotland, 1645–1653* (Oxford: Basil Blackwell, 1992), 246. The sole account of this meeting was written and published by William Allen eleven years later as *A Faithful Memorial of that remarkable Meeting of many Officers of the Army . . . at Windsor Castle* (April 1659); Austin Woolrych scrupulously examines its reliability in *Soldiers and Statesman: The General Council of the Army and its Debates, 1647–1648* (Oxford: Clarendon Press, 1987), 332–5.

52 David Underdown, *Pride's Purge: Politics in the Puritan Revolution* (London: Allen & Unwin, 1985), 96.

53 Ian Gentles, 'The Impact of the New Model Army', in *The Impact of the English Civil War*, ed. John Morrill (London: Collins & Brown, 1991), 90, 99.

54 David L. Smith, 'The Impact on Government', in *Impact of the English Civil War*, ed. Morrill, 44.

55 Morrill, *English Revolution*, 23.

56 Thomas Hobbes, *Leviathan*, ed. Richard Tuck (Cambridge University Press, 1996), 488.

57 W. C. Abbott, ed., *The Writings and Speeches of Oliver Cromwell*, 4 vols. (Cambridge, MA: Harvard University Press, 1937–47), II, 189–90.

58 C. H. Firth, ed., *The Clarke Papers*, 4 vols. (London: Camden Society, 1891–1901), I, 417.

59 John Price, *Clerico-Classicum, or, The Clergi-allarum to a third war* (London, [1649]), 33; see John Ponet, *A Shorte Treatise of politike power* (n.p., 1556), sig. Gviiiv.

60 John Goodwin, Ὑβριζτοδικαι: *The Obstructours of Justice* (London, 1649), 43.

61 Samuel Richardson, *An Answer to the London Ministers Letter* (London, 1649), 2–3.

62 Troubled by the absence of resistance theory in 1642, Conrad Russell argues (*Civil War*, 136) that if 'these men were closet resistance theorists, the trial of the King in 1649 should have given them a belated opportunity to come out' but that none did. However, this gets things the wrong way round: in 1649, it was the opponents of the trial – the displaced inferior magistrates – who had most to gain from the Calvinist theory of resistance.

63 *A serious and faithfull Representation of the Judgements of Ministers of the Gospell Within the Province of London* (London, 1649), 6.

64 Underdown, *Pride's Purge*, 123.

65. A. S. P. Woodhouse, ed., *Puritanism and Liberty*, 2nd edn (London: J. M. Dent, 1974), 462.

66 See *An Abridgment of the late Remonstrance of the Army* (London, 1648), sigs. A3v–4, B1v. I am grateful to Austin Woolrych for the suggestion about authorship.

67 Ibid., sig. A3.

68 These were key features of what has recently been labelled 'the neo-roman theory of free states'; see Quentin Skinner, *Liberty before Liberalism* (Cambridge University Press, 1998), 1–57. I am grateful to him for sending me an advance copy of his book, though it arrived too late for me to take proper notice of its findings.

69 See Woodhouse, *Puritanism and Liberty*, 58, 60, 63, 72–3.

70 Ibid., 456.

71 Ibid., 456–7.

72 John Milton, *Paradise Lost*, ed. A. Fowler (London: Longman, 1971), 218 (IV, 394).

5

The king among the radicals

GODLY REPUBLICANS, LEVELLERS, DIGGERS
AND FIFTH MONARCHISTS

David Loewenstein

In a book about diverse and conflicting representations of Charles I, a chapter on the king and radical writers during the English Revolution is bound to present a particularly negative account of his image and inadequacies as a ruler. Nevertheless, these writers responded more complexly and diversely than might at first be supposed. Critics of the king during the 1620s and 1630s had tended to be more conservative, law-abiding citizens deeply alarmed by the innovative policies of Charles and the Laudian revolution against Calvinist orthodoxy.[1] Radical writers of the later 1640s and early 1650s, however, probed Charles's reign, his character, and his power and politics for sharply polemical purposes as they attempted to justify to the nation such daring and unprecedented events as the king's formal trial, conviction for treason, and public execution, as well as the uneasy authority of the experimental republic.[2] Their polemical and frequently retrospective representations of a tyrannical Charles hardly offers more 'truthful' images of an often inscrutable king who Kevin Sharpe recently concludes was not in any case absolutist nor autocratic.[3] Rather, these hostile representations served both to fuel political and religious revolution and to expose its ambiguous developments. This chapter examines a relatively neglected facet of the complex history of the king's representation by highlighting some of the iconoclastic responses in the radical political and religious literature of the Revolution. The hostile image of the king as the persecuting power of Antichrist, especially, was used by more visionary radical writers, including the Fifth Monarchists, to register the urgency of the great apocalyptic crises and transformations occurring in England during the 1640s and 1650s.

Moreover, radical writers as diverse as George Wither, John Cook, John Milton, Edmund Ludlow and Lucy Hutchinson (the latter two writing after 1660) depicted Charles as a master of political dissimulation, prevarication and treachery and were deeply troubled by his equivocal dealings with the Irish Catholic rebels during the 1640s. Recent work on the king's character and politics has suggested that he was 'a weak man' who preferred the private worlds of connoisseurship, hunting, and family life; consequently, he was 'not in any sense a political man' and 'did not understand the use of power'.[4] But that is not how radical contemporaries usually saw or represented Charles, though they certainly perceived him as politically inflexible and as authoritarian in temperament. More than any other king in recent history, Charles I, in the words of the radical solicitor Cook, embodied 'an absolute Tyrant . . . and all the subtilty, treachery, deep dissimulation, abominable projects, and dishonorable shifts, that ever were separately in any that swayed the English Scepter'.[5] In radical eyes, Charles's political style of secrecy and deviousness was almost always calculated[6] – a manifestation of treacherous Machiavellian designs to subvert fundamental laws, to destroy parliaments as well as the liberties and rights of his subjects, and to introduce arbitrary government and unlimited power in church and state.

Other radical writers used the hostile image of the king polemically in order to expose the failures of the Revolution and ongoing forms of treacherous kingly power in the new republic. In the eyes of Leveller writers and the Digger Gerrard Winstanley, Norman tyranny and kingly power did not end with Charles's defeat and dramatic execution: rather, their danger was greater than ever and continued to manifest itself in the Long Parliament and after the traumatic events of 1648–9 ('their chief Captain *Charles* be gone, yet his Colonells' remain, the Digger warned, referring to the orthodox clergy, lawyers, landlords and other professions and institutions contributing to sharp class conflict in the age.)[7] In his confrontational writings, Lilburne the Leveller considered how the dissimulating arts of power and politics were practised more treacherously under Cromwell and the Army Grandees than they were practised under the king and the bishops. Writing on behalf of the poor commoners during the revolutionary years, the Digger leader also found it no less easy to trust 'the fair words of a Parliament' than it was to trust the subtlety of a cunning Stuart king.[8] The haunting spectre of the late king appears frequently in Winstanley's works: it became a potent polemical means to challenge menacing forms of power which were compromising not only the Republic but also the most daring ideals of the Revolution.

'Idol-Majestie': kingly politics, tyranny and dissimulation

Radical writers were acutely sensitive to what they perceived as the treacherous political designs of a king who had proved so difficult to negotiate with during the upheavals of the 1640s (especially from November 1647 onwards). The publication by parliament of the king's captured correspondence at Naseby, *The Kings Cabinet Opened* (1645), only fuelled suspicions that the devious, furtive king was aligned with papist powers, including the Pope himself and the Catholic Irish who had begun their nightmarish antichristian rebellion in October 1641; and that the king was covering his 'acts of hostility . . . over with deeper and darker secrecy'.[9] The letters revealed that the king was a 'dissembler' – 'A quality', the astrologer and popular pamphleteer William Lilly observed, 'which indeed he was as sufficiently Master of as any Man living'.[10] Various radical writers such as Milton, Wither, Cook, Lilly, John Goodwin, Edmund Ludlow and Lucy Hutchinson sensed that this king, like other European monarchs, was indeed 'doubtfull and ambiguous in all [his] doings'.[11]

Charles's theatrical strain highlighted for radical writers his 'ambiguous doings'. Among mid-century writers, Milton and Marvell most famously caught the theatrical strain of 'the Royal Actor' – both in his life and at his death – though Milton would treat the king's last 'memorable Scene' performed at Whitehall more sardonically in the *Defensio Secunda*.[12] Other radical writers were equally struck by the king's theatrical strain in relation to his cunning designs, politics and character; and they noted his preference for entertainments and rituals emphasizing hierarchy, order and reverence. Thus in his lengthy commemorative verses on the new republic, his *British Appeals* (1651), the parliamentarian soldier and poet George Wither remarked on the dangerous power of 'Flattering' poetic representation and exaltation, as in the lavish Caroline masques of the 1630s and their visual symbolism. Such spectacles of state, symptomatic of the remote Caroline court culture, had promoted the image of the divine-right king and his queen, deifying them as earthly gods and goddesses with unlimited power:

> He, and his *Queen* became
> So often represented by the name
> Of *Heath'nish Deities*; that, they, at last,
> Became (ev'n when their *Mummeries* were past)
> Like those they represented; and, did move,
> Within their Sphears like *Venus, Mars,* and *Jove*.

Like Milton, who scornfully exposed the king's 'conceited portraiture' in *Eikonoklastes*, Wither was sensitive to the power of literary and visual representation to transform and conceal more treacherous political motives – the king was 'fairly painted, and well varnish'd over, / The wickedness of his *Designes* to Cover'.[13] Wither's *British Appeals* portrays a king who had contrived plots and resorted to secrecy to advance his arbitrary power no matter 'whatsoere it cost / In *Treasure*, or in *blood* by others Lost'.[14] Like Milton, he perceives how the Comus-like behaviour of a Stuart king was able to seduce the Protestant gentry and nobility to serve his designs with a prodigal court of 'vast expence and luxurie, masks and revels':[15]

> By *maskings*, and loose Revellings, at *Court*,
> He, closely wrought upon the yonger sort
> Of wanton *Students*; and allur'd thereby,
> The flower, of all the *yong Nobilitie*
> And *Gentry* of his *Kingdoms* to encline
> To him, in whatsoere, he should design.[16]

Moreover, like Milton and John Cook, Wither links the late king's theatrical strain to his skills as a notorious verbal and political prevaricator. A year earlier the prophetic poet had warned the king to refrain from 'all equivocations, / From all close ends, and mentall Reservations'.[17] Now, after the regicide, Wither concludes that with a cold '*Heart* so hard, so double, and unsound', the king had acted to enslave or destroy his people by means of his political '*Juglings*': 'What could we have expected from a *King*, / So wilful, and so false, in every thing? / Or from the *Off-spring* of a *Generation*, / So long time rooted in *Prevarication*?'[18]

If Wither recognized the capacity of poetry and symbolic representation to sustain arbitrary regal power, he also wanted to believe in the power of his own popular and plain prophetic verses – the 'power of *hallow'd-Poesie*' – to offer bold political counsel to the new Commonwealth and its people while the largely unpopular republican regime was struggling to assert its authority.[19] Wither was particularly distressed, as was the High Court prosecutor Cook, about 'so many murmurings' among his unthankful countrymen after the traumatic events of 1648/9, including direct military intervention and regicide: behaving like the murmuring Israelites, they, during the unrepresentative experimental regime, 'begin to dote / Upon an *Idol-Majestie*' and 'Render abuse, Reproaches, and despights, / To their Deliverers', thereby forgetting their 'former *Pressures*' under regal power.[20] While presenting recent events (including parliament's military victories) in terms of God's extraordinary providences and manifold mercies, Wither nevertheless refuses to idealize the social conditions in the new republic, reminding his complaining country-men that, like the ancient Israelites in the wilderness, they are still on a trying 'Path to *Rest*', having only just escaped Egyptian thraldom: God 'doth lead us through / Much *Hardship*, and great difficulties, now'.[21] At the same time, Wither writes as a visionary remembrancer in *British Appeals*, recalling the history of late griefs and regal tyrannies and thereby shattering the illusion that his fellow citizens might be better off under the power of 'an *Idol-Majestie*'.

As he addresses his murmuring countrymen, Wither presents a vast cat-alogue of abuses of power intended to recall the king's ravenous designs and expansive prerogatives during the Personal Rule and its aftermath, just as Cook, the Attorney-General at Charles's trial, had recently dis-sected the charge against the king and amassed a list of his 'pretended Prerogatives' which encroached on the people's liberties and defined him as an arbitrary ruler.[22] Godly republican writers like Wither and Cook thus concentrated more on justifying the execution and its causes than on elaborating the foundations of English republican ideology and theory.[23] Wither's sweeping catalogue of 'former *Burthens*' suggests how Charles's religious, political, and fiscal policies exacerbated tensions and precipi-tated civil war. It includes not only the extravagant court entertainments but the privileges bestowed upon the king's peerage; the collusion of the king and his ambitious prelates in acts of oppression and tyranny against the people; the bloody Irish Rebellion which Wither believed was 'con-triv'd / By [the king], or with his knowledge'; the encroachments of his financial measures, including the Forced Loan, the collection of tonnage and poundage (customs duties 'to the great abuse / Of Trade and *Merchants*'), and especially the imposition of ship money which 'was extreamly Grumbled at';[24] and his ruthless use of such prerogative courts as the Star Chamber and the High Commission during the 1630s to inflict barbarous punishments on his and Laud's puritan adversaries. Nor can Wither let his grumbling countrymen forget Charles's later secret Engagement with the Scots (in December 1647), an example of the king's capacity for dangerous intrigue and opportunism when 'he assayd / To tempt the *Scotish Nation* to give ayd / To his Designs'. As Wither focuses his vision retrospectively, he also challenges the tendency to let powerful feelings of nostalgia for a past that is shattered colour the providential significance of the triumphant if arduous present: he therefore addresses country citizens who complain about present taxes, look back nostalgi-cally to the days of the old monarchy (they 'sing *Thanksgivings* backward'), and 'with murmuring / Requite Gods *mercies*' as they forget how 'their late oppressive *Plunderings*, / *Large Contributions*, and *Free Quarterings*, / Were first occasion'd by his *Tyranies*'. 'To readmit a *Tyrannizing King*' would therefore cost the people dearly: the sobering aim of the Commonwealth's visionary remembrancer has been to recall 'what must be exacted to maintain / The boundless Cravings of his *hungry Train*'.[25]

More than Wither, however, the puritan Lucy Hutchinson acknowledged the decorous nature and changed moral tone of Charles's court as she looked back on it during the later 1660s when she was composing her *Memoirs of the Life of Colonel Hutchinson*: compared with his licentious father, the austere, self-controlled Charles was 'temperate and chast and serious; so that the fooles and bawds, mimicks and Catamites of the former Court grew out of fashion'. Furthermore, given that her own godly and cultured puritan husband was skilled in music and a keen appreciator of the visual arts (seeking out 'rare Artists', 'he became a greate Virtuoso and Patrone of ingenuity'), she could acknowledge all that the king himself had done to foster the arts during his reign: 'Men of learning and ingenuity in all arts were in esteeme, and receiv'd encouragement from the king, who was a most excellent judge and a greate lover of paintings, carvings, drawings, gravings, and many other ingenuities less offensive then the bawdry and prophane abusive witt which was the only exercise of the other Court'. Nevertheless, for Lucy Hutchinson the king's discerning aesthetic tastes could not conceal the fact that he was much more dangerous and satanic than his father: as a bitter persecutor of his godly subjects and at the centre of a sinister popish plot, Charles was by far a 'worse encroacher upon the civill and spirituall liberties of his people'.[26] Like Milton, whose depiction of the impenitent and hardened king bears some resemblance to his portrait of a wilful Satan, she highlighted Charles's obstinate will and his proclivity for absolute forms of power: 'he was the most obstinate person in selfewill that ever was, and so bent upon being an absolute uncontrowlable Soveraigne that he was resolv'd either to be such a King or none'.[27] In Charles's case, the 'sad desolations' of the kingdom during his reign were also a result of allowing himself, as 'a most uxorious husband', to become 'effiminate' under the domination and power of a queen of foreign birth and subversive popish religion, whose cruel designs included rooting the godly out of England.[28] Hutchinson is therefore particularly keen in her *Memoirs* to stress the king's devious allegiances and his plotting to use foreign forces to enslave the English to his yoke. She points to the king's 'falsehood and favour of the Irish rebels', as

did other alarmed radical writers (see below), and to the king's captured
cabinet letters at Naseby as evidence of his cunning designs since 'contrary
to his professions, he had endeavour'd to bring in Danes and Lorainers and
Irish Rebells to subdue the good people here, and given himselfe up to be
govern'd by the Queene in all affairs both of State and religion'.[29]

The publication of the Naseby letters prompted radical writers justifying the king's trial and the regicide to discover evidence of his equivocal
politics and treacherous designs early in his career as England's Protestant
king. The heavy English losses in 1628 at the Huguenot stronghold of La
Rochelle (the 'best defence of all the Protestants in France', in the words
of Lucy Hutchinson) thus became an important case in point for
Hutchinson, the regicide John Cook, the parliamentarian astrologer
William Lilly, and the fierce godly republican Ludlow, all of whom
regarded the defeat as an act of the king's early betrayal of the Protestant
cause and not simply a matter of his loss of honour: here was evidence
from the beginning of Charles's reign that 'the Protestants had his body,
but the Papists had his heart . . . That he loved a Papist, better then a
Puritan', as Cook put it.[30] Here was one of 'these darke prognostications',
Ludlow grimly recalled, 'when his bloody reigne was so legible', as if in
retrospect one could read and interpret an interwoven pattern of the
king's 'treacherous and horrid designes' and blood guilt that included the
Irish Rebellion and the war against parliament and the people of England
and Scotland.[31] In 1649 Cook, the prosecution's lawyer, was making his
case against the king by recalling in detail the humiliating failures of the
king's naval expeditions in 1627 and 1628 to assist the beleaguered
Huguenots in La Rochelle; though the Duke of Buckingham led the failed
siege of the Ile de Ré (the base from which to aid the Huguenots in La
Rochelle), the king ultimately took responsibility for it and chose to blame
himself and, in the words of Lilly, 'sent to comfort the Duke'.[32] In Cook's
retrospective eyes, Charles was guilty of these failures and of betraying
the distressed French Protestants who placed their trust in him since he
claimed that 'he would assist them to the uttermost against the French
King' Louis XIII and his Catholic policy: the disastrous campaign was
therefore evidence of 'the Kings horrid perfidiousness, and deep dissimulation'. For many years, Cook confesses, 'I was of that Opinion . . . that the
King was seduced by evil Councel', believing that Buckingham 'and
others ruled him as a childe'. But the discovery of the Naseby letters
prompted Cook to revise his judgement and to conclude that the king,
'too politique and subtile a man to be swayed by any thing but his own

judgement', was indeed 'principal in all Transactions of State' and the chief manager or architect of policy – 'he was the Master builder' (a view of the king's political involvement which modern historians still remain divided over). Like Milton's hardened and guileful Satan, Cook's subtle King Charles emerges as the political schemer who has 'first devis'd' the 'devilish Counsel' (*Paradise Lost*, ii, 379–80): the discovery of the king's 'serpentine turnings and windings' in the Naseby letters and in his earlier behaviour towards the French Protestants convinced Cook that 'none of his Councel durst ever advise him to any thing, but what they knew before he resolved to have done'.[33]

Most nightmarish from the retrospective vision of radical Protestant writers, however, was the king's apparent involvement in the bloody rebellion of the Irish Catholics which had broken out in October 1641. Might not a devious, untrustworthy king who first betrayed the suffering Huguenots in France, both Cook and Ludlow (who were friends) suggested, also have countenanced the massacre of many thousands of Protestants in Ireland and likewise contracted the guilt of their blood?[34] For Protestants deeply imbued with the Foxeian apocalyptic tradition, no crisis more vividly or urgently embodied the monstrous threat of antichristian powers to subvert English liberties and reformed religion. In *King Charls his Case*, John Cook estimated that no less than 152,000 Protestant men, women and children were 'most barbarously and satanically murthered in the first four months of the Rebellion', and estimates of the massacred dead regularly ran higher, thereby fuelling a sense of paranoia and helping to prepare the way for Cromwell's vengeful Irish campaign in the summer and autumn of 1649.[35] For radical writers, including Milton, Cook and Ludlow, the Irish Rebellion especially illustrated the king's equivocal politics and rhetoric during the 1640s, as well as his savage treachery and blood guilt since he would 'raise War on his own children' using 'men from Popish principles [to] assist him'.[36] Milton devoted a whole section of *Eikonoklastes* to the troubling question of the devious king and the Irish Rebellion, and as late as *The Readie and Easie Way*, when he was working on his epic about the equivocal genesis of Satan's rebellion, he would still vividly recall the king's 'occasioning, if not complotting, as was after discoverd, the *Irish* massacre, his fomenting and arming the rebellion, his covert leaguing with the rebels against us'.[37]

As he discusses the disturbing history of the Irish Rebellion, Cook confesses that he 'spent many serious thoughts' wondering about the nature and extent of the king's involvement in the massacre, since 'if the king had a hand, or but a little finger in that Massacre, every man will say, Let him dye the death': 'How often was that monstrous Rebellion laid in his dish? and yet he durst never absolutely deny it', the solicitor observes, adding that the king, reluctant to condemn the rebels ('never was Bear so unwillingly brought to the stake'), had 'above forty times called them his Subjects, and his good Subjects'.[38] In Cook's eyes, the Cessation of 1643, the king's cease-fire with the Irish rebels ('Hell-hounds' and 'accursed Devils in the shape of men', Cook calls them), was evidence of his equivocation and proclivity to engage in calculated conspiracy and perfidious plots, as well as evidence of the prominence of Catholics in Oxford and in the royalist forces: 'If the king had once in good earnest proclaimed them Rebels, they would have burnt their Scabbards, and would not have stiled themselves, The King and Queens Army, as they did.'[39] Looking back in 1651, Cook would conclude that the late king, who had brought misery upon his people and shed innocent blood crying out to God for vengeance, was nothing less than 'the Author' of 'so bloody a Rebellion' – 'as ever the Devill was the Author or first tempter to sin, for without his countenance they durst never have attempted it'.[40] Reviewing the evidence in 1649, the astrologer Lilly remained less certain about Charles's initial complicity in the horrifying Irish Rebellion, but he was nevertheless struck by the king's equivocal behaviour and language with respect to the Irish Catholics, to whom he seemed 'tender hearted'.[41] Wither likewise perceived 'the late Inhumane *Massacre*' of the English Protestants as another haunting instance of the king's tendency to prevaricate about his political allegiances, since there was evidence that 'he did palliate, and look thereon / Without Compassion, when the *Deed* was done'.[42]

By acting as a dangerous prevaricator who had caused so much bloodshed among the subjects of his kingdoms, the king had, in the eyes of radicals, committed treason punishable by death: 'when he or they that are trusted to fight the peoples Battles, and to procure their welfare, shall prevaricate, and act to the inslaving or destroying of the people,' Cook observed and John Goodwin agreed, 'this is high Treason'.[43] And because kings were nothing less than 'the manufacture, workmanship, or *creatures* of the people' – Goodwin thereby attributed decisive agency to the people – they as the supreme power had the right and authority to punish kings and hold them accountable for their actions: 'All Authority, and Power of Government being originally and fundamentally in the people . . . they have a just and legall power . . . to act and do, whatsoever they rightly judge conducible to their wealth and safety.'[44] Like the Levellers, Cook and Goodwin developed arguments based on doctrines of natural law, *salus populi*, and popular sovereignty that enabled these writers to justify the daring act of regicide and the immediate events that led up to it. The king's powers were conditional and limited and therefore not God-given; the same law for punishing a shoemaker could be applied to a king, so that the intense Caroline concern for propriety and decorum, hierarchy and degree, including Charles's insistence that he was answerable only to God, was sharply challenged by these antimonarchical writers who claimed the king was answerable to the people. 'Since there is a Law of the Land clear enough for the punishing of shoemakers or taylours with death', Goodwin asserted, 'why should not the same Law be conceived to lie as clear for the punishing of Kings with death, in case they murther.'[45] Indeed, unaccountableness of actions in kings could hardly be defended – this, after all, would make a king 'greater than God himself' – since even God, Goodwin noted, 'frequently . . . and most graciously subjecteth himself and his actions to the cognisance and judicature of men'.[46]

Godly regicides and republicans justifying the traumatic revolutionary events of December 1648 to January 1649 regularly emphasized the horrid blood guilt of the late king – 'that man of blood', as he was called – who as an agent of Antichrist and a latter-day Pharaoh had furiously and cruelly turned the three kingdoms into a *'sea of blood*, which by his wilfullnesse hath overflowed these *Islands'*.[47] The blood of thousands, Cook pleaded with the High Court of Justice trying the king, 'demands Justice' and 'cryes aloud . . . much louder then the blood of *Abel'*, so that the fiercely antimonarchical writings of Cook and other godly radicals helped to generate an atmosphere of sanctified, Old Testament vengeance that enabled the saints to act out and justify a primitive and savage ethic of blood guilt and punishment.[48] Unavenged blood of an idolatrous tyrant, Ludlow asserted with the authority of ample Old Testament texts wherein he found the express words of God's law, would only bring guilt upon the whole land and divine indignation, and so the saints must take righteous action much as the revolutionary Jehu had executed divine vengeance by the command of God himself on the house of Ahab: 'Ye shall not pollute the land wherein ye are, for blood it defiles the land; and the land cannot be cleansed of the blood that is shed therein, but by the blood of him that shed it' (see Numbers 35:33).[49] Goodwin likewise conveyed an Old Testament sense of horror at the king's bloody pollution of the land and its urgent need for cleansing; introducing the theatrical language often used to characterize Charles's political behaviour, he depicted the king as 'not onely the Supreme Person, but the Supreme Actour also in the tragedie of bloud, which hath been lately acted upon the stage of this Nation; yea and had more of the guilt of the bloud shed in it, upon his conscience, than all his fellow-Actours besides, put together.'[50] Milton, whose antimonarchical and anti-Presbyterian writing influenced Goodwin's, showed a keener literary sensibility in *The Tenure of Kings and Magistrates*, where he linked the prevaricating king and the Presbyterian clergy supporting him by recalling the blood guilt of Lady Macbeth; he thereby highlighted the relation between equivocal political behaviour and blood guilt. If the king was responsible for 'so great a deluge of innocent blood' of God's chosen people and 'polluting with [his subjects'] slaughterd carcasses all the Land over', then the incendiary puritan ministers who wished to negotiate with him 'cannot with all thir shifting and relapsing, wash off the guiltiness from thir own hands'.[51] In the eyes of radical writers, moreover, the bloody king was 'that great *Nimrod*' of their age, to use Cook's words, because he had made 'the People . . . his Venison to be hunted at his pleasure': the comparison made grim reference to the king's chief recreation – hunting – and reinforced the urgent duty to avenge bloodshed and therefore (in Ludlow's words) 'appease the justice of the Lord'.[52]

The Bible, then, provided the primary impetus for various radical godly writers to urge the saints to execute bloody vengeance and 'to bind their kings with cheynes and their nobles with fetters of iron'.[53] Psalm 149 was a particular source of encouragement to the saints who yearned for the imminent reign of Christ and also wished to affirm their own agency in shaking and confounding the monarchies of the earth. In response to earthly kings 'doubtfull and ambiguous in all thir doings', Milton along with Ludlow, Cook, Mary Cary, John Canne, Henry Vane and Henry Stubbe cited this text with relish and prophetic authority since it 'never was yet so eminently fulfilled', in the view of Cary, 'as it shall be in these latter daies'. The agency of the saints was nothing less than the righteous duty of God's chosen ones, especially against the powers of Antichrist: this 'is an honour belonging to his Saints; not to build *Babel* . . . but to destroy it . . . and first to overcome those European Kings, which receive thir power, not from God, but from the beast'.[54] Indeed, as Cary reminded the saints by citing Psalm 110, in the day of the Lord's wrath, when Christ 'shall strike through Kings', the saints themselves will have a crucial role to play – 'the sons of Sion are & shal be the Lords instruments, the rod of his strength'.[55] Goodwin, moreover, found plenty of compelling scriptural evidence that a vengeful God would 'cut off the spirit of princes' and prove 'terrible to the kings of the earth' (Psalm 76:12) in such Hebrew prophets as Jeremiah, Hosea, Amos and Ezekiel, as well as in the Psalms.[56] When it came to the instrument of judgement, Canne the Fifth Monarchist was able to identify the 'high Court of Justice . . . before which the last of our kings had his tryal and sentence' as no other than the majestic '*throne* of God mentioned in *Dan.* 7.9, 10.'[57] Though the regicide was viewed with dismay by the majority of the population, a fearless and militant saint like Ludlow regarded 'that eminent act of justice upon the late King' as the most conspicuous example of special providence: 'I am assured it was done by the wise disposing hand of God, without whose providence not a sparrow falls to the ground, much less the blood of any of his pretious saints and faithfull witnesses' (echoing Matthew 10:29).[58] The events of the late 1640s, especially the Purge and the regicide, did indeed bring some radicals to a new pitch of excitement as they eagerly anticipated the accession of King Jesus.[59]

But their writings could register political tensions and unease about the king's death at the same time that they flaunted the regicide. Goodwin, like Wither, anxiously perceived that in an age when 'the judgements and consciences of the generalitie of men in the world have been overshadowed with Prerogative Divinitie', the regicide would greatly test the political will and spiritual strength of the nation: the king's public trial and execution, he wrote to the House of Commons, 'whereunto your hearts and hands were lifted up by God', would 'for a season exercise and trouble the fancies of many', and he therefore sought to present the recent traumatic events of the Revolution in heroic and even mythic terms, observing 'how unaccustomed the present Age is to bear the weight of such Heroique transactions'.[60] Like Ludlow, Wither configured the history of the king's fall and destruction in providential terms; moreover, in his highly self-conscious role as the republic's remembrancer, he was sensitive to how the Revolution's most daring events would later be configured and interpreted by other poets and historiographers, writing that 'twill be to the *Glory* / Of this our *Nation*, in their future *Story*' that the tyrannical king had not been removed '*Clandestinely*' or 'secretly'. The king's prosecutors had thereby refused to resort to the deviousness and secrecy that were disturbing hallmarks of his political style 'rooted in *Prevarication*'. The republic may have been founded upon an act of bloody vengeance, its origins accounting for the regime's uneasy authority and the people's murmurings; nevertheless, its self-appointed prophetic poet flaunted the fact that its regime had performed the unprecedented trial and shocking spectacle openly for the whole world to behold:

> We, with *open face*;
> By *Publick Justice*; in a *Publick place*;
> In presence of his *friends*, and, in despight
> Of all our *foes*, and ev'ry opposite,
> Try'd, Judg'd, and Executed, without fear;
> The greatest *Tyrant*, ever reigning here.[61]

Levellers and Diggers: kingly power in the Revolution

In the case of both the Levellers and the Diggers, Charles did not represent the only kind of treacherous kingly power and oppression endangering the people's liberties and the stability of the nation: rather, kingly power had begun to take on new forms and locations during the English Revolution and could not easily be contained. There was, in any case, more than enough blood guilt to go around in the kingdom – so William Walwyn feared. 'All you Soldiers and People, that have your Consciences alive about you', he pleaded in *The Bloody Project* of August 1648, 'let not the covetous, the proud, the blood-thirsty man bear sway amongst you.' In Walwyn's eyes, 'the King, Parliament, [and] great men in the City and Army', including the magistrates of London and the self-serving Presbyterian party, share blame for bringing misery upon the nation and imperiling the people's safety since 'they have [all] mounted to Honor, Wealth and Power'.[62] Walwyn wrote these anxious words of warning at the time of the renewed violence and bloodshed of the second Civil War, whose just cause he believed had not been well considered nor plainly stated, and more than a year after the House of Commons, influenced by the Presbyterian majority, had voted to burn the Levellers' Large Petition (May 1647). Walwyn's words register his fear, one that Lilburne, as well as Winstanley and the Diggers, would also sharply voice, that 'all the quarrell we have at this day in the Kingdome, is no other then a quarrel of Interests, and Partyes, a pulling down of one Tyrant, to set up another'. Walwyn's text was 'Printed in this Yeare of dissembling, 1648' – a grim reminder that its author considered the relocation of tyrannical power in the form of 'Grandee Factions' ominous, and that 'greater threatned dangers . . . like an inundation begin to break in upon us'.[63]

In Lilburne's fiercely combative pamphlets of the revolutionary years, regal tyranny was also to be discovered in many interconnected forms and

shapes in the kingdom, including the House of Lords, monopolizing merchants, the orthodox clergy, professional lawyers and judges, Cromwell
and the Grandees, the rule and authority of the new republic – all would
receive his sharp polemical lashings. Thus the crafty Presbyterian ministers of his age were at least as treacherous and antichristian as the monstrous Charles I: their 'various double dealings, turnings and windings,
self-seeking, and advantage-making in every businesse they transact or
negotiate with us', Lilburne lashed out in 1647 (thereby anticipating
Milton's analysis in *The Tenure*), compelled him to conclude that they were
men of satanic ambition who aimed to usurp power – 'Nay yee your selves
exercise the Kingly office; yee, I say it againe, yee your selves exercise the
Kingly office'.[64] Earlier in the same year, Lilburne, imprisoned in the
Tower by the House of Lords, published *Regall Tyrannie Discovered*, in
which he presented Charles Stuart as a monstrous tyrant guilty of treason
and produced the first Leveller work calling for the trial, deposition and
execution of the king. Lilburne waged his battle with a range of textual
authorities: armed with scriptural texts on the destruction of kings by
God's agents (e.g. Numbers 32:33; Deuteronomy 3:2–3; Joshua 8:29, 10:26,
28, 39; Judges 1: 6–7), constitutional and legal authorities or sources (e.g.
Magna Carta, Edward Coke, the Petition of Right, the *Book of
Declarations*), Charles's own words on the king's prerogative, other
Leveller tracts and petitions (including his own previously published
pamphlets), and historical works by Daniel and Speed, Lilburne possessed
the polemical weapons to challenge vigorously regal conceptions of
power, especially the notion that there is 'some superlative naturall,
inbred, inherent diety, or excellency in Kings above other men'. Not only
was Charles 'not God but a *meer man*': he had also broken the contract
between himself and his subjects. Lilburne's prolix and unsystematic text
of vehement self-justification, Leveller political theory ('Power is originally inherent in the People, and it is nothing else but that might and
vigour'), and historical analysis of tyrannical kingship from William the
Conqueror to the present king, moreover, addressed a series of interconnected evils. Norman oppression now included the treacherous judicial
and legislative powers of the House of Lords, whose title was by blood
'not by *common consent* or choyce of the People': 'trust them not', Lilburne
contends in homely yet pungent prose, 'no more then you would do a *Fox*
with a *Goose*, or a *devouring Wolfe*, with a *harmlesse Lambe*'. It included as
well the avariciousness of lawyers with their ambiguous laws and techni-
calities, the monopolies of merchant adventurers, and the self-interested

pursuit of the Westminster divines. With indignation and sometimes prophetic fervour, Lilburne struggled to combat the multiple forms and new
locations of 'the *King-Prerogative Tyranny*' with his pen as he dramatized
his own persecution under its arbitrary tribunals.[65]

Lilburne's profound distrust of Cromwell and the Army Grandees
remained unabated, so that the Purged Parliament and Republic began to
seem even more treacherous and dissembling than the king himself.[66]
Though kingship and the House of Lords were formally abolished by the
Rump Parliament in March 1649, Lilburne could use the hostile image of
the late king as a polemical weapon to assail the contradictions of a free
Commonwealth ostensibly based on the authority of the people and
established to protect their liberties. Several months after the defeat of the
Levellers at Burford by Cromwell in May 1649, Lilburne, once again a prisoner in the Tower of London, found himself engaging contentiously and
dramatically with the authorities of the new republic. Thus in a vivid
printed account of his verbal sparring with parliament's Attorney-General
Edmund Prideaux, Lilburne challenged the legitimacy of the republic
whose purged House of Commons – 'a mock Power or a mock
Parliament', as he called it – had unilaterally assumed sole legislative
power: 'the People chuse you, and yet you are absolute', he boldly confronted the Attorney-General – 'I pray Sir reconcile me these contrarie-
ties.' The Attorney-General's attempt to contrast the Commonwealth to
the government under Charles only fuelled Lilburne to attack more heat-
edly the treacherous state of power under that unicameral sovereign body,
the Rump, and its rule of 'arbitrary will': 'I tell you Sir, the same principle
that led me to hate [Arbitrary and Tyrannical] Will in the King, leads me a
thousand times more to hate Will in you, seeing you have promised better
things, ye absolute Freedom, and yet perform nothing, but do worse then
ever he did; by Governing us purely by the Sword and your own Wills.'[67]
After the hard-won defeat of King Charles, the sensitive issue of the
republic's performance was indeed an acute one in the eyes of radical
writers: writing from the perspective of the poor commoners, none confronted it more daringly than Winstanley the Digger.

Even more than Lilburne's pamphlets, Winstanley's Digger writings are
pervaded by a sense of Civil War history perceived in terms of acute class
conflict; but once again the hostile image of the king as a treacherous
Norman power is used for sharply polemical purposes to expose the
contradictions of the Revolution and the shortcomings of the new republic. Like Lilburne, Winstanley perceives multiple forms of oppression in

the Commonwealth, yet it is the poor who suffer the most from the powers of the earth, including landlords, the law and private property, a national ministry, and a conservative Rump Parliament which claimed its authority and all just power derive from the people. Like Cook, Goodwin, Ludlow and other godly radicals who defended the regicide, Winstanley could invoke the haunting theme of blood guilt in 1649, but in his case the aim was to fuel his prophetic appeal to the House of Commons in the new republic and sharply challenge the regime's ambiguous commitment to social revolution:

> If you establish the old *Norman* laws, and this especially, That the Lords of Manors shall still be the Lords of the Common land, and the Common people be still enslaved to them, then you pull the guilt of King *Charles* his blood upon your own heads; for then it will appear to the view of all men, That you cut off the Kings head, that you might establish your selves in his Chair of Government, and that your aym was not to throw down Tyranny, but the Tyrant.[68]

Without breaking the Norman yoke, the Rump could hardly expect the common people to trust the words of the new regime any more than parliament had been able to trust the empty language of a shifty and treacherous king: 'if you will not, you give a just occasion to the common people of *England*, never to trust the fair words of a Parliament any more, as you were always very slow in trusting the King, when he swore by the word of a King, because you found that subtilty and Self lay under, and no reality'. Acutely conscious of class inequalities and injustices, Winstanley warned the Rump Parliament that it could not afford to cheapen the truly revolutionary significance and symbolism of the regicide: 'Let it not be said in the ears of posterity, That the Gentry of England assembled in Parliament, proved Covenant-breakers . . . and promise-breakers to God, and the Common people, after their own turn was served; and killed the King for his power and government, as a thief kils a true man for his money.'[69]

Though the regicide seemed like an exhilarating triumph to godly republicans, England, in Winstanley's view, was still under siege by Norman powers whose ranks were swelling: it was being assaulted by Charles's 'Colonells, which are Lords of Mannours, his Councellours and Divines, which are our Lawyers and Priests, his inferiour officers and Souldiers, which are the Freeholders, and Land-lords.'[70] In *A New-Yeers Gift for the Parliament and Armie* (January 1650), Winstanley reminded the military and political rulers of the so-called free Commonwealth that the gentry and common people had once lived in bondage under Charles's 'Prerogative-tyranny' and that parliament and the common people had banded together to defeat the Norman king. Using a homely yet ominous metaphor – the kind we would expect from an author working hard to cultivate the commons – he underscores the present crisis in the Commonwealth by observing that the 'top-bow is lopped off the tree of Tyrannie, and Kingly power in that one particular is cast out; but alas oppression is a great tree still, and keeps off the sun of freedome from the poor Commons still, he hath many branches and great roots which must be grub'd up'.[71] Moreover, like the Levellers and other radicals justifying the violent revolution against the king, Winstanley can also resort to the language of *salus populi*, but he gives such political terminology a more provocative and challenging interpretation after the regicide and in the context of his agrarian communist convictions: for the poor people '*Salus populi* is the fundamentall Law, that gives that life and strength and courage to build upon and plant the common Land.' *Salus populi* is therefore not simply the law that justifies armed resistance, as well as the trial and execution of a tyrannical king; it is also the law that justifies the eradication of private property and class hierarchies and thereby 'breakes in pieces the Kingly yoake, and the lawes of the Conquerour' by enabling the poor to share freely in the land as a common treasury.[72]

However much Winstanley yearned to believe it, the conquering 'Kingly and Lordly Power', as he called it, was not cast out of the 'Free State' or Commonwealth by its new regime. Even in November 1651, when he dated the dedicatory epistle to his last published work, *The Law of Freedom in a Platform*, Winstanley dared to warn Cromwell of the precarious spiritual state of the Commonwealth, which had failed to answer the cries of the poor commoners and relieve their burdens, especially after they had assisted the army and parliament by risking their lives in war and by planting the earth and paying taxes. The hostile image of the king thus remained a potent polemical weapon in the hands of the defeated Digger writer, who possessed no real power himself. Although victory over the royalists at Worcester had occurred only two months earlier – an event that exhilarated radical millenarians like the Fifth Monarchists[73] – Winstanley soberly suggested to the godly puritan leader that the Commonwealth had still not freed itself from the oppressions and entanglements of kingly power:

> You know that while the King was in the height of his oppressing Power, the People only whispered in private Chambers against him: But after-

wards it was preached upon the house tops, That he was a Tyrant and a Traytor to *Englands* peace; and he had his overturn.

The righteous Power in the Creation is the same still: If you, and those in power with you, should be found walking in the Kings steps, can you secure your selves or posterities from an overturn? Surely NO.

Winstanley's tone here is both deferential and sharp as he maintains his vigilance: Cromwell has yet to prove his ways are 'more righteous then the Kings'. The problem, as Winstanley sees it, is that the gentry and political leaders have perpetuated the troubling ambiguities of the Commonwealth by acting as though one could steer a 'middle path' between being 'a free and true Commonwealths man, or a Monarchial tyrannical Royalist'.[74] The burdens of complex laws and oppressive tythes meant that while civil war had recently destroyed the king and the institution of monarchy, 'Kingly Power remains in power still', especially in the form of legal and clerical institutions, so that the poor are enslaved as much as ever. 'And so,' Winstanley grimly observes, 'as the Sword pulls down Kingly Power with one hand, the Kings old Law builds up Monarchy again with the other.'[75] Moreover, though the senior church court and instrument of royal power used to coerce Laud's opponents had been abolished by Long Parliament in 1641, Winstanley could still evoke its ominous spectre ten years later – but now to convey the sinister power of the established puritan clergy: 'their High Commission Courts Power remains still, persecuting men for Conscience sake, when their actions are unblameable'.[76] Thus by repeatedly evoking the highly charged spectre of the oppressive and persecuting King Charles and by identifying that hostile representation with the entrenched legal and ecclesiastical powers in the Commonwealth itself, the defeated Digger was able to subject the republic and its contradictions to one of its most acute contemporary critiques.

The king, millenarianism and Fifth Monarchist prophecy

Millenarian enthusiasm during the Civil War and Interregnum years stimulated many radical writers to associate the king's power and its destruction by means of the regicide with the vivid and fiery prophecies of Daniel and Revelation. As one future regicide observed, their age had witnessed a particularly dangerous 'conjunction' of Antichrist and 'men in places of power or authority in the world . . . kings and great men'.[77] Not only Winstanley, but the Buckinghamshire Diggers, Milton, Cook,

Ludlow and other radicals represented the king as Antichrist, his power derived from the nightmarish apocalyptic beasts of Scriptures who were persecuting the saints.[78] After the traumatic events of 1648–9, some of the most colourful radical apocalyptic discourses on the king were written by Fifth Monarchist authors, violent revolutionaries who envisioned the destruction of earthly kings as essential to the establishment of the kingdom of Christ, which they believed was imminent. The Fifth Monarchy movement was stimulated by the dramatic regicide and the intense hopes it aroused for the coming of King Jesus and the fulfilment of Daniel's everlasting kingdom (Daniel 7:27): 'The *power* and *spirit* of our *Cause*, was *great* and *high* after the *Kings Death*', Christopher Feake recalled at the end of the Interregnum, 'more then at any time before.'[79] Earlier in the decade, the visions of the prophet Daniel had an extraordinary immediacy for the Fifth Monarchists, who wished to explain the fierce struggles of recent history in eschatological terms:

> For though *Daniel* knew not *England*, *Scotland*, nor *Ireland*, much less the house of the *Stuarts*, nor *Charls* the late King . . . yet by a Spirit of Prophesie and Revelation, *Daniel* did foresee all these things. He saw this Princes ambition, his oppression of his Subjects, his wilfulness, and malignity against the people of God, and the ways of God, and the different degrees of the sufferings of the three Nations, the beheading of the Prince, and [the] abolition of all Kingly power.

So William Aspinwall wrote in 1654, believing that the great apocalyptic Beast was now slain by the saints. The Book of Daniel thus provided a crucial interpretive key to history and a powerful means of political speculation, for 'if *Daniel* had lived in this very age, and seen the transactions of things', Aspinwall excitedly added, 'he could not (without Divine assistance) have given a more exact and ample description of things . . . then here he hath done'.[80]

One of the Fifth Monarchy's more remarkable radical religious interpretations of the reign of Charles I, stimulated by a myth-making account of the prophecies of Daniel as well as of Revelation, was undertaken by Mary Cary in her lengthy millenarian commentary of over 300 pages entitled *The Little Horns Doom & Downfall: or a Scripture-Prophesie of King James, and King Charles* (April 1651). Daniel's prophecy of the four great beasts and world monarchies (in chapter 7) especially addressed the great urgency of Fifth Monarchists to explicate the political and religious struggles of England's mid-century crisis. The most dreadful of the beasts – the fourth

or Roman beast – and its little horn envisioned in Daniel 7:8 was to be associated with the persecuting monarchy of the late Charles: for like that
horn, the king 'did make War against the Saints, and that in such a
manner, as no King, Prince, or Potentate ever yet did'.[81] A principal aim of
her ambitious visionary commentary was to analyse the unfolding eschatological drama, including 'the late Tragedies that have been acted upon
the Scene of these three Nations: and particularly the late Kings doom and
death, was so long ago, as by *Daniel* predeclared'.[82] She therefore produced one of the most ingenious and acute Fifth Monarchist interpretations of Charles's reign in terms of God's millenarian designs and his
apocalyptic wrath. Her *Little Horns Doom* shows how the combination of
the late king's history of persecution and warfare against the godly, the
fantastic apocalyptic visions of the Bible, and a fertile imagination could
indeed generate an inspired work of political speculation and commentary.

Cary subjects the individual verses of chapter 7 of Daniel to great scrutiny, using them to explicate the king's recent history of advancing his prerogative and the fierce persecution suffered by the godly. She thus
considers in relation to verse 25 the ways in which a king 'shall wear out
the Saints of the most High': here she recalls the reissued Book of Sports
(1633), in which Charles provocatively 'constrained . . . the people of the
Kingdom to a prophane & loose life, to dishonour God, by inviting and
requiring of them to practice prophane and wicked sports upon that day,
which was appointed for a holy worshipping of God'; and she recalls how
he supported 'many wicked and abominable Priests' who drove the godly
and faithful from the land. As for the prophecy that he 'shall think to
change times and lawes' (Daniel 7:25), here Cary finds evidence for the late
king who 'made sad times for all circumspect and holy Christians, whom
he called Puritans; and times of joy, and rejoycing for all popish and prophane persons', as he 'ruled all by his own will, and made the people slaves
thereunto'.[83] When it came to making war with the saints, the little horn
and his armies were particularly cruel, 'so that where ever his Armies
came, their greatest hatred and malice was against' those they termed
'Puritans, Roundheads, and Sectaries'.[84] Although her prophetic commentary reveals 'that the King of *England* was one of those that was of one
mind with the Beast . . . and overcame them for a season as the Beast did',
by degrees, as Daniel 7:26 predicted so strikingly, the saints took away the
horn's great dominion: and so the late king 'lost City after City, and Towne

after Towne, and County after County, untill he came to have dominion over none at all'.[85] In Cary's apocalyptic scheme, 1645, the year the New Model Army was established, marked a crucial point when the Beast ceased to prevail against the saints and parliament: this was when Charles's antichristian power expired and when Jesus Christ began to set his saints free and assume his kingdom.[86] Parliament and the army were thus instruments of God's millenarian designs and terrible judgements against the powers of the earth. Daniel 7:11 predicted the most traumatic moments of the Revolution, justifying them in fiercely apocalyptic terms: the 'man of blood' should be slain, 'his body destroyed and given to the burning flame of justice'.[87] Again and again, the vivid and provocative scriptural language, imagery and prophecy of Daniel (and other prophetic parts of the Bible, including Revelation 11, which receives detailed analysis) enabled the Fifth Monarchist to explain the bitter history of the little horn and the saints at the same time that they fuelled Cary's anticipation of the New Jerusalem after the destruction of the apocalyptic Beast and all the unconverted kings of the earth – 'at least', she eagerly could imagine, 'these are the beginnings of that time'.[88]

Yet despite the new pitch of apocalyptic excitement generated by Charles's defeat in the Civil War and the revolutionary events which followed, the millennial age never arrived. Nevertheless, Cary and other radical religious writers questioned the very foundations of the political and social order as they offered daring new interpretations in writings of remarkable visionary power.

Notes

1 See the account of Charles's critics in L. J. Reeve, *Charles I and the Road to Personal Rule* (Cambridge University Press, 1989), chapter 6. See also Kevin Sharpe, *The Personal Rule of Charles I* (New Haven and London: Yale University Press, 1992), 953.

2 For discussion of earlier hostile images of the king, see Martin Dzelzainis's chapter in this volume.

3 Sharpe, *Personal Rule*, especially 193–6, 929–31.

4 I quote from Reeve, *Road to Personal Rule*, 4, 176; cf. 173–4, 197. See also Conrad Russell, *The Causes of the English Civil War* (Oxford: Clarendon Press, 1990), chapter 8; Derek Hirst, *Authority and Conflict: England, 1603–1658* (London: Edward Arnold, 1986), 138; and the conclusion to Sharpe, *Personal Rule*, 954, where, however, Charles emerges as a man of 'profound conscience and deep principle', deficient in the art of politics but committed to principles of 'honour and order (his own and the commonweal's)'.

5 John Cook, *King Charls his Case* (London, 1649), 39.

6 See Reeve, *Road to Personal Rule*, who portrays these qualities as a manifestation of

Charles's lack of confidence: 175. On the king's Machiavellian policies and encroachments, see Cook, *King Charls his Case*, 14, 20; on his 'learning and dexterity in State Affairs', see 35.

7 *The Works of Gerrard Winstanley*, ed. George Sabine (Ithaca, NY: Cornell University Press, 1941), 330.

8 Ibid., 306.

9 *The Kings Cabinet Opened* (London, 1645), 44.

10 William Lilly, *Monarchy or no Monarchy in England* (London, 1651), 76.

11 *Eikonoklastes*, in *Complete Prose Works of John Milton*, ed. Don M. Wolfe, 8 vols. (New Haven: Yale University Press, 1953–82), III, 598–9 (hereafter *CPW*).

12 Ibid., *passim*; *Defensio Secunda*, *CPW*, IV, 646–7; *An Horatian Ode upon Cromwel's Return from Ireland*, lines 53–8.

13 George Wither, *British Appeals with Gods Mercifull Replies, on the behalfe of the Common-wealth of England* (London, 1651), 11; *Eikonoklastes*, *CPW*, III, 342. See also John Goodwin, *The Obstructours of Justice* (London, 1649), 96. For the dangers of flattery and kingship, see as well George Wither, *Prosopopoeia Britannica: Britans Genius* (London, 1648), 10.

14 Wither, *British Appeals*, 12.

15 *The Readie and Easie Way*, *CPW*, VII, 425, 426 (where Milton is commenting on the debaucheries of the court of Louis XIV as he contemplates another Stuart monarch in England).

16 Wither, *British Appeals*, 13–14.

17 Wither, *Prosopopoeia Britannica*, 24.

18 Wither, *British Appeals*, 29, 28; I have silently removed distracting punctuation. See Cook, *King Charls his Case*, 5, on 'his notorious Prevarications'. On the king's hardened heart, see also Lilly, *Monarchy or no Monarchy*, 81–2.

19 See Wither, *British Appeals*, 2, as well as his verses addressed 'To the Soveraigne Majesty of the Parliament of the English Republike'. On the part played by the pen in an age of civil war and revolution, see Wither's self-conscious comments in *Campo-Musae* (London, 1643), 2, 4, 48, 73. For valuable recent accounts of Wither's poetry in the English Revolution, see David Norbrook, 'Levelling Poetry: George Wither and the English Revolution, 1642–1649', *ELR* 21 (1991): 217–56; Nigel Smith, *Literature and Revolution in England, 1640–1660* (New Haven: Yale University Press, 1994), especially 230–2, 261–2, 291–3.

20 Wither, *British Appeals*, 33, 21, 23. For similar concerns a year earlier, see Wither's *Prosopopoeia Britannica*, 27. On Cook's concerns about the people murmuring, see *King Charls his Case*, 17.

21 Wither, *British Appeals*, 18. On the unpopularity of the Rump, see Blair Worden, *The Rump Parliament* (Cambridge University Press, 1974), 87; Austin Woolrych, *Commonwealth to Protectorate* (Oxford: Clarendon Press, 1982), 387.

22 Wither's account may be compared with Cook's in *King Charls his Case*, 17–20; see also Wither's *Prosopopoeia Britannica*, 27–30. Modern historians are less harsh in their conclusions about the Personal Rule: see, e.g., Gerald Aylmer, *Rebellion or Revolution? England, 1640–1660* (Oxford University Press, 1986), 7; Sharpe, *Personal Rule*, *passim*.

23 Here I agree with Thomas Corns that 'the vision is trained backwards' in much of the revolutionary pamphleteering of 1649 focusing on regicide: *Uncloistered Virtue: English Political Literature, 1640–1660* (Oxford: Clarendon Press, 1992), 195–6.

24 See also the Fifth Monarchist William Aspinwall who likewise recalled, in his

apocalyptic commentary, the king wearing out the saints 'with Taxes, Impositions, Loans, Shipmonies &c. And all this he did by his Prerogative Royall': *An Explication and Application of the Seventh Chapter of Daniel* (London, 1654), 14; also 16.

25 Wither, *British Appeals*, 10–23; see also 28 for the king 'laying Plots / To make a *Rent*, betwixt us, and the *Scots*'.

26 Lucy Hutchinson, *Memoirs of the Life of Colonel Hutchinson*, ed. James Sutherland (Oxford University Press, 1973), 46; for Colonel Hutchinson's interests in the various arts, see 25, 207. See Lilly, *Monarchy or no Monarchy*, 82, on the king's sober behaviour. On decorum and order at the king's court, see Carlton, *Charles I*, 129; and Sharpe, *Personal Rule*, 209–35. On Charles and popery, see especially Caroline Hibbard, *Charles I and the Popish Plot* (Chapel Hill: University of North Carolina Press, 1983).

27 Hutchinson, *Memoirs*, 47; for Milton, see *CPW*, III, 231, 445, 527, 545, 547, 570, 576. See also Lilly, *Monarchy or no Monarchy*, 74.

28 Hutchinson, *Memoirs*, 48, 46. See, for a recent reconsideration of Henrietta Maria's political influence over the king, Sharpe, *Personal Rule*, 172–3.

29 Hutchinson, *Memoirs*, 127, 160; also 52.

30 Cook, *King Charls his Case*, 31. See Lilly, *Monarchy or no Monarchy*, 89. Hutchinson writes that the interest of the Protestants abroad were 'sadly betrey'd' (*Memoirs*, 47).

31 Edmund Ludlow, *A Voyce from the Watch Tower, Part V: 1660–1662*, ed. A. B. Worden, Camden 4th series, 21 (London: Royal Historical Society, 1978), 274, 131; also 130 and esp. 206. For Lilly's account, see *Monarchy or no Monarchy*, 86–9, 115 (with reference to the king's 'Legerdemaine and treachery').

32 Cook, *King Charls his Case*, 31–5, for his full account; Lilly, *Monarchy or no Monarchy*, 87. On Cook and Ludlow, see *Voyce from the Watch Tower*, 76, 87, 236. For recent assessment of the failures at Ile de Ré and La Rochelle and Charles's dishonour, see especially Reeve, *Charles I and the Road to Personal Rule*, 15–16, 41–51; Sharpe, *Personal Rule*, 42–3, 45, 65–6. See also Sharon Achinstein's chapter in this volume, p. 155.

33 Cook, *King Charls his Case*, 32, 35; see Goodwin, *The Obstructours of Justice*, who likewise sees the king as 'the great Architect of all the late and present miseries and calamities of the Nation' (67; also 97). For modern arguments that question Charles's personal involvement and initiatives in the business of government, see Charles Carlton, *Charles I: The Personal Monarch* (London: Routledge and Kegan Paul, 1983), 157–8; Reeve, *Charles I and the Road to Personal Rule*, 199. See also Kenneth Fincham and Peter Lake, 'The Ecclesiastical Policies of James I and Charles I', in *The Early Stuart Church, 1603–1642*, ed. K. Fincham (London: Macmillan, 1993), 23, 45. See Sharpe, *Personal Rule*, 198–208, on the king's involvement.

34 See Ludlow, *Voyce from the Watch Tower*, 274, for the connection; on Cook and Ludlow, see 76, 87, 236.

35 Cook, *King Charls his Case*, 28. John Canne and Lucy Hutchinson both estimated 200,000 Protestants massacred: John Canne, *The Golden Rule, Or, Justice Advanced* (London, 1649), 17; *Memoirs*, 51. Milton's estimates fluctuated wildly from 140,000 to 600,000 killed: see *CPW*, III, 308, 470; IV, 430–1, 522–3. See Wither, *British Appeals*, 12.

36 Cook, *King Charls his Case*, 29; Ludlow, *Voyce from the Watch Tower*, 206, 280 (as well as 274 cited above, n.34).

37 *CPW*, III, 470–85; VII, 410. For a full discussion of Milton and the Irish Rebellion, see David Loewenstein's forthcoming book, *Representing Revolution in Milton and his Contemporaries: Literature, Rebellion, and Radical Puritan Culture*, chapter 2.

38 Cook, *King Charls his Case*, 28. See also Milton, *CPW*, III, 526; Lilly, *Monarchy or no Monarchy*, 104–5; [John Lilburne], *Regall Tyrannie Discovered* (London, 1647), 51; *The Kings Cabinet Opened*, 45, 55.

39 *King Charls his Case*, 29, 30.

40 Cook, *Monarchy No Creature of Gods making* (London, 1651), 96.

41 *Monarchy or no Monarchy*, 105: 'I know he obliterated with his owne hands the word *Irish Rebells*, and put in *Irish* Subjects, in a Manuscript discourse writ by Sr. *Edward Walker*, and presented to him.'

42 Wither, *British Appeals*, 12–13.

43 Cook, *King Charls his Case*, 24. See Goodwin, *Obstructours of Justice*, 42.

44 Goodwin, *Obstructours of Justice*, 20, 39. On the people as the makers of kings, see also 15–16, and Canne, *Golden Rule*, 28. See also Goodwin's earlier radical Protestant defence of forcible resistance, *Anti-Cavalierisme* (London, 1642).

45 Goodwin, *Obstructours of Justice*, 7.

46 Ibid., 85–6. Lilly considered Goodwin's argument for regicide on the basis of accountability 'unanswerable' and his polemical treatise 'incomparably well penned': (*Monarchy or no Monarchy*, 119).

47 Wither, *British Appeals*, 'To the Wel-affected of the Common-wealth of England', 13. On this topic, see also Patricia Crawford, '"Charles Stuart, That Man of Blood"', *Journal of British Studies*, 16 (1977): 41–61; Stephen Baskerville, 'Blood Guilt in the English Revolution', *Seventeenth Century*, 8 (1993): 181–202. On blood guilt in relation to arguments for resistance, see Martin Dzelzainis's chapter in this volume.

48 Cook, *King Charls his Case*, 36; see Cook, *Monarchy No Creature of Gods making*, 96–7, and Goodwin, *Obstructours of Justice*, 98. See also H. N. Brailsford, *The Levellers and the English Revolution* (Stanford University Press, 1961), 332–3.

49 Ludlow, *Voyce from the Watch Tower*, 132–3 (citing Gen. 9:5–6, Exod. 21:12, Deut. 19:10–13, and other passages), 136, 137 (for Jehu), 141–3, 145, 200, 205. See also Goodwin, *Obstructours of Justice*, 41, 67, and his comment in the Whitehall debates: *Puritanism and Liberty: Being the Army Debates (1647–49) from the Clarke Manuscripts*, ed. A. S. P. Woodhouse (London: J. M. Dent, 1938), 168; see also Milton, *Eikonoklastes*, *CPW*, III, 586. For Jehu the godly regicide, see Milton, *CPW*, III, 215–16, 224, 463; IV, 407; Canne, *Golden Rule*, 13; Algernon Sidney, *Court Maxims*, ed. Hans Blom, Eco Haitsma Mulier and Ronald Janse (Cambridge University Press, 1996), 60–1.

50 Goodwin, *Obstructours of Justice*, 61–3; also 89, 92, 97.

51 *CPW*, III, 197, 214, 227. See also *Eikonoklastes*, *CPW*, III, 376.

52 Cook, *King Charls his Case*, 13; Ludlow, *Voyce from the Watch Tower*, 143. On hunting as the king's chief recreation, see Carlton, *Charles I*, 129.

53 Ludlow, *Voyce from the Watch Tower*, 138; also 234.

54 Mary Cary, *The Little Horns Doom & Downfall* (London, 1651), 34–5, 60–2, 127, 262–3; *Eikonoklastes*, *CPW*, III, 598–9 (cf. IV, 359). See also Mary Cary, *The Resurrection of the Witnesses* (London, 1648), 74; John Canne, *A Voice From the Temple to the Higher Powers* (London, 1653), 30; Cook, *Monarchy No Creature of Gods making*, 113–14; Henry Vane, *Retired Mans Meditations* (London, 1655), 392, 411; Sidney, *Court Maxims*, 56; Henry Stubbe, *Malice Rebuked . . . A Vindication of the Honourable Sr. Henry Vane* (London, 1659), 2. On Psalm 149 and Fifth Monarchists, see B. S. Capp, *The Fifth Monarchy Men* (London: Faber & Faber, 1972), 142.

55 Cary, *Little Horns Doom*, 128–9.

56 Goodwin, *Obstructours of Justice*, 65.

57 Canne, *Voice From the Temple*, 14.

58 Ludlow, *Voyce from the Watch Tower*, 87, 149. Mary Cary agreed (*Little Horns Doom*, 31–2).

59 Bernard Capp, 'The Fifth Monarchists and Popular Millenarianism', in *Radical Religion in the English Revolution*, ed. J. F. McGregor and B. Reay (Oxford University Press, 1984), 169–70. See, e.g., John Spittlehouse, *The first Addresses to his Excellencie the Lord General* (London, 1653), 23.

60 Goodwin, *Obstructours of Justice*, 'The Epistle Dedicatorie'. See also *Right and Might Well Met* (1649), in Goodwin, *Puritanism and Liberty*, 219–20.

61 Wither, *British Appeals*, 29. See also Canne, *Golden Rule*, 36.

62 *The Bloody Project; or, A Discovery of the New Designe, in the Present War* (1648), in *The Writings of William Walwyn*, ed. Jack R. McMichael and Barbara Taft (Athens: University of Georgia Press, 1989), 306.

63 Ibid., 301, 296, 304.

64 John Lilburne, *Plaine Truth without Feare or Flattery* ([London], 1647), 5, [20].

65 For quotations from Lilburne, *Regall Tyrannie Discovered*, see 9, 40–1, 44, 45, 65. For Lilburne's citations of scriptural texts on the destruction of kings, see 12–13.

66 Hence under the Purged Parliament, though invited to join his brother Robert on the High Court of Justice, Lilburne stressed the illegality of the Rump's trying of the king until 'a new and unquestionable Representative was sitting': John Lilburne, *The Legall Fundamentall Liberties of the People of England Revived, Asserted, and Vindicated* (London, 1649), 34; see also 42–3.

67 John Lilburne, *Strength out of Weakness* (London, 1649), 4, 12.

68 Winstanley, *Works*, 307.

69 Ibid., 306, 308.

70 Ibid., 330.

71 Ibid., 369, 357.

72 Ibid., 430.

73 Christopher Feake, *A Beam of Light, Shining in the Midst of much Darkness and Confusion* (London, 1659), 37.

74 Winstanley, *Works*, 502, 513.

75 Ibid., 507, 505. On the cautious Rump's shortcomings in law reform, see Worden, *Rump Parliament*, chapter 6.

76 Winstanley, *Works*, 504.

77 Colonel William Goffe in the Putney Debates: Goodwin, *Puritanism and Liberty*, 39.

78 *More Light Shining in Buckingham-shire*, in *Works*, 631; Cook, *Monarchy no Creature of Gods making*, 112; Ludlow, *Voyce from the Watch Tower*, 144; Milton, *CPW*, III, 598–9. Christopher Hill, *Antichrist in Seventeenth-Century England* (1971; revised edn, London: Verso, 1990), 105, 107–10.

79 Feake, *Beam of Light*, 36. Capp, *Fifth Monarchy Men* remains the best treatment of this movement's emergence after 1649 and its ideas.

80 William Aspinwall, *An Explication and Application of the Seventh Chapter of Daniel* (London, 1654), 29–30. See also Aspinwall's *A Brief Description of the Fifth Monarchy, or Kingdome* (London, 1653).

81 Cary, *Little Horns Doom*, 12–13, alluding to Daniel 7:21. See also Aspinwall, *Explication and Application*, for a similar association of the little horn with Charles.

82 Cary, *Little Horns Doom*, title page.

83 Ibid., 9–11.

84 Ibid., 13.

85 Ibid., 118, 40.

86 Ibid., 119, 133, 202, 219; and her concluding verses 'Unto the Armies faithful Leaders, and Unto the Faithful under their Command.'

87 Ibid., 41–2.

88 Ibid., 281.

6

Eikon Basilike and the rhetoric
of self-representation

Elizabeth Skerpan Wheeler

A modern brand manager would call it 'the King Charles experience'. *Eikon Basilike. The Pourtraicture of His Sacred Maiestie in His Solitudes and Sufferings*, offered on the streets on the very day of his execution, was never merely Charles Stuart's own apologia for his life and reign. Nor, as time passed, was it merely a book. Its generic affinities with Protestant historiography and spiritual autobiography appealed to a wide spectrum of readers, and allowed numerous accretions to and transformations of the original text, rendering the 'king's book' a phenomenon of true collective authorship. Its adaptation of established genres of political discourse altered the representation of the cultural relationship between ruler and ruled, resulting in a popular commodification of Charles I and kingship itself. *Eikon Basilike* was a cultural event that signalled a rupture with past discourses of kingship: it enabled its readers to become participants in a political culture that it helped redefine.

In contrast to the earlier, carefully manipulated images of Elizabeth I, James I, and Charles I himself, reinforced and enhanced with each public appearance of the monarch, *Eikon Basilike* appeared without an enveloping royal context. Because it appeared on the day of the king's execution, *Eikon Basilike* literally took the place of the king. In the absence of direct royal control or effective government censorship, this image immediately developed an autonomous life, appropriated by readers and the book trade to create a publishing phenomenon.[1] According to Francis Falconer Madan's magisterial *New Bibliography of the Eikon Basilike of King Charles the First*, the book went through thirty-five English editions in 1649 alone. In the ensuing decade, it was translated into Latin, French, German, Dutch and Danish, transformed into verse, and set to music.[2] Even in 1649, *Eikon Basilike* had no single physical appearance. Madan's work catalogues

Fig. 6.1 William Marshall, frontispiece to *Eikon Basilike*, 1649.

numerous accretions of both text and illustrations, as well as cheap and de luxe printings. Thus, there is no single, unified, 'official' version of the text. From the start, the image was democratized. The king's subjects bought the image, created new illustrations and poems, and added them to the king's book. Printers added previously published materials and compilations of sayings garnered from the original narrative, and then issued new editions. To speak of self-representation in *Eikon Basilike*, as if it were simply a work of autobiography, is therefore misleading. In both inception and reception 'self-representation' in *Eikon Basilike* was a collaborative project.

As its title page announces, *Eikon Basilike* is a 'portraicture' of Charles I, and begins, not with any kind of introductory note or preface, but with the famous, fold-out frontispiece engraved by William Marshall (fig. 6.1), table of contents, list of errata, and chapter 1, '*Upon His Majesties calling this last Parliament*'.[3] All the chapter headings are in third person, while the remaining narrative and meditations, with the exception of the final chapter to the Prince of Wales, are written in first person. The narrative and meditations are presented as the king's, but there are clearly other hands shaping the book and giving it its final form. Certainly there was at the outset a decision not to allow any material beyond the basic design of the book and the chapter headings to intervene between king and readers. Madan argues persuasively that the foundation of the king's book was, as numerous royalists insisted, Charles's own memoranda, and that the book was given its final form by the Presbyterian divine John Gauden, later bishop of Exeter. As H. R. Trevor-Roper and Philip A. Knachel have since agreed, the idea of dual authorship accords well with both published royalist accounts, testifying that their authors had seen Charles writing, and the information contained in the 1690 Anglesey Memorandum, detailing the contribution of Gauden.[4]

Thus, from the outset, the initial issue of the book presents itself as a picture in a frame, a central figure presented to the reader by some anonymous, intervening person. The words require a context. For their effect they depend on the reader's response to the context as much as to the words. As the initial authorship controversy of 1649 illustrates, the words by themselves carry only limited power. Their ultimate success or failure rests upon whether they correspond to already existing understandings of the nature of Charles's personality: whether the representation of Charles in *Eikon Basilike* is in a profound sense *true*. The Charles of *Eikon Basilike* rests his entire case on presenting the motives for his actions – what he believes his actions meant. What power the narrative possesses depends on its presenting an internally consistent picture of one man's point of view, rather than on its historical accuracy.

In chapter 3, '*Upon His Majesties going to the House of Commons*', for example, the main topic at issue is not what Charles did, or what evidence he had against John Pym, John Hampden, Arthur Hesilrige, Denzil Holles and William Strode, but rather the king's feelings about the event and the motives behind his actions. The narrative explains, 'Nor had I any temptation of displeasure, or revenge against those mens persons, further then I had discovered those (as I thought) unlawfull correspondencies they had used, and engagements they had made, to embroyle my Kingdomes.'[5] Insisting on his lack of personal animus, the narrator carefully qualifies even his own knowledge of the political context of the event. The members' 'correspondencies' were '(as I thought) unlawfull': whether they were in fact unlawful is irrelevant to the narrative. So is the members' relative guilt or innocence or the ultimate validity of the king's actions. The point is the king's belief at that moment. In fact, the narrator uses the king's actions as a justification of his sincerity rather than the other way around. Conceding his lack of success in apprehending the five members, the narrator concludes,

> Providence would not have it so, yet I wanted not such probabilities as were sufficient to raise jealousies in any Kings heart, who is not wholly stupid and neglective of the publick peace, which to preserve by calling in Question half a dozen men, in a fair and legall way (which God knowes was all my design) could have amounted to no worse effect, had it succeeded, then either to do Me, and my Kingdom right, in case they had been found guilty; or else to have cleared their Innocency, and removed my suspicions; which, as they were not raised out of any malice, so neither were they in Reason to be smothered.[6]

The action, then, disastrous as it was, is presented as proof of the king's desire to protect the public peace. The narrative even qualifies the king's perception of the five members: his action could as easily have proved their innocence as their guilt, as there were grounds for suspicions but nothing more. While not a direct admission of error, this account of the king's entry into the House of Commons concedes the disastrous consequences as the narrator strives to prove not the legitimacy of the action but the sincerity of the king's desire to govern well and protect the welfare of the country.

The accompanying prayer underscores this point.

> But thou, O Lord, art my witnesse in heaven, and in my Heart: If I have pur-posed any violence or oppression against the Innocent: or if there were any such wickednesse in my thoughts . . . Save thy servant from the privy conspiracies, and open violence of bloody and unreasonable men, according to the upright-nesse of my heart, and the innocency of my hands in this matter.[7]

Bringing the focus into the present, the prayer sets up a contrast between the king and his captors. These 'bloody and unreasonable men' are indeed purposing violence and oppression against the king, who proves his inno-cence by insisting that he lacked the evil intent that would make him guilty. The narrator does not name names in his prayer, nor does he directly blame others, as he asks God to judge his intentions rather than the results of his actions.

As do all the prayers of *Eikon Basilike*, this meditation echoes the Psalms of David. The royalist author of *The Princely Pellican*, a defence of Charles's authorship, explains the choice of inspiration:

> But such was Gods goodnesse ever to him, as his afflicted soul was never so much depressed, but by repairing to those Rivers of Divine Comfort, the *Psalmes* of *David*, he became infinitely refreshed: So as, the *burthen* of his *griefs* was nothing so heavy, as the *Solace* which that Book afforded him, was delightfully stored with all Spirituall Melody.
>
>   This it was which induced His Majesty to end every *Meditation* with a *Psalme*: that as the *former* lay open to the world his distressed Condition: so by acknowledgement of Gods mercy, and resignation of his will to his all-sufficient Mercy, he might returne Comfort to his thirsty Soul in the conclusion.[8]

In the meditations of *Eikon Basilike*, the words of Charles merge with the words of David, another king whose actions sometimes brought about catastrophe and whose motives were often maligned by others. The prayer for chapter 3 closes with an almost direct quotation of Psalm 7:5: '*Then let the enemy persecute my soule, and tread my life to the ground, and lay mine Honour in the dust.*'[9] In all the penitential Psalms, David himself regrets his mistakes, but pleads with God to judge his heart, offering his piety as proof of his own sincerity in his request for God's aid. Just as the narrative of *Eikon Basilike* requests that God judge '*rightly*', so David asks, 'judge me, O LORD, according to my righteousness, and according to mine integrity *that is* in me' (Psalm 7:8). Neither Charles nor David seeks forgiveness for his actions; both ask that God judge their hearts.

   This emphasis upon piety serves as the anchor of the climactic section of *Eikon Basilike*, the address '*To the Prince of VVales*'. Fully one-third of the chapter directly concerns maintenance of the Church of England and the proper devotion a king should feel and show toward God. Invoking the suffering of David, the narrator advises, 'The true glory of Princes consists in advancing Gods Glory in the maintenance of true Religion, and the Churches good; Also in the dispensation of civill Power, with Justice and Honour to the publick Peace. Piety will make you prosperous; at least it will keep you from being miserable; nor is he much of a loser, that loseth all, yet saveth his owne soule at last.'[10] As I have argued elsewhere, this chapter offers a positive programme for the future, assuring readers that their late king did concern himself with equity, peace and true faith, and that he attempted to instil these values in his son.[11] Urging moderation in religion and the extension of Acts of Indemnity and Oblivion to as many people as possible, the narrator recommends forgiveness, bemoaning 'faction' but making no harsh accusations. Like David, the narrator offers no excuse for his actions but pleads his good intentions and the sincerity of his effort to do what he believed was right. As in *Eikon Basilike* as a whole, the narrator presents not a justification of royal politics or actions, but a defence of the king's character. This Charles is pious, humanly limited and perplexed that his decisions and plans could go so seriously wrong. Confronted with the gulf between intention and result, the narrator can only pray that God will understand him and hope that his assurances to the Prince of Wales will ultimately restore the House of Stuart. The repeated evocation of the Psalms, the emphasis on conscience, the insistence on the depth of sorrow at his suffering, all present a vision of Charles the man, rather than Charles the king, a figure at once accessible to ordinary readers and impossible to refute.

This appeal to conscience was precisely what enraged such contemporary critics as the anonymous author of *Eikon Alethine* (first issued 26 August 1649) and John Milton, whose *Eikonoklastes* (first issued 6 October) indignantly contrasts King Charles's representation of his conscience with the historical fact of his actions.[12] As Sharon Achinstein has recently noted, Milton had particular reason for being anxious about the claim of conscience: he and fellow radicals themselves employed just this appeal in their own justifications of resistance to monarchy and an established church. Hence, Milton needed to prove that Charles must be judged solely by his deeds. Therefore, Milton's critique of Charles's style – especially his paraphrases of the words of David and Jesus – must call into question the king's sincerity.[13] The author of *Eikon Alethine* offers a similar strategy of attack, decrying gullible and uncritical readers ('understanding Animals, with whom every thing in Print goes for Gospel'), the king's 'shew of piety', and 'allurements of effeminate Rhetorick'.[14] Both Milton and *Eikon Alethine* challenge the 'king's book' by pointing out inconsistencies in the narrative, producing evidence that the king acted tyrannically, and arguing that the king's conscience fails to justify his actions.

The fundamental problem of this line of attack, for both Milton and modern critics, is that it shifts the ground of argument. As described above, *Eikon Basilike* in fact attempts to justify not the king's actions but his character, to refute the charge that Charles Stuart was a 'Man of Blood'.[15] Royalist defenders clearly recognized that the popular appeal of *Eikon Basilike* lay not in any supposed justification of action, but in the depiction of Charles's character. They therefore concentrate on responding to the attacks on the king's devotional practice. The anonymous *Eikon*

E Piste (issued 11 September 1649), a response to *Eikon Alethine*, insists that the internal consistency of the narrative, conceded by *Alethine*, proves Charles's lack of criminal intent.[16] Similarly, Joseph Jane's anonymously published *Eikon Aklastos* (issued in 1651) responds to Milton by underscoring the decorum of Charles's use of the Psalms: 'as the Kingly Prophet David sang to his harpe, and wrote his Divine meditations, while his Enemies sent foorth *their sharpe Arrowes, bitter words against him,* and that of so much venom, as he sajes, *the poyson of Aspes was vnder their lipps*: so his late Majest: composed those his meditations'.[17] Jane's careful interweaving of the words of the Psalms with his own answers effectively rebuts Milton's and later critics' charge of plagiarism. As indeed he should, Jane presumes readers' ready familiarity with David's words, and their ability to recognize immediately the king's employment of them. The charge of plagiarism implies that Charles was attempting to pass off David's words as his own; rather, as Jane and the author of *The Princely Pellican* argue, the king depended on readers' identification of their source. As for Milton's triumphant identification of the 'Pamela prayer', appropriated from Sidney's *Arcadia, The Princely Pellican* emphasizes the fact that it, along with the other three prayers, is an accretion to *Eikon Basilike*, not an integral part of the narrative. Meant to be private, these prayers, 'annexed to his *Divine Meditations* . . . might with more discretion have been silenced, then published'.[18] The narrative itself, the author explains, is a series of 'Essayes', those explorations of personal knowledge that incorporate extensive quotations of and allusions to the works of authoritative authors. Quoting Sir Francis Bacon, the author argues that Charles's use of the Psalms demonstrates how thoroughly the king digested that 'Store-house' of good things written by a king whose troubles mirrored his own.[19]

   The power of the king's self-representation, then, lies precisely in its lack of originality. In employing readily recognizable models as the basis for the king's meditations, *Eikon Basilike* accommodates Charles into a pattern long established as an example for Christians to follow. The penitential model permits the direct identification of readers with the king, spanning the gulf between ruler and subject. When Milton insists that the king be judged by his actions alone, without consideration of his intent, he makes the serious error of failing to consider the rhetorical context of *Eikon Basilike*. What readers, especially from 30 January onwards, would want themselves to be judged by their actions without consideration of their state of mind at the time of those actions? Under normal circum-

stances, the seventeenth-century English legal system, as well as all standard treatises on judicial rhetoric, recognized the importance of state of
mind in determining the degree of criminality in an action.[20] How many
of those who initially took up arms against the king intended his death
when they did so? How many readers, shocked and disoriented by the
king's execution and the sudden alteration in the form of their government, searched their own consciences with the suffering depicted in *Eikon
Basilike*? How many readers, in their own times of trouble, turned to the
penitential Psalms for comfort, finding their own anguish echoed in
David's?

Further investigation of possible models for *Eikon Basilike* suggests its
kinship with traditions of English Protestant writing that may be deemed
interactive genres: Protestant historiography and spiritual autobiography.
Numerous recent studies demonstrate how the first overtly encouraged
discovery of a larger narrative pattern harmonizing apparently random
events, while the second urged individuals to find connections between
their own lives and consciences and those of biblical models. As *The
Princely Pellican* explains, 'His *Majesty* . . . desired nothing more then to be
understood by His People'; for a seventeenth-century reader, to understand – whether oneself or another – meant to recognize the model or
pattern behind word or deed, to see the deeper structure and larger
context of one's life and experiences.[21]

To the Protestant historiographer of sixteenth- and seventeenth-
century England, the purpose of writing history was to manifest the evidence of God's purpose for his people. The narrative of individual events
was thus deliberately subordinated to the grander, eternal narrative of
Divine Will. *Eikon Basilike* deliberately depicts Charles as struggling with
forces beyond his control and hoping to discern a higher purpose to his
suffering. As David Loewenstein observes, the book 'challenges the perception of history as a dynamic and unsettling process of change: rather it
encourages its readers to perceive that, in the violent clash between monarchy and revolution, the authentic view is one which affirms history as
predictable and fixed'.[22] Further, it allows the king's words to supply a
coherent vision of the events of the 1640s. Loewenstein points out that all
the forces opposing the king have no names: they are an anonymous,
amorphous 'they'.[23] As a result, in Charles's narrative, his opponents do
not even indirectly present alternative perspectives on each episode.[24]
The only fully articulated point of view is the king's. As God's plan for
England provides the motivating force behind Protestant history, so

Charles's conscience and intentions supply the unity and coherence that so often equates with truth.[25]

With its carefully structured, episodic chapters and experiential presentation, *Eikon Basilike* mirrors the great work of Protestant martyrology, John Foxe's *Ecclesiasticall History*, known also as *Acts and Monuments* and 'Foxe's Book of Martyrs'.[26] Foxe's episodic narrative accommodates each individual example of religious persecution, from the beginnings of Christianity to the accession of Queen Elizabeth I, to his overarching purpose of telling the story of the ultimate triumph of the Protestant church. As I have argued elsewhere, the power of Foxe's narrative derives from his dramatic presentation of the martyrs' own words and representations of their suffering.[27] Each event is transformed into a new chapter of *Acts and Monuments*; as Foxe explains, 'The elder the World waxeth, the longer it continueth, the neerer it hasteneth to his end, the more Sathan rageth, giving still new matter of writing Bookes and Volumes.'[28] Subsequent editions followed Foxe's suggestion, continuing the narrative up to 1621 and adding a biography of Foxe himself in 1641, demonstrating how readily readers and publishers converted current events into new instalments of the grand narrative. In similar fashion, each signal event of the 1640s becomes a chapter of *Eikon Basilike*. Each event becomes meaningful when filtered through the perspective of the king's conscience. And, like *Acts and Monuments*, *Eikon Basilike* became an open invitation for supplementation, encouraging readers to make the king's experiences their own by bringing their own sensibilities – and compositions – to each new edition.[29]

The popular attraction to spiritual history corresponded to the rising popularity of spiritual autobiography. Cynthia Garrett has recently shown how seventeenth-century devotional treatises – 'how-to books' – gave detailed advice on how to structure a private prayer. Even puritans, she demonstrates, endorsed set prayers such as, but not limited to, those in the Prayer Book.[30] Use of others' meditations, the Bible, and other models served as an aid to prayer. Thus, even the appearance of the 'Pamela prayer' from Sir Philip Sidney's *Arcadia* – Milton's trump card – in various editions of *Eikon Basilike* cannot properly be construed as plagiarism or cynical misuse by someone unfamiliar with the distinctions between reality and fiction. In the spiritual autobiography, a genre increasingly popular with both puritans and Anglicans throughout the seventeenth century, a confluence of prayer and personal narrative, the pre-existing model performs an even more crucial service in the writer's structuring of

his or her life. The whole purpose of the spiritual autobiography is to discover the meaning of one's life, especially the pattern that may indicate
one's election. Hence, writers examine their consciences to discern patterns, which are then confirmed in their significance when they correspond to scriptural or other models. Biblical models – especially the Psalms
and the Book of Job – proved to be especially important to those attempting to make sense of their own suffering, whether spiritual or physical.[31]

Spiritual autobiographers, therefore, deliberately wove quotations
from the Scriptures into their own texts, establishing the authority of their
experiences and thoughts by demonstrating their familiarity. Writers
modelled their lives on older texts; in turn, readers of the published works
could apply the lessons of others' lives to their own. As Foxe's *Acts and
Monuments* recast public events as providential history, so spiritual auto-
biographies organized individual private lives as exemplary and implied
that readers, with careful examination, could discover the divine structure
of their own lives as they prepared their own stories. With their familiar
formulas, these books suggested the basic similarity of Christian lives.

The only chapter to depart from these two models – the final address to
the Prince of Wales – reinforces the interactive nature of the previous narrative through its pointed use of deliberative discourse.[32] Employing the
genre traditionally associated with advice, the chapter is written throughout in the second person. As a result, the words of the king often appear as
if they could be addressing the reader, as in these words counselling
against vindictiveness:

> When these mountains of congealed factions shall by the sunshine of
> Gods mercy, and the splendor of Your virtues be thawed and dissipated;
> and the abused Vulgar shall have learned, that, none are greater
> Oppressours of their Estates, Liberties, and Consciences, than those
> men, that entitle themselves, The Patrones and Vindicators of them,
> onely to usurp power over them; Let then no passion betray You to any
> study of revenge upon those, whose owne sinne and folly will
> sufficiently punish them in due time.[33]

These words simultaneously reassure readers that Prince Charles will not
punish them and suggest that their own loyalty ('the splendor of Your
virtues') will ultimately be valued. Moreover, the passage affirms those
values of property, liberty and conscience that had been the parliamentary
rallying cry in 1642.

The addressee / reader becomes part of a systematic discussion of political and religious values – values that, by implication, are more likely to be

upheld by the House of Stuart than the current government. In evaluating the king's advice, readers in effect participate in creating a vision of a desirable future government. Moreover, as all rhetoric textbooks inevitably pointed out, the deliberative genre explicitly invites the audience to consider future action.[34] The deliberative speaker or writer suggests and counsels, but it is the audience that ultimately must decide. The Charles of *Eikon Basilike*, therefore, offers readers what many could think the Commonwealth was denying them: a voice in determining their future and that of their country.[35]

Readers responded by making *Eikon Basilike* their own. The first edition, published by Richard Royston, contained no more than the twenty-seven chapters and the William Marshall frontispiece. But, when William Dugard published his more elaborate, rubricated edition around 15 March, the original chapters had been joined by numerous accretions that transformed the appearance of the book from a personal narrative to an 'experience' that attempted to recreate Charles's last days, give a fuller picture of his character, and intensify the perception of wisdom in the king's words.[36] The concluding section, 'Meditations upon Death, after the Votes of Non-Addresses, and *His Majesties* closer Imprisonment in *Carisbrooke-Castle*', now has its own chapter number, becoming number 28; this section now introduces a collection of four prayers, designated 'A Perfect Copie of Prayers Vsed By His Majesty In the time of His Sufferings: Delivered to Doctor Juxon, Bishop of London, immediately before His Death'. These include the famous 'Pamela prayer', which was attacked by Milton. After the prayers are five other works, some published separately after the king's death, a short epitaph beginning 'So fall's that stately Cedar', and, finally, with a separate title page, *Apophthegmata Aurea, Regia, Carolina*.[37]

Taken together, the prayers and the five short narratives present an intimate portrait of Charles as seen from the outside. The prayers – never identified as being of the king's own making, despite Milton's claim of plagiarism – give additional insight into Charles's preoccupations in captivity, words that inspired and comforted him. In keeping with the tradition of the Prayer Book and prayer manuals, they provide a model for devotion that readers may follow themselves; if readers use the prayers their king used, they in effect join him in a community of believers, entering imaginatively into his last days as they face the confusing times ahead. Similarly, three of the narratives allow readers to witness intimate moments between the king and his children. In these accounts, Charles becomes less a king and more a father, fearing that his two young children will forget him and that they will shortly be facing their own spiritual struggles as captives of the army.[38] As conversations with, and written by, children, these narratives are stripped of the formal language of royal ideology even as they discuss monarchy:

> His children being come to meet him, he first gave his blessing to the Lady Elizabeth and bade her remember to tell her brother James whenever she should see him that it was his father's last desire that he should no more look upon Charles as his eldest brother only but be obedient unto him as his soverign, and that they should love one another and forgive their father's enemies. Then said the King to her, 'Sweetheart, you'll forget this.' 'No,' said she, 'I shall never forget it while I live', and pouring forth abundance of tears promised him to write down the particulars.[39]

Instead of a king, a princess and a prince, this narrative presents a suffering family in a scene that could well echo in tone if not particulars the sentiments of many English families after two civil wars. The scene thus provides validation for the confusion, doubts and fears of English readers.

That validation is reinforced by the inclusion of 'His Majesties Reasons against the pretended Jurisdiction of the high Court of Justice, which he intended to deliver in Writing on Munday, January 22, 1648' and *Apophthegmata*. If readers had not known before the publication of *Eikon Basilike*, they discovered upon reading the accretions that Charles had been prevented from delivering a speech in his own defence at his trial. Through the medium of the king's book, readers are able to offer sympathetic ears, becoming parties to a speech that had never occurred in public and witnesses to the king's position. Together with the narratives, the speech turns readers into participants in Charles's final days, allowing ordinary people the privilege of observing the private thoughts of a king and the opportunity to hear words of self-defence that the court of high commission itself never heard. The *Apophthegmata* reverses the process. As their separate title page informs readers, these apophthegms are '[c]ollected out of' *Eikon Basilike*, and arranged under three headings: theological, moral, and political. Dugard's edition thus provides readers with their own commonplace book for ready reference. Like any commonplace book, *Apophthegmata* dignifies the entries as expressions of wisdom that readers may then apply to their own writings or review for insight into their own thoughts and experiences.[40] The accretions thus actively encourage readers' further participation in turning Charles into a symbol of goodness betrayed.

The various editions of *Eikon Basilike* reveal readers transformed into participants in the co-creation of the royal image. The book acquires several poetic additions in 1649: the 'Stately Cedar' epitaph mentioned above; a second epitaph beginning 'Whom *Scotlands* ayre brought forth'; 'The Frontispiece unfolded', explaining the Marshall engraving; and a tribute to the book itself – 'Upon His Sacred Majesties incomparable ΕΙΚΩΝ ΒΑΣΙΛΙΚΗ.'[41] This last poem in particular emphasizes the process by which the book bridges the gap between king and people. An apostrophe to the king, the poem opens:

> Couldst thou before thy death have *giv'n*, what wee
> Might *ask*, thy *Book* had been the *Legacie*.
> Thy *Will* can make but *Heirs* of *Monarchie*;
> But this doth make each man an Heir of *thee*.

So the Charles of *Eikon Basilike* is more important as a model of devotion and right conduct than as a king. As the poem explains, 'The *Style* betraie's a *King*, the *Art* a *Man*, / The high *Devotion* speake's a *Christian*' (lines 15–16). While the words of *Eikon Basilike* encourage readers to join the king in meditation and prayer, these accretions overtly turn Charles into an object of worship, not as a king, but as an exemplary human being, a pattern which a reader may emulate as his 'Heir'. By composing poems or adding illustrations to the king's text, readers actively become the king's heirs, taking the words as inheritance, not simply venerating them but building upon them, using the book as their property and their own vehicle for meditation and political expression.

Eikon Basilike thus effectively authorizes the many imaginative recreations of the king's image. William Marshall's frontispiece illustrates no scene from the book: instead, it renders overt the martyrology of the text, deliberately comparing the king to Christ and transforming Charles into a prisoner of conscience.[42] The author of 'The Frontispiece of the Kings Book opened' intensifies the king's Christlike posture in the Marshall engraving.[43] As the frontispiece mirrors Christ, so, the poem tells us, the book mirrors the Bible: 'His *Golden Manual*, so divine, so rare, / As, save God's booke, admits of no compare' (lines 5–6), except to Charles II. Unusual in its politics, this poem overtly advocates an active royalism instead of prayer. As Milton comments in *Eikonoklastes*, the words of the king were also transformed into poetry: Thomas Stanley versified the meditations following each chapter, thus allowing the eventual movement of *Eikon Basilike* from words and pictures to music. *Psalterium Carolinum*, composed by John Wilson, former member of the King's Musicke and former Professor of Music at Oxford, from Stanley's versifications, and published in 1657 with a dedicatory poem by Henry Lawes, literally turned the king's psalm-like meditations into psalms, to be sung by three voices.[44] With the advent of *Psalterium Carolinum*, the king's book went from private to public: from an individual reading experience to a group singing experience. Anthony Wood recalled that Wilson participated in afternoon 'musick meetings' at Oxford, and musical gatherings were common in many homes. The words of *Eikon Basilike* could thus have literally come out of others' mouths in song, in the part-singing of social gatherings that could have taken on a political dimension in their choice of music.

Subsequent issuings of *Eikon Basilike* throughout the reigns of the later Stuarts maintained their collective character, always with accompanying materials – some the accretions of 1649, some newly composed. A version issued in 1681, published by Richard Royston, included for the first time a poem – 'Majesty in Misery' – attributed to Charles I.[45] In 1693, Joseph Hindmarsh reissued the book as an accompaniment to Richard Perinchief's biography of Charles; the same edition included a 'Vindication' of Charles's authorship, responding to the Anglesey Memorandum. A Dublin edition of 1706 added 'A Character of the ROYAL MARTYR'.[46] By the early eighteenth century the book itself had become such a powerful symbol that the anti-Whig *Secret History of the Calves-Head Club* depicted it as being ritually burned by republican club members, before they swore an oath on a copy of Milton's *Defensio Populi Anglicani*.[47] On the other hand, the royal image also lent itself to satire. The year 1694 produced ΕΙΚΩΝ ΒΑΣΙΛΙΚΗ ΔΕΥΤΕΡΑ. *The Pourtraicture of His Sacred Majesty King Charles II*, a clever parody of *Eikon Basilike*, down to its frontispiece and chapter headings such as 'On his Majesty's being proclaim'd by the Parliament: His magnificent Entrance into London, and injoying the Countess of Castlemain the first Night'.[48] Meant to contrast the son's vice with the father's virtue, the book clearly presumes readers' ready familiarity with the appearance of the original work.

From the start *Eikon Basilike* was greater than the sum of its parts, both for how it represented King Charles and what it represented in the developing political discourse of the nation. In its portrait of the king, it illustrates the problem of authorship that confronts modern critics. Milton attacked the book as if it had a single, autonomous author (whether Charles or John Gauden), someone who can be guilty of plagiarism and bad faith in self-representation. As its history shows, however, the authorship of *Eikon Basilike* is collective, collaborative and participatory. There is no single, authorized version or 'work'.[49] Instead, the king's book is a 'text' in the current, critical sense of the word: it is the totality of its editions, accretions, illustrations and the experiences of its various readers. In the most fundamental way, there is no single *author* of the text of *Eikon Basilike.*

Further, the king's book offers something truly new in political propaganda: a democratized image of the king. For ultimate proof of its 'truth' it depends upon readers' perception of a connection with their own, personal truth. Many had seen Charles's dignified conduct on the scaffold and heard his moderate, irenic speech. Many more must have felt their own suffering, confusion and helplessness during the civil wars, regardless of their initial feelings about either king or parliament. Such perceptions could have easily led to sentimental identification with Charles, whom *Eikon Basilike* depicts as a man, father and Christian who happens also to be a king. As such, he becomes a suitable candidate for joining Foxe's martyrs, an ordinary / extraordinary figure persecuted by arbitrary authority.

In its many and varied editions, as well as its personal, familiar king, *Eikon Basilike* represents also the commodification of kingship. Issued in many forms, from cheap quartos to elaborate, rubricated octavos, illustrated with careful engravings or crude woodcuts, the book obliterated the distinction between 'high' and 'low' culture. The vast number of editions in 1649 alone suggest that the market was there, and that, through purchase or creative contribution to a new edition, English readers wanted to connect themselves to the king and whatever he represented to them.

Ironically, the democratized vision of kingship enabled the empowerment of readers. The famous hagiography associated with *Eikon Basilike* was, after all, the product of publishers and readers – a response to the 'work' of Gauden's edition of Charles's memoranda. In a sense, the 'text' of the king's book illustrates what may be called the conservative paradox: it is simultaneously safe and exhilarating. It prompts active involvement and even daring of those who advocate hierarchy, passivity and obedience. Participation in the 'text' of *Eikon Basilike* created the experience of political participation in readers feeling disfranchised by recent events and ignored by those in power. Like Sir Robert Filmer's *Patriarcha,* another royalist product of the times, *Eikon Basilike* signals the end of the royalism it celebrates.[50] Mere obedience and worship of authority are inadequate responses to the times; even the most dedicated supporters of kingship must acknowledge the need for popular sympathy.

Eikon Basilike thus represents a true break in traditional royalist culture – a critical cultural event. It radically departs from traditional political decorum. Abandoning the formal genres of parliamentary and ceremonial discourse for the popular genres of religion and sensibility, it becomes a model of intertextuality in its broadest sense. Emerging from a wide range of cultural, political, religious and literary forms the king's book moves the variegated languages of critique and protest into the heart of conservative politics, ultimately changing them in the most fundamental way. This royal image was a popular project, ironically illustrating the most basic argument of its most radical opponents: people make kings.

Notes

1 On the explosion of pamphleteering in the 1640s see Christopher Hill, *Milton and the English Revolution* (Harmondsworth: Penguin, 1979), 65; and Fredrick Seaton Siebert, *Freedom of the Press in England, 1476–1776: The Rise and Decline of Government Controls* (Urbana: University of Illinois Press, 1952), 166–7.

2 Francis F[alconer] Madan, *A New Bibliography of the Eikon Basilike of King Charles the First*, new series 3 (Oxford Bibliographical Society Publications, 1949; Oxford University Press, 1950).

3 Unless otherwise noted, when quoting from *Eikon Basilike* I use Madan, *New Bibliography* 1, printed by Richard Royston, British Library shelf mark C. 59. a. 24.

4 Madan, *New Bibliography*, 126–33; see further H. R. Trevor-Roper, '*Eikon Basilike*: The Problem of the King's Book', in his *Historical Essays* (London: Macmillan, 1957), 211–20; and Philip Knachel, 'Introduction', *Eikon Basilike: The Portraiture of His Sacred Majesty in His Solitudes and Sufferings*, ed. Philip Knachel, Folger Documents of Tudor and Stuart Civilization (Ithaca, NY: Cornell University Press for the Folger Shakespeare Library, 1966), xx–xxxii. A member of the Assembly of Divines in 1643, Gauden supported episcopacy and opposed changes in religion being made in the House of Commons. *The Religious & Loyal Protestation of John Gauden Dr of Divinity* appeared on 5 January 1649, describing Charles in '*Agony, solitude, and expectation of an inforced death*' (sig. A2v) in an appeal to Fairfax to spare the king's life.

5 Paragraph 4, sig. B7r.

6 Paragraph 5, sig. B7r.

7 Sigs. B8r–v.

8 *The Princely Pellican. Royall Resolves Presented In Sundry choice Observations, Extracted from His Majesties Divine Meditations: With Satisfactory Reasons to the whole Kingdome, that His Sacred Person was the onely Author of them* (n.p., 1649), 12. The author is unknown, although Madan believes him to be John Ashburnham, Groom of the Bedchamber, appointed 1628.

9 Sig. B8v; cp. 'Let the enemy persecute my soul, and take *it;* yea, let him tread down my life upon the earth, and lay mine honour in the dust' (Authorized Version).

10 Sig. Q5v.

11 Elizabeth Skerpan, *The Rhetoric of Politics in the English Revolution, 1642–1660* (Columbia: University of Missouri Press, 1992), 107–9.

12 Εικων Αληθηινη . *The Pourtraiture of Truths most sacred Majesty truly suffering, though not solely. Wherein the false colours are washed off, wherewith the Painter-steiner had bedaubed Truth in his counterfeit Piece entitled* Εικων Βασιλικη . The literature on *Eikonoklastes* is extensive, particularly in the past decade. See Sharon Achinstein, *Milton and the Revolutionary Reader* (Princeton University Press, 1994); Jane Hiles, 'Milton's Royalist Reflex: The Failure of Argument and the Role of Dialogics in *Eikonoklastes*', in *Spokesperson Milton: Voices in Contemporary Criticism*, ed. Charles W. Durham and Kristin Pruitt McColgan (Cranbury, NJ: Susquehanna University Press, 1994), 87–100; Skerpan, *Rhetoric of Politics*, 113–24; David Loewenstein, *Milton and the Drama of History: Historical Vision, Iconoclasm and the Literary Imagination* (Cambridge University Press, 1990), 52–73; Nancy Klein Maguire, 'The Theatrical Mask/Masque of Politics: The Case of Charles I', *Journal of British Studies*, 28 (1989): 1–22; Lois Potter, *Secret Rites and Secret Writing: Royalist Literature, 1641–1660* (Cambridge University Press, 1989), 156–93.

13 Achinstein, *Milton and the Revolutionary Reader*, 162–8.

14 *Eikon Alethine*, sigs. A1v, A3v.

15 For a full account of Charles's trial, including the accusation that he was a 'man of blood', see C. V. Wedgwood, *The Trial of Charles I* (London: Collins, 1964), 155–61.

16 Εικων η Πιστη. *Or, the faithfull Pourtracture of a Loyall Subject, in Vindication of* ΕΙΚΩΝ ΒΑΣΙΛΙΚΗ *Otherwise Intituled, the Pourtraicture of his Sacred Majestie, In his Solitudes & Sufferings. In Answer to an insolent Book, Intituled* ΕΙΚΩΝ ΑΛΗΘΙΝΗ: *whereby occasion is taken, to handle all the controverted points relating to these times* ([London], 1649), sig. N4.

17 ΕΙΚΩΝ ΑΚΛΑΣΤΟΣ *the IMAGE VNBROAKEN. A Perspective of the Impudence, Falshood, Vanitie, and Prophannes, Published in a Libell entitled* ΕΙΚΟΝΟΚΛΑΣΤΗΕ *against* ΕΙΚΩΝ ΒΑΣΙΛΙΚΗ *Or the Pourtraicture of his SACRED MAJESTIE in his solitudes and Sufferings* (n.p., 1651), 17, sig. C.

18 *Princely Pellican*, 28; the 'discretion' on the part of the publishers, that is. The accretions first appeared in William Dugard's edition of 15 March (Madan, *New Bibliography*, 22).

19 Ibid., 1, 10–11.

20 See for example Aristotle, *'Art' of Rhetoric*, I.10. Technically, King Charles was convicted because he refused to plead; the court thus never considered his state of mind. *Eikon Basilike* in effect provides the exploration that did not occur at the trial.

21 *Princely Pellican*, 26.

22 Loewenstein, *Milton and the Drama of History*, 54.

23 Ibid., 52.

24 Contrast Fabian Philipps, *King Charles the First, no Man of Blood: but a Martyr for his People*, issued 25 June 1649, which, in explaining and justifying the king's actions, presents the actual and imagined arguments that parliamentary leaders had against him.

25 On Protestant historiography, see further Richard Helgerson, *Forms of Nationhood: The Elizabethan Writing of England* (University of Chicago Press, 1992), especially 247–94; Nicholas von Maltzahn, *Milton's History of Britain: Republican Historiography in the English Revolution* (Oxford: Clarendon Press, 1991), 49–59; Joseph M. Levine, *Humanism and History: Origins of Modern English Historiography* (Ithaca, NY: Cornell University Press, 1987), 73–106.

26 *The Ecclesiasticall History: Containing the Acts and Monuments of Martyrs With the*

Persecutions Stirred Up by Romish Prelates in the Church. The eighth edition was published in London in 1641. See John R. Knott, *Discourses of Martyrdom in English Literature, 1563–1694* (Cambridge University Press, 1993), 33–83.

27 Skerpan, *Rhetoric of Politics,* 45–8.

28 8th edn, 1026.

29 Knott suggests that Charles may have actually read *Acts and Monuments* while in captivity, so the parallels may be deliberate. See *Discourses of Martyrdom,* 161.

30 Cynthia Garrett, 'The Rhetoric of Supplication: Prayer Theory in Seventeenth-Century England', *Renaissance Quarterly,* 46 (1993): 328–57; see especially 329, 345–52.

31 See Steven Mailloux, 'Persuasions Good and Bad: Bunyan, Iser, and Fish on Rhetoric and Hermeneutics in Literature', *Studies in the Literary Imagination,* 28.2 (1995): 43–61; Kathleen M. Swaim, *Pilgrim's Progress, Puritan Progress: Discourses and Contexts* (Urbana: University of Illinois Press, 1993), 18–41, 132–59; David Dawson, 'Allegorical Intratextuality in Bunyan and Winstanley', *Journal of Religion,* 70 (1990): 189–212; J. Samuel Preus, 'Secularizing Divination: Spiritual Biography and the Invention of the Novel', *Journal of the American Academy of Religion,* 59 (1991): 441–66.

32 For an extended discussion of the lack of deliberative discourse in royalist tracts of 1649 see Skerpan, *Rhetoric of Politics,* 107–11.

33 Sig. R2.

34 The classical loci for definitions of the oratorical genres are Aristotle, *'Art' of Rhetoric,* I. S3.1–6; Cicero, *De Oratore,* I.xxxi.141, and *Partitiones oratoriae,* IV.11; Quintilian, *Institutio oratoria,* III.iv.9.

35 According to several accounts, at Charles's sentencing, when John Bradshaw read the judgement 'in the name of the people of England', a lady in the gallery cried out 'not half the people!' See *The Trial of Charles I: A Documentary History,* ed. David Iagomarsino and Charles J. Wood (Hanover: University Press of New England for Dartmouth College, 1989), 110. Others note the great groan of the crowd at the moment of Charles's execution.

36 See Knachel, 'Introduction', 171–84. In the Royston edition, the meditations are not given a separate chapter heading.

37 'His Majesties Reasons against the pretended Jurisdiction of the high Court of Justice, which he intended to deliver in Writing on Munday, January 22, 1648', Thomason 669. f. 13. (81.), dated 5 February; 'A Copie of a Letter which was sent from the Prince to the King'; 'A Relation of what passed between His Majesty, the Lady Elizabeth, and the Duke of Glocester, the day before His Death', Thomason 669. f. 14. (9.), dated 24 March; 'Another Relation from the Lady Elizabeths own Hand'; and 'Another relation from the Lady Elizabeth'.

38 So important is the image of the children that portraits of three of the children appear in Joseph Earle's Latin translation of 1649 (E. 1384), commissioned by Charles II, although it includes none of the accretions of the Dugard edition.

39 *Eikon Basilike,* ed. Knachel, 192.

40 For an excellent recent study of the rhetorical functions of commonplace books, see Mary Thomas Crane, *Framing Authority: Sayings, Self, and Society in Sixteenth-Century England* (Princeton University Press, 1993), 12–38.

41 'Scotlands ayre' and 'Frontispiece Unfolded' appear in Madan, *New Bibliography,* 29, an edition published in late April. 'Upon *Eikon Basilike*' is in Dugard's edition, Madan, *New Bibliography,* 22, signed F. N. G.

42 On the Christology of the frontispiece see Loewenstein, *Milton and the Drama of*

History, 53; Knott, *Discourses of Martyrdom*, 161; Roy Strong, *Van Dyck: Charles I on Horseback* (London: Allen Lane, 1972), 29–30. Knott observes that the engraving echoes themes in the emblems of George Wither, while Strong points to numerous representations of Christ in the garden. In tone and composition, the engraving mirrors Giorgio Vasari's *Christ in the Garden of Gethsemane*, with its darkness, the right profile of the main figure, the extension of the right arm, and the appearance of a heavenly vision (in this case angels) in the figure's line of sight.

43 [William Somner], *The Frontispiece of the Kings Book opened. With A Poem annexed: The Insecurity of Princes. Considered in an occasionall Meditation upon the King's late Sufferings and Death* ([London, 1650? 1649]), see 3–4. So identified in the British Library catalogue, it is not listed in Thomason. Madan, *New Bibliography*, 140.

44 See Susan Treacy, '*Psalterium Carolinum*: Music as Propaganda in Seventeenth-Century England', *Explorations in Renaissance Culture*, 19 (1993): 45–69.

45 Madan, *New Bibliography*, 66. Royston is identified as 'Bookseller to His most Sacred Majesty'. The poem follows the table of contents and precedes the text. There are no other accretions. Significantly, there is no explanation of provenance of the poem, other than the explanation that it was composed 'during his Captivity at *Carisbrooke* Castle'. The poem regularly appears in subsequent editions as late as 1879.

46 Hindmarsh: Madan, *New Bibliography*, 67; Dublin: Madan, *New Bibliography*, 69, dedicated to James, Duke of Ormonde, overtly identified as a Loyalist document in the dedication.

47 [Edward Ward], *The Secret History of the Calves-Head Club, or the Republican unmasq'd*. 4th edn (London, 1704), 10.

48 Madan, *New Bibliography*, 132. The title page continues the parody by indicating that the manuscript was 'Found in the Strong Box' like the king's cabinet at Naseby.

49 I follow the distinction described by Margreta de Grazia, 'What is a Work? What is a Document?', in *New Ways of Looking at Old Texts: Papers of the Renaissance English Texts Society, 1985–1991*, ed. W. Speed Hill (Binghamton, New York: Renaissance English Text Society, 1993), 199–207.

50 *Patriarcha and Other Political Works*, ed. Peter Laslett (Oxford: Basil Blackwell, 1949); see Quentin Skinner, 'Some Problems in the Analysis of Political Thought and Action', *Political Theory*, 2 (1974): 277–303.

7

Milton and King Charles

Sharon Achinstein

That the King's Majesty, under God, is the only supreme governor of this realm, and of all other his Highness's dominions and countries, as well in all spiritual or ecclesiastical things or causes as temporal; and that no foreign prince, person, prelate, state, or potentate hath, or ought to have, any jurisdiction, power, superiority, pre-eminence, or authority, ecclesiastical or spiritual, within his Majesty's said realms, dominions and countries. *John Milton (1632)*

A Parliament is, by all equity and right, above a King, and may judge him. *John Milton (1649)*

Two statements authorized by John Milton could not be wider apart in sentiment, yet only seventeen years separated them. In 1629, and again in 1632, John Milton willingly put his hand to the first, his subscription undertaken to receive academic degree standing at Cambridge University. The second words are taken from his *Eikonoklastes*, the government's hired response to the *Eikon Basilike*.[1]

As a sign of the importance of public opinion in their revolution, the regicides searched for a champion, and their first choice was probably not John Milton. That commission was offered to John Selden, who reportedly refused the honour.[2] They turned then to Milton, who had published *The Tenure of Kings and Magistrates* just two weeks after Charles's execution. Looking at the two statements above, we might well wonder how did Milton arrive at this second position? It has been suggested that Milton himself refashioned his life story to suit a revolutionary trajectory, and that his political expressions were more often the result of topical pressures rather than a sustained political programme.[3] Beginning his career as a polemical writer with pamphlets urging an ecclesiastical revolution in 1640–1, Milton arrived in print controversy at the same time as the outbreak of hostilities between king and parliament. Strikes against the institutions of marriage and censorship followed in the early and mid 1640s. A period of relative silence ensued, not fully explained in Milton scholarship, until the author unleashed his pen in February 1649.

This chapter pictures Milton looking at King Charles, something he was paid to do repeatedly. It needs to be remembered that Milton's regicide tracts aimed at a goal far greater than attacking Charles; they meant to destroy the institution of monarchy in England. Much recent critical attention has underscored the presence of classical republican thought in Milton's political writing against kingship in general and Charles in particular.[4] Milton's re-imaging the king cannot be separated from the political theory underpinning the attack.

The account of Milton's republican principles can be enhanced by understanding how Milton viewed the king in the international political situation of Counter-Reformation Europe. In *The Tenure of Kings and Magistrates*, Milton observed, 'look how much right the King of *Spaine* hath to govern us at all, so much right hath the King of *England* to govern us tyrannically' (*CPW*, III, 214). There is of course the topical reference to Spain, a summoning of fears about Charles's 'Spaniolization'. But there is a political theory point as well. The repulsion of a tyrant is the same as the repulsion of a foreign king: 'the Law of civil defensive warr differs nothing from the Law of forren hostility. Nor is it distance of place that makes enmitie, but enmity that makes distance' (*CPW*, III, 215). If civil war and foreign war are given identity, we can properly regard the status of the English civil wars in a new light. Not only were they a domestic struggle, they were also an international one.

In seeking to explain how Milton came to see King Charles as a tyrant in the first place, this chapter attends to the phenomenon, sometimes dismissed as a 'hysteria' and rarely examined a legitimate interpretation, one that erupted periodically across the whole of the seventeenth century in more or less vocal and violent explosions. Reduced to a single nominative, nonetheless it encompassed thousands of instants, and that is the Popish Plot. By placing Milton's attitude towards King Charles in light of the Popish-plot interpretation of history, we can see how foreign affairs played a key role in perceptions of Charles, and how the story of Charles is deeply imbricated in the story of Counter-Reformation Europe. We can also see that Popish-plot thinking was not merely a result of apocalyptic rhetoric or irrational fears; it was, rather, a rational and highly effective means of political analysis.[5]

This context can complement studies of early modern opposition that focus on constitutionalism or republican political theory; the Popish Plot, moreover, supplied a motive to action perhaps more powerful than these as an ignition for radical change. Since it drew upon a mode of interpretation vital to English history since the Reformation, the Popish Plot worked to fire revolutionary action not only because it could explain the present; it also reawakened memories of past events, fears and self-perceptions deeply rooted in collective memory so as to seem naturally woven into the fabric of English identity.

Anti-popery needs some delineation here. Milton's response to the Irish Rebellion is one instance of his anti-popery, and the narrow, cruel prejudice in relation to Ireland can neither be underestimated nor forgotten. But it is not merely a response to Catholic religion. Even though Catholicism in England concentrated in the gentry and thus may have been a more powerful force among the political elite than numbers alone would suggest, nonetheless, the numbers of Catholics in England did little to warrant the tremendous fears generated by anti-popery. Because the numbers of Catholics do not seem to match the intensity of fears about them, historians have sought to explain anti-popery as something other than hatred of actual Catholics. Peter Lake has argued that it was a means by which puritans defined their own self-image through a negative mirror; Kevin Sharpe uses a 'scapegoat' model; and Robin Clifton has seen it as a useful 'stalking horse for Parliamentarians wishing to alter the balance of the constitution'.[6]

I take a different approach in this chapter, exploring the hermeneutic value of what I call Popish-plot thinking. 'As Englishmen looked across to the continent', writes John Elliott, 'they saw, in one part of Europe after another, the triumph of popery and arbitrary power'.[7] If we explore the Englishman's view of Counter-Reformation Europe, with its religious and dynastic warfare, as creating a powerful perspective glass for interpreting events both at home and abroad, we begin to see anti-popery less as paranoia than as a response to something truly threatening. It was not only a religious programme, it was also a way of interpreting events in history, a means of assigning causes. To return to the Irish for a moment: in chapter 12 of *Eikonoklastes*, Milton charges that Charles himself was the author of the Irish Rebellion, despite the king's protestations to the contrary. Popish-plot thinking then, was partially a fear of a Catholic invasion from within Britain, and also an account of the monarch's complicity in that invasion, an exposure of his secret relations with foreign powers, and a denunciation of the guile and surreptitiousness by which that invasion was to take place.

As with fears of popery, fears in excess of true referents, Milton's violent iconoclasm is very often out of proportion with the perceived threat. Looking to explain its intensity, current literary scholars have suggested that apocalypticism aroused Milton's creative potential.[8] If we turn away from generalized apocalypticism to the more precise historical framework of Europe during the Thirty Years' War, we can reassess Milton's apocalyptic view of Charles's designs as a rational response to a real political situation. Further, Milton can be seen as engaging both with the political and religious conflicts within England, and also with those of mid-century Europe. The procedure here will be diachronic and genetic. I wish to observe Milton over time since the interpretive scheme of the Popish Plot worked through accretion of disparate instances, drawn together in retrospect in an act of interpretation and demystification.

Even if Popish-plot thinking seems a quaint historical accident, its presence in early modern English political culture is hard to overestimate; with its suspicion of the motives of political leaders, its critical interpretation of the king's choices, its ability to mobilize citizens for collective action, and its wide play in an international press, against a background in which the fate of the Protestant Reformation had not yet been settled in Europe, it proved a force powerful enough to pull down the institution of monarchy in one European country.

Coming of age with the Good Old Cause

Milton's political coming of age mirrored the rise of the Good Old Cause, parliament's bid for sovereignty. It also coincided with that great international crisis of the seventeenth century, the Thirty Years' War. I wish to dwell on the early Milton to see how his Popish-plot thinking developed over time. I am aware that a narrative of 'development' risks a facile teleology. However, the very nature of Popish-plot thinking is developmental, that is, it is a hermeneutic in which present historical instances are related to past ones. Popish-plot thinking always works in retrospect before casting its fears into the future; the accretion makes a coherent narrative out of apparently discrete elements, and gives the present the power to alter the past. In his later writings, and especially his writings on King Charles, Milton returns to his early concerns. But the return is repetition with a difference, as the present deepens and fortifies his understanding of contemporary political events.

Even from his early poetry, Milton viewed earthly events through the rhetoric of Counter-Reformation Protestant militancy. With his 1626 Latin poetry commemorating the Gunpowder Plot, written against 'all the brutish gods in profane Rome', King James was pitted against the 'fierce tyrant who controls Acheron's flaming currents', who 'arms invincible nations for a deadly war one against the other and overturns kingdoms hitherto flourishing under the olive-branch of peace'.[9] The Gunpowder Plot had been exposed in 1605. By 1626, however, its commemoration had become politically charged, as puritans grasped its symbolic power as a story of England's Providential deliverance from an international Catholic enemy. Milton himself acknowledges the European stakes, as his poem recreates the fabled plotting of Satan stirring up followers. After the Houses of Parliament are to be destroyed, Satan promises the rebels that the foreign powers will rush to conquer: 'Afterwards let the fierce Frenchman or the cruel Spaniard invade the Britons while they are still panic-stricken . . . Thus the Marian regime will at last be re-established in that land.'[10] The beginning of the Thirty Years' War in 1618, a conflict which in its initial stages divided Europe along confessional lines, renewed the cult of the Gunpowder Plot in England, when James's apparent *rapprochement* with Catholic Spain alarmed puritans. Gunpowder poetry, unlike Armada celebrations, did something other than celebrate monarchical authority; it celebrated institutions of English government, as the plot was aimed against the government as a whole, against its central institution of parliament. Gunpowder commemorative poetry under Charles spoke a parliamentary, and even an anti-Laudian interest, as puritan preachers increasingly used 5 November sermons as a warning against the rise of popery; notably, Laud ignored the date.[11]

The young Milton saw the fortunes of England linked with those of Europe. To be sure, he could be flippant regarding warfare on the continent, as in his reply to a letter from Alexander Gill in May 1628, praising his old teacher's poetical tribute to the success of the allies: 'I know not truly whether I should more congratulate Henry of Nassau on the capture of the city or on your verses.' But he could also be deadly serious and sharply critical of England's continental role. He registered intimately the presence of war in Germany in a letter to his old tutor dating from 1627, distressed that Thomas Young, then pastor to the English Merchants at Hamburg, was living where 'all around you echoes the horrifying noise of war'. Milton voiced outrage that England itself had banished Young to that place, betraying and leaving stranded a worthy subject: 'O native country, hard-hearted parent [*patria, dura parens*], more cruel than the

white cliffs of your coastline, battered by foaming waves, is it fitting that
you should expose your innocent children this way? Is this the way you
treat them, iron-hearted land, driving them on to foreign soil and allowing
them to search for their food on distant shores?' Likening Young's plight to
that of Paul and Jesus, exiled prophets of old, but especially to that of
Elijah, fleeing 'from the hands of King Ahab', the poem leaps out of its
third-person narrator into direct address, 'and from your hands too,
beastly woman of Sidon', speaking directly to Jezebel. Moving from the
intimate to the political, Milton lays blame on Charles and Henrietta
Maria in the figures of Ahab and Jezebel. Even from this early date, the
king's household is not above criticism.[12]

Milton's European tour of 1638–9, whether intended as a culmination of
his humanist studies or as a flight from familial responsibilities, was something more, perhaps an awakening to the international dimension of
domestic political conditions. Milton's travel route on the continent was
determined by the fighting in the Thirty Years' War.[13] There he experienced first-hand the effects of Counter-Reformation persecution in Italy,
where he visited 'the famous *Galileo* grown old, a prisner to the
Inquisition', and there he sat among those Italian academicians who
'themselvs did nothing but bemoan the servil condition into which
lerning amongst them was brought'. There, he vouched later, plots were
laid against him by English Jesuits, 'because of the freedom with which I
had spoken about religion' (*CPW*, IV, 619; II, 537–8). He had left England
while conflict between Scotland and the king was already turning violent;
however, his return was, as he reported later, on account of that very
conflict, perhaps now seen in a different light. The European journey was
not only a chance to mingle with the international *literati*; it was also a
chance to observe up close the Counter-Reformation European political
landscape. For the rest of his writing life, Milton could not keep the
spectre of Europe at bay, and indeed in his writing on Charles, he is watching Europe, warily, mistrustingly.

Foreign policy in the Personal Rule: WAR IS PEACE

England's mid-century troubles have, until very recently, been viewed as a
constitutional struggle within the context of England's state-building, as a
crisis of three kingdoms rather than as part of a general European experience.[14] Along the same lines, Milton's contribution to the thought of the
English revolution has been seen in his defence of English liberties against

the encroachments of tyranny. I want to turn away from this important domestic constitutional context and cross the channel. Charles's foreign policy relations with the continent formed a central plank of parliamentary resistance in the parliaments of the early 1640s.[15] Whether through deliberate policy or ineptitude, Charles refused to engage significantly in the great cataclysm on the continent. His neutrality has been understood recently as pragmatic diplomacy; at the time, English citizens interpreted his repeated non-intervention as his rejection of the Protestant cause.[16] Either story does not entirely square with the reality. Indeed, far from being isolated, Charles's subjects were seriously involved in the fighting in the Thirty Years' War, as English, Scottish and Irish recruits peopled the armies of Europe. Many English royalists hired themselves as mercenaries to the Habsburg Empire following the end of the first Civil War; royalists in 1644 were reported to have greeted the recruiting agent of the Habsburg emperor with the remark that 'Emperors and Kings must help each other against their treacherous vassals.'[17] Fifty thousand Englishmen had fought abroad in the 1620s, in Germany or in France; from Ireland, between 1644 and 1649, France recruited over 7,000 troops and Spain recruited approximately 4,000; from Scotland alone, 25,000 recruits, or one adult male in ten, estimates Geoffrey Parker, had fought for the Protestant alliance on the continent between 1625 and 1632.[18] Men from the British Isles had been fighting hard on the continent all through the halcyon days of the Personal Rule.

Far from being isolated, England under Charles nonetheless seemed to abandon the tradition of Elizabeth's confessional, or apocalyptic, foreign policies. Running out of money to finance his Scottish campaign, Charles had reopened negotiations with Spain in 1638, and by 1640 there were three Spanish ambassadors in London, a situation Milton denounced in *Of Reformation*, recoiling at their warm reception by the Laudian prelates, 'a Tympany of *Spanioliz'd Bishops* swaggering in the fore-top of the State, and meddling to turne, and dandle the *Royal Ball*' (*CPW*, I, 587). English citizens rioted at the Spanish ambassador's residence in April 1641, one of a series of mob anti-popery actions.[19] Henrietta Maria, in the meantime, was seeking assistance against the Scots from the Pope.[20]

The early Stuart monarchs shrunk from confessional engagement. In the vacuum created by this withdrawal, argues Simon Adams, leading members of parliament took up the Protestant cause.[21] So did John Milton. When he recalled modern history, it was consistently ideologically marked by the Counter-Reformation binarism between Catholic and

Protestant.[22] It is true that the war between Spain and the Netherlands, in the 1560s and in the 1640s, did polarize international politics both inside and outside of Europe.[23] In England, however, there were complicating factors resisting a strict confessional policy, such as Charles's search for support from a series of European powers for restitution of the Palatinate, or his fears about the rising power of the Dutch (Protestant), due to their alliance with the French (Catholic). Charles repeatedly sought Spanish aid. Nonetheless, Milton saw Europe through the early allegiances of the Thirty Years' War, when sides could be more easily drawn on confessional lines, and when the centre of power of the Habsburgs was Spain; later, however, as the theatre of power shifted away from Spain to Germany, politics, not solely religious divisions, were increasingly the prime motives for allegiance.[24]

These changes were beyond Milton's interpretive scheme. He saw instead a betrayal of confessional interest. Milton's attention to foreign policy in the early 1640s was of a piece with the political leaders of his day, who were mounting a case against the king, as evident in Commons' petitions, the Grand Remonstrance and the Nineteen Propositions. As early as *Of Reformation*, Milton attacked those 'priestly policies' which have 'gone the way also to leave us as naked of our firmest, & faithfullest neighbours abroad, by disparaging and alienating from us all protestant Princes, and Commonwealths . . . preferring the *Spaniard* our deadly enemy before them' (*CPW*, I, 586).

Milton's ample anti-Spanish rhetoric indeed touched a nerve of national memory: Elizabeth's glorious defeat of the Spanish Armada, and, by contrast, Charles's appalling attempt at a Spanish match. As early as 1641, Milton drew upon that national memory to launch a critique of Charles's foreign policy. In a plea recalling the success of the Spanish Armada, Milton hoped to revive that ideal of Protestant militancy abroad, reminding readers in *Of Reformation* of a seascape where 'for us the *Northern Ocean* even to the frozen *Thule* was scatter'd with the proud Ship-wrecks of the *Spanish Armado*, and the very maw of hell ransack't'. In contrast, the contemporary Spanish fleet 'lies thirsting to revenge his Navall ruines that have larded our Seas' (*CPW*, I, 615). This comes in 1641, when another, perhaps more pressing, communal memory of Spanish boats was the presence of the Spanish fleet at Dover in 1639, where they had found temporary refuge from the Dutch.[25]

While the Armada was a memory that appealed to English citizens of all stripes, Spain had also served to galvanize public opinion in the 1630s in the propaganda opposing Charles's match with the Spanish Infanta, indeed the first organized public opposition in English political history.[26] In calling to mind the 'Ship-wracks of the *Spanish Armado*' (*CPW*, 1, 615), Milton reactivates multiple responses, appealing to an already ingrained oppositional tradition.

Not only was Charles friendly to the Spanish in his foreign affairs, his church policy seemed an imitation of the Spanish model. Instead of 'No Bishop, no King' – the conservative defence of episcopal government in England – Milton substitutes, 'One Pope, and one King', vouching that Charles's church, 'finding the Spaniard their surest friend, and safest refuge . . . to uphold the decrepit Papalty have invented this super-politick Aphorisme' (*CPW*, 1, 582). It is true Charles was hispanophilic between 1625 and 1640, even resisting joining the Protestant leadership of Gustavus Adolphus, but Milton, in his interpretation of this foreign policy, saw menace, not reason of state, in these choices. This friendship with Spain was emblematic of Charles's willingness to betray Protestantism: it meant a turn to popery in religion and arbitrary power in government.

In this context, where Charles appeared too friendly to Spain, the rhetorical situation of *Of Reformation* bears remark. The tract is 'written to a friend', and in it Milton reminds his readers that it is one of the state's chief interests to determine who are friends, and who enemies. It should be noted that Milton takes aim not merely at the domestic affairs. England's abandonment of its international allies is another defect of 'priestly policie':

> Hence it is that the prosperous, and prudent states of the united Provinces, whom we ought to love, if not for themselves, yet for our own good work in them, they having bin in a manner planted, and erected by us, and having bin since to us the faithfull watchmen and discoverers of many a Popish, and Austrian complotted Treason, and with us the partners of many a bloody, and victorious battell, whom the similitude of manners and language, the commodity of traffick, which founded the old Burgundian league betwixt us, but chiefly Religion should bind to us immortally, even such friends as these, out of some principles instill'd into us by the Prelates, have bin often dismist with dreadful answers, and somtimes unfriendly actions. (*CPW*, 1, 586–7)

In this charge against those setting English foreign policy, Milton conceives of foreign relations in terms of popish plotting, with Austria (Habsburgs) at odds with the Dutch. Friends watch out for each other, especially friends bound by a long history of watchful amity. Such an ideal of an international Protestant community was bandied about in the early

1640s; John Dury and Samuel Hartlib had devised schemes for a union with the Dutch in 1641–2.[27] Parliament suggested close affiliation in June 1642 in the Nineteen Propositions, 'That Your Majesty wil be pleased to enter into a more strict alliance with the States of the United Provinces and other neighbouring princes and states of the Protestant religion, for the defence and maintenance thereof, against all designs and attempts of the Pope and his adherents to subvert and suppress it.'[28]

How much awareness did Milton have of events abroad, and of Charles's foreign policy? A great deal, it seems, from the collection of facts presented in his prose writings. But the nature of his political information is worth evaluating. His tracts are peppered with allusions to materials in the popular press, those pamphlets written against Charles's foreign policy. Milton was not only a defender of pamphlets (*Areopagitica*); he was a reader of them. From his communication of facts and rumours, it is also clear that Milton was a reader of newsbooks. The spread of information is a part of his Gunpowder poem, as Fame 'wings her way through the yielding air . . . she spreads contradictory rumours and vague murmurings through the English cities, and then in a clear voice she makes public the plots and the foul working of treason . . . Her reports caused utter amazement.'[29]

The Thirty Years' War had inaugurated a new era in the dissemination of political information in England. Even English ballads and prodigies boasted events on the continent.[30] The newsbook came of age with the Thirty Years' War; the first publicly disseminated news in England was that of foreign affairs. The earliest English corantos in the late 1620s contained a Protestant bias, and fed 'the appetite for participation in the Thirty Years' War'. There is no evidence of Milton's subscribing to manuscript newsletters, but a well-loved fellow of Christ's, who may have been a tutor to Milton, was a prolific author of them while Milton was there. Joseph Meade digested extensive reports on foreign affairs in the 1620s, registering doubt about the king's loyalty to the Protestant cause abroad.[31]

Revolutions and revolts seized Europe in the 1640s, and news of these were received in England with great interest. In diaries, newsletters, and in printed pamphlets, English men and women were aware they were living in a volatile world, and their news of foreign events was sometimes better than news of home affairs. Continental news was of particular relevance to the struggle between king and parliament, as it provided the millennialist impulses driving many in England to revolt: 'These days are days of shaking . . . and this shaking is universal: the palatinate, Bohemia, Germania, Catalonia, Portugal, England', preached a fast sermon to the House of Commons on 25 January 1642/3.[32] John Rous remarked on revolts in Portugal and Aragon, watching foreign events as closely as he did speeches at Westminster. Thomas Carew and Aurelian Townshend exchanged poems debating the significance of the death of Gustavus Adolphus for England; Ben Jonson's poem, penned in 1620 and published in 1640 urged:

> Wake, friend, from forth thy Lethargie: the Drum
> Beates brave, and loude in *Europe*, and bids come
> All that dare rowse: or are not loth to quit
> Their vitious ease . . . [33]

The horrified royalist James Howell published a 146-page account of the 'monstrous successes' of the Neapolitan revolt.[34] News of the revolt in Naples and a peasant revolt in Danzig appeared in the same newsbooks as the terms of the Peace of Westphalia in late autumn 1648.[35] The *Tenure* registers the optimism and the uncertainty of 1649, the year of revolutions. Milton presents the dangers of Spanish tyranny and perfidy by citing the examples of the Dutch revolt and the recent insurrection in Naples (*CPW*, III, 240). Given this political situation, and the quality of his political information, it is no wonder that a view of foreign affairs would prove vital to Milton's case against Charles.

When put in relation to his foreign policies, Charles's cultural policies thus may be seen as a species of double-speak: war is peace. The cult of irenicism and the myth of England's halcyon era played over and over in court masque, painting and poem, Charles's avowed pacifism and repudiation of the military slaughters taking place in Europe, could be seen at best as a wishful idyll, at worst as an out-and-out lie. It was certainly a politically charged portrait. Very early on in his writing career, Milton saw the cultural policy in the worst light, as an instance of Charles's mendacity. 'Having fitted us only for peace, and that a servile peace', Milton moans (*CPW*, I, 595), Charles's prelacy has renounced that 'good warfare' of the 'Church militant' (*CPW*, I, 758, 757). His own 'martial muse', in sharp contrast, presents the English very often with the epithet, 'warlike'.[36] The closing prayer in *Of Reformation* embraces a vision, where 'amidst the *Hymns* . . . this great and warlike nation . . . shall put an end to all Earthly *Tyrannies*' (*CPW*, I, 616).

Court culture and the European Match

Charles I was the first English monarch since Henry VIII to set foot outside of the British Isles, and his aesthetic taste did nothing but strengthen cultural links with the great European courts.[37] The influence of Charles's French queen, too, contributed to this Europeanization of the English court. Not only Henrietta Maria's taste for pastoral drama and masque, but the material conditions of her religious observance, with her Catholic chapel, replete with images of the Virgin and other elements of visual and musical display, all duplicated the aesthetic bounty of Counter-Reformation baroque Catholicism. This bounty, it has been argued, found its correlate in Laudian ritual, the spiritual counterpart to the new courtly aesthetic, with its emphasis on ceremony and 'the beauty of holiness'.[38]

Even in his early writings, Milton noted displeasure in this situation at court: 'A dangerous thing, and an ominous thing. to imitate with earnestnesse the fashions of neighbor nations. so the english ran madding after the french in Edward the confessors time': so Milton added to his Commonplace Book, sometime between 1639 and 1641, citing the example of King Edward's French upbringing, and his importation of French customs to England. Unusually for Milton's book, editorializing follows: 'Speed. god turn the omen from these days' (*CPW*, i, 429–30), perhaps reflecting on the French remnants of the 'Norman Yoke' in the English law courts, but more likely thinking of Charles's infatuation with European manners, his match to his French queen, and possibly of the offspring whose upbringing was a source of dispute in the royal marriage contract.

This royal marriage gave Milton much to ponder, both in practice and in theory. In practice, he considered the consequences for the religious settlement of the state; in theory, since Charles's defenders had staked his political identity on a theory of patriarchal authority, order inside the household was a fair topic of political analysis. 'Marriage with Papists dangerous to England', Milton wrote in his Commonplace Book between 1641 and 1643, adjudging that Philip II's marriage to Mary was 'for no other end than to reduce that Island to that religion' (*CPW*, i, 402). The monarch's choice of spouse could threaten the identity of the nation, as attested by the Act of Settlement of 1701, when this danger was eliminated by law barring Catholic succession.

In the late 1630s or early 1640s Milton already harboured suspicions about Charles's allegiance to the Protestant religion. Marriage 'with one of a different religion dangerous', noted Milton in his Commonplace Book sometime between 1639 and 1641, 'for hence Gregory the 15th is so bold as to count Prince Charles a favourer of the Catholic cause, as he calls it, and of the Roman prelacie, because he sought in marriage a daughter of Spain'. In his distinction between the 'Catholic cause' and the 'Roman prelacie', Milton recognizes that the conflicts on the continent and the question of religious settlement within states were two distinct, though equally important, matters. The details of the French Match however offer little consolation: 'the marriage with France also was no lesse dangerous if the conditions obtained by the marquesse D'Effiat, and Richelieu be true. as amoung the rest that the children should be bred in the papists religion till 13 years old' (*CPW*, I, 399). Though summarizing a source, the language here shows something of Milton's view: the word *dangerous* appears repeatedly. This danger was of national and international dimensions. As time went on, Charles's history of matrimonial designs looked more ominous; new pieces of evidence could be added to those already collected. The interpretation gained power through revising the past to explain the present. In *Eikonoklastes*, the interpretation is full-blown, as an entire chapter is devoted to Henrietta Maria.

Fashioning Charles's image

If *The Tenure of Kings and Magistrates* was a defence of the liberties of the subject and an account of sovereignty in a high language of humanist and republican political theory, then *Eikonoklastes* was an all-out assault on Charles's reputation. In it, Milton sought to put to a halt the rising cult of King Charles the martyr.[39] Taking his title from the Greek emperors, who 'broke all superstitious Images to peeces' (*CPW*, III, 343), Milton's work aimed to demolish. It cast doubt on the authorship of the King's Book and condemned those readers who had made the work a 'shrine' (343). It indulged in rumour mongering, repeating the charges that Charles was complicit in the murder of his father (351–2) and that Henrietta Maria was adulterous (419). It assaulted Charles for his plagiarism, seen as equivalent to theft of his subjects' property.[40]

But the book also makes a positive construction. Milton's demolition may be seen more accurately as a demystification, and a substitution of his 'true' account for a false one. Both the King's Book and Milton's response fought over the interpretation of a history which dated back to the king's calling the Long Parliament. Milton hoped to show that events in

Charles's reign, when seen properly, might be woven together so as to reveal a larger, sinister, design. 'These were not *some miscarriages* onely of Goverment, *which might escape*', Milton asserts in refutation of Charles's denial that these instances formed a pattern, 'but a universal distemper, and reducement of law to arbitrary power; not through the evil counsels of *some men*, but through the constant cours & practise of al that were in highest favour' (438). The essence of popery was its combination of Catholicism in religion and absolutism in politics, but the crime of the King's Book was to disguise these evils under a penitential coat. In its reading of past events in light of the present, in its assumptions of a coherence to that history, and in its single-minded hermeneutic of demystification, Milton's *Eikonoklastes* is a masterpiece of Popish-plot thinking.

Milton's reply to the King's Book was published in October 1649, and it is in many ways a defensive work, doggedly responding to the text of *Eikon Basilike* chapter by chapter. Yet Milton's rhetorical stance addressed the double charges of tyranny and popery by a hermeneutic supplied by Popish-plot thinking, so that 'these his fair spok'n words shall be heer fairly confronnted and laid parallel to his own farr differing deeds, manifest and visible to the whole Nation' (347), an exposure of a secret history. Milton wanted to alter the stance of the viewer, to reclaim the king's image from that of being an object of worship to one that could be subject to scrutiny.[41] His writing thus should be placed into that tradition Annabel Patterson has called 'secret history' writing, one that includes *The Kings Cabinet Opened* (1645) (a subject of chapter 21 of *Eikonoklastes*), and Marvell's *Account of the Growth of Popery and Arbitrary Government* (1677).[42] Repeatedly Milton finds the secret motives and deeds underlying Charles's public statements. In looking at the Uxbridge treaty, for example, Milton shows that Charles 'for fashions sake call'd a Parlament, yet by a Jesuitical slight not acknowledg'd though call'd so; but privatly in the Counsel Books inroull'd no Parlament' (526), that Charles gave parliament some say only for appearances' sake. Milton repeatedly draws the distinction between Charles's public and private actions. Thus the theme of the king's theatricality is a cornerstone of Milton's charge.

All the elements are here, at last: the culture war against theatricality, Charles's 'licentious remissness of his Sundays Theater', and his '*Dominical* Jiggs and May-poles'; the accusation of Catholic worship at court, 'the superstitious rigor of his Sundays Chappel', (358); the denunciation of Charles's marriage, attacks on Henrietta Maria (chapter 7);

Charles's subjection to her political influence (538), where 'that *constancy to his Wife* is set in place before Laws and Religion' (541). There are reminders of Charles's support of the Irish rebels (chapter 12); his extortions and breaches of law, 'the abolishing of Parlaments, the displacing of honest Judges, the sale of Offices, Bribery and Exaction not found out to be punish'd, but to be shar'd in' (435), his seeking support from foreign powers (538), his episcopacy tending towards popery, his breaking of the coronation oath to preserve religion (443), his correspondence with the Pope (499), his 'Antichristian fraud' (510), 'his good affection to Papists and Irish Rebels' (537), his likeness to Ahab (393), his fashioning 'both Interests of Tyrannie and Episcopacie . . . incorporat into each other' (511), his failure towards the Protestants of Europe, 'weakning and deserting his Confederats abroad, and with them the Common cause of Religion' (463; also 513–14). Even the Gunpowder Plot (597) is evoked, all amidst the political charges of tyranny.

Popish-plot thinking involves a retrospective gaze, one through which events from the past rise in significance in light of those of the present. In retrospect, the most spectacular instances of Charles's betrayal of the Protestant cause on the continent were the botched expeditions to relieve distressed Huguenots in France. In *Eikonoklastes*, Milton summoned up old memories of La Rochelle, Cadiz, and the Ile de Ré to write a prehistory of Charles's disloyalty to the Protestant cause. Rochelle indeed provided marked evidence for many puritans that England had failed the churches abroad.[43] Buckingham had led the expeditions, becoming the target for opposition to Charles in the late 1620s.[44] As an instance of Popish-plot thinking, where present needs rewrite past history, even Buckingham's name has disappeared from the picture by the time Milton blames Charles for the affair in 1649 (*CPW*, III, 436–7; also 375). Likewise, Milton stands by his 1641 analysis of England's 'Spaniolization' in religion, but in 1649 he lays blame not on the bishops (as he did in 1641), but on the king himself. Charles 'professes *to own his Kingdom from Christ, and to desire to rule for his glory, and the Churches good*: The Pope and the King of *Spain* profess every where as much; and both his practice and all his reasonings, all his enmitie against the true Church we see hath bin the same with theirs' (*CPW*, III, 536–7).

Milton takes pains to counter Charles's self-image, reworking many of the king's favoured images to show either that they are crafty distortions or that they do not suit at all. As if recalling the ceiling of the Banqueting House at Whitehall, Milton makes ample use of the analogy between

James and Solomon. Even in his earlier antiprelatical pamphlets, Milton used this analogy to glance disparagingly at Charles (*CPW*, I, 584, 860), but in *Eikonoklastes* Solomon is remembered for his court, in which Charles, in his upbringing, had been 'soft'nd by a farr wors Court then *Salomons, and so corrupted* by *flatteries*' (*CPW*, III, 569). Milton emphasizes Charles's likeness to Solomon's offspring, the tyrannical Rehoboam, who, when he assumed rule, threatened to 'chastise his people with scorpions' (1 Kings 12:15). Charles indeed 'acted in good earnest what *Rehoboam* did but threat'n, to make his little finger heavier then his Fathers loynes, and to whip us with his two twisted Scorpions, both temporal and spiritual Tyranny, all his Kingdoms have felt' (*CPW*, III, 570; this figure repeats in *Tenure*, III, 208; and twice in *A Defense*, chapter 4). Milton turns the Solomonic analogy into an object of critique.

On another cultural front, Charles's myth of halcyon days comes in for a challenge:

> For the peace we had, what peace was that which drew out the English to a needless and dishonourable voyage against the *Spaniard* at *Cales*? Or that which lent our shipping to a treacherous and Antichristian Warr against the poore Protestants of Rochell our suppliants? What peace was that which fell to rob the *French* by Sea, to the imbarring of all our merchants in that Kingdom? which brought forth that unblest expedition to the Ile of *Rhee*, doubtfull whether more calamitous in the success or in the designe, betraying all the flowre of our military youth, and best Commanders to a shamefull surprisal and execution. This was the peace we had, and the peace we gave, whether to freinds [*sic*] or to foes abroad. (*CPW*, III, 436–7)

Milton not only attacks Charles's foreign policies, he also responds to a cultural war over their representation.

The aim of *Eikonoklastes* is to instigate a re-representation, in aesthetic, hermeneutic and political terms. Satiric in his assessment of the king's self-constructed image, Milton questions both its aesthetic success and its hermeneutic ground: 'He who writes himself *Martyr* by his own inscription, is like an ill Painter, who, by writing on the shapeless Picture which he hath drawn, is fain to tell passengers what shape it is; which els no man could imagin' (*CPW*, III, 575). Fundamentally concerned with the hermeneutic question of how to interpret events, *Eikonoklastes* asserts that the king's image is not self-evident, as the king himself is aware: he needs an inscription to explain himself. Further, the aesthetic charge does not merely call into question matters of artistry, but also the political implications of any poor representation of majesty: 'If the Parliament represent the whole Kingdom, as is sure anough they doe', Milton avers, 'then doth the King represent onely himself; and if a King without his Kingdom be in a civil sense nothing, then without or against the Representative of his whole Kingdom he himself represents nothing, and by consequence his judgement and his negative is as good as nothing' (*CPW*, III, 410). Good representation, then, is that which is truly representative, not the false image of the king presented in *Eikon Basilike*. Thus loyalty is not to that king, nor to his image, but to what the king represents, the people, bound by that Oath of Coronation. When Charles broke that oath, the subjects' obligations to him were also broken: 'the Oathes then were interchang'd, and mutual; stood and fell together' (*CPW*, III, 592–3). If we recall the oath signed by Milton in 1632, we can now see how he might imagine himself disobliged from it in 1649.

In all, the king had pursued a 'privat interest of his own' (*CPW*, III, 383). In another language, at another time, all this might be a precise summary of the charge in Andrew Marvell's *Account of the Growth of Popery and Arbitrary Government*, published anonymously, and a forerunner of the Exclusion Crisis; except that Marvell's work ends with an appeal to his majesty to remedy the evil. In the case of Milton's writing, remedy had already been taken, to execute the king and to abolish monarchy in England.

Milton's approach to Charles in *Eikonoklastes* ought to be seen not merely as an attack against the iconic nature of kingship or against theatricality. It ought, instead, to be considered in light of a history of representations of Charles, built up over the years of his Personal Rule, and responding directly to Charles's policies both political and cultural. In challenging the king's theatricality, Milton takes notice that the chief campaign of the monarch had been a private war against Protestant ideology in favour of continental absolutism and popery, and he recognizes that Charles's cultural policies were indeed a part of his political policies. In this battle over which memories of Charles's reign would survive, at base there was a fundamental disagreement over the nature of political representation, taken in the broadest sense. Would the English be represented by a wilful monarch, or by an accountable representative, parliament? The unmasking of popery was one step towards accountability. With Charles's domestic tyranny seen as a reflection of his relations with Europe, Milton calls up a powerful interpretive scheme. The particular forms taken up by Milton in his challenge to the king's representation were those bequeathed to him by England's fund of national memory.

Notes

I wish to thank David Norbrook for reading a draft of this chapter.

1 David Masson, *The Life of John Milton Narrated in Connexion with the Political, Ecclesiastical, and Literary History of his Time*, 6 vols. (New York: Peter Smith, 1946), I, 217, 257–8; John Milton, *Eikonoklastes*, in *Complete Prose Works of John Milton*, ed. Don M. Wolfe, 8 vols. (New Haven: Yale University Press, 1953–82), III, 589 (hereafter *CPW*).

2 Wilbur Cortez Abbott, ed., *The Writings and Speeches of Oliver Cromwell* (Oxford: Clarendon Press, 1988), II, 1.

3 Paul Stevens, 'Discontinuities in Milton's Early Public Self-Representation', *Huntington Library Quarterly*, 51.4 (1988): 261–80.

4 Martin Dzelzainis, 'Defining Milton's Republicanism', in *Milton and Republicanism*, ed. David Armitage, Armand Himy, and Quentin Skinner (Cambridge University Press, 1995), 3–24; Blair Worden, 'Milton's Republicanism and the Tyranny of Heaven', in *Machiavelli and Republicanism*, ed. Gisela Bock, Quentin Skinner and Maurizio Viroli (Cambridge University Press, 1990), 225–45; Janel Mueller, 'Contextualizing Milton's Nascent Republicanism', in *Of Poetry and Politics: New Essays on Milton and his World*, ed. Paul G. Stanwood (Binghamton, New York: Medieval and Renaissance Texts and Studies, 1994), 1–20; Nicholas von Maltzahn, *Milton's History of Britain: Republican Historiography in the English Revolution* (Oxford: Clarendon Press,1991); and David Norbrook, *Writing the English Republic: Poetry, Rhetoric and Politics, 1627–1660* (Cambridge University Press, 1999).

5 Too often in contemporary scholarship has the Popish Plot been written out of serious analysis by language that stigmatizes it as irrational; words such as 'panics', 'hysteria' and 'fears' downplay the legitimacy of the phenomenon and dismiss it as an object of rational analysis, as did Samuel Butler's opening lines of *Hudibras*. Caroline Hibbard, *Charles I and the Popish Plot* (Chapel Hill: University of North Carolina Press, 1983) and Jonathan Scott, 'England's Troubles, 1603–1702', in *The Stuart Court and Europe: Essays in Politics and Political Culture*, ed. R. Malcolm Smuts (Cambridge University Press, 1996), 20–38, attempt the necessary work of recovery.

6 Peter Lake, 'Anti-Popery: The Structure of a Prejudice', in *Conflict in Early Stuart England: Studies in Religion and Politics, 1603–1642*, ed. Richard Cust and Ann Hughes (New York: Longman, 1989), 72–106; Kevin Sharpe, *The Personal Rule of Charles I* (New Haven: Yale University Press, 1992), 908; Robin Clifton, 'Fear of Popery', in *The Origins of the English Civil War*, ed. Conrad Russell (London: Macmillan, 1975), 162. See also Anthony Milton, *Catholic and Reformed: The Roman and Protestant Churches in English Protestant Thought, 1600–1640* (Cambridge University Press, 1995), 52.

7 J. H. Elliott, 'England and Europe: A Common Malady?', in *Origins of the English Civil War*, ed. Russell, 253.

8 On Milton's iconoclasm, see C. A. Patrides, '"Something like Prophetic Strain": Apocalyptic Configurations in Milton', in *The Apocalypse in English Renaissance Thought and Literature*, ed. C. A. Patrides and J. Wittreich (Manchester University Press, 1984), 207–37; David Loewenstein, *Milton and the Drama of History: Historical Vision, Iconoclasm, and the Literary Imagination* (Cambridge University Press, 1990); or, for a deconstructive approach, Lana Cable, *Carnal Rhetoric: Milton's Iconoclasm and the Poetics of Desire* (Durham, NC: Duke University Press, 1995). On the radical apocalyptic tradition, see David Loewenstein's chapter in this volume.

9 'In Eandem' ['In Proditionem Bombardicam'] and 'In Quintum Novembris (On the
Fifth of November)', in *The Poems of John Milton*, ed. John Carey and Alastair Fowler
(London: Longman, 1968), 34, 45. David Quint explores literary influences on Milton's
Gunpowder poetry, in 'Milton, Fletcher, and the Gunpowder Plot', *Journal of the
Warburg and Courtauld Institutes*, 54 (1991): 261–8; and Stella Purce Revard, the context of
sermons on which Milton draws, in *The War in Heaven: Paradise Lost and the Tradition of
Satan's Rebellion* (Ithaca, NY: Cornell University Press, 1980), 89–93.

10 *Poems of John Milton*, ed. Carey and Fowler, 47.

11 David Cressy, *Bonfires and Bells: National Memory and the Protestant Calendar in
Elizabethan and Stuart England* (London: Weidenfeld & Nicolson, 1989), 150–4.

12 Letter to Alexander Gill, in Masson, *Life of John Milton*, I, 191; Letter to Thomas Young,
'Elegia Quarta', in Carey and Fowler, *Poems of John Milton*, 60. The early date for the
Ahab and Jezebel outburst disputes the idea of Milton as pro-monarchical until quite
late, as in Don M. Wolfe, *Milton in the Puritan Revolution* (New York: Nelson, 1941), 209.
Milton later noted Ahab as a possible topic for his biblical epic (*CPW*, VIII, 556), and the
allusion to 2 Kings 19:2 recurs in his writings about Charles and Henrietta Maria, for
example in *Eikonoklastes*, *CPW*, III, 393.

13 See John T. Shawcross, *John Milton: The Self and the World* (Lexington: University of
Kentucky Press, 1993), 84–92, on familial reasons for his journey. On route disruptions
due to war-torn Europe, see John W. Stoye, *English Travellers Abroad, 1604–1667* (London:
Jonathan Cape, 1952), 176.

14 Righting this balance is Smuts, ed., *Stuart Court and Europe*.

15 Simon L. Adams, 'Spain or the Netherlands? The Dilemmas of Early Stuart Foreign
Policy', in *Before the English Civil War: Essays on Stuart Politics and Government*, ed. H.
Tomlinson (London: Macmillan, 1983), 79–102.

16 Sharpe, *Personal Rule*, 70, 89.

17 J. V. Polišenský, *The Thirty Years' War*, trans. Robert Evans (London: New English
Library, 1974), 238–9.

18 Geoffrey Parker, 'The World Beyond Whitehall: British Historiography and European
Archives', in *Stuart Court and Europe*, ed. Smuts, 281; Jane Ohlmeyer, 'Ireland
Independent: Confederate Foreign Policy and International Relations during the Mid-
Seventeenth Century', in *Ireland: From Independence to Occupation, 1641–1660*, ed. Jane
Ohlmeyer (Cambridge University Press, 1995), 107.

19 Brian Manning, *The English People and the English Revolution* (London: Bookmarks,
1991), 72.

20 Sharpe, *Personal Rule*, 828; S. R. Gardiner, *History of England from the Accession of James I
to the Outbreak of the Civil War, 1603–1642*, 10 vols. (London, 1891), IX, 131–2.

21 Adams, 'Spain or the Netherlands?' See also Simon Adams, 'Foreign Policy and the
Parliaments of 1621 and 1624', in *Faction and Parliament: Essays on Early Stuart History*,
ed. Kevin Sharpe (London: Macmillan, 1978), 139–72.

22 For this tradition, see Paul Christianson, *Reformers and Babylon: English Apocalyptic
Visions from the Reformation to the Eve of the Civil War* (University of Toronto Press, 1978);
B. Capp, 'The Political Dimension of Apocalyptic Thought', in Patrides and Wittreich,
eds. *Apocalypse*, 93–124; and Christopher Hill, *Antichrist in Seventeenth-Century England*
(London: Verso, 1990).

23 Geoffrey Parker, 'The Dutch Revolt and the Polarization of International Politics', in
Geoffrey Parker, *Spain and the Netherlands, 1559–1659* (London: Collins, 1979), 66.

24 Leopold von Ranke, *A History of England Principally in the Seventeenth Century*, 6 vols. (Oxford, 1875), II, 29; Geoffrey Parker, *The Thirty Years' War* (London: Routledge, 1997), 192–202.

25 Hibbard, *Popish Plot*, 30.

26 Martin Butler, *Theatre and Crisis, 1632–1642* (Cambridge University Press, 1984); Thomas Cogswell, 'England and the Spanish Match', in *Conflict in Early Stuart England*, ed. Cust and Hughes, 107–33; Frederick S. Siebert, *Freedom of the Press in England, 1476–1776* (Urbana: University of Illinois Press, 1965), 148–54.

27 H. R. Trevor-Roper, 'Three Foreigners: The Philosophers of the Puritan Revolution', in H. R. Trevor-Roper, *Religion, the Reformation and Social Change* (London: Macmillan, 1967), 252; and Masson, *Life of John Milton*, II, 367–8, 517–18 on Dury; III, 231–5, on Hartlib.

28 S. R. Gardiner, *Constitutional Documents of the Puritan Revolution, 1625–1660* (Oxford: Clarendon Press, 1979), 253. See also Adams, 'Spain or the Netherlands?', 79.

29 *Poems of John Milton*, ed. Carey and Fowler, 48.

30 William E. Burns, 'Signs of the Times: Thomas Jackson and the Controversy over Prodigies in the Reign of Charles I', *Seventeenth Century*, 11.1 (1996): 21–33; Marvin A. Breslow, *A Mirror of England: English Puritan Views of Foreign Nations, 1618–1640* (Cambridge, MA: Harvard University Press, 1970).

31 Siebert, *Freedom of the Press*, 150; on manuscript news, see Harold Love, *Scribal Publication in Seventeenth-Century England* (Oxford: Clarendon Press, 1993), 9–22; Joad Raymond, *The Invention of the Newspaper, 1641–1649* (Oxford: Clarendon Press, 1996), on the newsbook's importance for the outbreak of the Civil War. Meade's newsletters are in Thomas Birch, ed., *The Court and Times of Charles I* (London, 1848); Meade's connections with Milton are explored in Marjorie Hope Nicolson, 'Milton's "Old Damoetas"', *MLN* 41 (1926): 293–300; and John P. Rumrich, 'Mead and Milton', *Milton Quarterly*, 20.4 (1986): 136–41.

32 Jeremiah Whitaker, *Eirenopoias. Christ the Settlement of Unsettled Times*, quoted in Trevor-Roper, *Religion, the Reformation and Social Change*, 46.

33 Ben Jonson, 'An Epistle to a Friend, to perswade him to the Warres', *The Underwood*, in *Ben Jonson*, ed. C. H. Herford and Percy and Evelyn Simpson, 11 vols. (Oxford: Clarendon Press, 1925–63), VIII, 162.

34 *Diary of John Rous, 1625–1642*, ed. M. A. Everett Green, Camden Society, 66 (London, 1856), 101, 121; James Howell, *An Exact Historie of the Late Revolutions in Naples*, trans. Alexander Giraffi (London, 1650).

35 *Moderate Intelligencer*, 190, 191 (2–9 November 1648; 9–16 November 1648).

36 Contrast James A. Freeman, *Milton and the Martial Muse: Paradise Lost and the European Traditions of War* (Princeton University Press, 1980), whose Milton is hostile to war, against Robert Thomas Fallon, *Captain or Colonel: The Soldier in Milton's Life and Art* (Columbia: University of Missouri Press, 1984).

37 Hibbard, *Popish Plot*, 22. R. Malcolm Smuts, *Court Culture and the Origins of a Royalist Tradition in Early Stuart England* (Philadelphia: University of Pennsylvania Press, 1987), 183–5. See also the chapter by Jonathan Wainwright in this volume.

38 Smuts, *Court Culture*, 227–8. See also Gordon Albion, *Charles I and the Court of Rome* (London: Burns, Oates & Washnourne, 1935), 395–8.

39 Florence Sandler, 'Icon and Iconoclast', in *Achievements of the Left Hand: Essays on the Prose of John Milton*, ed. Michael Lieb and J. Shawcross (Amherst: University of

Massachusetts Press, 1974), 160–84, and John R. Knott, Jr., '"Suffering for Truths Sake": Milton and Martyrdom', in *Politics, Poetics, and Hermeneutics in Milton's Prose*, ed. David Loewenstein and James Turner (Cambridge University Press, 1990), 153–70.

40   Richard Helgerson, 'Milton Reads the King's Book: Print, Performance, and the Making of a Bourgeois Idol', *Criticism*, 29.1 (1987): 1–25.

41   Thomas N. Corns, *Uncloistered Virtue: English Political Literature, 1640–1660* (Oxford: Clarendon Press, 1992), 217–20; see my *Milton and the Revolutionary Reader* (Princeton University Press, 1994), 162–8. As Elizabeth Skerpan Wheeler shows in this volume, *Eikon Basilike* rapidly developed an autonomous life; and as Joad Raymond argues, this out-of-controlness of images was true throughout Charles's reign.

42   Annabel Patterson, *Early Modern Liberalism* (Cambridge University Press, 1997), 183–231.

43   Simon L. Adams, 'The Protestant Cause: Religious Alliance with the West European Calvinist Community as a Political Issue in England, 1585–1630' (Oxford, D.Phil. thesis 1972), 420; see C. H. Firth, ed., *The Memoirs of Edmund Ludlow*, 2 vols. (Oxford, 1894), I, 12; and Lucy Hutchinson, *Memoirs of the Life of Colonel Hutchinson*, ed. James Sutherland (Oxford University Press, 1973), 46–7.

44   On Buckingham as a figure for opposition, see James Holstun, '"God Bless Thee, Little David!": John Felton and his Allies', *ELH*, 59 (1992): 513–22.

8

The King's Music

Jonathan P. Wainwright

Any examination of the musical culture at the court of Charles I must begin with an assessment of his musical achievements during the period of his term as Prince of Wales (1616–25). Charles's elder brother, Prince Henry, had formed his own household in the winter of 1609/10 and, until his untimely death in the autumn of 1612, his household was the focus of many important artistic and scientific developments.[1] Prince Henry's musical activities were also noteworthy: his household musicians formed the first new group to be added to the royal music since Henry VIII's reign (a group mainly of singer-lutenists),[2] and his musical patronage is notable for its Italianate interests (particularly in his employment of the musician Angelo Notari).[3] After Charles was created Prince of Wales, on 3 November 1616, he appointed seventeen musicians to his household.[4] He inherited six singer-lutenists from his brother's musicians (Angelo Notari, Thomas Day, Jonas Wrench, Robert Johnson, John Sturt and Thomas Ford) and added six more of his own (Richard Ball/Balls/Bales, his nephew Alfonso Ball, John Coggeshall/Coxall, John Drew, John Daniel and Robert Marsh);[5] however, it was in the field of string consort music which Prince Charles's musicians really made their mark.

Charles employed four of the most eminent composers of consort music, Alfonso Ferrabosco the younger, John Coprario, Orlando Gibbons and Thomas Lupo, and together they were responsible for extending the range of scorings employed in the English fantasia idiom and for the introduction of the violin into contrapuntal music. Prince Charles was himself a skilled performer on the bass viol (having been taught by Alfonso Ferrabosco) and according to John Playford, 'could play his part exactly well on the Bass-Viol, especially of those Incomparable Fancies of Mr Coperario to the Organ'.[6] Coprario was one of the first composers to use the violin in contrapuntal consort music. Although the violin had first appeared at the English court in 1540, it had been used almost exclusively for dance music until about 1620.[7] In 1622 Prince Charles formed a violin and viol ensemble[8] – 'Coperario's Musique' – which consisted of Lupo, John Woodington and Adam Vallet (violins), Ferrabosco II and Coprario (viols) and Gibbons (keyboard).[9] Once the violin had become established as an instrument for 'serious' contrapuntal chamber music, court composers began experimenting with new forms and scorings using mixed groups of violins and viols with keyboard (usually organ) and/or theorbo continuo. One of the new forms to emerge was the fantasia-suite,[10] a fixed three-movement sequence of fantasia and two dances (alman and galliard), which was created by Coprario and seems to have remained a court genre until the Civil War, after which it was more widely disseminated. Another new fantasia scoring that appears to have had its origins in the experiments which were taking place in court circles in the 1620s was that of the 'Great Dooble Base' fantasies, so-called because they use – together with a violin (or treble viol), tenor and/or a bass viol – an instrument a size larger, and tuned a fourth lower, than the normal bass viol. The best-known examples are Orlando Gibbons's three- and four-part 'Great Dooble Base' fantasies.[11] The importance of these court consort pieces cannot be overestimated, for they stand at the head of a tradition that was to culminate in the trio sonatas of Henry Purcell and, as such, perhaps herald the beginnings of the English musical Baroque.

Charles's accession to the throne on 27 March 1625 created a problem. The new king already had a sizeable household of his own that he needed somehow to amalgamate with the personnel inherited from his father. His solution was to retain most of both households, with their existing salaries; only seven of his musicians from his time as Prince of Wales were not reappointed.[12] The extra numbers of musicians necessitated a reorganization of the royal music and the various groups of musicians (such as the 'Musicians for Lutes and Voices' and the 'Musicians for the Violins') came under the overall control of the 'Master of the Musicke', Nicholas Lanier, whose duty it was to oversee both the 'public' and the 'private' secular music-making at court.[13] The 'King's Musicke' provided musical entertainment for court dinners, for dancing, for masques, 'play nights', and intimate chamber music. The public image of the King's Musicke was best displayed in the masques, the most elaborate being James Shirley's *Triumph of Peace*, which was performed at the Banqueting House at Whitehall under the auspices of the Inns of Court on 3 February 1634.[14]

The songs and choruses that survive from the masque – a number of which include instrumental 'simfony' – were composed by William Lawes and are fairly conventional. It seems that the most progressive music was reserved for the more intimate surroundings of the privy chamber. The 'Private Musick' performed chamber music and vocal pieces for the king's private delectation and the musicians continued the innovative work pioneered when Charles was still Prince of Wales.

The adventurous and sophisticated musical tastes of Charles I are revealed in a set of four part-books in Christ Church, Oxford (Mus. 732–5) and a companion organ-book in the Royal Music Library (Manuscript R.M. 24.k.3, housed in the British Library, London) which contain Coprario's fantasia-suites for one or two violins, bass viol and organ, and Orlando Gibbons's fantasies for one or two treble viols, bass viol and 'Great Dooble Basse'. Whereas the Royal Music organ-book is finely bound in black morocco and bears the arms of Charles I, the four Christ Church part-books remain in their original paper covers. The inside front cover of Mus. 732 contains the name 'John Wodenton', and the back cover of Mus. 734 – in a different hand and in very faded ink – is signed 'Woodington'; the latter inscription is very similar to Woodington's signature as found in the Whitelocke Papers at Longleat.[15] Woodington – who appears to have been the owner of the manuscripts – was a violinist at court and was also a vicar choral at St Paul's Cathedral.[16] Christ Church Mus. 732–5 and Royal Music Manuscript 24.k.3 were copied by four scribes, but only one of the copyists has been identified for certain: Stephen Bing, a colleague of Woodington's at St Paul's, contributed a single piece to three of the Christ Church part-books.[17] (We return to Stephen Bing's copying activities and his links with the court below.[18]) Manuscripts such as Christ Church Mus. 732–5 and Royal Music Manuscript 24.k.3 are the only tangible evidence we have for the music performed to – and perhaps even by – the king in his privy chamber.

The confidence of the Caroline court's musical establishment must have taken a knock in the later 1620s with the deaths of a number of its foremost musicians: Orlando Gibbons died suddenly at Canterbury on 5 June 1625 while the court was awaiting the arrival of Queen Henrietta Maria from France, Coprario died in the summer of 1626, Lupo in the winter of 1627/8, and Ferrabosco in March 1628. But the court's musical identity was reaffirmed in 1635 with the appointment of William Lawes as a 'musician in ordinary for the lutes and voices'[19] and the image of a progressive musical culture was secured. William Lawes's consort music represents some of the most adventurous instrumental music of the time and his fantasia-suites and Harp Consorts, in particular, single him out as the heir to Coprario.[20] Towards the end of the 1630s Lawes returned to the composition of fantasies in more traditional scorings with his Consort Setts for five and six viols and organ.[21] This may at first seem surprising, but it appears that the more old-fashioned viol fantasies remained in the court repertoire and were performed alongside the more progressive pieces until the outbreak of the Civil War in 1642 (and possibly beyond, at the Oxford Court).

There survive today in the library of Christ Church, Oxford three inter-related manuscript sets – Mus. 2, 397–408 and 436 ('The Great Set'); Mus. 417–18 and 1080; and Mus. 432 and 612–13 – which have recently been the subject of intense musicological enquiries.[22] The three manuscript collections were copied by two scribes, Stephen Bing (1610–81) and John Lilly (1612–78), whilst working for Christopher, First Baron Hatton (1605–70).[23] The set Mus. 432 and 612–13 is the one most obviously linked with Baron Hatton, for the dark-blue morocco bindings of the three books (an organ-book and two bass viol parts) contain the full Hatton coat of arms.[24] The original contents of the part-books (untitled and unascribed fantasies and ayres for two bass viols and organ by Coprario, Jenkins and Ward) were copied by John Lilly and, at a later date, Stephen Bing added Mico's three-part fantasies to the organ-book (Mus. 432). The Mico fantasies were not, however, copied into the companion part-books (Mus. 612–13), but they do appear in Mus. 417–18 and 1080, which were copied entirely by Stephen Bing. This set, which is incomplete (lacking the tenor book for the four-part pieces), contains three- and four-part viol-consort music by Bull, Coprario, Ferrabosco II, Orlando Gibbons, Jeffreys, Lupo, Mico and Ward. With the exception of the six three-part fantasies by George Jeffreys, the whole contents of Mus. 417–18 and 1080 are duplicated in another collection of instrumental music copied jointly by Bing and Lilly: Mus. 2, 397–408 and 436, the 'Great Set'. This comprehensive collection of larger-scale viol-consort music from the earlier Stuart period consists of a score-book (Mus. 2) and an organ-book (Mus. 436) copied by Stephen Bing, and three sets of part-books copied by John Lilly (Mus. 397–400: four-part works; Mus. 401–2: three-part works, incomplete; and Mus. 403–8: five- and six-part works).[25]

It is important, at this point, to note the fact that Christopher Hatton, the patron of the copyists of these sets, was closely connected with the court during the 1630s and rose to prominence during the Civil War as the king's Comptroller of Household during the years of the Oxford Court, 1642–46.[26] Indeed, it seems from the contents of the manuscripts – a large proportion of the three- to six-part English viol-consort repertoire written before the mid to late 1630s [27] – that their most likely provenance was the court or the household of a nobleman with strong links with the court musicians. This suggestion is supported by the repertoire of the sets. Four of the most eminent composers of consort music are represented: Ferrabosco the younger, Coprario, Orlando Gibbons and Lupo, all of whom had been employed by Charles I when he was still Prince of Wales. The repertoire contained in the Christ Church manuscripts of viol-consort music suggests that they are the product of a court-related circle of scribes working in the mid to late 1630s. This proposed dating is supported by the physical evidence offered by the manuscripts. All three sets of part-books are made up of the best quality royal paper – the type of paper often used for presentation manuscripts – that contains watermarks which can be dated to before 1640.[28] Thus evidence offered by the paper types of the Bing and Lilly manuscripts reinforces the mooted copying date of the mid to late 1630s. This view represents a substantial revision of the previously accepted datings of the 'Great Set' and related manuscripts. It had, until recently, been argued that the sets were retrospective collections copied after 1656.[29] In light of Christopher Hatton and Stephen Bing's links with court musicians, it is now possible to suggest that the manuscripts are of London provenance and were copied in the mid to late 1630s. It is even possible that the Christ Church consort manuscripts were intended as a presentation set for the king but, at the outbreak of Civil War and the disbandment of the regular court musical establishment, the project floundered and was left unfinished. Whatever the true *raison d'être* of the Christ Church sets of viol-consort music, we should be grateful to Christopher Hatton and his copyists, John Lilly and Stephen Bing, for preserving such a complete record of the instrumental music performed at court before the 'hostilities'. Indeed it seems that the Christ Church consort manuscripts represent one of the last great musical enterprises of the royalist court before the outbreak of the Civil War.

Instrumental music was not the only type of music heard in the privy chamber. The king would have been entertained regularly with songs by the likes of Henry Lawes. Over 430 songs by Lawes survive and many were the product of court circles in the 1630s. He set over forty poems by Carew and at least fourteen by Herrick, as well as poems by Suckling, Waller, Milton, Lovelace and Cartwright. The musical style that Lawes adopted in

his songs – often freely declamatory, sometimes even approaching recita-
tive – was ideally suited for an effective and direct projection of the text.[30]
The close relationship between Lawes and the Caroline court poets is
reflected in the title pages of the printed song-books and poetry collections and, in the words of David Greer, 'in this courtly milieu . . . it is possible to discern something of that rapport between writer and musician
that had earlier been a feature of French and Italian cultural life'.[31]

We have so far been concerned with the King's Musicke, whose duty it
was to provide secular music for the king and court. The other musical
establishment at court was the Chapel Royal, a body of persons within the
Royal Household responsible for the ordering and performance of divine
service in the sovereign's presence (whether it be at Whitehall, Hampton
Court, Windsor or elsewhere). In the seventeenth century the Chapel
Royal comprised (with occasional fluctuations) a dean and thirty-two
'Gentlemen', of which seven or eight were chaplains and the rest 'singing-
men'. A sub-dean, who was responsible for the daily running of the
chapel, was elected from the chaplains, and the organists and a Master of
the Children, responsible for the twelve choristers, came from the ranks of
the singing-men.[32] The basic musical duties of the Chapel Royal were the
performance at morning and evening prayer, but they also performed at
royal christenings, weddings and funerals and at state occasions such as
coronations. Gentlemen were paid £40 a year and, according to the
'Orders for the Attendance' drawn up while William Laud was dean, were
required to attend daily, one month on and one month off (i.e., only half
the Gentlemen were on duty), except for Sundays and major festivals,
when all were required to attend.[33] This system, together with the good
holidays (three months in the summer and eight other weeks over the
year), enabled some Gentlemen to also hold posts at nearby foundations
such as St Paul's or Westminster Abbey. The prestige and attractive rates
of pay meant that many of the country's best composers and singers were
employed as Gentlemen and, in both repertoire and performance standards, the Chapel Royal provided a model for cathedrals and collegiate
establishments to follow.

However, the repertoire of the Chapel Royal in the 1630s – although
more adventurous than many cathedrals – was still relatively conservative.[34] Sacred and devotional music in England, it seems, remained fundamentally old-fashioned in approach and showed little or no awareness of
the Italianate *stile nuovo*. It has been noted that the only publications to
contain *stile nuovo* sacred compositions before the Commonwealth period

were Walter Porter's *Madrigales and Ayres* (London, 1632)[35] – a single sacred work, 'Praise the Lord' – and William Child's *First Set of Psalmes of III. Voyces Fitt for Private Chappels or Other Private Meetings with a Continued Base either for the Organ or Theorbo Newly Composed after the Italian Way* (London, 1639).[36] It is noteworthy that as late as 1639 Child is describing his Psalms as 'after the Italian Way', as if it was something unusual. The title of Child's publication also emphasizes the private nature of his music, as if 'modern' Italianate music was considered best suited to private devotional meetings rather than public liturgy. With just a few exceptions, the Anglican liturgical repertoire, as performed in cathedrals and the Chapel Royal, was extremely conservative.[37] This is reflected in the contents of John Barnard's *First Book of Selected Church Musick* (London, 1641): of the twenty-one composers represented in the publication, nine were born before 1550 and none was born after 1600.[38]

Recent research has, however, revealed a hitherto unnoticed area of court musical activity which was closely in touch with the latest progressive musical styles. Charles I's queen, Henrietta Maria, maintained her own household, a court within a court. One of the principal articles of Henrietta Maria's marriage treaty was that she could have her own chapel in which she was free to exercise her Roman Catholic faith. Her private chapel, at Somerset House, was staffed by an entourage of Capuchin friars, and the music was provided by French musicians and an English organist: first Richard Dering (1625–30) and then Richard Mico (1630–c.1642).[39] Dering was one of the earliest English composers to contribute to the new genre of the small-scale *concertato* motet, and his Latin motets for two and three voices and basso continuo were most likely written for performance at the queen's Roman Catholic services.[40] Dering spent time in both Venice and Rome in the second decade of the century, and the influence of the most up-to-date Italian music is apparent in his motets.[41] It seems, then, that the interest in Italian music (which had perhaps reached its zenith in Elizabeth I's reign) did, in court-related circles, continue in the first half of the seventeenth century. This is further indicated by the fact that the London bookseller Robert Martin thought it worthwhile to publish five catalogues of Venetian music between 1633 and 1650.[42] It has been demonstrated that one of Martin's main customers was the aforementioned Christopher Hatton (see page 165, above), and that most of his music library – perhaps as many as 200 items, the great majority of which are Italian publications – survives today in Christ Church, Oxford.[43] What is more, manuscripts of Latin motets and a Latin

Mass which also survive were copied from these printed sources by Hatton's musicians, George Jeffreys and Stephen Bing. In light of Hatton's court associations, I have suggested that this up-to-date Italian music represented the repertoire of Henrietta Maria's Roman Catholic chapel.[44] The music – by Claudio Monteverdi's contemporaries, such as Alessandro Grandi, Agostino Facchi, Francesco Maria Marini, Tarquinio Merula and Giovanni Felice Sances – was designed for performance by only a handful of singers and a continuo player, and this most progressive Italian repertoire would be most suitable for the educated tastes of noblemen. The manuscripts contain a substantial number of motets with Marian texts, such as Marian antiphons, Song of Songs texts, and Litanies of our Lady and a Latin Mass by Alessandro Grandi.[45]

Henrietta Maria had been at the height of her power and influence in England in the 1630s. She had, on 14 September 1632, laid the foundation stone for her chapel at Somerset House, which was designed by Inigo Jones and dedicated to the Virgin. The chapel was opened with conspicuous ceremony on 8 December 1636 and thereafter became an embarrassingly public magnet for Roman Catholics and a large number of converts.[46] The discomfiture of the Anglican establishment was such that Archbishop Laud was forced to issue a proclamation against taking Mass. The queen promptly held a Midnight Mass at the Somerset House chapel for all recent converts in defiance of Laud. This was also the period when statues to the Virgin, which had been broken or defaced after the Reformation, began to return to public prominence, and in 1635 a discourse, 'wherein . . . the *B. Virgin Mary* Mother of God, is defended, and vindicated', was published under the title *Maria Triumphans*. The anonymous author dedicated the book to Henrietta Maria and in the dedication he explicitly associated the queen's name with that of the Virgin. Indeed there can be little doubt that the author was intending the 'Maria' in his title to be dually interpreted as the Blessed Virgin Mary in Heaven and Queen Henrietta Maria, the Virgin's champion and representative on earth. (Incidentally Maria was the king's preferred name for his queen.) The presence of so many Marian pieces in the manuscripts demonstrates that we have here the remnants of the musical repertoire of Henrietta Maria's Roman Catholic chapel – a repertoire that was a symbolic representation of not only the Virgin Mary but of the queen herself.[47] There are, too, a few hints that this progressive repertoire was used in the king's presence. In a number of the manuscripts certain texts are different from their original printed versions; for example, Alessandro Grandi's two-voice motets 'Ave sanctissima Maria' and 'Tu pulchra es Maria' have become 'Ave sanctissime Messia' and 'Tu dulcis es, Messia'. The original Marian versions would be unacceptable for the king's worship and thus it appears that the texts were modified to suit a more Protestant taste. Perhaps we have here an indication of the music that was performed to 'his Sacred Majestie in his Solitudes and Sufferings'.[48]

As research has progressed on the music manuscripts associated with the Caroline court, more and more we have come to realize that Charles I's adventurous and sophisticated artistic tastes were of immense significance in the development of English music. The king was surrounded by the best musicians of the age and was able to create an active and progressive musical culture at court, and it was to the court which the country looked for the latest musical fashions. The system of manuscript dissemination produced by the court network – the web of contacts created by movement from the provinces to London of patrons and their households (including musicians) – was perfect for insuring the spread of up-to-date styles of composition, and there can be little doubt that, had it not been for the Civil War and the Commonwealth years, England would have been at the forefront of the musical Baroque.

The King's Music, in some ways, is less tractable to ideological interpretation, than, for example, the images produced by the king's painters, or the texts of masques or panegyrical lyrics. Moreover, in the context of musicological research, we are, perhaps, both more aware of what we do not yet know about the conditions of cultural production in the early Stuart period, and more actively engaged in the recovery of a proper understanding of those conditions. Nevertheless, the musical dimension must be seen as a vital component in the life of the courts of Charles I and Henrietta Maria, and one which both reflected their own cultural agendas and shaped how they were perceived.

Musicians and composers under royal patronage led and dominated their disciplines at least as surely as court painters set standards and objectives in the visual arts for the contemporary cultural and social elite. Music and poetry had in the context of Caroline song an interanimating relationship more productive, probably, than at any other time in English musical – and literary – history. Masque, so often interpreted as the paradigmatic early Stuart literary form and so often squeezed to give up its political messages, owed as much to dance, to music, and to song as to the stage designs of Inigo Jones or the texts of court poets. The splendour of masque, its display and celebration of regal power, were underwritten by the achievements and the assurance of the King's Music. Again, musico-logical research is currently disclosing in the music associated with the queen's chapel a significant manifestation in the heart of the Stuart estab-lishment of a different aesthetic, based on Italianate values and assump-tions, and motivated by the spirit of the Counter-Reformation. The disruption of the displacement of the king's court to Oxford, Henrietta Maria's return to France, and the eventual dispersal of what remained of the King's Music constituted as poignant a symbol of the impact of civil war as the fate of the Caroline literary culture, and its impact on English musical development was arresting. The fulfilment of the Caroline court's musical promise had to wait until the Restoration.

Notes

1 See in particular Roy Strong, *Henry, Prince of Wales and England's Lost Renaissance* (London: Thames and Hudson, 1986).

2 Peter Holman, *Four and Twenty Fiddlers: The Violin at the English Court, 1540–1690* (Oxford University Press, 1993), 197–211.

3 Ian Spink, 'Angelo Notari and his *Prime Musiche Nuove*', *Monthly Musical Record*, 87 (1957): 168–77; Pamela Willetts, 'A Neglected Source of Monody and Madrigal', *Music & Letters*, 43 (1962): 329–39; 'Autographs of Angelo Notari', *Music & Letters*, 50 (1969): 124–6; Holman, *Four and Twenty Fiddlers*, 201–5; and Jonathan P. Wainwright, *Musical Patronage in Seventeenth-Century England: Christopher, First Baron Hatton (1605–1670)* (Aldershot, VT: Scolar Press, 1997), 162–5 and 191–4.

4 For details see Andrew Ashbee, *Records of English Court Music*, IV (Snodland: the author, 1991), 216–30.

5 Holman, *Four and Twenty Fiddlers*, 198.

6 John Playford, *An Introduction to the Skill of Musick* (London, 10/1683). This is the first edition to make reference to the king's performing ability; previous editions which contain the section are concerned only with the king's musical preference: 'And for Instrumental Musick none pleased him like those incomparable Fantazies for one Violin and Basses Viol, to the organ, Composed by Mr Coprario' (4th–7th editions; 1664, 1666, 1667 and 1670). All editions subsequent to 1683 repeat the version of the 10th edition.

7 See Peter Holman, 'The English Royal Consort in the Sixteenth Century', *Proceedings of the Royal Musical Association*, 109 (1982/3): 39–59, and Holman's *Four and Twenty Fiddlers*, *passim*.

8 Dated from John Woodington's petition to Charles I (12 May 1625), in which he states that he had been a member of 'Coperario[']s musique 3 yeres' (BL Add. MS 64,883, fo. 57).

9 See Ashbee, *Records*, IV, 217–30.

10 The term *Fantasia-Suite* is modern; see Christopher D. S. Field, 'Fantasia-Suite', *New Grove Dictionary of Music and Musicians*, ed. Stanley Sadie (London: Macmillan, 1980), VI, 392–3.

11   Gordon Dodd, ed., *Thematic Index of Music for Viols* (London: Viola da Gamba Society, 1980–), Gibbons nos. 1–4 (*a* 3) and nos. 1–2 (*a* 4). Gibbons's four three-part fantasies for the 'Great Dooble Base' in Ireland, Dublin, Archbishop Marsh's Library, MS Z2.1.13 are followed by three anonymous fantasies with the same scoring (treble, bass and 'Great Dooble Base' viols); these three anonymous fantasies had – until recently – been attributed to Gibbons due to their scoring and position in the manuscript. However, Richard Charteris – 'A Postscript to John Coprario: A Thematic Catalogue of his Music with a Biographical Introduction (New York, 1977)', *Chelys*, 11 (1982): 16–17 – has recently discovered a fragment of one of the three fantasies attributed to Coprario. This fragment, inserted between the pages of a copy of Ernest David and Mathis Lussy, *Histoire de la Notation Musicale* (Paris, 1882) in Case Western Reserve University Library, Cleveland, Ohio, suggests that the three three-part fantasies for the 'Great Dooble Base' (*Thematic Index*, 'Gibbons' nos. 5–7) are actually by Coprario. See also Oliver Neighbour, 'Orlando Gibbons (1583–1625): The Consort Music', *Early Music*, 11 (1983): 355–6, where it is argued, on stylistic grounds, that the three anonymous fantasies are by Coprario. Peter Holman – 'George Jeffries and the Great Dooble Base', *Chelys*, 5 (1973/4): 79–80 – noted that George Jeffreys calls for a 'Great Basse' viol in the 'Symphonies' to 'Felice Pastorella' (BL Add. MS 10,338, fos. 51v–6) and, due to the Hatton family's patronage of Orlando Gibbons, speculated that the Hatton family were the owners of a single example of the 'Great Dooble Base'. He has since withdrawn this suggestion – *Four and Twenty Fiddlers*, 216–17 – in light of the recently discovered references to a 'greate base Vyall' at court (see Ashbee, *Records*, III, 134 and 138, and IV, 215) and the identification of pieces by Coprario which use the instrument.

12   Holman, *Four and Twenty Fiddlers*, 226.

13   Lanier, the first holder of the post of Master of the King's Musicke, was appointed in 1626 at a salary of £200 per annum (see Ashbee, *Records*, III, 19). His service to the king extended beyond musical matters for he was sent to Italy a number of times between 1625 and 1628 to negotiate the purchase of paintings from the Gonzaga collection at Mantua (see Ian Spink, 'Lanier in Italy', *Music and Letters*, 40 (1959): 242–52). See also Michael I. Wilson, *Nicholas Lanier: Master of the King's Musicke* (Aldershot, VT: Scolar Press, 1994).

14   *The Triumph of Peace* is not, strictly speaking, a court masque, for although it was presented to the court, it was not performed entirely by courtiers. However, many members of the King's Musicke were involved; for details see Murray Lefkowitz, 'The Longleat Papers of Bulstrode Whitelocke: New Light on Shirley's *Triumph of Peace*', *Journal of the American Musicological Society*, 18 (1965): 42–60; A. J. Sabol, 'New Documents on Shirley's Masque *The Triumph of Peace*', *Music and Letters*, 47 (1966): 10–26; T. Orbison and R. F. Hill, eds., 'The Middle Temple Documents Relating to James Shirley's *The Triumph of Peace*', *Malone Society Collections*, 12 (1983): 31–84; and J. Limon, 'Neglected Evidence for James Shirley's *The Triumph of Peace* (1634)', *Records of Early English Drama Society Newsletter*, 13.2 (1988): 2–9. See also Kevin Sharpe, 'The Caroline Court Masque', in *Criticism and Compliment: The Politics of Literature in the England of Charles I* (Cambridge University Press, 1987), 179–264.

15   Longleat, Whitelocke Papers, parcel II, no. 9, item 6 f. 5. Woodington's signature is reproduced in Lefkowitz, 'The Longleat Papers', plate 1, no. 5.

16   In a petition to Charles I dated 12 May 1625, Woodington describes himself as 'Musician to K[ing] James 6 yeres, and to His Ma[jes]tie in Coperario[']s musique 3 yeres' (BL

Add. MS 64,883, fo. 57) and his name appears in court records until 1647 (see Ashbee, *Records*, III, *passim*). Woodington was a vicar choral at St Paul's from *c*. 1628 to 1645 (see Pamela Willetts, 'John Barnard's Collections of Viol and Vocal Music', *Chelys*, 20 (1991): 34–6).

17   Willetts – 'John Barnard's Collections', 35 – has suggested that the main scribe may be John Tomkins (1586–1638), a court musician and also a colleague of Bing's and Woodington's at St Paul's Cathedral. The circumstantial evidence makes this an attractive proposition. John Woodington's handwriting does not appear to be present in the manuscripts despite the fact that, on 15 February 1635, Woodington was paid £20 'for a whole sett of Musicke Bookes by him p[ro]vided & prickt w[i]th all Coperaries & Orlando Gibbons theire Musique, by his Ma[jesty's] speciall Com[m]and and Warr[an]t' (Public Record Office AO1/394/72; see also Public Record Office LC 5/134, p. 43: 'A Warr[an]t for paym[en]t of XXli unto Mr John Woodington for a new sett of bookes for Cooperarios Musique, by his Ma[jes]t[y's] speciall com[m]annd. Febr[uary]. 20. 1634 [NS 1635]'). For full details, see Wainwright, *Musical Patronage*, 61–3.

18   For details of Bing's career and copying activities see Sarah Boyer and Jonathan Wainwright, 'From Barnard to Purcell: The Copying Activities of Stephen Bing', *Early Music*, 23 (1995): 620–48, and Wainwright, *Musical Patronage*, 52–114 and 160–77.

19   See Ashbee, *Records*, III, 82. William Lawes's links with the court must predate his appointment in 1635. The earliest version of his Royal Consort (suites of dances) appears to date back to the early 1630s and thus it is possible that he was composing for the Lutes and Voices several years before his official court appointment. His elder brother, Henry, was appointed as 'a musician for the voices' in 1631 (see Ashbee, *Records*, III, 57); this would presumably have given William access to court musicians, if not to the court itself.

20   See Murray Lefkowitz, *William Lawes* (London: Routledge and Kegan Paul, 1960), 88–125; Holman, *Four and Twenty Fiddlers*, 262–5; and David Pinto, *'For ye Violls': The Consort and Dance Music of William Lawes* (Richmond: Fretwork, 1995), *passim*.

21   See Pinto, *'For ye Violls'*, 70–140.

22   See Jonathan P. Wainwright, 'The Christ Church Viol-Consort Manuscripts Reconsidered: Christ Church, Oxford Music Manuscripts 2, 397–408 and 436; 417–18 and 1080; and 432 and 612–13', in *John Jenkins and his Time: Studies in English Consort Music*, ed. A. Ashbee and P. Holman (Oxford University Press, 1996), 189–241; and Wainwright, *Musical Patronage*, 66–90.

23   See Pamela Willetts, 'John Lilly, Musician and Music Copyist', *Bodleian Library Record*, 7 (1967): 307–11; 'Stephen Bing: A Forgotten Violist', *Chelys*, 18 (1989): 3–17; D. Pinto, 'The Music of the Hattons', *Research Chronicle [of] The Royal Musical Association*, 23 (1990): 79–108; and Pamela Willetts, 'John Lilly: a Redating', *Chelys*, 21 (1992): 27–38.

24   Wainwright, *Musical Patronage*, plate 2.

25   For full descriptions and inventories of the manuscripts of viol-consort music copied by Bing and Lilly see Wainwright, *Musical Patronage*, part 2, *passim*.

26   For full details of Hatton's career see ibid., 3–24.

27   Five of the eleven composers of viol consort music represented in the sets died before the third decade of the seventeenth century (Bull, Coprario, Ferrabosco II, Orlando Gibbons and Lupo); Ward died in 1638; and all the works of the younger composers in the set (Coleman, Jeffreys, Jenkins, Mico and White) appear to be early works written before *c*. 1640: see, e.g., Andrew Ashbee, 'The Four-Part Consort Music of John

Jenkins', *Proceedings of the Royal Musical Association*, 96 (1969/70): 29–42; 'John Jenkins, 1592–1678: The Viol Consort Music in Four, Five and Six Parts', *Early Music*, 6 (1978): 492–500; John Bennett and Pamela Willetts, 'Richard Mico', *Chelys*, 7 (1977): 43–6; Ernest H. Meyer, rev. Diana Poulton, *Early English Chamber Music* (London: Faber & Faber, 1982), *passim*; Andrew Ashbee, *The Harmonious Musick of John Jenkins*, 1, *The Fantasias for Viols* (Surbiton: Toccata Press, 1992), *passim*; and Wainwright, *Musical Patronage*, 132–59.

28   For full details of the watermarks in the sets, see Wainwright, *Musical Patronage*, 82–3; and the first instalment of the Viola da Gamba Society *Index of Manuscripts Containing Music for Viols*, ed. Andrew Ashbee, Robert Thompson and Jonathan P. Wainwright (forthcoming).

29   See for example: Willetts, 'John Lilly', 311; John Harper, ed., 'Orlando Gibbons: Consort Music', *Musica Britannica*, XLVIII (London: Stainer and Bell, 1951–), xv–xxix; Michael Hobbs, ed, *Orlando Gibbons: Six Fantasies* (London: Faber & Faber, 1982), viii; John Harper, 'The Distribution of the Consort Music of Orlando Gibbons in Seventeenth-Century Sources', *Chelys*, 12 (1983): 3–22; and Pinto, 'Music of the Hattons', 79–80.

30   For full details, see Ian Spink, *English Song: Dowland to Purcell* (London: Batsford, 1974), 75–99.

31   David Greer, 'Vocal Music I: Up to 1660', in *The Blackwell History of Music in Britain: The Seventeenth Century*, ed. Ian Spink (Oxford: Basil Blackwell, 1992), 169.

32   See Edward F. Rimbault, *The Old Cheque-Book . . . of the Chapel Royal* (London, 1872); and David Baldwin, *The Chapel Royal: Ancient & Modern* (London: Duckworth, 1990).

33   Rimbault, *Old Cheque Book*, 71–3.

34   For an indication of the Chapel Royal repertoire in the 1630s, see G. E. P. Arkwright, 'The Chapel Royal Anthem Book of 1635', *Musical Antiquary*, 2 (1910/11): 108–13.

35   See Ian Spink, 'Walter Porter and the Last Book of English Madrigals', *Acta Musicologica*, 26 (1954): 18–36; and 'An Early English Strophic Cantata (Porter's Farewell)', *Acta Musicologica*, 27 (1955): 138–40. Spink stresses the progressive Italianate elements of the madrigals and cantata in Porter's *Madrigales and Ayres*.

36   Robert Thompson, 'George Jeffreys and the *Stile Nuove* in English Sacred Music: A New Date for his Autograph Score, British Library Add. MS 10,338', *Music & Letters*, 70 (1989): 318.

37   The exceptions include William Child's anthems 'Bow down thine ear' (4vv), 'O God, wherefore art thou absent' (4vv), 'Turn thou us' (verse anthem) and 'Woe is me' (4vv), which are 'successful essays in the *stile nuovo*'; and Child's Te Deum and Jubilate 'for Dr Cosin' include *stile concitato* choral writing (see Peter le Huray, *Music and the Reformation in England, 1549–1660*, 2nd edn (Cambridge University Press, 1978), 360–3).

38   It should be noted that Barnard purposely excluded works by living composers, but even so the conservative nature of the Anglican liturgical repertoire is revealed.

39   For details of Henrietta Maria's musical establishment see Ian Spink, 'The Musicians of Queen Henrietta-Maria: Some Notes and References in English State Papers', *Acta Musicologica*, 36 (1964): 177–82; Bennett and Willetts, 'Richard Mico', 35–40 and 46; and Ashbee, *Records*, III, 244–52. It seems that the French musicians left England in 1642–3.

40   Dering's motets appear to have remained in the repertoire throughout the 1630s and 1640s and, surprisingly, were even popular during the Commonwealth; their appeal

was such that John Playford published a substantial number of them in two publications entitled *Cantica Sacra* in 1662 and 1674.

41 For full details see Peter Platt, 'Richard Dering: An Account of his Life and Work', B.Litt. thesis (Oxford, 1951/2); 'Dering's Life and Training', *Music & Letters*, 33 (1952): 41–9; 'Perspectives of Richard Dering's Vocal Music', *Studies in Music*, 1 (University of Western Australia, 1967): 56–66; and 'Dering, Richard', *New Grove Dictionary*, v, 382–3.

42 See Donald W. Krummel, 'Venetian Baroque Music in a London Bookshop', *Music and Bibliography: Essays in Honour of Alec Hyatt King*, ed. O. Neighbour (London: Saur, 1980), 1–27, and Wainwright, *Musical Patronage*, 28–30.

43 For full details of the Hatton collection see Wainwright, *Musical Patronage*, *passim*.

44 Wainwright, *Musical Patronage*, 169–77, and Jonathan P. Wainwright, 'Images of Virtue and War: Music in Civil War Oxford', in *William Lawes, 1602–1645: Essays on His Life, Times and Work*, ed. Andrew Ashbee and Lynn Hulse (London and Brookfield, VT: Ashgate, 1998), 121–42.

45 Included in Grandi's *Il Primo Libro de Motetti* (Venice, 1610).

46 The chapel had been planned as early as 1623 as part of Charles's scheme to entice the Spanish Infanta into marriage. See [Cyprien de Gamaches], *Mémoires de la Mission des Capucins*, ed. A. de Valence (Paris, 1881), 29 and 34–7; and Thomas Birch, *The Court and Times of Charles I*, II (London, 1848), 176 and 310–12.

47 See also Erica Veevers, *Images of Love and Religion: Queen Henrietta Maria and Court Entertainments* (Cambridge University Press, 1989), 75–109.

48 From the subtitle to John Wilson's *Psalterium Carolinum* of 1657, which was, in turn, taken from the title of John Gauden's recasting of Charles I's record of his sufferings and religious meditations: *Eikon Basilike, The Pourtraicture of his Sacred Majestie in his Solitudes*.

9

The visual image of Charles I

John Peacock

Like his father, Charles I was not given to appearing before his people, however successful such public self-exposure might have been for their predecessor Queen Elizabeth. Nor was he very keen to make himself available to his courtiers, at least not as freely as King James was: within the palace of Whitehall, entry to the royal presence was carefully regulated, as were the King's appearances before the court, both for the diurnal routine and for special ceremonial occasions. But Charles's reticence in exhibiting his person was complemented by a close attention to the ways in which that person was represented. As a connoisseur, collector and patron of the visual arts, he was well qualified to plan and oversee the formulation of his own image. In facile historical retrospect, this image has become equated with the portraits of Van Dyck; but Charles employed other artists both English and European to help carry out his cultural policies, and concerned himself with other visual media besides painting, from the small-scale imagery of coins and medals to the hugely spectacular projects of self-representation in the court masques. While the royal person was relatively secluded, the royal image was made manifest.

This contrast, given a highly personal accentuation by Charles I, was endemic in the institution of early modern kingship. The King's existence was protected and enclosed by a privileged group of courtiers, household officials and servants, while the signs of his power were, as far as possible, broadcast to his subjects at large. How far this was in fact possible is not altogether clear. John Donne, as a politically aspiring subject of James I, makes an aggressive joke on this point in 'The Canonization'. When the harassed poet-lover tries to divert his imaginary critic's attention elsewhere, by urging

> get you a place,
> Observe his honour, or his grace,
> Or the King's reall or his stamped face
> Contemplate,[1]

there is a sneering hint that accumulating wealth would be a vulgar second best to advancement at court, but he basically implies that gloating over the royal countenance impressed on one's money or seeing it in the flesh are closely related forms of gratification, available only to a fortunate minority. The poet is obviously not referring to someone who handles halfpennies or farthings, which were not 'stamped' with the King's 'face' but made do with simple heraldic symbols, nor pieces of a penny or twopence, where the 'face' was on a tiny scale; he refers to someone familiar with silver crowns and gold sovereigns, where the King's 'portrait' (a term with a very general sense in this period) appears skilfully designed and ideologically charged. In other words, some of the signs of the King's power, such as his portrait on the coinage, may operate within quite a narrow scope, as if being a target of ideological pressure were an aspect of social privilege. The diffusion of the royal image did not always maximize the effect of political symbolism in promoting political power.

Given the doctrine of divine right, disseminating the King's image could not be a matter of simple advertisement. If the office and the person of the King were sacred, then his image, however far it partook or did not partake of this sacred quality, required a certain reverence. Contemporaries noted that this reverence could be compromised in two obvious ways, by unauthorized (and therefore probably unskilful) representation or by a demeaning environment. They knew that the Elizabethan government had acted to suppress clumsily painted portraits of the Queen, which, according to Walter Raleigh writing in the next reign, 'by her own commandment were knockt in pieces, and cast into the fire'.[2] John Evelyn, in a later generation, told a racier version of the story, with criticism of a monarch who had let her image become too available:

> Had *Queen Elizabeth* been circumspect, there had not been so many vile
> *copies* multiplied from an ill Painting; as being call'd in, and brought to
> *Essex*-house (Where my L. of *Leicester* then lived), did for several years,
> furnish the *Pastry-men* with *Peels* for the use of their Ovens.[3]

Evelyn was writing just after the Restoration, and pleading with Charles II to follow the well-known example of Alexander the Great, who granted monopolies in representing his person to the best available artists: Apelles the painter, Lysippus the sculptor, and Pyrgoteles the gem engraver, who was licensed 'to carve his Effigies' on a small scale:

> We wish the same might please his *Majesty*, and that none save such as for their excellent tallent had particular indulgence, might any more dare to represent his sacred person in *painting*, or *Carving*, then in his *Coyne* and Royal Signature: for it is seriously a reprochfull thing only, to behold how it is profan'd by the hand of so many vile, and wretched Bunglers . . . as blush not daily to expose their own shame, in so precious and rever'd a Subject.[4]

Evelyn's major points of reference are not aesthetic taste or political effect, but the sacred and the profane.

He goes straight on to complain of a second danger to the royal image: that it may be displayed in an ignominious setting. In a scandalized tone, he singles out the habit of using the monarch's portrait as an inn sign: 'that the Heads of *Kings* and *Heros* should be permitted to hang for Signes, among *Cats*, and *Owles*, *Dogs* and *Asses*, at the pleasure of every *Tavern* and *Tippling-house*, we have frequently stood in admiration of'.[5]

James Howell, travelling on the continent some decades earlier, had contrasted this popular, undisciplined English custom with a more seemly method of diffusing the royal image throughout France. Observing the many commemorative pictures and statues of the assassinated Henri IV to be seen in the localities, he wrote to a friend: 'there's scarce a Market-Town, but hath him erected in the Market-place, or o'er some Gate, not upon sign-posts, as our *Henry VIII*'.[6] Howell identifies two potentially conflicting attitudes: one shows a proper deference to the ruler of the state, made visible through the regulated structures of civic society; the other assimilates the ruler's portrait into popular culture, making it familiar and commonplace, and leaving it to jostle for attention amidst a mob of images.

This conflict was dramatized in an episode of the 1630s involving a statue of Charles I. The King had presented his bust, cast in bronze by the court sculptor Hubert Le Sueur, to the town of Portsmouth. Its ostensible purpose was to commemorate his safe return to England in 1623, after his romantic but imprudent journey, while Prince of Wales, to woo the Infanta in Spain; it may also have been a covert tribute to the unpopular favourite Buckingham, the moving spirit of the Spanish adventure, who had been stabbed to death in Portsmouth in 1628. The bust was placed in the Square Tower, facing up the High Street, which was unsurprisingly

punctuated with inn signs. Lord Wimbledon, the royal governor and com-
mander of the garrison, decided that these signs had now become an
affront to the King's bust, and wrote to the corporation accordingly:

> Whereas at my last being at Portsmouth I did recommend the beautify-
> ing of your streetes by setting in the Signes of your Innes to the houses
> as they use in all Civill Townes, Soe now I must recommend it to yo.ᵂ
> more earnestly in regard of his Ma.ᵗˢ figure or Statue that it hath pleased
> his Ma.ᵗⁱᵉ to honor your Towne with more then any other, for that those
> signes of your Innes doe not onely obscure his Ma.ᵗˢ figure but outface it
> as yo.ᵂ yourselves may well perceive.⁷

This is not merely a complaint about visibility. The key word is 'outface',
which vibrates not just with emphatic reproval but with excessive
meaning: it declares that there is a hierarchy even among images, while
admitting that they are all in competition, and envisages them confronting
each other with challenging looks. The letter goes on to address this
anxiety with a sturdy argument: the King's statue is equivalent to the King,
'for that any disgrace offered his Ma.ᵗᵉˢ figure is asmuch as to himselfe'. To
reinforce this point, the governor concludes by ordering the garrison to
doff their hats whenever they pass the statue, and by hoping (but in a que-
rulously insistent tone) that the citizens will do the same without his
having to command it.

   This directive is couched in terms of respect for the King's honour
rather than reverence for his sacred nature, although it worries at the same
problem identified by Howell and Evelyn. How can the dissemination of
the King's image be regulated and made most effective? How can that
image, even if sent into the public domain by royal policy, be guaranteed
to exercise the numinous power which is its *raison d'être*? How can it assert
its primacy in the general populace of representations?

Coins

Many of the king's subjects would habitually see a representation of him
on the coinage. Some of the humblest coins, such as the half-groat (twopence) and the penny, usually bore a profile portrait of the monarch;
although on the denominations that were larger both in value and size the
image would be more finely designed and eloquently presented. The portrait was sometimes an equestrian figure, and on one issue during the Civil
War a half-length,⁸ but most frequently it was a bust – what Donne had
brusquely called 'his stamped face'. It was Henry VII, founder of the

modern English monarchy, who had initiated the practice of showing a realistic profile portrait on his coins; this superseded the medieval use of a generalized royal image in full face, and, by taking up the Renaissance interest in Roman coins and medals, gave to the King of England's image associations of imperial power. The succession of the Stuarts and the union of England and Scotland reinforced these associations; and James I issued one set of coins which showed him as a Roman emperor wearing a laurel wreath, an image which had already been used on his coronation medal. Charles I continued and consolidated the use of a realistic portrait with imperial associations. Since his profile was always facing left, his characteristic 'lovelock' (the fashion of wearing the hair longer over the left shoulder), adopted early in the reign, was thereafter always visible, and helped to impart to what was necessarily a quasi-stylized rendering of individual features a distinctive trait. And although he never appeared on his coins dressed *à l'antique* (as he did, for example, in the court masques), he always wore a crown closed by two arches, signifying imperial rule. The consistent use of this type of image ensured that, even on the small scale of the coinage, both the King's person and his authority were instantly recognizable.

Charles had a large collection of coins and medals, both antique and modern; many of these were eventually arranged in the New Cabinet Room at Whitehall, alongside pictures and other *objets d'art*, and accompanied by treatises on numismatics purchased when he was still Prince of Wales. His interest in coins as aesthetic and historical objects took a practical turn when he became king; and the cultural policy which informed the royal collection as a whole, and stimulated his patronage of the most advanced artists – such as Rubens, Van Dyck and Inigo Jones – to formulate his image, represent his regime, and celebrate the Stuart dynasty, can be discerned in the design and production of the Caroline coinage.

Just as Charles entrusted the execution of his portraits to court painters recruited from the continent – first Mytens and then Van Dyck – whom he judged more capable and more stylistically advanced than English artists, so he employed a foreigner to attempt improvements in the production of his coins. This was Nicolas Briot, a native of Lorraine, who had worked both for the Duke of Lorraine and as engraver-general at the royal mint in Paris.[9] Briot arrived in London in 1625, the year of Charles's accession and marriage to the French king's sister. He may have left France under a cloud; even so, in 1626 he was entrusted with the design of the Great Seal of England, along with a privy seal for the King and a council seal for the

Fig. 9.1 Nicolas Briot, silver crown of Charles I, 1631–1632.

Queen; and in the following year he made the Great Seal of Scotland.[10] The royal image on the Great Seal was necessarily traditional and medievalizing, to emphasize the age-old continuity of the sovereign power; but Briot was also encouraged to turn his attention to the coinage, where innovation was in order, and in his opinion necessary. In 1628 he submitted proposals to revise the weight of silver coins, and to introduce brass or copper money for small denominations;[11] although these practical measures were not adopted, he was granted a patent allowing 'full Power and Authority to Frame and Engrave the first Designs and Effigies of the King's Image, in such Sizes and Formes as are to serve in all sorts of Coins of Gold and Silver'.[12]

It was in the design rather than the overall reform of the coinage that Briot was to make his mark. His chief campaign – to introduce mechanical methods of production into the Royal Mint at the Tower of London, where coins were still struck by hand – promised well. In 1631–2 he produced a trial issue of coins using a rotary press; the increased definition and regularity of appearance ensured that his designs were exceptionally well executed. An equestrian image of the King on the silver crown[13] (fig. 9.1) is realized with great subtlety, the animation of the horse and the composure of its rider in the same instant being convincingly suggested. By an illusionistic effect, the point of the King's upraised sword crosses the boundary between the field of the image and the space of the inscription around it, linking the realism of the figure to the more abstract textual

formulation of his sovereign status. The deeper relief given to the lettering of these coins, and the absence of irregularities caused by manual production,[14] helps the Latin inscription of the royal titles, neo-antique both
in language and in lettering, not merely to narrate but to represent the
idea of monumental permanence that is implicit in the obdurate metallic
substance of the royal money. Briot's new production process, by display-
ing his designs to their fullest potential, gave his representations of the
King an intensified reality.

Nonetheless his enterprise was frustrated. From the first he had come
up against the vested interests of the officers of the Mint, and had to petition the king strenuously to get the necessary facilities (already granted
him by royal warrant) made available in the Tower for his experiments.[15]
Once his new mechanized process had been tried, despite the superior
quality of the results it was not adopted, possibly because it proved too
slow at producing the requisite volume of coins. A later opportunity did
come in 1635, when royal sponsorship had a freer hand in a different situation: Briot was appointed Master of the Mint in Scotland, and could eventually set up his machines in Edinburgh.[16] But in the initial moment of
success the artist's talent and the King's favour had not been sufficient to
overcome the institutional and material constraints on the production of
the 'King's' money.

As late as 1638 the King was ordering the officers of the Tower Mint to
make another trial of Briot's methods 'without delay or further excuse';[17]
there is no record of the result, nor was there any change in established
practices. But if royal authority could not bring about an immediate
reform in the quality of production, it could still prescribe the images and
inscriptions on the coinage, and combine both to make powerful statements for its own ends. James I had set a strong example in 1604, the
second year of his reign over both England and Scotland, when in spite of
the Commons' reluctance he proclaimed himself King of Great Britain,
and issued new English coins to represent his new title. The gold sovereign
was renamed (again by proclamation) the 'unite', and the royal style encir-
cling the King's image changed from 'ANG. SCO. . . . REX' to 'MAG. BRIT.
. . . REX'; on the reverse appeared a new legend, 'Faciam Eos In Gentem
Unam', from Ezekiel 37:22: 'I will make them one nation in the land upon
the mountains of Israel; and one king shall be king to them all: and they
shall be no more two nations, neither shall they be divided into two kingdoms any more at all.'[18] The ruler who figures at first sight as, in the traditional formula, 'D[ei]. G[ratia]. . . . REX', king by the grace of God, goes on

to speak with the voice of God himself. The tiny scope of the coin compels a resort to abbreviation and allusion, but the tendentious announcement of the royal will exerts a peculiar pressure in this condensed form. Charles maintained his father's insistence on the idea of a composite realm of Great Britain, but while his Scottish coinage kept the imperious quotation from Ezekiel, the gold unites of his English coinage, including those struck by Briot, carried a new and more relaxed legend: 'Florent Concordia Regna' (May the kingdoms flourish in harmony).[19] It is the widely circulating silver coins – the crown, half-crown, shilling and sixpence – which best express his personal view of monarchy; backing the crowned image of the King are the royal arms with the legend 'Christo Auspice Regno' (I reign by Christ's favour).[20] Here without his father's Old Testament portentousness, Charles displays a transparent faith in the doctrine of divine right.

The representation of the King on his coins faced new challenges during the Civil War. Separated from his capital, and involved in shifting military campaigns, Charles had to set up new, temporary royal mints to assist in financing his armies. The first of these was established at York; Briot was summoned to take charge of it, bringing his own machinery.[21] The war had given him a belated opportunity to meet the King's wish for finer standards of production, unhampered by the vested interests and conservative practices of the London moneyers. Designs already familiar were reissued, although the crisis gave a new urgency to the images of the King – especially that of him mounted on horseback, armed, crowned and wielding a sword – and to the favoured motto, 'Christo Auspice Regno'; while the clarity with which the designs were struck renewed the force of their message.[22] At the same time, the Welsh branch of the Tower Mint was moved from Aberystwyth to Shrewsbury, and new designs supporting the royalist cause were devised. Now some of the equestrian images of the King showed him riding through a field strewn with armour and weapons;[23] and on the reverse of all the coins the royal arms were replaced by the legend 'REL. PROT. LEG. ANGL. LIBER. PARL.', with minor variants (fig. 9.2), referring to the solemn declaration on 19 September 1642 at Wellington that he would 'defend and maintain the true Reformed Protestant religion . . . govern according to the known laws of the land, maintain the just privileges and freedom of Parliament'.[24] This legend was set out in a centrally placed horizontal band, easily read, and encircled by a more aggressive motto from Psalm 68:1: 'Exurgat Deus Dissipentur Inimici' (Let God arise, let his enemies be scattered). The latter was copied

Fig. 9.2 Shrewsbury mint, silver twenty shillings of Charles I, 1642.

from the inaugural issue of coinage by James I, the founder of the dynasty – a reminder that any readiness on Charles's part to explain himself and conciliate was bound up with his divine right to rule.

The import of this new design was quickly spread abroad. From London the Venetian ambassador wrote:

> Upon the money coined at Sirosberi the King has had another motto printed instead of the usual inscription, to wit Exurgat Deus et Dissipentur inimici ejus, and another in the middle Pro Religione et Parliamento, all in order to make it more and more patent to his people that his intentions are directed solely to the preservation of religion and the privileges of the country.[25]

Given that he might not have seen the new coins, and could be relying on reported information, his 'reading' of the inscriptions is significant: he puts the Psalm text emphasizing divine right and sovereign power first, and the words of justification and reassurance second, reversing the ostensible emphasis of the design. There may have been other contemporaries who read the King's new presentation of himself as less reassuring than it purported to be, sensing in it the dissembling and intransigence which were to discredit him as a negotiator. Later variants of his patriotic dedication to Protestantism and parliament, stamped on splendid gold coins of £3 value minted at Oxford, show the letters undulating between wavy lines as if inscribed on a scroll or a battle standard; in the final version they appear on the tail-end of a bannerol with the 'Exurgat' legend coming first

Fig. 9.3 Bristol mint, gold twenty shillings of Charles I, 1645.

– an elegant but not conciliatory visual conceit.[26] On the obverse of these
Oxford coins a half-length figure of the King brandishes a sword while
holding a less discernible olive branch; the ostensibly even-handed but
ambivalent offer of war or peace ironically reflects the claim made by the
inscriptions that the King is only fighting for the war aims of his misguided
opponents.

Charles continued to issue the 'Exurgat' coinage from Oxford when it
became his capital, and from Bristol, his principal port after its capture in
July 1643. He used the coinage as a propaganda weapon in the war, not by
associating his image with an obvious *parti pris*, but by suggesting that the
differences seemingly manifested in the conflict were in reality reconciled
in his sacred person and his divinely guaranteed sovereignty. The contradiction involved in fighting his enemies with a doctrine of transcendental
détente left traces on the coins which were its vehicle. The most notable of
the coins produced at Bristol (fig. 9.3) uses the Oxford design of the King
with sword and olive branch, proffering war or peace, backed by the declaration for Protestantism and parliament tacked on to the decorative royalist bannerol.[27] This is a gold piece of twenty shillings, the coin which
Charles's father had renamed by proclamation the 'unite', and the effort of
the design to juggle with dualities and divisions is replete with unintended
irony.

A more blatant irony of the divisions of warfare was that both sides
continued to mint the 'King's' money. Parliament had control of the

Fig. 9.4 Thomas Simon (attributed), crown of Charles I, *c.* 1646.

Tower Mint,[28] and since it professed to be fighting in the King's name, coins were still produced as before, bearing his portrait and titles, and backed by the royal arms and his personal mottoes. The only sign of the new regime was a new 'privy mark' (the mint mark stamped on each year's coins), a *P* in brackets, which signified parliament's control and minimized it at the same time. A talented new designer was emerging in London, Thomas Simon, who, while not officially apprenticed to Briot, had evidently learnt much from him in the later 1630s.[29] After Lord Keeper Lyttleton had removed the Great Seal to York in 1642, Simon was commissioned to engrave a copy for parliament's use, an act of forgery and high treason from the King's point of view. Ironically, when in 1646, the year of the King's surrender and confinement, Simon redesigned the equestrian image on the Tower coinage (fig. 9.4),[30] he produced a masterpiece. Previous versions had fudged differences of scale between horse and rider, making the King's figure more imposing and the horse's body less bulky and more visually engaging. Simon made this relationship, and the horse's body, more realistic, so that the highly bred animal and the uncommon dignity of its rider become metaphorically associated. This motif and the figures themselves suggest a careful study of Van Dyck's *Charles I on Horseback*, then at Hampton Court. Simon's ability to transmute Van Dyck's magnificent portrayal of the King into a miniature compass and a different medium anticipates Marvell's fine vignette of Charles's execution in the *Horatian Ode*, in making cultural gain from political defeat, and acknowledging a new phase in which the King's image becomes common property – it can belong to his opponents, and to history.

Medals

Charles I inherited a large collection of medals and antique coins from his brother Prince Henry. This may not have been eventually conserved in its entirety, as various courtiers competed to get hold of parts of it, supposedly for purposes of assessment and cataloguing, to the distress of the curator Abraham van der Doort.[31] In his own catalogue of the royal collections, compiled at the end of the 1630s, van der Doort lists various antique medals, and some modern ones, kept in the Cabinet Room at Whitehall, along with a number of books 'concerning antiquity of medals'. Some of the medals are noted as gifts to, or purchases by, Charles, and five of the books are described as 'bought by your Majesty when you were Prince'[32] – which suggests that he took an interest in the collection, especially by keeping up with specialist publications or else purchasing books on medals that were not already in the library which he had also inherited from his brother. Since some of the medals issued during his own reign were also kept in the Cabinet Room, we may assume that Charles's interest in medals was not just an antiquarian diversion but a concern with their historical continuity and contemporary function.

Looking back from the end of the seventeenth century, John Evelyn observed that Charles I was the first English monarch who consistently issued medals on significant occasions throughout his reign. In his *Numismata. A Discourse of Medals, Antient and Modern* (1697), Evelyn reproduced and described many of these issues, in the context of a more general treatise on the subject. His book was published to fill a gap – the absence in English of any studies 'concerning antiquity of medals' like those which had been appearing in various European languages since the mid-sixteenth century – and it therefore offers near contemporary discussion of the design and function of medals pertinent to the Caroline regime. Above all, Evelyn stresses the importance of medals as historical records, given their durability and the valuable information they convey: 'they are . . . the most lasting and (give me leave to call them) Vocal Monuments of Antiquity'.[33] Their 'Vocal' quality Evelyn associates with what he calls 'Character' and 'Soul'; by 'Character' he means the lettering of the inscriptions, by 'Soul' the texts which the inscriptions record, drawing on the traditional association of visual images with the body and of words with the soul.[34] This implicitly literary, northern European view of medallic imagery (and of images in general) would not have been shared by Charles I; but on another important point he and Evelyn would have seen eye to eye. Speaking of the influence exerted by the representations of renowned figures from the past, Evelyn compares medallic portraits with antique portrait sculpture, and makes an analogy with the moral and political significance of collections of portrait sculpture among the ancient Romans: 'in that point ART became a piece of *State*'.[35] King Charles showed himself well aware of the use of medallic 'Art' for purposes of 'State', especially for the promotion of his own designs.

As medals bearing the King's image were in most cases issued by royal command, in numbers sufficient for a preconceived group of recipients, their design and distribution could be fairly carefully controlled. Those which marked celebratory occasions, such as the birth of royal children, might be designed on the modest scale of coins, and struck in large numbers. So the medals struck to celebrate the birth of a male heir in 1630 were described as 'Pieces of Coyne made in the manner of Largesses to express the joy of yo^re Maties happy issue',[36] and the idea of largess, of the monarch's bounty to his subjects, was exemplified by the wide distribution of these pieces, which bore a profile bust of the King probably designed by Briot. In 1626 Briot had been paid for producing 'certain pieces of largess of gold and silver in memory of his Majesty's Coronation, as also . . . for the shaping of his Majesty's picture and the other device upon the said pieces of largess'.[37] The 'other device' on the obverse of the coronation medal, signifying that England was at war with Spain, was an arm emerging from a cloud and wielding a sword. The *bras armé* was a traditional heraldic badge of the Dukes of Lorraine,[38] and it looks as if Briot, a native of Lorraine, had come up with the image himself. This was probably exceptional, as most of the 'devices' on the royal medals suggest careful deliberation by the King and his advisers.

Signs of this deliberation appear in the very first medal of his reign, marking his marriage to Henrietta Maria of France. Most examples of this medal show facing profile portraits of the couple, backed by a cupid with a bunch of lilies and roses, symbolizing their union. But one variant (fig. 9.5) replaces the portraits with two infants, male and female, standing with hands joined on a flowery island, from which a chain descends into the sea.[39] The inscription reads 'Stat Prole Hac Altera Delos' (For these offspring stands fast another Delos). The spouses are allusively represented as Apollo and Diana, born on the floating island of Delos, which

Fig. 9.5 Marriage of Charles I and Henrietta Maria medal, 1625.

Zeus later chained to the seabed. This mythological conceit is not a spontaneous fancy; it derives from a masque performed at Whitehall a few months earlier, in anticipation of the marriage, *The Fortunate Isles and Their Union*. This had presented Charles, as chief masquer, on the floating island of Macaria ('the Blessed'), a frank paraphrase of the Delos of mythology; when the island appeared the chorus were invited to

> sing the present prophecy that goes
> Of joining the bright lily and the rose.[40]

The medal simply repeats this symbolism in a different medium, scaling it down from the grandiose spectacle of the masque to the terseness of the numismatic format.

Further appearances of the Apollo and Diana theme show how transposing images in this way could produce complex interrelationships. An allegorical painting of 1628 by Honthorst shows the Duke of Buckingham as Mercury presenting the Liberal Arts to Apollo and Diana, who are idealized portraits of the King and Queen in classicizing costume.[41] They sit to one side, holding hands and watching the allegorical presentation as if it were a masque; the masques of the 1630s reiterate this motif of the royal couple as idealized siblings (and patrons of the arts), one masque concluding with an invocation of 'Hymen's twin, the Mary-Charles'.[42] The theme evidently had powerful associations for the King, as it reappears in a medal struck during the Civil War (fig. 9.6). This was made to commemorate the reunion of the King and Queen at Kineton on 13 July 1643, the same day that the parliamentary forces were defeated at Roundway Down.[43] The reverse has a Latin inscription recording the auspicious coincidence. On the obverse Charles and Henrietta Maria are seated, clasping each other's

Fig. 9.6 Medal to commemorate the meeting of the King and Queen at Kineton, 1643.

right hand, with the sun and the moon over their respective heads, identifying them once more as Apollo and Diana; at their feet lies a dragon
with a spear through its neck. The legend, 'Certius Pythonem Iuncti'
(United they more surely [will destroy] the Python), identifies this creature with the python slain by Apollo, here symbolizing the monster of
rebellion. This is a stern revision of the original Apollo and Diana medal
for the marriage of 1625. The first medal had symbolized an untried relationship with factitious and innocent images of children and flowers. The
second affirms the close bond between the King and Queen, variously
expatiated upon in the cultural propaganda of the pre-war regime, and
refocuses the imagery of that propaganda into a new, concise, and appropriately more challenging form.

Given that medals were to take on a fresh function as ideological
weapons in the Civil War, their use as 'pieces of State' was well established
in the earlier years of the reign. In the domestic sphere they could play an
affirmative role in celebrating the royal offspring, or marking special
events such as the reform of the Order of the Garter in 1629, or the
deferred Scottish coronation at Edinburgh in 1633.[44] In the wider world
they might publicize and reinforce policy initiatives, although here their
confident imagery might turn out to be misplaced: on a medal of 1628,
announcing the interrupted and eventually unsuccessful expedition to La
Rochelle, the martial image of the King on horseback, accompanied by a
Virgilian invocation to Caesar Augustus, must soon have jarred.[45]
Between festivity and policy there was a shifting middle ground, opened

Fig. 9.7 Nicolas Briot, Dominion of the Seas medal, 1630.

up by debates about prerogative, about what were the powers intrinsic to sovereignty, and some medals occupy this ambiguous space.

The most interesting of these relate to the political doctrine known as 'the sovereignty of the seas', that is, the putative dominion of the English crown over the seas between England and its immediate continental neighbours. A medal of 1628 showed on the reverse a sceptre and a trident crossed and bound by a cord, with the royal monogram and the motto 'Regit Unus Utroque' (One rules with both).[46] The King's head on the obverse was a classicizing portrait bust, with neo-antique drapery and a radiate crown (as found on Roman imperial coins), an image evidently meant to express the idea of time-honoured *imperium*. This was pertinent not only to foreign states but, more immediately, to the parliament of 1628, which the King hoped would grant revenues to finance the navy. The persuasions he applied were unsuccessful; new ones were tried when parliament reassembled in 1629, an effort marked by the reissue of the medal, with the royal arms replacing the neo-antique bust of the King,[47] as if the wider perspective of international jurisdictions was being narrowed down so as to focus on exigencies at hand. Briot, who designed the medals, prepared corresponding patterns for half-groat coins;[48] these would have spread the message on a more popular level, and so the King's bust was in contemporary costume, familiar and easily recognizable.

The following year, Parliament having been dissolved, saw the issue of an entirely new medal (fig. 9.7), again designed by Briot.[49] It was much larger in size, and cast rather than struck, allowing the imagery to be more intricately detailed and in higher relief. The reverse shows a warship at sea, executed by the artist with exceptional bravura; the inscription reads 'Nec Meta Mihi Quae Terminus Orbi' (Nor to me is that a limit, which is boundary to the world). The King's bust on the obverse has decorated armour, a large ruff, and an elaborately embroidered cloak; these are all rendered in realistic detail, while the head is boldly designed in a modern French portrait style which, although not very idiomatic, is more forceful than the portrait patterns produced so far by the painters Mytens and Honthorst. The doctrine of marine sovereignty is here related in a magnified format and in frankly triumphal vein, sponsored as it now is by the King ruling alone, without the concern to recommend its sustenance to an unresponsive parliament. Humbler variants of this medal were also produced,[50] but the scale and virtuoso workmanship of the original (which seems to have circulated quite widely) make it uniquely imposing. Behind the figure of Charles, Briot's signature is unusually prominent, identifying the artist's ambition with the monarch's political vaunt.

A copy of this medal was issued in 1639, probably to stress the King's principal role in a crisis unfolding in the English Channel. A large but disabled Spanish fleet, transporting troops to the southern Netherlands, was sheltering in English waters from a Dutch fleet determined to destroy it; Charles had ordered his own navy to hold the ring, while attempting to extort political concessions from Spain through opportunistic negotiations. As if to dignify this opportunism, the medal reasserts his sovereign authority over the English seas. Briot repeats his previous design, only bringing the King's image up to date.[51] He is shown dressed only in armour, worked with a design of military trophies; and the portrait type is now derived from Van Dyck. Both revisions have an ambivalent effect. The armour may symbolize Charles's resolve to dictate terms to the Spanish and Dutch, but it inevitably recalls the recent campaign against his own subjects, the Scots. And the Van Dyckian countenance shows a new psychological subtlety, but for that reason scarcely reinforces the assertiveness of the medal's programme.

Whatever the relation of medals to political crises, the King was also concerned with the image of him which they projected in a longer historical perspective. Both the medals of 1630 and 1639 seem to have chimed with this concern, as he gave them a special place in his own collection. They were included in a particular series of medals representing modern European sovereigns: Holy Roman Emperors, Kings of France, Grand Dukes of Tuscany.[52] Charles evidently thought that Briot's portraiture dis-

Fig. 9.8 Nicolas Briot, Return to London medal, 1633.

played him worthily in this context. Other medals which ended up in the collection bore physical traces of the King's attachment to them. For his return to London after the Scottish coronation in 1633, Briot produced a bravura design (fig. 9.8) with a detailed view of the city, including London Bridge and St Paul's, and two alternative obverses: an equestrian image of the King on a rearing horse, and a boldly conceived portrait bust.[53] Both variants figure in van der Doort's catalogue among a group of Scottish coins and medals; they are described as 'much worne in the Kings pockett' and 'another the like worne'.[54] Both portraits were inscribed 'Carolus Augustissimus Et Invictissimus'; and van der Doort's naively scrupulous observation allows us to glimpse Charles fondling in thought this glorious view of himself on the stage of history.

The Civil War gave a special impetus to the use of medals for propaganda. It also broke the King's virtual monopoly on his own medallic image; since parliament professed to be fighting in his name, it used his image to support its cause. This paradox is exemplified in a medal issued by parliament probably just before the start of hostilities in 1642 (fig. 9.9).[55] The reverse shows, in the lower half, a stylized but detailed representation of the House of Commons with the Speaker and, above that, the House of Lords presided over by the King. On the obverse is a profile bust of the King, robed and crowned, encircled by a legend which reads: 'Should hear both houses of parliament for true Religion and subiects freedom stand.' The admonitory message in the vernacular breaks the usual convention of oblique or condensed Latin mottoes, and suggests

Fig. 9.9 Thomas Rawlins, Declaration of Parliament medal, 1642.

that one side of the dual representation is speaking plainly to the other. The medallic form, with its two aspects back to back, is used to point up the constitutional contradiction underlying the political crisis: that the split between King and parliament, which can have no reality in principle, is becoming only too real in practice. In that it heralds the war, this medal exhibits an awkward fact: the King is on both sides.

The imagery used to express this fundamental dilemma seems to have had a compelling effect, as it was reiterated and paraphrased in different contexts and combinations, especially after the conflict began. A variant of the original medal substituted for the English legend a terser Latin one, 'Pro Religione. lege. Rege. et Parliamento', again enclosing the King's bust.[56] This more 'corporatist' version emphasizes the overlap rather than the difference between the two sides, opting for a tautology which suggests that King and parliament have distinct identities but identical aims. Thereafter the two sides of the medal undergo various transformations and permutations, as parliament chooses other figures to represent its *alter ego*. Its own image, as the two Houses – or more precisely, the image of the King in parliament – is now combined with portraits of its chief generals, the Earls of Essex and Manchester, in medals designed as military badges to be given to their officers. One version of the Essex medal, on which he is shown at half-length holding a sword erect in his right hand, surrounds his figure with both legends from the original, one inscribed inside the other;[57] the warning in English, now overtaken by events, suggests alienation from the King, while the declaration in Latin affirms loyalty. Another version spreads the ambiguity more evenly.[58] It adds to Essex's portrait a second sword, brandished above his head by a heavenly hand, with a quotation from the English Bible, 'The sword of the Lord and of Gydeon', referring to the rout of the Midianites in Judges 7:18–20. The reverse legend, around the image of parliament, points to a more sober alternative: 'In the multitude of councellors there is peace.' The offer of war or peace is properly the monarch's prerogative; and this doubling of the King's role is compounded by the continuing play with the duality of the medallic form.

Charles himself used his profile portrait from parliament's original medal on a badge commemorating the Battle of Edgehill,[59] the inscription now consisting of his titles. On the reverse is an armed knight on a rearing horse inscribed 'C P', to denote the Prince of Wales, who was present at the battle. This image was immediately appropriated for a parliamentary medal;[60] it serves now as the obverse, inscribed 'Robertus Comes Essexiae', and is backed by Essex's coat of arms. A competitive touch appears in the execution of the commandeered design: one of the rearing horse's hooves crosses the frame which bounds the image, increasing the illusion of animated movement, and revealing an aesthetic rivalry in each side's attempts to fix what had been an indecisive battle with definitive symbols. This symbolic strife – with images being seized, exchanged, substituted or reversed – charged the innate dualism of the medium with the alternating fortunes of war.

Aside from these hostile exchanges, the King's medals take up images from the 1620s and 1630s, and adapt them to a war situation. One oval piece (fig. 9.10) associated with a battle, possibly again Edgehill, uses a half-length portrait by Van Dyck, showing Charles as sovereign of the Order of the Garter (fig. 9.11), and reproduces it in miniature;[61] the medallist gives full value to Van Dyck's composition by inscribing the King's titles in the background of the original picture space, on a curtailed curve which runs less than halfway round the edge. On the reverse the King appears in armour on a rearing horse, a winged genius flying above him with a palm and a garland; the inscription is the Garter motto, 'Honni Soit Qui Mal Le Pans'. One image is majestically unperturbed, the other in

Fig. 9.10 Thomas Rawlins (attributed), Battle of Edgehill military badge, 1642.

vigorous motion, and the meaning emerges from their contrast: the ceremonial chivalry of the 'halcyon days' has been roused to action and
success. The emphasis is not on disruption but on continuity, the war seen
as vindicating the values of the Personal Rule. Another telling image from
the past is seen on a series of medals dated 1643. Two of these celebrate
the taking of Bristol by Prince Rupert, and they show a classicizing bust of
the King closely imitated by Thomas Rawlins from the obverse of a Briot
medal of 1628 which has already been noted.[62] Two further medals by
Rawlins imitate the entire design of the Briot original, which had
announced the King's desire to raise parliamentary revenues that would
allow him to augment the navy and so rule by sea as well as by land. The
reverse of the original shows a crossed sceptre and trident, with the legend
'Regit Unus Utroque' (One rules with both). The new medal[63] signifies
the King's readiness to negotiate peace from his position of strength: the
reverse shows a sword and olive branch crossed, with the words 'In
Utrumque Paratus' (Prepared for both). The portrait bust on the obverse
replaces the radiate crown which Briot had given the King with a laurel
wreath, figuring him not just as a Roman emperor but an imperial conqueror – again reviving a favourite characterization from the cultural

Fig. 9.11 After Anthony van Dyck, *Charles I wearing the Garter Star*, c. 1632.

propaganda of the Personal Rule (used repeatedly, for example, in the
court masques) and insisting that the war has tested and proved its truth.

Among the exceptional volume of imagery provoked by the King's
death, it was the medals which revealed a peculiar fitness to represent the
traumatic event. Whether one views the mode of execution in a physical
or a supernatural perspective – the King's head was separated from his
trunk, or moreover, his soul was separated from his body – the fact is that
he was cut in two. And the signifying format of the medal, which worked
through patterns of duality, was only too apt for this situation. It used
both images and texts, and so comprised a 'body' and a 'soul', according to
a commonplace of Renaissance aesthetic theory which we have seen
Evelyn invoking still at the end of the seventeenth century. It also combined portraiture and symbolic imagery, although the separation of the
head and the corpus of illustration on opposite sides always had the potential to produce not the expected alikeness but, as we have seen, a
discomfiting dichotomy.

Commemorative medals issued by the dead King's supporters do their
utmost to resist this tendency, as they attempt to deny on the symbolic
level the appalling dichotomization of the King's sacred person. They
stress invulnerability and integrity, with images of the salamander thriv-
ing amid flames and the rock unmoved by storms, also used in *Eikon
Basilike*. The boldest in conception actually paraphrases the image of the
axe and the block. A bust of the King is inscribed with the epithets 'Divus'
and 'Pius', blending antique Roman apotheosis with Christian sainthood.
On the reverse a diamond is struck by a hammer on an anvil, with the
legend 'Inexpugnabilis' (Unconquerable), referring to Pliny's account of
the absolute infrangibility of the diamond, 'for strike as hard as you will
. . . it scorneth all blowes . . . and the very anvill itselfe underneath cleaveth
in twain'.[64] The crucial resistance to 'cleavage' is not matched in medals
issued at the same time on the continent, which, at a greater emotional
distance, tend to acknowledge rather than deny the horrific split in the
English body politic. A Dutch medal backs the King's bust with a Medusa
head,[65] appropriately symbolizing anarchy while unguardedly reproduc-
ing the dreadful motif of decapitation. Another, issued in Germany (fig.
9.12), actually shows the King's severed head exulted over by the Hydra of
rebellion;[66] as the obverse depicts conjoined busts of Charles and
Henrietta Maria, the image of the many-headed monster acquires an
unconscious air of hysterical parody. Imaginative excess unfolds the
potential incoherence of medallic representation, and the retrospective
irony of its many puissant renditions of 'the King's head'.

Fig. 9.12 Heinrich Reitz the younger, Charles I memorial medal, 1649.

Prints

Next after the coinage, which was an object of desire for ulterior motives, the royal image was most widely diffused and most sought after in the medium of engraved or etched prints. The London print trade catered for a wide spectrum of purchasers, from the few who could afford luxuriously illustrated folio volumes to the many whose interest might be seized by cheaply produced portraits of famous contemporary figures, and who might wish especially to possess a picture of their sovereign. So a modest coin bearing an officially sanctioned image of the King, familiar and disregarded, could be exchanged for an engraved portrait on a larger scale, enlivened by ingenious technique, arresting detail, and perhaps a reference to topical events. Given that prints might be attractive as commodities and possessions, the desire for them was still different from that for the King's 'stamped face', since it was a desire for the representation itself. Writing in a later generation, Pepys put his finger on it when describing – with a typical mixture of gratification and guilt – a visit to his bookseller, 'there finding plenty of good pictures, God forgive me how my mind run upon them'.[67] Pepys was a well-paid government official; even so, for many low-paid subjects of Charles I, the pleasure of owning and looking at an engraved portrait of the King must have been comparable to that taken by the courtiers in their Van Dycks (which were often studio repetitions anyway).

Because of its manageable technology and flourishing market, print production was able to represent political change without being unduly susceptible to political control. The Civil War presents an extreme case of this combination of topicality and freedom; but even in the pre-war years, within a framework of consensus and obedience to the royal government, there was the readiness to respond quickly to changing events, a tendency in which subversive possibilities lay dormant. The royal image was especially subject to change at the engraver's hand, as the significant stages of a reign were pictured and publicized: accession to the throne, marriage, upbringing of royal children, wars, parliaments, and so on – at least some of which would require a newly current portrayal of the monarch. So, in the period immediately following the accession of Charles I in 1625 many engraved portraits of the King were produced by reworking previous engravings of him as Prince of Wales. Crispin van de Passe contrived such a portrait[68] by lengthening the former Prince's hair (unevenly, so as to show the lovelock over his left shoulder) and giving him a pointed beard; but while the inscription of his titles was revised, the accompanying Latin verses praising Charles as 'the hope of his father' were left untouched, a remnant of an immature past self. A twice-revised equestrian portrait by Renold Elstrack[69] had first shown Charles in his teens, about ten years before his accession, and then been reworked to show him as a young adult, by changing the head, hat and ruff. To depict him at last as King (fig. 9.13), the hat and ruff were altered slightly again, and the head reworked, with longer hair, a pointed beard and a larger moustache. The original print had been an elaborate but stylistically consistent image. In the third and final state there is an incoherence between the King's fashionable coiffure and his outdated Jacobean costume, and a disproportion between the mature, fuller face and the slight, younger body. These rifts may have been scarcely remarked in a situation where the patriotic acumen of the publisher matched the loyal curiosity of the buying public; but they imply the capacity of the medium to chronicle events in an awkwardly peremptory fashion.

Generating the royal image from imperfectly adapted portrayals of the king's younger self was politically gauche, since it disclosed the contingencies of human development rather than affirming the mystique of monarchy. The problem is compounded in prints which include Charles in a dynastic context. An elaborate engraving by Willem van de Passe, probably issued in 1624 and headed *Triumphus Jacobi Regis Augustaeque Ipsius Prolis*,[70] depicts the first Stuart King of England enthroned amid his family

Fig. 9.13 Renold Elstrack, *Charles I on Horseback*, engraving, third state.

both living and dead. On his left are the King and Queen of Bohemia with their children, and on his right, in front of the deceased Queen Anne and Prince Henry, the hopeful Prince Charles. A second state of the engraving has James holding a skull to signify his demise, and includes Henrietta Maria with Charles, who is now crowned. As the two states were produced within five years, the dress of the figures has not especially dated; and the composition is skilfully handled, with the figure of Charles in a favoured position and a lively attitude. But a mediocre imitation of van de Passe's design by Gerrit Mountin[71] (fig. 9.14) gives away to the viewer some of the problems inherent in a dual representation of sovereignty and dynasty. Mountin makes the central figure of James much larger than the others, blatantly using an antiquated convention which van de Passe had subtly hinted at, while that of Charles receives no special treatment; and in the second state of the print, dating from the mid 1630s, Charles's figure is crowned but otherwise unchanged, so that his clothes look old-fashioned and his face implausibly youthful. His identity is figured as utterly derivative from his looming father; and, although now accompanied by three children, he manifests none of that patriarchal gravity which Van Dyck had rendered in the 'great piece' of the royal family, and which had become a keynote of the Personal Rule.

Van Dyck's official images of Charles as paterfamilias, imperial cavalier, sacred majesty or *re galantuomo*, translate the doctrine of divine right into the glorious amenities of baroque portraiture, creating an imaginative world in which the King's identity is defined first and foremost by his relationship to God. The unsanctioned images of the print trade often inhabit a world of contingency, where identity depends on merely human relationships being given meaning by shifting political circumstances. As time passes and events unpredictably unfold, these images need to be revised, supplemented or replaced; and the practice of producing new images by reworking the engraved plates from which the old ones were printed, too aptly points up the accidents of life and the vicissitudes of history.

Engravers nonetheless designed portraits of the King which were adequate to their purpose, combining mastery of the medium, recognizable likeness and the necessary air of regality; this last quality was often sustained by reverential and laudatory inscriptions. A full-length portrait by William Hole of Charles as Prince of Wales is altered in a second state to celebrate him as king.[72] He is shown crowned and standing under a cloth of estate; a heraldic tapestry behind him is inscribed, around its border, 'Behold Great Britaine This Is Charles The Faire, / His Brothers Partner &

Fig. 9.14 Gerrit Mountin, *James I and his Descendants*, engraving, *c*.1634–1635.

His Fathers Heire'. The second line of this distich has been obviously reworked on the plate, and must originally have read 'His Fathers Partner & His Brothers Heire'. The interests of both are symbolized by books and pieces of armour on a table next to the King; and the suggestion that he is both an intellectual like James and a man of action like Henry applies whichever way round the text is read. A contemporaneous portrait by Willem van de Passe[73] shows the King enthroned, with the Greater George worn over an ermine robe, and the regalia. This is an original design; but under it are four lines of verse copied from an earlier portrait of James I by Cornelis Boel:[74]

> Crownes have their compasse, length of dayes their date,
> Triumphes their Tombes, felicitie her fate:
> Of more then earth, can earth make none partaker,
> But knowledge makes the KING most like his maker.

The only change made is 'KING CHARLES' for 'the KING'. The reassertion of the monarch's quasi-divine nature is entirely appropriate to the van de Passe image of majesty, while the gratuitous change of wording leaves a trace of the power of mortality and the engraver's attempt to tamper with it.

This portrait was copied by another, unidentified engraver, adapted to a half-length format, with a decorative frame incorporating the King's titles in Latin and English.[75] He is now wearing armour, and the most prominent words on the frame are 'Fidei Defensor Potentiss[imus]'. Since the print is dated 1627, we may conclude that it refers to the military expedition of that year to the Ile de Ré, to relieve the Protestants of La Rochelle. This image in turn was adapted by the Dutch engraver Cornelis van Dalen, who arrived in England in 1633, to record another major event in the King's reign[76] (fig. 9.15). He is depicted at full-length astride a rearing horse, still crowned, but with his ermine robe restored and a sceptre in one hand; in the background is a city view inscribed 'Edynburgh'. The print must record Charles's Scottish coronation of 1633; and the triumphal equestrian motif is found on one of Briot's medals for that occasion.[77] Van Dalen does update the portrait head, slightly changing the hairstyle and ageing the face, but it is essentially van de Passe's image derived through his anonymous imitator of six years before. Copying a portrait in this way is a similar expedient to reworking it on the engraver's plate, but as an implicit metaphor of representation it works more positively, suggesting that the regal identity is constant and continu-

The high & mighty Monarch: CHARLES by y^e grace of GOD king of Great Brittaine France & Ireland Defendor of the Fayth. etc.

EDYNBURGH

C: v. Dalen fculp:

Fig. 9.15   Cornelis van Dalen, *Charles I Crowned King of Scots*, engraving, 1633.

ous rather than subject to vicissitude, revision or even (in the last resort) erasure.

The prints so far discussed were issued as separate sheets; but many engraved images of the King were published in books, either as a separate frontispiece or within an engraved title page. This could be a way of bidding for royal patronage, or engaging the King's attention; at the least, it might give one's work enhanced credentials by associating it with the monarchy. As a result, royal endorsement was assumed for arguments or projects which Charles might have regarded with reserve or antipathy. One form which this practice took was to picture the King together with his immediate predecessors, thereby suggesting that he follow their example along whatever line the author had to recommend. John Smith's *Generall Historie of Virginia*, first published in 1624, carried on its title page three portraits, of Queen Elizabeth, James I and Prince Charles, superimposed on a map of Virginia and New England. In quickly succeeding reissues of 1626 and 1627, the portrait of 'Carolus Princeps' was reinscribed 'Rex' and a crown simply added to the head; while in the later 1632 edition a portrait of the mature Charles was finally substituted.[78] To solicit the King's interest in colonization seemed proper enough; but on other programmatic title pages he was made to appear in more contentious settings. Christopher Lever's *History of the Defendors of the Catholique Faith* came out in 1627, the year of the expedition to the Ile de Ré. The title page[79] shows the King in armour, standing in an aggressive attitude, behind him the English fleet and a fortress under siege. There are portraits of his predecessors back to Henry VIII, who tramples on a pope, a cardinal and a friar; the other monarchs are accompanied by vignettes of Romish depravity, such as the Armada and the Gunpowder Plot, Queen Mary being exonerated by the inscription 'Non natura sed pontificiorum arte ferox' (Fierce not by nature but because of priestly cunning). But Lever's tactful patriotism has an over-insistent edge. Edward VI stands by a scene of liturgical objects being removed from a church, a cause not obviously appealing to King Charles, whose motto 'Donec pax reddita terris', recently adopted for the coronation medal of the previous year, is confidently appropriated to underline his melodramatically martial figure, as if the author can confidently declare the King's own mind. Remaking the monarch in the image of one's convictions carried the risk of presuming too much.

To position the King in a political picture of one's own devising was a form of implicit counsel, which could be drawn out more clearly in the succeeding text. This is how the print and book publisher Henry Holland presents an English version of Xenophon's *Cyropaedia* in 1632, by his father, the celebrated translator Philemon Holland.[80] Two pairs of portraits on the title page (fig. 9.16) convey the idea of bringing back to life the values of the classical past. A head of Xenophon is posed in profile within a classical niche, detached in a timeless enclave, while a half-length portrait of his translator, in the style of a modern miniature painting, looks out at the spectator. Full-length figures of Cyrus and Charles I dominate

Fig. 9.16 William Marshall, engraved title page to Xenophon, *Cyropaedia*, trans. Philemon Holland, 1632.

the design. Cyrus, on the left, wearing antique armour, appears lively and resolute, but the figure style is conventionalized and the expression remote, fixed on some timeless horizon. Charles, in the place of honour on the right, is crowned and wearing robes of state, with the ermine trimming folded back to reveal fashionable contemporary dress. He looks straight at the spectator, and his pose is gracefully animated, as if he could easily walk out of the picture space; the engraver, William Marshall, has rendered the figure and costume as realistically as possible. Under both figures are panels depicting battle scenes, a cue taken up in the dedicatory preface to the King by Henry Holland. He recalls that his father began the translation for Prince Henry, whose death interrupted it, and he now offers it for the future benefit of Charles's infant son; but he turns out to be aiming it at Charles himself. He recommends the example of Cyrus as 'a warlike Monarch . . . now in these dayes (not without Gods providence,) of Action', referring to Charles's indirect support for Gustavus Adolphus and those 'who fight *the Lords Battailes*'. In effect, Holland is urging the King to commit himself whole-heartedly to the Protestant cause in the Thirty Years' War; but he takes care to argue in what he calls 'the submissive voice of a loyal subject'.[81] His carefully diplomatic address enables us to read the representation of the King which precedes it on the title page: it is both flattering and admonitory, within a topical context to which the military motif gives the key. Contemporaries were probably skilled in reading the imagery straight off, with all its risky nuances.

This portrait of the King had an ironic reincarnation during the Civil War. It was copied, with minor changes, on to the frontispiece of an Irish pamphlet of 1646,[82] put out in response to the treaty signed between Lord Lieutenant Ormond and the Confederate Catholics. Charles stands to the left of a prone female figure inscribed 'Hybernia'; opposite him an allegorical figure of Faith represents the Catholics, next to the armorial bearings of the papal nuncio Rinuccini. The arms of Pope Innocent X dominate the whole scene, which is crowded with scrolls inscribed in Latin with pious hopes for the Catholic cause. Charles's borrowed image is now printed in reverse, and so has to 'change sides' in the design, becoming a vehicle for anti-Protestant aspirations.

Not all engraved images of the King were produced in a commercial or political context beyond his control. The best printmakers resident in London during the pre-war part of his reign – the engravers Lucas Vorsterman and Robert van Voerst, and the etchers Jan Lievens and Wenceslas Hollar – worked in the ambience of the court, and sometimes issued prints bearing a royal privilege. Vorsterman engraved a handsome portrait of Charles,[83] although, perhaps because it was done in Antwerp after he left England, it is not an accurate likeness. Van Voerst was official engraver to the King and collaborated with Van Dyck, whose early double portrait of Charles and Henrietta Maria (1632) he reproduced in a brilliant print (fig. 9.26),[84] probably the most sympathetic engraved image of himself which the King was ever to see. Hollar in turn adapted the heads from this portrait in an etching of 1641,[85] which again gives a sympathetic portrayal of the King (if not particularly of the Queen). And he made a further use of Van Dyckian imagery in a memorial print of 1649 (fig. 9.17), after Charles's death.[86] Although the plate is inscribed 'Ant: van Dyck pinxit', the overall design is of mixed origin: partly based on Van Dyck's Garter portrait (already used for a Civil War medal), but partly also on an idiosyncratic etching of the king published in 1630 as frontispiece to a book[87] (fig. 9.18). Hollar's final portrayal has a grim, courtly aloofness which seems to deter undue curiosity about its provenance in the urban print trade, which had traduced the royal image in so many ways.

Sculpture

To approach the court is to come to the more costly and prestigious representational arts of sculpture and painting, over which the King could exercise a deliberate control. In 1625, the year of his accession, he acquired a court sculptor, Hubert Le Sueur, who had until then been in the service of Louis XIII. Le Sueur was a skilled bronze founder, but his first commission in London was to work on the funeral catafalque of King James, which was made of temporary materials. Inigo Jones had designed it as a classical *tempietto*, adorned with twelve allegorical statues, which Le Sueur executed in plaster and calico.[88] This project, perishable as it was, nonetheless looked forward to an important theme in the imagery of the Caroline regime: the interest in antiquity, especially in the idea of imperial Rome, which would be developed both in the temporary tableaux of the court masques, constructed from much the same materials as the catafalque, and in the more enduring forms of classical architecture, which could be adorned with Le Sueur's bronze statues of King Charles.

Le Sueur was employed not only to produce new work, such as these portrait statues, but also to supplement the royal collection of antique sculpture, most of it acquired from the Duke of Mantua in the late 1620s. In 1631 he was sent to Italy to take 'moulds and patterns of certain figures

Serenisſimus Princeps, Carolus D. G: Angliæ,
Scotiæ, & Hiberniæ, REX, etc. ☙

Ant: van Dyck pinxit. Ioan: Huÿſſens excudit Antuerpiæ. W: Hollar fecit, 1649

Fig. 9.17 Wenceslas Hollar, *Charles I*, etching, 1649.

and antiques there',[89] including the Spinario, the Belvedere Antinous, and the Borghese Gladiator, only recently excavated in Rome. The bronze casts made from these moulds were set up in the garden of St James's Palace; Henry Peacham, writing 'Of Antiquities' in 1634, praised both the statues and their procurer, 'Hubert le Sueur, his Majesties Servant . . . the most industrious and excellent statuary in all materials, that ever this country enjoyed.'[90] The stress on 'industry' and 'materials', on workmanship, suggests a particular view of Le Sueur's function as 'his Majesties Servant'. This view is reinforced by a document of 1636, an order in the

Fig. 9.18 George Lid, *Charles I*, etched frontispiece to
Thomas May, *A Continuation of Lucan*, 1630.

King's name to pay him for 'several busts of Brasse (Viz.) two Bustes of
our own Pourtrait, one Bust of Brutus, and one of Agrippina . . . the sum
of £200'.[91] The indifferent tone of the list, which barely distinguishes each
item and implies that each is routinely rated at the same price,[92] is not
flattering to the artist. It appears that his portrait busts of the King are no
more valued than his casts or pastiches after the antique. What is acknowledged is not quality of design but workmanship and iconography: the
sculptor is rewarded for expertly producing portraits of the King which
may be associated with the imagery of ancient Rome.

The prototype for these portraits appears to be a marble bust of Charles (fig. 9.19), signed on the back by Le Sueur in Roman majuscule lettering and dated 1631.[93] The King wears armour embossed with neo-antique ornament, notably a grotesque Medusa mask on the breast and an overall pattern of rinceaux, in which the flowers have been adapted into heraldic roses, no doubt an allusion to his Tudor ancestors.[94] This piece can probably be identified with 'ye late Kings head in Marbell', noted in the Commonwealth sale inventories of the King's goods, in a long list of statues from St James's Palace.[95] Since the head is very weathered, it must have been displayed in the garden of St James's, keeping company with Le Sueur's successful casts after the antique. In fact the population of sculpture around it was made up largely of antique figures, including the companion pieces of its bronze offspring mentioned above: next to each other in the same list are 'Brutus in brass' and 'Agrip[p]ina in brass'.[96]

This marble bust, which records Le Sueur's habitual image of the King, is old-fashioned in its treatment of both the head and the body. The face is simplified and abstracted to a disconcerting degree, recalling sixteenth-century Mannerist portraits of rulers which emphasize a superhuman aloofness; this may be owing as much to the sculptor's limitations as to the King's preferences. The decoration on the armour is similarly out of date; but Le Sueur, whose father had been a master armourer, would have been aware of this, and the reason lies elsewhere. The use of Mannerist ornament on costume was standard practice in another area of royal image-making, the court masques, and it is there that the decorative and symbolic elements of Le Sueur's imagery can be matched. In *The Triumph of Peace*, a masque staged before the King and Queen at Whitehall in 1634 by the Inns of Court, the principal masquers wore a costume based on antique armour, designed by Inigo Jones.[97] On the decorated cuirass is a pectoral mask and rinceaux with five-petalled heraldic roses, like those on Le Sueur's marble bust. There are clusters of similar roses around the shoulders, and, as the text describes the colour scheme as 'carnation and white',[98] they would appear to be Tudor roses, paying a compliment to the King. The allusion is not at all remote, since both Stuart monarchs, following their predecessors from Henry VII onwards, had used the Tudor rose on their coinage.[99] We can see, then, that Le Sueur's old-fashioned ornament harks back to the past with intent, to signify dynastic continuity, and that this symbolic language works across a spectrum of representations, from coins to masques.

Symbolic cross-reference appears in other portrait busts of the King. In

Fig. 9.19 Hubert le Sueur, Charles I, marble, 1631,
V and A Museum

Fig. 9.20 Hubert le Sueur, Charles I, bronze, 1635,
Bodleian Library

the variants which Le Sueur produced of the marble exemplar, all in
bronze, the treatment of the head remains constant while the accessories
and the detailing of the armour sometimes change. One variant (fig. 9.20)
has pauldrons consisting of lions' faces, with gaping upper jaws that
define the truncated contours of the armoured shoulders. This dramatic
motif appears in another masque of 1634, *Coelum Britannicum*, in which the
King and his attendant lords represent 'ancient heroes' from Roman
Britain. The costume (fig. 9.28), again based on antique armour, has rin-

ceaux with roses on the cuirass and lion-mask pauldrons, over which Inigo Jones took special care, sketching and revising them several times. His final design shows one of the two lion masks more emphatically delineated than the rest of the costume, with an almost sculptural plasticity; and the accounts reveal that the pauldrons were modelled by the sculptor Nicholas Stone.[100] They are so close to Le Sueur's image that they may well be copied from it. But Le Sueur in turn owes a debt to Jones, since the symbolic meaning of the motif derives from the masques, which Jones had been designing for decades.

Charles appeared in the masques of the 1630s under different guises, but the role he took was always the same: an imperial ruler from an idealized Romano-British past. This was the same role as that taken by his dominant but short-lived elder brother Henry in the court entertainments of a generation earlier, during the brief period of his coming of age and his sudden death. In designing Henry's persona, Inigo Jones drew on the imagery of ancient Rome and the iconography of the Caesars. His principal reference was a set of equestrian portraits of the Twelve Caesars engraved by Antonio Tempesta,[101] which mixed historical evidence with visual invention in the extravagant idiom of Cinquecento Italian court festivals, and made liberal use of the grotesque ornament favoured in Mannerist art. Jones's most complete surviving design for Henry depicts him in the masque *Oberon the Fairy Prince* (1611). Here he is the protagonist of a composite classical/Arthurian scenario; his costume, paraphrasing Roman armour, is a pastiche of Tempesta's Caesars, including prominent lion-mask pauldrons.[102] This 'Caesarean' motif, associated in Jones's design vocabulary with a romantically British, chivalric idea of imperial power and with Henry's self-image as future king, recurs when his younger brother Charles actually becomes king and adopts the same self-image. Its use by Le Sueur indicates how the royal image which Henry began to develop in the masques is extended by Charles into more lasting forms, including in this case the obdurate medium of bronze sculpture.

Bronze was also a medium which lent itself to reproduction; Le Sueur's skill in casting and working it meant that his busts of the King could be multiplied. He designed several related types and produced numerous replicas. A few examples were retained in the royal collection, but most were spread abroad, to be displayed either in public or in the houses of courtiers. One version of the 'Caesarean' type with lion-mask pauldrons was presented to Oxford University by its chancellor, Archbishop Laud, in 1636 (the year of the royal visit to the university) and eventually set in a niche in the

Bodleian Library; another exists at Wentworth Woodhouse, Strafford's seat in Yorkshire, and is said to have been given him by the King.[103] The choice of type may well have been adapted to the recipients, Laud calculating that neoclassical ornament would appeal to an academic audience, and Strafford being predisposed to appreciate the symbolism of imperial autocracy. A different type shows the King with the accoutrements of royalty, wearing the crown, and the chain of the Garter over an ermine cape. One cast of this started off in the royal collection, but was given to the Earl of Holland in exchange for a Venetian landscape painting;[104] another was sent to Chichester in the late 1630s, perhaps as a signal that conflicts between the corporation and the cathedral chapter were an affront to royal authority and should be settled.[105] Such gifts were not always successful in their intended context, as we have seen with 'the image of his Majesty's own head, in brass, for the town of Portsmouth ... made and delivered by his Majesty's command'.[106] The documents do not specify which type of bust this was, but it seems that the hostile reaction of the citizens was not to nuances of meaning but to the symbolic imposition of the King's presence and the governor's demand for visible signs of respect.

The more indispensable Le Sueur became in broadcasting the King's image, the more manifest were the aesthetic limitations of his work. In the 'Caesarean' type of bust, for example, the head is much less expressive than the armorial ornament, the bland features contrasting with the animistic power of the lion faces and the grimacing pectoral mask. The 'royal' type is frankly an assemblage of parts, with the crown fitted separately on to the head, and the Garter chain made of individual links attached to each other and pinned to the cape underneath. Its banality is attested on one of the sculptor's bills, annotated by the King. An item reads: 'his Majesty's image, with the crown and order well gilt, £60'; the price is struck through, with a note 'This I will not have.' Le Sueur offered it again, addressing the King as 'your poor petitioner' and leaving the price open: he got £30 only.[107] This unwanted piece is very likely the one which the King swapped with Lord Holland for a picture.

Le Sueur's 'industrious and excellent' efforts were being overshadowed by the negotiations with the papal court for a bust of the King by Bernini. Van Dyck's portrait of Charles in three positions, which was to serve as a model, aroused high expectations.[108] Before being sent to Rome in 1636 it was probably used by the Flemish sculptor François Dieussart, who carved a marble bust of the King in that year.[109] This was made for the Earl of Arundel, who had brought Dieussart to England from Rome, and was evidently set on employing a sculptor with an Italian training and a more

Fig. 9.21 Hubert le Sueur, Charles I in antique military costume, gilt-bronze,
c. 1638, Stourhead.

advanced style than Le Sueur. When eventually Bernini's bust arrived in
the summer of 1637 it caused a sensation; before it was even out of its
packing case Inigo Jones, always eager to trumpet his knowledge of
modern art, 'exclaimed with an oath' that it was 'a miracle'.[110]

In response to this challenge, Le Sueur made an attempt to see the King
afresh. Instead of trying to engage Charles's interests as a connoisseur and
to compete with the modern, baroque style of Van Dyck, Dieussart and
Bernini, he played to his own modest strengths and to the King's self-
image with an entirely new portrait in a neo-antique idiom (fig. 9.21). It

employs a more historically correct version of Roman military dress: a plain breastplate with a square-cut neckline and the edge of a shirt visible underneath, and decorated only with a lion mask; a cloak fastened with a round brooch; and 'labels' at the shoulders.[111] All these details recall the busts of Roman emperors in the royal collection; the slight turn of the head and the further sideways glance of the eyes show that Le Sueur has also attended to the expressive qualities of Roman portrait sculpture.[112] The only Mannerist, pseudoclassical touch is a decorated helmet topped by a rearing dragon, but this must allude to the legend of St George and the King's role as Garter knight, so that it complements metaphorically the antique military costume. The overall conception obviously struck a chord with the King: the bust was displayed at Whitehall in the royal collection, and the entry describing it in Abraham van der Doort's inventory shows that its point was appreciated: 'Y. [Majesty's] owne Picture cast in brasse wth a helmett upon his head whereon a dragon, after the Auncient Roman fasshion.'[113]

Although in eclipse as an artist, Le Sueur was too useful to be easily supplanted. He was, for example, increasingly called upon for full-length sculptures of the King. The first of these had been an equestrian statue, commissioned by Lord Treasurer Weston for the garden of his house at Roehampton.[114] It was evidently meant to emulate similar statues in Florence of Cosimo I and Ferdinando I by Giambologna and Pietro Tacca, and that of Henri IV by Tacca on the Pont Neuf in Paris; Peacham wrote that it would 'compare with that of the New Bridge at Paris, or those others at Florence, and Madrid'.[115] The statue at Madrid was of Phillip III, again by Tacca, and it stood in the garden of the Casa del Campo, the royal retreat across the river from the Alcázar.[116] Charles must have seen it in 1623, and would have appreciated the compliment paid him by Weston in following it as a precedent. He had Le Sueur make a miniature version of Weston's statue, which he kept in the royal collection,[117] so that the new equestrian image became his own possession as well as a semi-public project.

There were also life-size standing sculptures executed for architectural settings. For the new Canterbury Quadrangle, which he added to St John's College, Oxford, Laud commissioned statues of the King and Queen; they were placed high up in classical aedicules, in the centre of facing *baroquisant* frontispieces.[118] When Inigo Jones by royal command designed a classical choir screen for Winchester Cathedral (fig. 9.22), it incorporated statues by Le Sueur of James I and Charles I, as supreme governors of the

Fig. 9.22 Inigo Jones, choir screen of Winchester Cathedral, 1637–1638, Royal Institute of British Architects.

Church. Jones's preliminary sketch gives each an individual pose, but in the event Le Sueur only differentiated the heads, casting the bodies from the same mould.[119] Two similar statues (or perhaps replicas of the earlier ones) were placed above Jones's new portico for St Paul's Cathedral;[120] and a Latin inscription on the frieze under them celebrated King Charles's work of re-edification.

All these statues showed the King armed, invested with the regalia, and wearing the insignia of the Order of the Garter, that is, as head of church and state. After his death they were viewed with hostility by the new republic, which set about removing them. In 1650 the Commonwealth Council of State ordered both statues on the portico of St Paul's 'to be thrown down and broken to pieces, and the inscription on the stone work under them deleted'.[121] Another statue of Charles at the Royal Exchange was 'to be demolished, by having the head taken off, and the sceptre out of his hand, and this inscription to be written "Exit tyrannus Regum ultimus"'.[122] But not every public sculpture of the King fell victim to icon-oclasm. The equestrian statue at Roehampton had been expropriated by order of parliament, and ended up with a Holborn brazier called John Revett. He was ordered 'to breake the said statue in peices to the end That nothing might Remaine in Memorie of his . . . Majestie'. Instead he buried it, dug it up at the Restoration, and published an engraving to advertise its return to life.[123]

Of all the images of the King, these sculptures most resembled his physical body, and came to have his own fate visited upon them. As they underwent deposition, decapitation and resurrection they figured the death and rebirth of monarchy.

Painting

King Charles loved the art of painting above all things; one of his earliest biographers represented him as a painter *manqué*.[124] His passion had a practical bent, as painting was the chief medium by which early modern rulers transmitted their image to each other and established vicarious presences in the complex network of international politics. It was important to secure the services of artists whose portrayal of the ruler would be powerful and persuasive, who could command a visual language which would be intelligible on a European scale. In early seventeenth-century England this meant employing foreigners.

The historic centres of modern painting were Italy and the

Netherlands. After his accession, Charles had tried but failed to attract two Italian painters to his court: Francesco Albani, the pupil of the Carracci, and Guercino.[125] In the event, his court painters, whose periods of service overlapped, were respectively Dutch and Flemish: Daniel Mytens from Delft and Anthony van Dyck from Antwerp. Van Dyck, who overshadowed and effectively displaced Mytens, had the advantage of a lengthy residence in Italy.

Mytens had been in London since 1618. His first patrons were the Earls of Arundel and Southampton; but he let it be known that he wished to work for Charles, then Prince of Wales,[126] and he seems to have achieved his wish. There are two portraits of Charles dated 1623, probably painted after his return from Madrid; a replica of one of them was despatched to Spain, as a sequel to the negotiations for the Prince's marriage to the Infanta.[127] Mytens's employment at court was confirmed in 1624 when James I awarded him a yearly pension of £50 and a grant of denization 'by direction from ye Princes highnes'.[128] When the prince became king in 1625, he commissioned Mytens to produce 'a coppy of Titians great Venus', that is, the *Venus of the Pardo*, which he had brought back as a gift from Madrid, and he paid the unusually large sum of £120 for it (although the original was an unusually large picture).[129] Soon after authorizing this payment the King appointed Mytens 'one of our picture-drawers of our Chamber in ordinarie'.[130] In effect he had become court painter.

Charles's patronage of Mytens suggests that he had recognized his talent and was deliberately fostering it; the grant of a pension had designated it 'for his better encouragem^t in the art and skill of picture drawing'.[131] To choose a Mytens portrait to send to Spain was to recognize the quality of his work, since Phillip IV's collection of pictures had made an overwhelming impression on the young prince. He was perhaps trying to turn this experience to practical advantage when he set Mytens to copy one of the great Titians out of that collection; whatever the destination of the copy (which we do not know), the work of producing it would have posed an unusual challenge to the painter, compelling him to extend his range beyond his chosen specialism of portraiture. A year later, in the summer of 1626, he was given leave of absence; the Privy Council approved a passport for 'Daniell Mitten, his Majesty's picture drawer, to goe over into the Low Countries and to remaine there for the space of six months.'[132] Since his pension was explicitly tied to his continued residence in England, this journey has the appearance of a study trip approved by the King. Mytens had not crossed the Channel for eight years; apart from the studios of his fellow painters, the court of the Archduchess in Brussels and the household of the Prince of Orange at The Hague would both provide opportunities to learn more of fashionable portraiture.

It is worth saying – in the face of the praises routinely heaped upon Van Dyck – that Mytens was a very good painter. His most accessible work today is the early portrait of the King's cousin, the young Marquess of Hamilton, in the Tate Gallery.[133] The design is sober and restrained; the only dramatic accent is the sitter's red stockings, but the treatment of the dully coloured slate pavement on which he stands is equally engaging. It is not so much the conception of the image that makes the picture a success, as the relation between the quality of painting and the social distinction attributed to the sitter. The portrait of Charles as Prince of Wales which (as far as we can tell) was sent to Spain in 1623 (fig. 9.23) is similarly restrained, although more elaborately composed.[134] He stands on a patterned carpet; on one side is a velvet curtain and a table fitted with a gold-embroidered velvet cloth, on the other a view of the Thames and Westminster. The dominant colours, defined by Charles's costume, are dark red and black; and the overall effect, rich but sombre, is no doubt meant to accord with the grave decorum of the Spanish court on which the portrait had to make its impression.

The careful hopes which Charles invested in Mytens were well founded. He was grooming his painter to be a kind of ambassador, to represent him (in both senses) to the states of Europe. Although he kept Mytens's self-portrait in the royal collection, and in the most honourable company, alongside those of Rubens and Van Dyck, his own portraits were made to travel. One portrait type from the early years of the reign shows the King in an interior (fig. 9.24), standing on a black and white marble pavement.[135] He looks straight at the spectator. Behind him a red velvet curtain is raised to reveal a classical balustrade of white marble with a landscape beyond. The pale, sharp tones of the landscape contrast with the dark curtains and the rich fabrics of the King's costume, and the light from outside cuts through the shadows of the room. There is evidence to suggest that this setting represents the Queen's House at Greenwich, with its view across the river. Since the Queen's House was used to receive visitors from abroad, who would come either over land from Dover to Blackheath or else up the Thames,[136] the motif of an opening to the world outside has not just a topographical reference but international bearings, by symbolically placing the King on a line of communication to the continent. A variant of this design, which shows him in a less specific interior,

Fig. 9.23 Daniel Mytens, *Charles I as Prince of Wales*, *c.* 1623, Royal Collection.

Fig. 9.24 Daniel Mytens, *Charles I*, 1628, Royal Collection.

has the curtain raised to reveal a Salomonic column (a European, in fact Catholic, motif) and beyond it a view of foreshore and sea,[137] repeating the theme of the *invitation au voyage* or opening to Europe.

The lines of communication which Mytens suggested in his portraits were used not only by diplomats but by artists, one of whom, ironically, displaced him. Van Dyck had already spent the winter of 1620/1 in England, heralded as 'Rubens . . . his famous Allievo (pupil)' and granted a pension of £100, twice what Mytens was to receive in 1624. When he returned to settle in 1632, he was knighted and became 'Principal Painter in Ordinary to their Majesties' with a pension of £200 a year.[138] Although both artists coexisted for two years, Van Dyck's ascendancy was at once evident, and can even be seen charactered in paint on one of Mytens's royal portraits.

Not long before Van Dyck's arrival, Mytens had painted a double portrait of Charles and Henrietta Maria.[139] The Queen holds an olive branch, which the King has just given to her, while she hands him a wreath of laurel. The exchange celebrates their dynastic union, as the symbolic gifts recall their fathers, the olive the peace-loving James I and the laurel the valorous Henri IV. This programme is developed in *Albion's Triumph*, the Twelfth Night masque of 1632. Charles, the chief masquer, is the emperor Albanactus, while Henrietta Maria, the principal spectator, is the goddess Alba, as her 'native beauties have a great affinity with all purity and whiteness'[140] (and she wears white in the portrait). The masque stages the triumph of Albanactus, expounded allegorically as his conquest of vices and passions; and he is conquered in turn by the beauty of Alba. The conclusion celebrates the calm and prosperity of Charles's Personal Rule; Peace appears, to a song which plays on the qualities of the laurel and the olive:

> 'Tis not the laurel tree that brings
> Anointing oil for sacred kings;
> Those princes see the happiest days
> Whose olive branches stand for bays.[141]

The King's olive branches are his laurels, his peace is his victory: with courtly adroitness the masque allows him the role of triumphator and peace-maker at the same time; the Mytens portrait, produced alongside it, is not up to such agile transpositions. In the copy of it which survives, the sense of interaction is minimal, and the gaze which the Queen exchanges with her husband is quite prosaically, even unattractively, rendered. Her figure seems to have caused displeasure, as it was obliterated, and repainted in the style of Van Dyck (fig. 9.25). We can view on Mytens's own canvas the moment of his eclipse, as he is literally painted out by his successor, on whose newly resplendent work the King's loving regard now falls.

The double portrait was intended for a particular room in Somerset House, the Queen's residence,[142] but its stay there, even after being emended, was short. It was replaced by Van Dyck's own reworking of the composition, in colours more closely associated with the masque: the Queen is in white, the King's suit is carnation (the colour worn by Peace in *Albion's Triumph*), and the curtain behind them, red in Mytens, is now olive green.[143] The loving rapport of the royal couple is much more convincingly suggested; the masque had praised it extravagantly, along with the prosperity of their realm, here evoked by a landscape added in the background. Van Dyck's picture notably surpassed Mytens's and made a considerable impression. It was published in a handsome engraving by Robert van Voerst in 1634[144] (fig. 9.26). Nicolas Briot reproduced the figures on a series of medals in 1635, staying as close as possible, on this tiny scale, to the detailing as well as the poses in Van Dyck's painting.[145] A miniature copy was painted by the limner John Hoskins in 1636, and kept in the Cabinet Room at Whitehall:[146] this treatment was reserved for favourite pictures in the King's collection, so that he could have the pleasure of possessing them twice over.

Van Dyck's prodigious talent had been enhanced by his cosmopolitan experience. Mytens could create a sense of presence, individuality and status. But Van Dyck had learned from Venetian Renaissance painting how to endow his figures with subjectivity, and to relate them, not just through physical attitude in the Florentine and Roman way, but with implicit ties of empathy. He had also learned how to paint landscape, and to use it as a metaphor of subjectivity and empathy. Nicholas Hilliard compared the restless animation of the human face to changes in the weather, but the restricted economy of miniature painting left no scope to work out such an idea; Van Dyck could realize the distilled subtleties of English limned portraiture on the scale of life, and make shifting skies figure the motions of the mind. Finally, he had learned, while painting the noble families of Genoa in the 1620s, to represent aristocracy as a condition above ordinary human existence, to suggest that the power of a ruling elite is justified by the exalted quality of its inner life.

Fig. 9.25 Daniel Mytens and a later hand, *Charles I and Henrietta Maria*, c. 1630–1632, Royal Collection, Hampton Court Palace.

Fig. 9.26 Robert van Voerst after Van Dyck, *Charles I and Henrietta Maria*, engraving, 1634.

The Charles portrayed by Mytens is the Charles of the 1620s, involved in dynastic courtship, warfare, tough diplomacy and the accompanying parliamentary conflict. The new Charles overpainted by Van Dyck on the old one is the monarch of the Personal Rule, and Van Dyck's function is to picture his power as sympathetically as possible, especially to himself. Van Dyck's most ambitious portraits of the King were not sent out into the world but were kept and displayed in the royal palaces, where they helped to magnify the ruler's splendour and diffuse his quasi-divine presence throughout the precincts of government. Each was carefully adapted to its setting. The 'great piece' of the royal family in the Long Gallery at Whitehall had a view of nearby Westminster in the background. The equestrian portrait in a landscape was displayed in the country palace of Hampton Court. And the picture of the King riding through a triumphal arch was at the end of the Gallery at St James's, forming a climax to the double series of the *Twelve Caesars* by Titian and Giulio Romano, and representing him as an imperial *princeps*.[147]

But while the King retained the originals, copies were made of these beguilingly potent images. The poet Waller, in a conceit not quite far-fetched enough, called Van Dyck's studio a 'shop of beauty'. It was certainly run on business-like lines, and its products could be ordered in bulk. Royal portraits could be reproduced, to be sent abroad as gifts to foreign rulers, or to be presented to (or purchased by) courtiers and others. The quality of these multiples depended on their place in the King's scheme of things. Full-length portraits of the King and Queen in robes of state were sent in 1638 to the Prince of Orange; these would have been carefully supervised studio replicas of the originals kept at Somerset House.[148] Lord Wharton, a regular masquer who collected Van Dycks, was actually presented with original portraits of the royal couple, paid for by the Queen;[149] but it was more usual for courtiers to make their own arrangements. The Marquess of Hamilton and the Earl of Northumberland both had versions of the St James portrait, which omitted the arch appropriate for its original setting: Hamilton's was painted by Remee van Leemput, a professional copyist (who may have started out as an assistant to Van Dyck), and Northumberland's (fig. 9.27) was obtained from Van Dyck's estate after his death.[150]

Wharton and Northumberland were both keen admirers of the artist's work, but not such admirers of the King as to take his side during the Civil War. When Northumberland acquired his version of the St James portrait, he was acting as guardian of the King's two youngest children, who were

Fig. 9.27 Anthony van Dyck and a later hand, *Charles I on Horseback*,
c. 1633–1640, Petworth House.

now in the custody of parliament, but his motives were aesthetic rather than pious. His picture was inventoried as 'The King . . . on a White Horse the face not finished by Van Dyke': its head was lacking, and its owner left it like that, presumably unwilling to have a lesser painter intervene.[151] Paradoxically, Van Dyck's images of the King were too distinguished to be sure of retaining their political potency beyond the calculated *mise-en-scène* of the Caroline court.

Masques

The most magnificent images of the king were to be seen in the court masques. As a medium for representing royalty the masque was unique, in that it did not need to fabricate a simulacrum of the monarch: the King appeared in person. Although in the allegorical fiction which generated the action of a masque he might have a named part – Albanactus, Britanocles, Philogenes – or else, with the masquers who attended him, be the principal in a group of 'perfect lovers' or 'ancient heroes', these were conventionally transparent disguises, and his role was to be himself. It is important to remember that masquers did not speak or sing, or engage in any kind of dramatic impersonation. They could only do what was compatible with the decorum of the court; so they appeared in symbolic costume, and thereafter they danced. They were set apart from the professional performers elsewhere in the action by their silence and their splendour. When the King appeared in a masque he was at the centre of a spectacular tableau vivant.

Inigo Jones, who designed and produced the Caroline masques, wrote that they were 'nothing else but pictures with light and motion'.[152] This was a partisan assertion, a challenge to his discarded colleague Ben Jonson, who had always argued that the text was the vital element. Since masques relied on music and dancing, as well as text and visual spectacle, the argument was wide open. But during the 1630s, when Jones was in the ascendant, he made sure that the masques became more and more pictorial in character, a tendency which accorded with Charles's love of the visual arts and his use of them to make statements of his political objectives and ideals. *Coelum Britannicum* (1634), a masque about the reforming intentions of the King's Personal Rule, has a very wordy text by Thomas Carew; nonetheless Jones contrived that the opening scene, a grand prospect of a ruined Roman city, 'detained the eyes of the spectators for some time' before any performer came on stage and the dialogue was allowed to begin – that is, the action began with a picture.[153] As the initial speeches got under way the scene changed to show the celestial sphere, held up by a giant figure of Atlas wearing a crown,[154] an emblem of the burden of monarchic rule; so that even before the King appears his symbolic double has preceded him. Often when the King makes his eventual appearance in a masque, it is at the centre of a static group. In *Albion's Triumph* (1632), as the emperor Albanactus, he is revealed sitting in a sacred grove, 'attended by fourteen consuls', symbolizing the Privy Council; and in *Salmacida Spolia* (1640), 'the King's majesty and the rest of the masquers were discovered sitting in the Throne of Honour, his majesty highest in a seat of gold'.[155] The texts make clear that, before the King rises to initiate a formal dance, these group poses were held for some time, again inviting the audience to react as if to a picture.

Such moments were arresting because otherwise a masque was constantly on the move, not only with dancing but with scene changes, Jones's major contribution. When he spoke of 'pictures with light and motion', Jones was invoking an idea of the pictorial which included not only 'stage-pictures' or posed tableaux, but reached out to that dynamic quality which was fundamental to contemporary art – the art we now call 'baroque' – and came to be seen in the portraits of Van Dyck or the ceiling of the Banqueting House by Rubens. Caroline England produced no monumental baroque art of its own: Van Dyck's project for a set of tapestry cartoons celebrating the Order of the Garter, with the King at the centre, came to nothing.[156] But in the spectacular transformations of the masque, designed by Jones to look like baroque paintings come to life, the King could figure as gloriously as any continental sovereign, with the added advantage of figuring authentically as himself.

Precisely what image of the King emerged from the masques is hard to say. Masques were occasional and ephemeral. They were also ambivalent in function and form. They were festive entertainments to be enjoyed, but also political parables which might require sharp attention. They addressed topical events, but articulated more general philosophical themes. They treated their royal protagonists with adulation, but might also intimate advice or criticism. Their main purpose at the Stuart court was to celebrate divine right monarchy, and during the 1630s to present an apologia for the Personal Rule. But quite early the masque form had developed a double structure: the main masque, in which sacred royalty triumphed, was preceded by the antimasque, a contrasting action in a comic or grotesque vein. The characters in the antimasque might be drolls or plebeians, or more sinister figures like magicians or rebels, but they were all, in Ben Jonson's phrase, 'imperfect creatures'[157] who were eventually dismissed by the dazzling epiphany of the masquers. The antimasque was in a dramatic mode which threatened conflict, the main masque in a symbolic mode which achieved transcendence. So the masque form offered to produce its meaning dialectically, and then went back on its offer.

The apotheoses of the masque were witnessed by an elite. Although the texts were often printed, and so made more accessible, the performances were for 'spectators of quality',[158] courtiers and privileged outsiders. Those excluded, such as citizens and the common people, often cropped up irrepressibly as comic characters in the antimasque, encouraging the courtly elite to see the majority of their compatriots as part of a bumptious social subplot.

In one way the masque was too complex a form to be always constrained by these conditions. The scenario of *Salmacida Spolia* has been linked by Martin Butler to the summoning of the Short Parliament soon afterwards, and the King's need to conciliate and compromise.[159] This was in response to a crisis; but Kevin Sharpe has argued that all the masques of the 1630s offer counsel to the King as well as praise, and that the text of *Coelum Britannicum* even hazards parody of his style of government, and its high-minded rhetoric of reform.[160] The use of parody, especially, seems to qualify the image of the King formed in such a context. The problem is that these qualifications are made in the antimasque; when the King himself appears in the main masque, and overlays with his presence the notion of him so far sketched in the course of the action, any scepticism must tend to give way to respect, the respect due to that presence. In *Coelum Britannicum* he was 'richly attired' as an 'ancient hero' (fig. 9.28), in a costume costing almost £90, much more than a full-length portrait by Van Dyck.[161] The effect, as always, was designed to be overpowering: here was majesty in excess, art and life compounded, a glorious representation which was also the real thing.

The masques provided the only images of the King from which the King was not absent; they figured him magnificently while sparing him the disadvantages of becoming the object of representation. The citizens of Portsmouth might begrudge deference to a statue; the courtiers of Whitehall could scarcely deny it to the real presence of their sovereign.

Fig. 9.28 Inigo Jones, ancient hero for *Coelum Britannicum*, 1634, Chatsworth.

Notes

1 John Donne, 'The Canonization', *The Elegies and the Songs and Sonnets*, ed. Helen Gardner (Oxford: Clarendon Press, 1965), lines 5–8.

2 Walter Raleigh, *The History of the World* (London, 1652), sig. A5v.

3 *Evelyn's Sculptura* ed. C. F. Bell (Oxford University Press, 1906), 25.

4 Ibid.

5 Ibid., 25–6.

6 James Howell, *Epistolae Ho-Elianae: Familiar Letters*, 10th edn (London, 1737), 42.

7 PRO SP 16/300/30; *Calendar of State Papers: Domestic* (hereafter *CSPD*), 1635 (London: Longman, –), 443, 22 October 1635, Edward Viscount Wimbledon to the Mayor of Portsmouth. Charles Avery, 'Hubert Le Sueur, the "Unworthy Praxiteles" of King Charles I, *The Forty-Eighth Volume of the Walpole Society, 1980–1982* (Glasgow, 1982): 184.

8 Herbert A. Grueber, *Handbook of the Coins of Great Britain and Ireland in the British Museum*, 2nd edn (London: Spink, 1970), 116, no. 626, plate XXVI.

9 Mark Jones, 'Nicolas Briot', in *The Dictionary of Art*, ed. Jane Turner, 35 vols. (London: Macmillan, 1996), IV, 818.

10 Helen Farquhar, 'Portraiture of our Stuart Monarchs on their Coins and Medals', *British Numismatic Journal*, 5 (1909): 175; *CSPD*, 1625–6, 573, 6 September 1626, Warrant to Nicholas Briot, etc.

11 *CSPD*, 1628–9, 428, 1628, Propositions . . . [of] Mons. Briot, made to the King; see *CSPD*, 1629–31, 353–4, 2 October(?) 1630, Nicholas Briot to the King.

12 Patent dated 16 December 1628 in Rymer, *Foedera*, XIX, 40, quoted in Farquhar, 'Portraiture', 175.

13 Edward Besly, *Coins and Medals of the English Civil War* (London: Seaby, 1990), 14, fig. 20; Grueber, *Handbook of Coins*, 111, no. 596, plate XXIV.

14 See, e.g., Besly, *Coins and Medals*, 13, fig. 18.

15 *CSPD*, 1629–31, 353, 2 October 1630, Petition of Nicholas Briot to the King.

16 Besly, *Coins and Medals*, 14–15.

17 *CSPD*, 1637–8, 498, 8 June 1638, The King to Sir William Balfour, *et al.*, quoted in Farquhar, 'Portraiture', 176.

18 Grueber, *Handbook of Coins*, 101, no. 533; see 197, no. 159, plate L, for the corresponding Scottish coinage.

19 Ibid., 200, no. 169, plate L; 106, no. 564; 110, no. 592, plate XXIII.

20 Ibid., 108–9, nos. 574–83, plate XXIII.

21 Besly, *Coins and Medals*, 57.

22 Ibid., 59, fig. 81, and plate VIII; Grueber, *Handbook of Coins*, 121, no. 650, plate XXVII.

23 Besly, *Coins and Medals*, 31, fig. 36 (see 37, fig. 42, for a more elaborate version designed for the Oxford mint by Thomas Rawlins); Grueber, *Handbook of Coins*, 119, no. 643.

24 S. R. Gardiner, *History of the Great Civil War*, new edn, 4 vols. (London, 1894), I, 24; Besly, *Coins and Medals*, 29 f.

25 Ibid., 31–2; *CSPV*, 1642–3, 186–7, 31 October 1642, Giovanni Giustinian to the Doge and Senate (wrongly dated 21 October by Besly).

26 Grueber, *Handbook of Coins*, 116, no. 26, plate XXVI; Besly, *Coins and Medals*, 37–8, plate IV.

27 Grueber, *Handbook of Coins*, 113, no. 610, plate XXV; Besly, *Coins and Medals*, 46–7, fig. 62, plate V.

28 Besly, *Coins and Medals*, chapter 10, 'The Tower Mint in the Civil War', 91 f.

29 Ibid., 94; Alan J. Nathanson, *Thomas Simon. His Life and Work, 1618–1665* (London: Seaby, 1975).

30 Besly, *Coins and Medals*, 95, fig. 131.

31 Roy Strong, *Henry, Prince of Wales and England's Lost Renaissance* (London: Thames and Hudson, 1986), 197–200.

32 *The Thirty-Seventh Volume of the Walpole Society, 1958–1960. Abraham Van der Doort's Catalogue of the Collections of Charles I*, ed. Oliver Millar (Glasgow, 1960), 124–5.

33 John Evelyn, *Numismata. A Discourse of Medals, Antient and Modern* (London, 1697), 1.

34 John Peacock, *The Stage Designs of Inigo Jones* (Cambridge University Press, 1995), 48–9.

35 Evelyn, *Numismata*, 69, following Henry Wotton, *The Elements of Architecture* (London, 1624), 106–7, who goes further by claiming that public portrait sculpture in Rome 'had . . . a secret and strong *Influence*, even into the advancement of the *Monarchie* . . . so as in that point ART became a piece of *State*'.

36 *CSPD*, 1633–4, 361, 1633(?), Petition of Edward Green, chief graver of the Mint and seals, to the King; Farquhar, 'Portraiture', 183, dates this to the birth of Prince Charles in 1630. Edward Hawkins, *Medallic Illustrations of the History of Great Britain and Ireland*, 2 vols. (London, 1885, and plates 1904–11), 254, no. 37, plate XX.18. See Millar, *Van der Doort*, 132 note 5: 'Item A Silver peece with a roase and a lillie *Coyned* uppon the duke of yorks Birthday 1633.'

37 Quoted in Farquhar, 'Portraiture', 188; Hawkins, *Medallic Illustrations*, 1, 243, no. 10, plate XX.1.

38 Paulette Choné, *Emblèmes et pensée symbolique en Lorraine (1525–1633)* (Paris: Klincksieck, 1991), 77–8.

39 Hawkins, *Medallic Illustrations*, 1, 238–40, nos. 1–5, plate XIX.7–11.

40 Stephen Orgel and Roy Strong, *Inigo Jones. The Theatre of the Stuart Court*, 2 vols. (London: Sotheby Parke Bernet; Berkeley and Los Angeles: University of California Press, 1973), 1, 374, lines 425–6.

41 Christopher White, *The Dutch Pictures in the Collection of Her Majesty the Queen* (Cambridge University Press, 1982), 53–5, no. 74.

42 Orgel and Strong, *Inigo Jones*, II, 457, line 441; the masque is *Albion's Triumph* (1632). See in *Coelum Britannicum* (1634) the conceit of the royal couple as 'CARLOMARIA', 572, lines 271–9.

43 Hawkins, *Medallic Illustrations*, 1, 306, no. 130, plate XXVI.15; Evelyn, *Numismata*, III, no. XXXII.

44 Hawkins, *Medallic Illustrations*, 1, 253, no. 14, plate XX.14; 265–6, nos. 59–60, plate XXII.1–2.

45 Ibid., 1, 252, no. 32, plate XX.13; the inscriptions repeat *Georgics* I.40: '[Caesar] da facilem cursum, atque audacibus adnue coeptis' (grant a smooth course, and give assent to bold undertakings).

46 Ibid., 1, 250, no. 26, plate XX.8.

47 Ibid., nos. 27–8, plate XX.9–10.

48 Ibid., nos. 29–30, plate XX.11–12.

49 Ibid., 256, nos. 40–1, plate XXI.1.

50 Ibid., 257, nos. 42–3, plate XXI.2–3.

51 Ibid., 285, no. 97, plate XXIV.10.

52 Millar, *Van der Doort*, 139.

53 Hawkins, *Medallic Illustrations*, I, 266, nos. 62–3, plate XXII.3–4.

54 Millar, *Van der Doort*, 137 note 1; see 130, where the actual Coronation medal is inventoried and also noted as 'much worne in yo$_r$ Ma$_{ts}$ pockett'.

55 Hawkins, *Medallic Illustrations*, I, 202, no. 108, plate XXV.5.

56 Ibid., I, 202, no. 109, plate XXV.6.

57 Ibid., I, 295–6, no. 113, plate XXV.10.

58 Ibid., I, 296, no. 114, plate XXVI.1.

59 Ibid., I, 299, no. 119, plate XXVI.6.

60 Ibid., I, 300, no. 120, plate XXVI.7.

61 Ibid., I, 298, no. 118, plate XXVI.5; Erik Larsen, *The Paintings of Anthony Van Dyck*, 2 vols. (Freren: Luca Verlag, 1988), II, 312, no. 788, illus. 297a.

62 Hawkins, *Medallic Illustrations*, I, 307, nos. 131–2, plate XXVI.16–17; see also note 44 above.

63 Ibid., I, 308, nos. 134–5, plate XXVI.18–19.

64 Ibid., I, 340, no. 186, plate XXIX.18; Pliny, *Historia Naturalis*, XXXVII.xv.57. The image of the diamond on the anvil comes from Gabriel Rollenhagen, *Nucleus emblematum* (Cologne, 1613; facsimile Paris: Aux Amateurs de Livres, 1989), Centuria secunda, 37.

65 Hawkins, *Medallic Illustrations*, I, 349, no. 208, plate XXX.18.

66 Ibid., I, 350, no. 209, plate XXXI.1.

67 *The Diary of Samuel Pepys*, ed. Robert Latham and William Matthews, 10 vols. (Berkeley: University of California Press, 1970–83), IV, 434, 26 December 1663, quoted in Alexander Globe, *Peter Stent, London Printseller* (Vancouver: University of British Columbia Press, 1985), 28.

68 A. M. Hind, *Engraving in England in the Sixteenth and Seventeenth Centuries*, vol. II, *The Reign of James I* (Cambridge University Press, 1955), 42, no. 5, plate 13.

69 Ibid., 168–9, no. 10, plates 90–1.

70 Ibid., 295–7, no. 15, plates 180–1.

71 Ibid., 311–12, no. 5, plate 192.

72 Ibid., 318, no. 4, plate 198.

73 Ibid., 287, no. 2, plate 174.

74 Ibid., 57–8, no. 12, plate 28.

75 Margery Corbett and Michael Norton, *Engraving in England in the Sixteenth and Seventeenth Centuries*, vol. III, *The Reign of Charles I* (Cambridge University Press, 1964), 342, no. 9, plate 180 (a).

76 Ibid., 253, no. 1, plate 133.

77 Hawkins, *Medallic Illustrations*, I, 266. no. 62, plate XXII.4.

78 John Smith, *The Generall Historie of Virginia, New-England, and the Summer Isles* (London, 1624, 1626, 1627 and 1632); Corbett and Norton, *Engraving in England*, 98, no. 10, plate 49.

79 Corbett and Norton, *Engraving in England*, 214, no. 4, plate 106 (b).

80 *Cyrupaedia; Or, The Institution and Life of Cyrus King of Persians. Written in Greek by Xenophon. Translated into English by Philêmon Holland* (London, 1632); Corbett and Norton, *Engraving in England*, 189–90, no. 251, plate 80.

81 *Cyrupaedia*, sig. qq8r.

82 Corbett and Norton, *Engraving in England*, 264, no. 2, plate 143.

83 Ibid., 198, no. 6, plate 95 (b).

84 Ibid., 203, no. 4, plate 99; Larsen, *Paintings of Van Dyck*, II, 318–19, no. 806, illus. 291; reproduced in colour in Arthur K. Wheelock Jr, *et al.*, *Anthony Van Dyck* (Washington: National Gallery of Art, 1990), 247.

85 Richard T. Godfrey, *Wenceslaus Hollar. A Bohemian Artist in England* (New Haven and London: Yale University Press, 1994), 68, no. 34.

86 Ibid., 114, no. 79.

87 Corbett and Norton, *Engraving in England*, 251, no. 1, plate 132 (a); the book is Thomas May, *A Continuation of Lucan's historicall poem* (London, 1630) and the etching is signed George Lid (perhaps an abbreviated form of a longer surname). See note 61 above.

88 Avery, 'Hubert Le Sueur', 141, 174, no. 11; John Harris and Gordon Higgott, *Inigo Jones. Complete Architectural Drawings* (London: Zwemmer, 1989), 186–7, nos. 53–4.

89 Avery, 'Hubert Le Sueur', 148; 178–9, nos. 16–20, plate 50.

90 Quoted ibid., 149.

91 Ibid., 204, Document 68; 180, nos. 23–24, plate 51 (d).

92 Ibid., Document 64, indicates that the standard payment for a bust of the king was £50.

93 Ibid., 153; 181–2, no. 29, plate 54 (a).

94 The same ornament is found on the armour of a bust of James I: Ibid., 189, no. 46. For rinceaux with roses used in Henry VII's Chapel, Westminster Abbey, see H. M. Colvin, ed., *The History of the King's Works. Volume III, 1485–1660 (Part I)* (London: Her Majesty's Stationery Office, 1975), plates 16–17.

95 Avery, 'Hubert Le Sueur', 153; *The Forty-Third Volume of the Walpole Society, 1970–1972. The Inventories and Valuations of the King's Goods, 1649–1651*, ed. Oliver Millar (Glasgow, 1972), 148, no. 189.

96 Ibid., 147, nos. 164–5.

97 Orgel and Strong, *Inigo Jones*, II, 536, 565, no. 274.

98 Ibid., 552, lines 635–46.

99 Grueber, *Handbook of Coins*, 105, nos. 559–60, plate XXII; 109–10, nos. 586, 589, plate XXIII.

100 Orgel and Strong, *Inigo Jones*, II, 590, 594–7, nos. 287–9; 569: 'To Nicholas Stone for enbossing the first patterns of the lions heads for the pouldrons and makeing of severall moulds upon them.'

101 Bartsch XVII.146.596–607, reproduced in Sebastian Buffa, ed., *The Illustrated Bartsch*, vol. XXXV (New York: Abaris Books, 1984), 325–7; Peacock, *Stage Designs of Inigo Jones*, 281–2.

102 Orgel and Strong, *Inigo Jones*, I, 204, 220, 225, 228, nos. 70–1.

103 Avery, 'Hubert Le Sueur', 182, nos 30B, 30C, plate 55. See 155–6 for the use of lion-mask pauldrons in actual armour.

104 Ibid., 156.

105 Avery, 'Hubert Le Sueur', 156–7, 182–3, no. 32A, plate 56 (d); David Howarth, 'Charles I, Sculpture and Sculptors', in *The Late King's Goods*, ed. Arthur MacGregor, (London and Oxford: Alistair McAlpine and Oxford University Press, 1989), 90.

106 Avery, 'Hubert Le Sueur', 183–4, no. 32D; 204, Document 64.

107 Ibid., 205, Document 75; 206, Document 81.

108 Oliver Millar, *Van Dyck in England* (London: National Portrait Gallery, 1982), 65–6, no. 22.

109 Oliver Millar, *The Age of Charles I* (London: Tate Gallery, 1972), 126, 128, no. 236. Charles Avery, 'François Dieussart', in *Dictionary of Art*, ed. Turner, XIII, 884–5.

110 R. W. Lightbown, 'The Journey of the Bernini Bust of Charles I to England', *Connoisseur*, 169 (1968): 220. In a letter to Cardinal Francesco Barberini this strong reaction is ascribed to 'the superintendant of the statues', which is most likely an inaccurate reference to Inigo Jones; there was a keeper of the king's statues, Isaac

Besnier, at a later date (later than van der Doort's inventory, where he is not mentioned): see Rupert Gunnis, *Dictionary of British Sculptors, 1660–1851* (London: Abbey Library, 1968), 50, 'Peter Bennier'.

111 Avery, 'Hubert Le Sueur', 158–9, 184–5, no. 33, plate 58 (a); the term 'labels' is used when describing Roman armour in, e.g., the masques: Peacock, *Stage Designs of Inigo Jones*, 298–9.

112 A. H. Scott-Elliott, 'The Statues from Mantua in the Collection of King Charles I', *Burlington Magazine*, 101 (1959): 218–27, plate 14.

113 Millar, *Van der Doort*, 70; Avery, 'Hubert Le Sueur', 158.

114 Avery, 'Hubert Le Sueur', 146–7, 176–7, no. 14, plate 48.

115 Quoted ibid., 147.

116 Jonathan Brown and J. H. Elliott, *A Palace for a King* (New Haven and London: Yale University Press, 1980), 35, 37, fig. 16.

117 Avery, 'Hubert Le Sueur', 147–8, 177–8, no. 15, plate 49.

118 Ibid., 161–2, 185–6, nos. 37–8, plate 62 (d); Howard Colvin, *The Canterbury Quadrangle* (Oxford University Press, 1988), 36–8, fig. 34.

119 Avery, 'Hubert Le Sueur', 165, 189, nos. 44–5, plate 62 (c); Harris and Higgott, *Inigo Jones Drawings*, 248–50, no. 81.

120 Avery, 'Hubert Le Sueur', 165–6 (with doubts that the statues were ever installed, but see below); Harris and Higgott, *Inigo Jones Drawings*, 238, fig. 75.

121 Howarth, 'Sculpture and Sculptors', 92; *CSPD*, 1650, 260–1, 31 July 1650, Council of State. Day's Proceedings.

122 *CSPD*, 1650, 260–1; David Norbrook, 'Marvell's "Horatian Ode" and the Politics of Genre', in *Literature and the English Civil War*, ed. Thomas Healy and Jonathan Sawday (Cambridge University Press, 1990), 151, identifies Henry Marten as the proposer of this republican gesture, imitating the defacement of Tarquin's statues by Brutus.

123 R. M. Ball, 'On the Statue of King Charles at Charing Cross', *Antiquaries' Journal*, 67 (1987): 97–101.

124 Richard Perrinchief, *The Royal Martyr; Or, The Life and Death of King Charles I* (London, 1676), 253–4, quoted in Arthur MacGregor, 'King Charles I: A Renaissance Collector?', *Seventeenth Century*, 11 (1996): 159 note 58.

125 Carlo Cesare Malvasia, *Felsina Pittrice Vite De Pittori Bolognesi*, 2 vols. (Bologna, 1678), II, 366.

126 Oliver Millar, *The Tudor, Stuart and Early Georgian Pictures in the Collection of Her Majesty the Queen*, 2 vols. (London: Phaidon, 1963), I, 84.

127 Ibid., I, 85, no. 117; Millar, *Age of Charles I*, 24–5, no. 18.

128 *Original Unpublished Papers Illustrative of the Life of Sir Peter Paul Rubens*, ed. W. Noel Sainsbury (London, 1859), 357.

129 Ibid., 358; Harold E. Wethey, *The Paintings of Titian*, vol. III, *The Mythological and Historical Paintings* (London: Phaidon, 1975), 161–2, no. 21, plates 74–6.

130 Millar, *Tudor, Stuart*, 84.

131 Sainsbury, *Original Unpublished Papers*, 356–7: the phrase is used in the document and then repeated in the endorsement.

132 Ellis Waterhouse, *Painting in Britain, 1530 to 1790*, 4th edn (Harmondsworth: Penguin, 1978), 54.

133 *Dynasties: Painting in Tudor and Jacobean England, 1530–1630*, ed. Karen Hearn (London: Tate Publishing, 1995), 218–19, no. 147.

134   Millar, *Tudor, Stuart*, 85, no. 117; reproduced in colour in MacGregor, *Late King's Goods*, plate 66.

135   Millar, *Tudor, Stuart*, 85–6, no. 118; reproduced in colour in MacGregor, *Late King's Goods*, plate 65.

136   Harris and Higgott, *Inigo Jones Drawings*, 226–7.

137   David Piper, *Catalogue of Seventeenth-Century Portraits in the National Portrait Gallery, 1625–1714* (Cambridge University Press, 1963), 61, no. 1246.

138   Millar, *Van Dyck in England*, 10, 14, 20.

139   Millar, *Tudor, Stuart*, 86, no. 119, plate 58 and fig. 12.

140   Orgel and Strong, *Inigo Jones*, II, 454, lines 10–11.

141   Ibid., lines 402–5.

142   Millar, *Tudor, Stuart*, 86.

143   Wheelock, *Anthony Van Dyck*, 246–9, no. 62; see note 84 above.

144   See above note 84.

145   Hawkins, *Medallic Illustrations*, I, 273–4, nos. 72–4, plate XXII.13–15; Briot omits the laurel and the olive, which on this scale would not register clearly, and has the royal couple clasping hands.

146   John Murdoch, *et al.*, *The English Miniature* (New Haven and London: Yale University Press, 1981), 100, fig. 111; Millar. *Van der Doort*, 106.

147   Millar, *Tudor, Stuart*, 93, no. 143, 98, no. 150; Gregory Martin, *National Gallery Catalogues. The Flemish School* (London: National Gallery, 1970), 44.

148   Millar, *Tudor, Stuart*, 95–6, no. 145.

149   Ibid., 95.

150   Ibid., 94; Jeremy Wood, 'Van Dyck and the Earl of Northumberland: Taste and Collecting in Stuart England', in *Van Dyck 350*, ed. Susan J. Barnes and Arthur K. Wheelock Jr (Washington: National Gallery of Art, 1994), 285.

151   Millar, *Tudor, Stuart*, 94; Wood, 'Van Dyck and Northumberland', 284–5, fig. 4 (the face completed in the late seventeenth century or thereafter).

152   Orgel and Strong, *Inigo Jones*, II, 480, lines 49–50; Peacock, *Stage Designs of Inigo Jones*, 35–54.

153   Orgel and Strong, *Inigo Jones*, II, 571, lines 37–8; see 547, lines 203–4: 'The spectators having entertained their eyes awhile with the beauty and variety of this scene . . .' (on the opening scene of *The Triumph of Peace*).

154   Ibid., II, 572, lines 189–94; 566, 580, no. 280.

155   Ibid., II, 456, lines 259–64; 733, lines 343–6.

156   Millar, *Van Dyck in England*, 86–7, no. 43.

157   C. H. Herford and Percy and Evelyn Simpson, eds., *Ben Jonson*, 11 vols. (Oxford: Clarendon Press, 1925–52), VII, 414, line 183.

158   Orgel and Strong, *Inigo Jones*, II, 662, line 33.

159   Martin Butler, 'Politics and the Masque: *Salmacida Spolia*,' in Healy and Sawday, eds., *Literature and the Civil War*, 59–74.

160   Kevin Sharpe, *Criticism and Compliment: The Politics of Literature in the England of Charles I* (Cambridge University Press, 1987), 239.

161   Orgel and Strong, *Inigo Jones*, II, 567–9, 578, line 951; Millar, *Van Dyck in England*, 22.

10

The royal martyr in the Restoration

NATIONAL GRIEF AND NATIONAL SIN

Lois Potter

Late in January 1661 the Reverend William Hampton of Bleechingly, Surrey, got word that the thirtieth of that month had been declared 'a day of fast and humiliation' for the execution of Charles I. Despite having already committed himself to preaching twice on Sunday, the sixty-year-old clergyman was determined to give both the morning and the afternoon sermon on Wednesday the thirtieth, and worked himself up to an effort which he himself, in retrospect, could hardly believe. When he published the sermon, with a dedication to Charles, Lord Cockain, he explained why he had been so eager to take on this task. Twelve years ago, he recalled, he and Cockain 'did in private pour forth our souls together in utter detestation of that horrid Fact, and in bitter lamentation for it'. What he had long wished for 'in my secret prayers' had at last come to pass: an opportunity to express those feelings 'in publick'.[1] Hampton says that he was in tears himself and also drew tears from his listeners. It is likely that the same experience was repeated in many parish churches around the country. What happened to this powerful collective emotion, and to the figure who inspired it, King Charles the Martyr, will be the subject of this chapter.

The celebration of the Restoration is remembered for 'the public communal response, the visible joy', that it inspired.[2] But it was also the first opportunity many people had had for a public communal mourning of Charles I. Theories about the role of the crowd in public spectacles of death are not designed for the special and unprecedented case where the condemned man is not 'the symmetrical, inverted figure of the king' (as Michel Foucault puts it),[3] but the king himself. The event seems neither to have created an unforgettable image of the power which ordered it, on the model described by Foucault, nor to have produced the carnivalesque reactions which, Thomas Laqueur argues, were more characteristic of the

240

English execution scene.[4] Instead, not only did royalists like William Hampton mourn in secret; even hostile members of the public were stunned into silence. C. V. Wedgwood quotes the reaction of a puritan in Yorkshire when the news arrived there: 'one neighbour durst scarcely speak to another when they met in the streets, not from any abhorrence at the action, but in surprise at the rarity and infrequency of it'.[5]

The aftermath of the king's death offered no opportunity for the public mourning which, as events of the late twentieth century have shown, can have a cathartic effect on the national experience of violent death and widespread grief. Troops dispersed the crowd as soon as the executioner had finished his work. The funeral was private; the procession from Westminster to Windsor took place in the dark and the service was entirely silent because Bishop Juxon, who officiated, was forbidden to use the Common Prayer service and refused to use anything else.[6] Parliament's allocation of £500 for all expenses was a sharp contrast not only with James I's funeral, estimated to have cost £50,000 and to have involved 9,000 people, but also with those given later to Ireton and Cromwell; the latter had cost even more than James's, on which it was modelled.[7] Clare Gittings, in her account of aristocratic and royal funeral ceremonies in the early modern period, has noted that the seventeenth century saw a movement away from rituals emphasizing status and continuity and towards those which allowed the expression of personal emotion. Ironically, Charles I, the king most concerned to preserve the public dignity of his role, was the one whose death was to be the most private and personal loss for many of his subjects.

This sense of private grief may explain something that puzzled Wedgwood, in her admirable account of the aftermath of the execution. While it is true that most memorial objects, such as medals and rings, are intended for individual use, many memorials of Charles I – pictures which showed his face only when seen from the correct direction or reflected in a silver tube, tiny editions of the *Eikon Basilike* and other 'royal' works – seem to have been designed for secrecy. Yet, as Wedgwood notes, 'no serious attempt seems to have been made to prevent the display of the King's portrait in private houses'.[8] Moreover, there was no ban on visits to the king's burial site at Windsor.[9] Yet some writers thought, or pretended to think, that their grief might be punished; the writer of an almanac of 1653 alludes briefly to Charles I and then breaks off, warning that 'there stands one near, / Will take thy eyes out, if thou shed a tear'.[10] It would seem that, except for the communities of royalists in exile, grief for the king was essentially the kind of private experience that William Hampton recalled. When attending illegal theatrical performances carried the minor risk of being caught and fined, people found it safer to create their own performances: they might gather in one another's houses to mourn and read aloud from the *Eikon Basilike*, or enjoy the illicit but not very dangerous pleasure of reading royalist pamphlets and verses. By the late 1650s the practice may even have grown. Pepys, who had once approved of the regicide, created a private commemoration ceremony on 30 January 1660 by singing his setting of 'Great, good and just', the Earl of Montrose's poem on the execution.[11] It is arguable, in fact, that such ceremonies were valued precisely because they *were* private.

The object of this solitary emotion was also its model, King Charles the Martyr. As Joad Raymond amply documents elsewhere in this volume, even before the execution, before the *Eikon Basilike* with its subtitle referring to the king's 'solitudes and sufferings', the image of the solitary and suffering king had been crucial to royalist propaganda in 1647–8.[12] Parliament unwittingly connived at the equation of king and Christ by scheduling the execution for a day when the prescribed Gospel, Matthew 27, opened with the words, 'When the morning was come, all the chief priests and elders of the people took counsel against Jesus to put him to death.' Laura L. Knoppers points out, rightly, that royalist iconography of the regicide 'recalls but does not represent actual physical suffering'.[13] At least as important as the *Eikon*, however, were the printed accounts of the trial and execution, at least some version of which can be found in most of the collected 'Works' of Charles I published in the 1650s and immediately after the Restoration. The brief final exchanges on the scaffold are varied slightly in different accounts by the shorthand writers, but in all versions Charles asks whether his hair will get in the way and warns others not to touch the axe (presumably, in case they should blunt it). The account printed after the Restoration in the sumptuous two-volume *Basilika* indicates the king's words by putting them into a larger typeface than the others, and the mixture of roman and italic dialogue seems meant to suggest a Prayer Book service. Yet this is real speech, not ritual, and not the written language of the *Eikon*. It requires an effort to 'hear' the tone in which it may have been said and has an extraordinary power to compel the reader's identification with the nervous awareness, the close relationship between victim and instrument of death, which once led artists to depict martyred saints clutching the symbols of their martyrdom. It is significant that at several crucial points in the next forty years it was the account of the trial and execution, not the serene *Eikon Basilike*, that was reprinted.[14]

As is well known, the imagery of the verse and prose responses to the execution compares Charles both to Christ and to an actor.[15] Laqueur's illuminating analysis of the iconography of executions shows that such imagery is inherent in the entire concept of carnival: 'feasting accompanied with much ribaldry, trial and sacrifice of a carnival king in whose disorderly demise the ultimate chaos of death is contained'.[16] The power of the martyr image was so strong that in the 1650s the late king was often attacked only within a context in which he could be seen as victim as well as cause of evil. The 'secret histories' of this period, many relying simply on hearsay, frequently blacken the memory of James I ('the Fountain of all our late afflictions and miseries'[17]) in order to make Charles into a victim of his father's crimes, like a hero of Greek tragedy with its family curses. Anthony Weldon's *Court and Character of King James* (1650) claims that the king had called down a curse 'on me and my posterity, for ever!' if he should (as he did) spare the convicted murderers of Sir Thomas Overbury.[18] Blame for recent events might even be laid on Charles's great-grandfather Henry VIII.[19] In the late 1650s some pamphlets begin to call Charles more saint than king.[20] By acknowledging both his private virtues and his failure as a ruler, these writers removed King Charles the Martyr from a political context. They were, perhaps without knowing it, participating in a collective project of conciliating the two sides in the late war, in the interest of the settled government which both sides seem to have wanted by the mid 1650s.

Thus Charles I was an important actor, not only on the scaffold, but in his son's restoration. The celebrations of 1660/1 conflate the restored king with the murdered king: the Restoration was, one preacher declared, 'the sweet fruit of his late Majesties prayers. He sowed in teares what we are now reaping in joy.'[21] Knoppers quotes many poetic examples showing how 'Charles I as crucified Christ gave way to Charles II as the resurrected Christ'.[22] The new ruler, arriving in London on his thirtieth birthday and crowned on St George's Day 1661, was beginning his ministry at the same age as Christ, and perhaps reminded some people that St George in Rubens's pre-war painting had been made to resemble Charles I. For those to whom he was an entirely unknown quantity, the knowledge of the king's long years of poverty-stricken exile inspired the hope that he had been purified by his sufferings. Bishop George Morley, preaching at the coronation, verged on blasphemy as he linked father and son, putting into the mouth of God the words 'Behold the Man; behold your King; Behold Charles the Sufferer, the Son of Charles the Martyr . . .'[23]

Thomas Laqueur's evocation of the sacrifice of the carnival king describes its typical ending: 'The wildness, inversion and feasting of the carnival finally gives way, and the proper world order is restored.'[24] But the definitions of carnival and proper world order depended on one's allegiance. For royalists, a country without a king was a carnivalesque world-turned-upside-down, plunged into anarchy worse than the most drunken cavalier could have imagined. For their opponents, the riotous celebrations of the Restoration were an obscene carnival. In fact the 'near-anarchy' of those early months also alarmed the new government, which saw itself as restoring order.[25] The fact that the first commemoration of the 30 January anniversary was also the day on which the exhumed carcases of Cromwell, Ireton and Bradshaw were hanged at Tyburn can be seen as a belated rewriting of the king's execution. Presented in 1649 as the will of the people, the regicide became, in the proclamation of the anniversary fast, the work of 'the Fanatick rage of a few miscreants'.[26] Now it was the regicides who became the expelled carnival kings; the grotesqueness of their hanging cancelled out their expensive funerals, creating a narrative of crime and retribution.[27] Another kind of narrative seems to have been involved in the decision to create two new holidays in 1661, each with its own order of worship – the fast for Charles I's execution and the celebration of Charles II's birthday and restoration. Since a king dated his reign from the death of his father, the normal day for celebrating a king's accession was the day on which his reign began. The separation of the end of Charles I's reign on 30 January from the beginning of Charles II's on 29 May was a deliberate separation of mourning from celebrating, winter from spring, dead king from restored king.[28] At times it seems that an unintended result was to allow Restoration congregations to indulge, and then forget, their mourning for Charles I. Henry King, in a sermon preached at Whitehall on 29 May 1661, used the Old Testament account of Saul (who, like Charles II, was taller than most of his subjects) as the basis for a definition of the true king that would certainly have disqualified the diminutive Charles I.[29]

An examination of the 30 January sermons bears out, and indeed helps to explain, the often noticed absence of tragedy in the Restoration. Nancy Maguire has suggested that the 'ludicrously extravagant revisionism' of the 1660s, with its demonizing of the regicides and idealizing of the dead Charles I,[30] exemplifies 'the psychological defence mechanism of "splitting" which, at a primitive level, dichotomizes experience into disparate and juxtaposed "good" and "bad" pairs of opposites'. The same kind of splitting, she argues, makes tragicomedy, with its serious high plot and comic low plot, the natural form for early Restoration drama: the period was simply unable to integrate the contrasting emotional experiences of mourning and celebration, seeking instead to undo tragic endings in a fantasy of wish-fulfilment. Perhaps, if the audience was, as Maguire suggests, 'politically sophisticated' but 'emotionally inaccessible',[31] it was because the opportunity for emotional abandonment available in church went far beyond anything the theatre could offer. An important aim of the 30 January sermons was that of uniting the whole congregation in a cathartic experience of grief and humiliation. As one preacher put it, evoking the full horror of the 1649 execution, 'We should not stand dumb spectators at such a wofull spectacle, but we should wail and howle . . .'[32]

National fasts were normally held to atone for the sins which might have brought misfortune on the country, but the regicide was the most spectacular example of National Sin yet to be impressed on a congregation. Fear of its consequences was based on the most often evoked prototype, the destruction of Jerusalem, widely regarded as God's punishment of an entire people for the crucifixion of Christ.[33] Thus the proclamation of the 30 January fast asks worshippers to pray that they and their posterity will not be punished for the king's death, and the first collect of the Common Prayer service for the day is a confession that 'the sins of this Nation have been the cause which hath brought this heavy judgment upon us'.[34] The Surrey clergyman William Hampton echoed its words as he advised his listeners not to blame the perpetrators of the regicide but to recognize that, 'for our personal sins, and for our National sins, we have all contributed to that stock of sin which brought that stroak of divine vengeance upon the Land'.[35] The sermon which Pepys heard from his parish priest at the first 30 January service in 1661 was on the text 'Lord forgive us our former iniquities', and Pepys approved of what was said about 'the justice of God in punishing man for the sins of his ancestors'.[36]

Persuading audiences to identify themselves with past sins and past sufferings was the aim of the two agencies most apparently opposed to each other: the pulpit and the stage. No one any longer wants to argue that Restoration drama was blithely apolitical and atemporal. Susan Staves and Nancy Maguire, among others, have effectively analysed the ways in which it alludes to or inscribes the topics and concerns of the day – suffering monarchs, usurpers, loyal generals, the crisis of authority, the disillusionment with the possibility of honesty and heroism.[37] But the relationship between theatre and collective consciousness was not simply based on the rational discussion and dramatization of themes of topical significance. It is interesting, for instance, that the first two Shakespeare tragedies known to have been performed in 1660 were *Othello*, which Pepys saw on 11 October 1660, and *Hamlet*, which was probably revived on 24 August 1661.[38] Reactions to plays in this period are hard to come by, and there may not be much significance in the fact that, with regard to *Hamlet*, Pepys's *Diary* and Downes's *Roscius Anglicanus* record only admiration of Betterton's performance, rather than comments on the appropriateness of a play in which the hero's grief for his father, at first repressed, finally becomes revengeful. It is clear, however, that it was *Othello* – the only tragedy not concerned with the killing of a ruler – that had the most compelling appeal for the Restoration and the greatest influence on other playwrights. It is also the tragedy that most powerfully depicts unrestrained rage and grief. How the Restoration actors expressed such emotions we do not know, but Snarl, in Shadwell's *The Virtuoso* (1676), scorns current actors by contrast with those he remembers from before the war: 'Pox, they act like poppets now, in sadness. I that have seen Joseph Taylor, and Lowin, and Swanstead! O, a brave roaring fellow would make the house shake again.'[39] Emotion, as expressed in public at least, is now identified with 'the last age' and 'the late king's days'.

The most elegant expression of the idea of an organic relationship between past and present theatre is the opening of the prologue to the Davenant/Dryden *Tempest* (1667), with its striking simile about the relationship between Shakespeare's play and its adaptation:

> As when a Tree's cut down the secret root
> Lives under ground, and thence new branches shoot;
> So from old *Shakespear*'s honoured dust, this day
> Springs up and buds a new reviving Play.[40]

As Dryden knew, this is an image with a biblical source (Job 14:7–9), and one which had been used for political purposes. Robert Vaughan's frontispiece to Anthony Sadler's *The Loyal Mourner* (1649) depicts exactly such a relationship between dead tree and new branches, with a fallen crown and sceptre in front of the trunk leaving no doubt about the nature of the analogy.[41] Michael Dobson has offered a reading of this link between the theatrical and political:

> 'Old' Shakespeare is here identified with the restored monarchy, likened
> to the oak tree which first protected and later came to symbolize

Charles II, but at the same time he is identified with the irretrievably dead Charles I – like the Globe, a victim of the axe during the Interregnum. In common with the monarchy itself, Shakespeare is indeed worth reviving, but with (officially unacknowledged) alterations.[42]

Though limited as an analogy – Shakespeare is not a martyr – Dobson's sense of the tone of these verses corresponds to something which is suggested about the cult of Charles I from early in the Restoration. Idealized and safely dead, both king and poet are important chiefly because they enable others to spring forth from their 'honoured dust'.

It was dust which some people would soon want to sweep away. Though the cult of Charles the Martyr and the 30 January service remained in the Book of Common Prayer until 1859, they were bound to become increasingly irrelevant to the reality of Restoration life. The regicide Edmund Ludlow says in his memoirs that even the first 30 January sermons were badly attended since the cavaliers spent the time drinking, while truly godly people stayed away and prayed in private, not for the sins which had led to the execution but for those which had brought about the Restoration.[43] He was probably exaggerating, at least with regard to the first year. But it is probable that the event lost its popularity when it lost its novelty. As early as 1664, Pepys and his wife fasted only because all the shops were shut and they had forgotten to buy any food in advance.[44] Throughout the period of the *Diary*, Pepys sometimes attended services and sometimes, when very busy, took the opportunity to catch up on his own work or do his accounts, though the more devout royalist John Evelyn seems always to have attended them, at least until his last years. But it is evident that, as the Civil War and regicide receded further into the past, it became harder to convince many congregations that they should still be doing penance for the death of someone they had never seen. This was particularly true after the revolution of 1688, when the difficulty of reconciling horror at the Civil War with rejoicing at the Glorious Revolution was sometimes resolved only by the reflection that both William and Mary were grandchildren of Charles I.[45] William Sherlock, Dean of St Paul's, testified to the strength of such views even as he tried to dismiss them in 1692: 'It is not enough to say, that we had no hand in it, that it was done before many of us were born, or before we could know and judge any thing about it, or that we did abhor and detest it when it was done.'[46] More typical of the age was a pamphlet printed and sold in 1694 by Richard Baldwin, the most influential Williamite publisher: the execution was indeed a 'Horrid Murther', but Charles I was only a man, not a proper object for devotion, and 'after 45 Years there ought to be an end'.[47] More substantial evidence of public unwillingness to take on collective guilt are preachers' frequent complaints of poor attendance at the anniversary sermons and their references to (possibly fictitious) people elsewhere who are feasting instead of fasting on the day of Charles the Martyr, or who call it a 'madding day'.[48] Dissenters openly complained of anniversary sermons which blamed them for the king's death, while one writer, referring to the fact that traditionalist Church of England clergymen used it to attack the political views of their superiors, compared 30 January with 'the Baccanalia of Rome, wherein Slaves and Servants might safely insult and hector their Masters'.[49] Thus an occasion which had originally been intended to reinforce obedience and restore order had come to be seen as potentially divisive, insubordinate, even carnivalesque.

Further, several events of the Restoration deprived Charles I's martyrdom of its uniqueness. If *Eikonoklastes* was, as John Knott says, Milton's attempt 'to protect the tradition of Protestant martyrdom from the efforts of Charles and his followers to appropriate it',[50] what Milton could not do was done by the Restoration itself and its reversal of the roles of pathetic sufferer and insulting conqueror. Many people were undoubtedly impressed by the unaffected and pious deaths of such figures as Thomas Harrison and Thomas Scot in 1660 and Sir Henry Vane in 1662.[51] Indeed, the reversal was often made more obvious by the deliberate creation of parallels, as when Vane's death was scheduled for the anniversary of the Battle of Naseby and on the spot where the Earl of Strafford had been executed in 1641.[52] But the parallel worked both ways: if Vane's death balanced Strafford's, Vane's sufferings mattered as much as Strafford's.[53] Just as with Charles I, accounts were published of the regicides' scaffold speeches, their conversations with their families, and their last letters. A curious publication of 1661, *Rebels no Saints*, was apparently intended to counteract the effect of these works. The compiler says in his introductory epistle that he produced this booklet in order to undeceive those who might be taken in by the feigned sanctity of the rebels, but its effect is so totally counterproductive, for any reader not already violently prejudiced against them, as to make one wonder whether it is ironically intended. It is a shock to move immediately from the last words of Major-General Harrison

> By God I have leaped over a Wall, By God I have runn'd through a Troop, and by God I will go through this death, and he will make it easy to me. Now into thy hands, O Lord Jesus, I commit my spirit.

to the comment:

> Kings are the only flowers in Gods terrestrial Garden, that wear the Inscription of *Noli me tangere*, warrented from Gods own mouth . . . Dye then, Mr *Harrison*, and let thy sin perish with thee, whilest thy memory shall want the mercy of a sigh to rescue thy abominable Name from putrefaction; and may all the rest of thy accursed crue dance at thy wedding.[54]

Faced with unexpected courage from people whose beliefs he abhorred, the author found himself making (in cruder terms) the same point that Milton had insisted upon in *Eikonoklastes* – that the important qualification for martyrdom was the cause, not the suffering.[55] Milton himself may well have tried, as Knoppers suggests, to argue his case again in *Paradise Regained*, where a deliberately low-key, untheatrical Jesus, who does not die, 'counters the pathos and dramatic appeal not only of the theatrical martyr-kings but of the Christ whom they imitate'.[56] Since what enabled both Charles and the regicides to die bravely, and what impressed the standers-by, was precisely their passionate belief in the cause for which they considered themselves to be dying, it was hard to argue that such passionate conviction was hypocritical or that, even if it were deluded, it deserved no sympathy.

In this context, the fascination with martyrdom, which appears both in the titles of plays of the early Restoration and in some of their most impressive scenes,[57] can be seen as part of an on-going debate about which sufferers really deserved that title. The torture scene of Dryden's *Indian Emperor* (1665) is often understood as simply anti-Catholic or sceptical in its treatment of religion. The Spaniards initially apply the torture in an attempt to get the emperor Montezuma and his high priest to reveal the whereabouts of hidden treasure, but, because the Christian (Catholic) priest urges Montezuma to be converted before he dies, the scene becomes a debate over religion. As one would expect in Dryden, Montezuma behaves with kingly courage and the high priest with priestly cowardice, though he is loyal enough to ask the emperor for permission to tell the torturers what they want to know and dies before he can reveal it. Both priests assure Montezuma that their religion is the true one; rather ineptly, the Christian priest goes on: 'But we by Martyrdom our Faith avow.' This allows Montezuma to reply, tellingly, 'You do no more than I for ours do now.' This line is often quoted, and interpreted as an impressive vindication of a non-Christian religion. But neither the emperor's sun-worship nor the fanatical Catholicism of the priest who supervises his torture are religions with which most of Dryden's audience would be likely to identify itself. The point is rather, as Montezuma goes on to say, that martyrdom in itself is not a useful test of the truth of any religion:

> To prove Religion true –
> If either Wit or Suff'rngs would suffice,
> All Faiths afford the Constant and the Wise.   (V.ii. 83–5)[58]

It might be a comment on the futility of comparing the respective merits of the Church of England martyr of 1649 and the sectarian martyrs of 1661–2. Dryden later gives Montezuma (who survives the torture but then kills himself) the still more cynical perception, which must have been evident to anyone who had watched the decline of interest in Charles the Martyr, that suffering is as much subject as anything else to the taste for novelty:

> I might have liv'd my own mishaps to Mourn,
> While some would Pity me but more would Scorn!
> For Pity only on fresh Objects stays:
> But with the tedious sight of Woes decays.   (V.ii. 244–7)

On the other hand, the death of St Catherine in Dryden's *Tyrannick Love* (1669), with its significant subtitle, *The Royal Martyr*, seems an unambiguous glorification of martyrdom: 'practically everyone in the play refers to the proto-martyr Charles I',[59] and the saint's decapitation, which happens offstage, is an apotheosis, with no grotesque or horrific elements. But it is significant that this martyr is female, as indeed are several other suffering rulers in early Restoration plays.[60] The first Restoration revivals had all-male casts; it is interesting that the first female role to be played by an actress seems to have been the martyred Desdemona. While women who suffer nobly are heroines, passively suffering men seem to arouse some uneasiness. One of many civil war pamphlets reprinted at the Restoration was a sermon which Bishop Brownrigg had preached, and for which he had been imprisoned, in 1644, on the anniversary of Charles I's coronation. Listing the king's many virtues, Brownrigg had stressed his chastity: 'What Virgin hath he deflowred? Whose bed hath he defiled? Whose Virginity hath he assaulted? . . . We may and should boast of God's mercy: All Christendome cannot afford such another' (31).[61] Only a year after Brownrigg preached that sermon, Charles I would be accused of weakness and uxoriousness because the letters found after the Battle of Naseby revealed the extent to which he confided in his wife.[62] The question of the martyr's virility is inadvertently raised even in 1660, when a biographer admits that his remarkable chastity had resulted in his being 'thought less than Man by some; till the happy fruit and satisfactions of a Matrimonial Bed vindicated that suspition'.[63] Another biography claims that some of those present after the execution tried unsuccessfully to examine the decapitated corpse in the hope – it was thought – of finding evidence of the pox or impotence.[64]

Such 'suspicions' about Charles I are particularly interesting, of course, in view of the revelations that his subjects were soon to have about Charles II's 'manhood'. The main effect of the royal martyr on his oldest son seems to have been one of polarization. Burnet's *History* of 1683 explains the famous good manners of the restored king as the result of his mother's determination that he should not be as stiff and remote as his father.[65] The image of the Merry Monarch, Harold Weber suggests, helped to counterbalance his embarrassing failure to produce a legitimate heir, a failure which enabled his opponents to ridicule him for precisely the qualities they had attacked in the cavaliers (and even in Charles I): 'effeminacy, impotence, and homosexuality'.[66]

Idealization of Charles I is an obvious way of rebuking Charles II, but even praise of the late king is sometimes a two-edged sword. When Le Sueur's pre-war statue of Charles I on horseback, hidden in 1649, was re-erected in Whitehall in 1675, it inspired a dignified poem by Waller, concluding that 'kings so killed rise conquerors again'.[67] A very different poem on the same subject, attributed to Marvell, opens with mock-naive speculations as to the intended purpose of the raised stage where the statue is to be erected: will the Italian comedians be performing on this tiny space? But surely this would be unfair competition with 'the Mimick so legally seiz'd [in possession] of Whitehall' (line 8). If the poem actually *is* by Marvell, the contrast would be devastating: Charles II is compared to a comic actor, and farcical mimics perform on the very site of the 'tragic scaffold' where the 'Horatian Ode', in a half-admiring phrase, had described the 'royal actor' playing his last part. At the end, presumably alluding to Waller's satisfaction that Charles I could now 'see his son reign where he a martyr died', the author suggests that, on the contrary, the late king should be placed with his back turned toward the palace because,

> Though of brass, yet with grief it would melt him away,
> To behold ev'ry day such a court, such a son.[68]

The contrast between the familiar image of the suffering king and that of his wastrel son replaces Waller's image of a conqueror with a feminized

Charles I, who not only grieves but weeps to see what is going on in his former residence.

Attempts to reclaim the martyr king for a heroic role probably lay behind the two statue poems. When the writers of the Proclamation of the 30 January fast claimed that the ceremony would be 'a lasting Monument of their otherwise inexpressible detestation and abhorrency of that villanous and abominable Fact' of regicide, they may have been alluding to the fact that Charles I, as yet, had no monument. Unlike James I, who had arranged for the burial of his executed mother, and a sumptuous tomb in her memory, in Westminster Abbey, Charles II seems to have felt no urgency about any ceremony for his own father, although in 1670 he gave an expensive military funeral to General Monk, Duke of Albemarle, the 'author' of the Restoration. There had been talk of both a funeral and a tomb since 1660, but it was not until 1678 that a serious proposal for one was finally made, coinciding with the 30 January sermon. The Commons voted the sum of £70,000, to be collected by a special tax over a four-year period, for both a funeral and a suitable memorial. Christopher Wren, who was commissioned at once, designed a domed mausoleum similar to those of other rulers in the period. It would have contained a statue of the king, 'in modern Armour', standing on a shield borne by the four Cardinal Virtues and being offered a crown by angels overhead.[69] The clever design (fig. 10.1) allowed the plinth beneath the Virtues to crush beneath it the four Vices most opposed to the king, including heresy and hypocrisy. Presumably the king was to be borne on the shield because he was a fallen hero, but the fact that he was to be portrayed not lying down but standing (though with a sheathed sword), and the fact that the crown above him was a martyr's rather than a victor's, would have been apparent only to those who already knew his story. It was, as has recently been argued, a 'militant' monument.[70] Charles II approved these plans, but the turmoil of the Popish Plot intervened; his relations with parliament deteriorated, and he finally returned the designs to Wren, telling him to keep them for the time being. 'In conclusion,' Wren's grandson wrote later, 'the whole Design of the Funeral and Tomb, through Incidents of the Times, or Motives unknown to the Publick, were laid aside.'[71] According to John Toland, at the time the monument for Charles I was being discussed, the publisher Richard Chiswell, who now held Royston's monopoly on printing the works of Charles I, made the obviously self-interested proposal that the funds should be applied instead toward placing a copy of this book, chained, in every church in the country, 'which in his Opinion,

94.

Fig. 10.1 Design for statue of Charles I. Proposed monument to Charles I by
Christopher Wren, *c.* 1678.

would prove a more glorious and lasting Monument than any could be fram'd of Brass or Marble'.[72] The account of the monument project published later on the basis of Wren's papers closes with a quotation adapted from Lucan's *Pharsalia* which applies to Charles the lines saying that Pompey the Great needs no tomb. As J. Douglas Stewart points out, this was quite probably written by Wren himself as a comment on the fiasco.[73] In fact, the commonplace topos about a writer erecting his own monument through his writings may have become literally true in Charles's case. The rotunda shape of Wren's design (fig. 10.2) corresponds to that of other royal monuments of the period, completed and projected,[74] but it also recalls the title page of volume I of *Basilika* (fig. 10.3), the magnificent two-volume collection of the works of Charles I published in 1662.

However, even the literary tomb did not last, and Milton had a posthumous revenge on the king he had been unable to defeat while he lived. When *Eikonoklastes* was republished, in the post-revolutionary climate of 1691, the publisher's advertisement included a brief memorandum said to have been found in a copy of the *Eikon Basilike* belonging to the Earl of Anglesey, whose books were being auctioned off following his death in 1686. Anglesey stated tersely that in 1675 he had heard from both Charles and James that the *Eikon* had been written not by their father but by Dr John Gauden. Gauden had indeed made his claim to authorship early in the Restoration and, according to some versions, had been promised rewards by Charles II himself. The correspondence on this subject in the state papers had been potentially embarrassing for years, though Anglesey's motives in leaving his note (which, as some writers pointed out, might easily not have been found at all) remain mysterious. A passionate controversy erupted, with writers on both sides producing their aged expert witnesses to testify that, yes, they had seen Charles writing something which they understood to be his memoirs, or, conversely, that they remembered hearing someone say that Gauden had written them. Stylistic comparisons between the *Eikon* and Gauden's other works did or did not prove his authorship, depending on the previous opinions of the reader. While there were many people who continued to believe both that the *Eikon* was the greatest piece of devotional writing in English and that Charles I was indeed its only author, it never regained its former status. What Elizabeth Skerpan Wheeler says elsewhere in this volume about the authorship controversy following the book's first publication is equally true of this second controversy: 'What power the narrative possesses depends on its presenting an internally consistent picture of one man's

92.

Fig. 10.2 Design for rotunda. Proposed monument to Charles I by Christopher Wren, *c.* 1678.

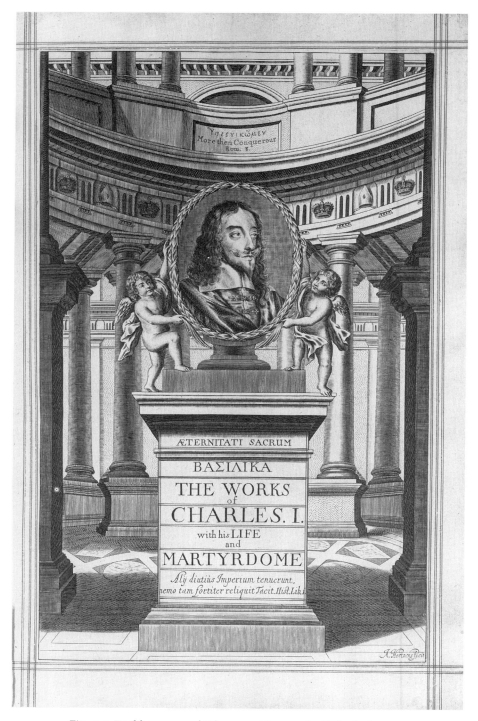

Fig. 10.3 *Basilika*, engraved title page with portrait of Charles I, 1662.

point of view.' In 1668, Pepys described a chance encounter in a coach with a lady 'tolerable handsome, but mighty well spoken, whom I took great pleasure in talking to, and did get her to read aloud in a book she was reading in the coach, being the King's Meditations'.[75] By 1668, Pepys and many others were disillusioned with the restored king, but it seems that to speak and hear the words of the dead king was still a pleasure – an example of what Skerpan Wheeler describes as readers becoming 'participants in the co-creation of the royal image'. Once the *Eikon* was dissociated from the voice of Charles I, it lost most of its interest.

A sermon dedicated to the Duke of York in 1661 had taken as its text: 'And by it he [the dead Abel] being dead yet speaketh' (Hebrews 11:4). At the end of the dedication the preacher assured James, 'Your Highness though you cannot see your Fathers face, yet you may hear his voyce; he made not his last Speech upon the Scaffold, *yet he speaketh*, yea he speaketh so loud that he may be heard throughout the whole Court, the whole kingdome, the whole world.'[76] If the echoes of Charles I's voice were dying out elsewhere during the course of the century, it would seem that his sons, at least, continued to hear them. Richard Ollard has noted a moment at which Charles II echoed a vehement expression used by his father in a similar context.[77] In James's case, the results were more dramatic. At a crucial juncture in his life, when he was confronted by the invasion of William of Orange and the desertions of many of his followers, this man, always hitherto known for his bravery, collapsed with terror and fled the country without a fight. J. G. A. Pocock has speculated entertainingly on what Charles I would have done in his son's place ('The first move would have been to offer battle'), and explained James's collapse as a result of his fear that he was about to see history repeat itself.[78] Pocock's theory is borne out by a letter which James wrote to the Privy Council, not long after his flight, explaining his action by 'a Saying of Our Royal Father of Blessed Memory, when he was in the like Circumstances, "that there is little Distance between the Prisons, and the Graves of Princes (which afterwards proved too true in his case)"'.[79] He was quoting the opening of chapter 28 of *Eikon Basilike*. The letter, assuming that it is entirely in James's words, suggests that he still thought of the book as his father's in every sense that mattered – or else, he was prepared to make cynical use of what he took to be a still-potent image of Charles the Martyr. In 1692 he published, or allowed to be published, *Imago Regis: or, The Sacred Image of His Majesty, in his Solitudes and Sufferings, Written during his Retirements in France*. Unlike the *Eikon* parodies mentioned in Skerpan

Fig. 10.4 Frontispiece to James II's *Imago Regis*, 1692.

Wheeler's chapter above (p. 135), this was a wholly serious imitation: ana-
lysing different episodes in James's life and reign, it alternates between
narratives and short prayers with frequent biblical quotations about the
sufferings of Christ. Its frontispiece (fig. 10.4) depicts the king in contemporary dress and perriwig, reading at a table, with a dog jumping up at the
side of his chair.[80] Though the dog, symbol of fidelity, might be intended
as a reproach to those who had abandoned James in his hour of need, the
picture differs from the famous frontispiece to the 1649 *Eikon* in that it has
no emblems. The appeal to a legend now over forty years old had some
success in James's own party: after his death, there were Jacobite attempts
to canonize him, and the poet Jane Barker linked father and son in her
elegy: 'Himself a saint, a martyr was his sire.'[81] But, as Laura L.
Knoppers's chapter in this volume makes clear, no romantic legend has
ever been able to establish itself around the figure of James II. The time of
the martyr was over; that of the patriot had come.

Notes

I should like to thank my research assistant, Barbara Silverstein, for her help with this chapter.

1 William Hampton, *Lacrymae Ecclesiae; Or, The Mourning of Hadadrimmon for England's Iosiah* (London, 1661), 'Dedication', n.p.

2 Laura L. Knoppers, *Historicizing Milton: Spectacle, Power, and Poetry in Restoration England* (Athens: University of Georgia Press, 1994), 68.

3 Michel Foucault, *Discipline and Punish: The Birth of the Prison*, trans. Alan Sheridan (Paris: Gallimard, 1975; New York: Vintage Books, 1979), 29.

4 Thomas W. Laqueur, 'Crowds, Carnival and the State in English Executions, 1604–1868', in *The First Modern Society: Essays in English History in Honour of Lawrence Stone*, ed. A. L. Beier, David Cannadine and James M. Rosenheim (Cambridge University Press, 1989).

5 *Memoirs of the Life of Mr Ambrose Barnes*, ed. Longstaffe, Surtees Society (1867), 108–9, quoted in C. V. Wedgwood, *The Trial of Charles I* (1964; Harmondsworth: Penguin, 1983), 196. See also Elizabeth Skerpan Wheeler's chapter in this volume.

6 Wedgwood, *Trial of Charles I*, 203–5. Some of these details were less strange than they may seem: nocturnal funerals were a common practice even for aristocrats in the seventeenth century, and they usually dispensed with a funeral sermon. See Clare Gittings, *Death, Burial and the Individual in Early Modern England* (London and Sydney: Croom Helm, 1984), 188–9, 195–6.

7 Gittings, *Death, Burial and the Individual*, 227, 229–31. She gives the estimated budget for Charles's funeral at £400, Wedgwood (see note 5) at not more than £500. For the relation of Cromwell's funeral to James I's, see Roy Sherwood, *The Court of Oliver Cromwell* (London: Croom Helm, 1977), 166, which makes the point that the protocol for James I's funeral was followed 'because they were burying a king'.

8 Wedgwood, *Trial of Charles I*, 209.

9 John Evelyn visited it in 1654; see *The Diary of John Evelyn*, ed. E. S. de Beer, 6 vols. (Oxford: Clarendon Press, 1955), III, 98–9.

10 'Raphael Desmus' [Samuel Sheppard], *Merlinus Anonymus* (London, 1653).

11 *The Diary of Samuel Pepys*, ed. Robert Latham and William Matthews, 10 vols. (Berkeley: University of California Press, 1970–83), I, 32–3. The editors suggest that this was John Wilson's setting, but Pepys says 'my song' and he did compose music for other verses.

12 See above pages 60–2. See also Lois Potter, *Secret Rites and Secret Writing: Royalist Literature, 1641–1660* (Cambridge University Press, 1989), 174–5.

13 Knoppers, *Historicizing Milton*, 19–20. See also Peacock's chapter in this volume pages 198–9, for the contrast between English and continental imagery of the decapitation.

14 In 1684 John Nalson published *A True Copy of the Journal of the High Court of Justice*, dedicated to James, Duke of York. After James's flight from the country, another, anonymously printed, account appeared, significantly called *A Looking-Glass for the Times in the Tryal and Martyrdom of King Charles the I of Glorious Memory* (London, 1689). At the end the editor wrote, '*Sic transit gloria mundi.*' The famous frontispiece to the *Eikon* reappears in the crucial year 1681, along with other royalist works, as part of a collection based on Wither's 1635 *Emblems*, called *Delights for the Ingenious*, by Nathaniel

Crouch. See Michael Bath, *Speaking Pictures: English Emblem Books and Renaissance Culture* (London and New York: Longman, 1994), 126–7.

15 See, e.g., Nancy Maguire, 'The Theatrical Mask / Masque of Politics: The Case of Charles I', *Journal of British Studies*, 28 (1989).

16 Laqueur, 'Crowds, Carnival and the State', 339.

17 Anon., *A Cat May Look Upon a King* (London, 1653), 2.

18 Anthony Weldon, *Court and Character of King James* (London, 1650), 409.

19 Anon., *A Messenger from the Dead* (London, 1657).

20 See, e.g., the anonymous *The Court Career* and *Bradshaw's Ghost* (both London, 1659).

21 Edward Boteler, *Jus Poli et Fori; Or, God and the King, Judging for Right against Might* (London, 1661).

22 Knoppers, *Historicizing Milton*, 32–3.

23 George Morley, *A Sermon Preached at the Magnificent Coronation of the Most High and Mighty King Charles the IId* (London: R. Norton for T. Garthwait, 1661), 58, sig. I1v.

24 Laqueur, 'Crowds, Carnival and the State', 339.

25 Ronald Hutton, *The Restoration: A Political and Religious History of England and Wales, 1658–1667* (Oxford University Press, 1983), 126.

26 Charles II, *A Proclamation for Observation of the Thirtieth Day of January as a day of Fast and Humiliation according to the late Act of Parliament for that purpose* (London, 1661).

27 See, e.g., Evelyn, *Diary*, III, 269 (entry for 30 January 1661).

28 It was so effective that John Evelyn was surprised to find James II declaring his accession day, perfectly correctly, as the day of Charles II's death: *Diary*, IV, 499.

29 Henry King, *A Sermon Preached at White-hall on the 29th of May* (London, 1661). In another phrase which would turn out to be ironic, he declared, 'When God is angry with a Land, he cuts off the Line of Succession' (23).

30 Nancy Maguire, *Regicide and Restoration: English Tragicomedy, 1660–1671* (Cambridge University Press, 1992), 147–9.

31 Ibid., 107.

32 Thomas Reeve, *A Dead Man Speaking, or the Famous Memory of King Charles I* (London, 1661), 9.

33 For example, in *A Solemn Humiliation for the Murder of K. Charles I* (London, 1686), sig. C1.

34 *The Book of Common Prayer* (London, 1662), sig. S[3v].

35 Hampton, *Lachrymae Ecclesiae*, 33–4.

36 Pepys, *Diary*, II, 26.

37 Maguire, *Regicide and Restoration*, *passim*; Susan Staves, *Players' Sceptres: Fictions of Authority in the Restoration* (Lincoln: University of Nebraska Press, 1979), especially chapters 1 and 2.

38 For dates of revivals and the comments on them referred to here, see *The London Stage, 1660–1800*, part 1, '1660–1700', ed. William Van Lennep (Carbondale: Southern Illinois University Press, 1965), under the relevant dates.

39 Thomas Shadwell, *The Virtuoso*, ed. Marjorie Hope Nicolson and David Stuart Rodes (Lincoln: University of Nebraska Press, 1966), 1.2.150–3.

40 John Dryden and William Davenant, *The Tempest; Or, The Enchanted Island*, in *Works of John Dryden*, ed. Maximillian E. Novak and George Rogert Guffey (Berkeley: University of California Press, 1970), x.

41 Reprinted as the frontispiece to Maguire, *Regicide and Restoration*.

42 Michael Dobson, *The Making of the National Poet: Shakespeare, Adaptation and Authorship, 1660–1769* (Oxford: Clarendon Press, 1992), 38–9.

43 Edmund Ludlow, *A Voyce from the Watch Tower, Part V: 1660–1662*, ed. A. B. Worden, Camden 4th series, 21 (London: Royal Historical Society, 1978), 283.

44 Pepys, *Diary*, IV, 29.

45 For the appropriation of the Stuart anniversaries by Williamites, see David Cressy, *Bonfires and Bells: National Memory and the Protestant Calendar in Elizabethan and Stuart England* (London: Weidenfeld & Nicolson; Berkeley and Los Angeles: University of California Press, 1989), 186–7.

46 William Sherlock, Untitled sermon preached at St Margaret's, Westminster, 30 January 1691/2 (London, 1692), 11.

47 *Some Observations upon the Keeping the Thirtieth of January, and Twenty ninth of May* (London, 1694), 1.

48 For example, William Lancaster, *Sermon Preached before the House of Commons* (London, 1697), 7; Lilly Butler, *Sermon Preached before the Lord Mayor* (London, 1698).

49 *A Modest Enquiry into the Causes of the Present Disasters in England* (London, 1690), 5.

50 John R. Knott, *Discourses of Martyrdom in English Literature, 1563–1694* (Cambridge University Press, 1993), 4.

51 See, e.g., Christopher Hill, *The Experience of Defeat: Milton and Some Contemporaries* (London: Faber & Faber, 1984), 72–5.

52 Ronald Hutton, *Charles II: King of England, Scotland and Ireland* (Oxford: Clarendon Press, 1989), 171.

53 Evelyn (and no doubt many others) later made the same parallel between the trial and execution of the Earl of Strafford in 1641 and that of the Earl of Stafford at the end of 1680. *Diary*, IV, 226.

54 'W. S.', *Rebels no Saints; Or, A Collection of the Speeches, Private Passages, Letters and Prayers of Those Persons Lately Executed*, by a Person of Quality (London, 1661), 14–15. For other attempts to counteract the spectacle of martyrdom, see Knoppers, *Historicizing Milton*, 50–1.

55 See also Joan Bennett, who quotes similar comments from Milton's *Defence of the English People* on the danger of confusing a hardened criminal with a courageous martyr: 'God, Satan, and King Charles: Milton's Royal Portraits', *PMLA*, 92 (1977), and *Reviving Liberty: Radical Christian Humanism in Milton's Great Poems* (Cambridge, MA: Harvard University Press, 1989), 445.

56 Knoppers, *Historicizing Milton*, 37.

57 Maguire, *Regicide and Restoration*, 152–3, 200–1.

58 *The Works of John Dryden*, IX, ed. John Loftis (Berkeley and Los Angeles: University of California Press, 1966), 29.

59 Maguire, *Regicide and Restoration*, 200.

60 For example, Edward Howard's *Change of Crowns* and John Dover's *The Roman Generalls; Or, The Distressed Ladies*, both dating from 1667; see ibid., 154–6.

61 *A Sermon Preach'd on the Coronation day of K. Charles I, March 7, 1644, in S. Mary's in Cambridge, by Bishop Brownrigg when he was Vice-Chancellor of the Vniversity, for which he was cast into Prison* (London, 1661), 31.

62 Potter, *Secret Rites*, 59–61.

63 Anon. [a Person of Quality], *The Faithful, yet imperfect Character of a Glorious King, King Charles I. His country's & religions Martyr* (London, 1660), sigs. C6 and D5.

64 Richard Perrinchief, 'Life', in *Basilika: The Works of Charles I*, 2 vols. (London, 1662),
    I, 93.
65 Richard Ollard, *The Image of the King: Charles I and Charles II* (New York: Atheneum,
    1979), quoted 172.
66 Harold Weber, *Paper Bullets: Print and Kingship under Charles II* (Lexington: University
    Press of Kentucky, 1996), 92.
67 Edmund Waller, 'On the Statue of King Charles I at Charing Cross', quoted in David
    Howarth, 'Charles I, Sculpture and Sculptors', in *The Late King's Goods*, ed. Arthur
    MacGregor (London and Oxford: Alistair McAlpine and Oxford University Press, 1989),
    109.
68 'The Statue at Charing Cross', lines 55–6, in *The Poems and Letters of Andrew Marvell*, ed.
    H. M. Margoliouth, rev. Pierre Legouis with E. E. Duncan-Jones, 2 vols. (Oxford:
    Clarendon Press, 1971), I, 199–201.
69 The sculpture design for the interior is usually attributed to Grinling Gibbons, but J.
    Douglas Stewart thinks it was by Gaius Cibber, though Wren may have been
    responsible for the overall concept. See J. Douglas Stewart, 'A Militant, Stoic
    Monument: The Wren-Cibber-Gibbons Charles I Mausoleum Project: Its Authors,
    Sources, Meaning, and Influence', in *The Restoration Mind*, ed. W. Graham Marshall
    (Newark: University of Delaware Press, 1997), 31–2.
70 Ibid., 29–33.
71 Christopher Wren, *Parentalia* (London, 1750), 332.
72 John Toland, *Amyntor; Or, A Defence of Milton's Life* (London, 1699), 150. However,
    Toland appears to be a very unreliable witness.
73 Wren, *Parentalia*, 322; Stewart, 'Militant, Stoic Monument', 53.
74 R. E. Beddard mentions, among many others, Inigo Jones's mausoleum for James I and
    the designs of François Mansart for a proposed Bourbon funerary chapel. See R. E.
    Beddard, 'Wren's Mausoleum for Charles I and the Cult of the Royal Martyr',
    Architectural History, 27 (1984): 36–49; 42.
75 Pepys, *Diary*, VI, 101.
76 Thomas Reeve, *A Dead Man Speaking* (London, 1661), sig. **2.
77 Ollard, *Image of the King*, 21.
78 J. G. A. Pocock, 'The Fourth English Civil War: Dissolution, Desertion, and Alternative
    Histories in the Glorious Revolution', in *The Revolution of 1688–1689: Changing
    Perspectives*, ed. Lois G. Schwoerer (Cambridge University Press, 1992), 56–7.
79 Letter of 14 January 1689, quoted in *Royal Tracts, in 2 Parts* (Paris, 1692), 28.
80 Titus Oates later published two virulent attacks on James, *Eikon Basilike* (1696) and
    Eikon Basilike Deutera (1697), but only the titles resemble the original.
81 Jane Barker, 'At the Sight of the Body of Our Late Gracious Sovereign Lord King
    James', in *The Galesia Trilogy and selected manuscript poems of Jane Barker*, ed. L. S. Olson
    (Oxford University Press, 1997), 313.

Reviving the martyr king:
Charles I as Jacobite icon

Laura Lunger Knoppers

On 30 January 1696 the following note was affixed to the church door at Whitehall:

> What, Fast and Pray,
> For the Horrid Murder of the day,
> And at the same time drive ye Son away,
> The Royal Father and the Royal Son,
> While by your praying you their Rights do own,
> Go ask your Learned Bishops, and your Dean,
> What these strange Contradictions mean,
> And cease to fast, and Pray, and Trouble Heaven,
> Sins, whilst unrepented, cannot be forgiven.[1]

Thirtieth of January sermons, as the anonymous critic pointed out, were at best an ambivalent public exercise after 1688. William and Mary observed the fast in mourning for the regicide, yet by supplanting Charles's son, James II, they seemed to contradict all that the day had come to stand for: divine-right monarchy, passive obedience and indefeasible hereditary rule. While most scholarly analyses of Charles the martyr have stopped in the early Restoration, the character and legacy of Charles I continued to be interpreted, contested and debated long after 1688.[2] Indeed, the most controversial legacy of the royal image – among Jacobites – has been largely overlooked. I shall explore how, in a pointed rebuttal to the 'Glorious' Revolution, Jacobite verse revived the martyr king Charles I to legitimate and sanctify the exiled Stuart family, true heirs to Charles's suffering and his crown.[3]

Rescued from its marginalized position on the periphery of English history and brought into the mainstream of late seventeenth- and early eighteenth-century politics, society and culture, Jacobitism has been much discussed – and debated – in recent years.[4] While studies by Paul Monod, William Donaldson, Murray Pittock, and Richard Sharp have moved away from a focus on Jacobite intrigue and uprisings to look at Jacobitism as an ideology, discourse or cultural practice, they have noted the Jacobite uses of Charles the martyr only in passing.[5] Yet closer examination of manuscript verse shows that Charles the martyr was repeatedly and powerfully evoked in Jacobite texts.

How did the Jacobites use Charles I? By reviving the martyr king in their private manuscript verse, Jacobites preserved their divine-right ideology through military defeat and political misfortune. Uses of Charles the martyr help explain such peculiar and puzzling characteristics of Jacobitism as its persistence and yet (especially in England) passivity, its conflation of high and low cultures, and its maintenance of divine-right ideology in face of the repeated diplomatic failure and military defeat. Reviving the martyr king enabled Jacobites to reconcile the appearance of defeat with the sanctity of divine right, to transform misfortune into moral and spiritual victory, shame into glory.

Indeed, this was precisely the transformation effected by Charles I and his supporters after military defeat in the English civil wars and the regicide.[6] In 1649 the *Eikon Basilike* and a host of attendant elegies and engravings rewrote Charles's military defeat and judicial execution as Christic suffering and martyrdom. The evocative and poignant image of the martyr king (fig. 11.1) haunted the Cromwellian regime. While it is recognized that Charles was thought to have gained a martyr's glory through suffering and death in 1649, and that the cult of the royal martyr flourished at the time of the Restoration, less well known is the fact that the same held true after 1688, for Charles the martyr king lived on in Jacobite song and ballad.

Recalled from early Stuart mythology, Charles I as martyr was used by the Jacobites to reinterpret diplomatic and military setbacks from the Battle of the Boyne in July 1690 through the failed uprisings in 1715 and 1745. Charles as icon conveyed the spiritual in the world of experience, the timeless in the apparent contingencies of historical time. Yet while the figure of Charles the martyr king could win sympathy for his heirs and supply an interpretive framework, it provided no rationale for action or call to arms. Ironically, their very reverence for Charles I may have embued the Jacobites with a faith in divine providence and ensuing passivity that contributed to the permanent exile and exclusion of the Stuart heirs.

Fig. 11.1 Engraving of Charles the martyr king, n.d.

'For I have lost my glory and my crown': James II

Once he finally fled to France in 1690 – without bloodshed in England, although blood was certainly shed in Ireland and Scotland on his behalf – the stubborn, controversial and fervently Catholic James II could be remade in the likeness of the most powerful image in Stuart iconography, the martyr king, Charles I. In an early manuscript poem, 'His Majestie's Royall Farewell to England, A Pindarique', James blames his troubles upon the falseness of the British people:

> Adieu false Brittains, False to your vows adieu!
>   And you
> Who closely do my Ruin still pursue,
>   By whom
> My Royalties are Trampl'd on;
> Which has Enforc'd me from my Throne,
> And I have lost my Glory and my Crown.[7]

Invoking a traditional sense of glory as linked with an earthly crown,
James portrays himself as victim, his ruin sought by subjects who have
betrayed him. By going on to recall the regicide, however, the poem
immediately reverses the assignment of glory and shame:

> Your Fame, by Forreign Nations, is Abhor'd
> For your past Murder of your Sovereign Lord
> > What was his Fault?
> > What was his Crime?
> When you his Sad Confusion wrought.
> And the most Just, most Sacred, most Divine,
> His Soul Angelick, Temper all Sublime,
> > Yet to the wonder of the world
> > And Englands shame,
> His sacred Person of Heroick Fame,
> Was Barbarously to a Scaffold brought.   (2)

In the highly emotive language of this verse, Charles I was, as in *Eikon
Basilike*, removed from the contingencies of time into the mythological
and sacred. The verse abstracted from the complexities of history the
single graphic moment of the execution in which the rebels 'Cutt off his
Royall Head: / And banish'd all the Royall Seed / To Begg their Bread / Oh
Cursed Deed' (2). James both shares in and outdoes the sufferings of the
earlier Stuart martyr: 'Where shall I go? where shall I flye? / And I expect
no Ease from you. / And of these wounds I cannot Dye' (3).

Jacobite verse on James II appropriated the tradition of martyrdom in
England, going back to Foxe's *Book of Martyrs* and expressed so powerfully
in *Eikon Basilike*.[8] That James II remained devoutly Catholic, despite his
later pledge to maintain the Church of England in the event of a Stuart
restoration, complicated his identification with Charles I as martyr. But
that James and his heirs were Catholic, increasingly Frenchified and associated with absolute monarchism also made the identification with the
British Anglican martyr king necessary and vital.

Another Jacobite verse, 'King James's Sufferings Describ'd by himself. A
Pindarique', linked Charles and James in their passive, undeserved
suffering:

> There's None of all the Royal Pedigree
> > From the Insults of Rebells free;
> And I my self Incur as the Suffering Progeny:
> > The same Disloyall Brood
> > Did shed my Fathers sacred Blood

> Whilst he their Hellish Black Designs withstood
>> Then the Rebellious Crew
>> Calls back his Sons again
>> Not for to reign
> But to be scorn'd and dispossest anew.
> And that my Royall Parent should not be alone
> I'm Heir both to his Suffring, and his Throne.[9]

Evoking the language of the crucifixion, James posits his own sufferings as beyond those of his father:

> Only the Angry Heavens have added to my fate
> Some grains of Gall to make it more compleat.
> Those who spring from my Loyns do head my foes
> Part of my self does now my very self oppose;
> Those who were born to be my Joys procure my Woes.
> My very flesh and Blood with Enemies Combine
> And those to whom I did give Life, do hunt for mine.   (10)

The language of the poem recalls the true icon that lies behind and legitimates the Stuart suffering: Christ, who was 'scorned' and at Golgotha given vinegar to drink mixed with gall (Matthew 27:34). Also like Christ, betrayed by Judas, James's life was sought by those closest to him.

In his passivity and patience in suffering, then, James followed not only the martyr king, Charles I, but Christ himself. Another Jacobite verse, 'A Song', described James in the language of the suffering servant of Isaiah, who was 'despised and rejected of men; a man of sorrows, and acquainted with grief' (Isaiah 53:3). Widely interpreted by Christian commentators as foreshadowing Christ, the 'man of sorrows', the passage found a typological parallel in the exiled James II:

> Would you see the Man of Sorrows,
>> Then behold great James the just,
> Tho' Grief his cheeks hath plowed in furrows,
>> Yet in him still put your trust.
> His Majesty's divinely sacred,
>> Which your conscious hearts must own,
> 'Twas your blind misguided hatred,
>> Drove him from his Lawful throne.[10]

This verse particularly evinces the combination of high and low culture in Jacobite verse. Although set in popular song and ballad forms, and ostensibly echoing the voice of the people, the verse was in fact an elite, written *representation* of an idealized popular view. Hence, the paternalistic tone:

'you' have something to learn, knowledge to gain by gazing upon James, remade in the image of Christ.

Yet the controversial actions of James II in his brief reign from 1685 to 1688 may have made it difficult to portray him fully as a passive, suffering martyr. Hence, Jacobite verse often employed the rhetorical obverse, blackening the actors of 1688–9 by linking them with the rebels of 1641:

> Curst be the starrs which did ordain
> That Whiggs in England ere should Reign
> Who by their Damn'd Rebellious Brood
> Laid the three Kingdoms all in Blood
> Curst be their Tribe yea Doubly curst
> Be those that murdered Charles the First
> And may their Names Recorded be
> In Hell to all Eternity.[11]

Although almost everyone would have shared this condemnation of the regicide, the Jacobites were distinct in linking the 'Tribe' of regicides with a Williamite 'crue':

> Curst be the crue that would have done
> The same to Charles the Martyr's son
> But Curst of all their Race be those
> Who Basely did King James depose
> Under Pretence to set us free
> They sold us into Slavery.   (472)

Blaming the enemies of the Stuarts allowed the verse writers to keep from looking too closely into James's actual character. The curse was an effective means of inversion, undercutting the providentialist rhetoric associated with William III.[12]

'The Whigg's Address' likewise identified Whigs with regicides. The Whig speakers ask to be appointed William's 'cheif Ministers of State / Or else your Person we shall hate', and they promise to be on their best behaviour: 'We'll be as faithful and as just / As to your Unkle Charles the first.'[13] Indeed, if William listens to them, they will make his crown 'the lightest e'er was worn / You'l scarcely know you've any on', making him as 'glorious' as they had made Charles I. The poem thus reveals Whig hypocrisy and perfidy even before they threaten William by reminding him that 'Tho' you are Lord yet we are Masters / Tis truth you cannot choose but know / We prov'd it sixty years ago.'

Similarly, the Jacobite author of 'Forty one Revivd' fused 1641 and 1688, both times during which 'Rebells Whiggs and Traytors' plagued the nation:

> Such Rogues in Grain
>   Serve God for Gain
>   Obey they Princes for fear
> Curse their Cause
> Damn their Laws
>   Gave'm Tolleration here:
> For their Murdering Charles and Royall James Abdication.[14]

Such verse evoked unchanging types to explain and interpret present history. The rebels and traitors – who defined by contrast the sanctified Stuart kings – included William III, as the poem makes clear:

> Then to Englands Royall Roses
>   Let us Drink a Flowing Bowl
> No fat Arses or Long Noses,
>   Shall subject a Loyall Soul.

Fat arse and long nose were only two of the graphic adjectives used to characterize the appearance of the usurper, William.[15] Drinking a toast to the exiled Stuarts, 'Englands Royall Roses', was likewise a common form of Jacobite protest.

The concluding lines of the poem show an equally characteristic and even more passive turn, to the divine:

> Since the Blessed Abdication
>   England Groans beneath her Lords
> Curses on Dutch Preservation
>   If there's Justice in the Gods
> Now they've scourg'd our Sinfull Nation
>   Heaven sure will burn the Rods.

The language itself is subversive and ironic: a so-called 'Abdication' under which England groans was clearly not 'Blessed', and William's action had gone far beyond simple 'Preservation' of English rights and liberties. William was, rather, a scourge sent to punish a sinful nation.

This Jacobite writer's acquiescence and faith that such scourging would surely cease with the destruction of the instrument (implicitly William himself) shows both the strength and the limits of the divine-right ideology employed against the Williamite regime. The indefeasible right, sacred monarchy and obedience associated with the figure of Charles I both legitimated the Jacobite cause and undermined its grounds for human action. The very strategy designed to win support for the exiled Stuarts did so at the cost of effecting any kind of real change.

'Let the whole Royal Martyr Shine': James Francis Edward

If James II was too controversial and too well remembered to assume the full lineaments of the royal martyr, his son, James Francis Edward, could be idealized because – not despite the fact – he was all but unknown to the British people. One Jacobite verse written during the reign of Queen Anne managed to portray the very quiescence of the self-styled James III as the patience of a martyr king:

> O may the hardships of an injured Heir
> Bring mercy down this guilty land to spare
> After the great example of my Sire
> With patience will I bear the Almightys Ire.[16]

James III as 'martyr' – suffering, patient and praying that his own suffering might vicariously redeem the guilty land – was remarkably well developed, especially given that in order to fit this picture, James needed to do essentially nothing at all. Such passivity allowed him to claim innocence and to identify with Charles the martyr king in a way never fully available to his father.

   If active Jacobitism abated under the firmly Anglican and Stuart Queen Anne, the Tory high church crisis of her last years brought a renewed interest in Charles the martyr. Thirtieth of January sermons by high Anglican clergy such as Luke Milbourne extolled the virtues of passive obedience and recounted the horrors of rebellion against divine-right monarchy: such views were, according to one contemporary, 'the declared Principles of Jacobitism'.[17] A broadsheet on the execution of Charles I (fig. 11.2) was reprinted in 1710, the critical year of the impeachment of high church divine Henry Sacheverell. And in 1713, John Faber reissued an engraving of the portrait of Charles I at his trial, sitting passive and melancholy yet marked by the timeless symbols of kingship – his lesser George and the Garter insignia on his sleeve (fig. 11.3). *The True Pourtraicture of ye Royall Martyr Charles 1st* depicted the king who had died for divine-right monarchy and for the Anglican Church, now allegedly in danger from Whiggish toleration and dissent. While not specifically Jacobite, such reprintings kept the image of the martyr king firmly in public view.

   Overtly Jacobite texts revived Charles the martyr (in manuscript) at the

Fig. 11.2 *The Black Memorial*. Broadsheet on the execution of Charles I, 1710.

Fig. 11.3 *The True Portraicture of ye Royall Martyr Charles 1st, King of England.*
Published by John Faber, 1713.

time of the Hanoverian succession. With the disappearance of the actual Stuart line, in accordance with the Act of Succession passed in 1701 that excluded the Catholic Stuarts in favour of the Lutheran German House of Hanover, Charles the martyr king reappeared in Jacobite song and verse. Hence, one writer used the death of Queen Anne to curse the 'villains, vipers, monsters of the age' who joy 'to see the exit of the Stuart race', exclaiming:

> How basely cruell have they been to those
> Whose vertues only rendered them their foes
> Can Royal Martyrs blood be yet forgott
> Or can our tears wash out so foul a blott.[18]

The Stuarts had erred, it seems, but only in the mercy they had shown. And they were marked by martyrdom from Mary, Queen of Scots to Charles I, 'butchered next' as 'Royalty was made the Traitors prey', through his exiled son and grandson. James III was given the full inheritance of Stuart martyrdom. And yet such a lineage only amounted to forbearance and patience, not action, as James is urged to 'Bear well thy sorrows bear them if you can / Look on the faithless with smiling scorn / And know you are to endless empire born.'

Jacobite verse lauded the virtues of the martyr king Charles I and his lineage to attack by contrast the mock king George I. One verse proposed an exchange between George and James Francis Edward: 'Give us the Hero of the Martyrs Line / To whom the Crown belongs by right divine.'[19] 'A Littany for the Year 1715' inverted sacred ritual, just as George himself parodied sacred kingship:

> From an high Court and that Rebellious Crew
> That did their Hands in Royal blood imbrue
> Defend us Heaven and to the Throne restore
> The Rightful Heir and we will ask no more.[20]

Going beyond even the sin of Pilate, who symbolically washed his hands before the multitude, saying 'I am innocent of the blood of this just person: see ye to it' (Matthew 27:24), the 'Rebellious Crew' of regicides – and their Hanoverian heirs – had imbrued their hands in royal blood.

The true king and martyr, Charles I, and his suffering lineage were also pointedly recalled to denounce the impious ceremony of thanksgiving for the Hanoverian succession planned for 20 January 1714/15. A number of Jacobite manuscript poems pointed out the 'contradictions' of the occasion, in which mourning for the royal martyr was incongruously and illegitimately replaced by thanksgiving for a usurper. One of these, 'On ye late Thanksgiving day on Jan. 20 1714/15', urged repentance:

> Ye loyal souls, at this detested time
> With sighs lament your guilty Countrys crime
> When Factions Rage and rebell Sons of war
> Brought Martyred Charles to the vindictive Bar
> When Hypocritick zeal for publick good
> Thirsted to drink the Godlike Stuarts blood.
> This day let us offended Heaven implore
> To charge this mockery at the Tyrants door
> So Thunder strike the bold Blasphemer down
> Whilst he triumphant wears an injured Monarchs Crown.[21]

Aligning the thanksgiving with the parody Eucharist in which the regicides 'thirsted to drink the Godlike Stuarts blood', the Jacobite observer undermined the appearance of peaceful succession and legitimacy. At the same time, however, the verse displaced its own ground for action. The divine-right ideology that revealed George I to be a 'bold Blasphemer' placed the responsibility for revenge not on human but on divine forces.

Similarly, 'A Form of Prayer for ye Sons of ye Church of England for Jan. 20' turned to a divine audience for forgiveness:

> Searcher of Hearts Almighty Providence
> That saw'st our Crimes now see our Penitence
> And let our scalding Tears at once attone
> For our forefathers Guilt and for our own
> Thy great Vicegerent fell by their rude hands
> By us his royal Offspring exil'd stands
> Made miserable by our own Consent
> Our Sin [is] now become our punishment.[22]

Indeed, this verse was concerned not with taking action, but with averting divine wrath while redirecting punishment on to the guilty Whigs.

> But if their Crimes afresh for vengeance call
> Oh let it only on the guilty fall
> Let Whiggs those harden'd Rebells feel the weight
> And on th' Usurpers head a double portion light.

Jacobite verses on the twentieth of January 1714/15 thus notably focused on the martyr king and the penitent people. References to the present Stuart line, 'his royal Offspring', were brief and generalized. George I was directly contrasted with Charles the martyr king and was found wanting.

Verses on the birthday of the 'Old Pretender', the 10 June – some specifically dated 1715 – began to fuse the martyr king and his suffering heir. One such verse, 'On ye 10th of June', drew upon royalist type to sanctify the present-day heir despite the vicissitudes of history:

> Our injur'd Sov'reign last of all that Line
> Which rul'd Brittania with a Right Divine
> Him in Exile his Subjects now bemoan
> Heir to the Stuarts suffrings and their Throne.[23]

'On ye Same' linked regicides and Whigs, for whom 'long has king killing been their practisd trade / They glory in the ruins they have made.' The times necessitated caution:

> Who would his secret Soul expose in times
> When Loyalty is held the worst of Crimes
> When sacred Kings are driven from their throne
> The Father murder'd and exild the Son
> Because they hold their Right from God alone.[24]

But the response, again, was to turn to the divine: 'But on this day lets fast and pray & mourn / Till Heaven our ravish'd Bliss again return.'

Another tenth of June poem written in 1715, however, actually urged James onward to 'just Conquest' and beseeched him to avoid the passivity that brought on Charles's 'shameful end':

> At length being settled on thy fathers throne
> Pull Whiggs and false Dissenters down
> Who princely power diswade
> And Monarchy invade
> See and beware
> Lest the same cruel fate
> Attend thy latter state
> By which the good King Charles a Shameful End did bear.[25]

Passivity was avoided, then, by contrast to Charles I: this verse advocating action also interpreted Charles's death as shameful, without the transfiguration of the martyr.

More characteristic of the uses of Charles the martyr in 1714/15 was the reissue in July 1715 of the visual image of the royal oak, first printed in 1649 after the regicide, and central to Stuart iconography (fig. 11.4). This text, then, did appear in print, albeit coded. A note under the visual text explained that 'This is the Chapter for the Day (Tenth of *June*) appointed by the Rubrick of the Church of *England*.' Like the fortuitous – or providential – coincidence of the passion narrative with the date of the execution of

For there is hope of a Tree, if it be cut down, that it will sprout again, and that the Tender Branch thereof will not cease.

Though the Root thereof wax old in the Earth, and the Stock thereof die in the Ground:

Yet through the Sent of Water it will bud, and bring forth Boughs like a Plant, Job xiv. 7, 8, 9.

Done from the Original of *Vaughan*, after the Murder of King *Charles* the First.

Note, This is the Chapter for the Day (Tenth of *June*) appointed by the Rubrick of the Church of *England*.

Fig. 11.4 Engraving of the Stuart Royal Oak, July 1715.

Charles I, the collect for the day of the birthday of James Francis Edward employed traditional Stuart iconography: 'For there is hope of a Tree, if it be cut down, that it will sprout again, and that the Tender Branch thereof will not cease.' Hence, both in visual form and biblical text, Charles I was evoked and linked with his exiled heirs, and again the proposed resolution was divine, not depending upon, or indeed even calling for human action.

Other undated Jacobite verse on the Hanoverians likewise had recourse to divine initiative. 'Britannia's Lamentation' charged: 'Rebellious Whigs of Oliver's brood, / You're hungry for murder and thirst after blood / You hate the true Grandson of King Charles the good.' The solution, however, was providential:

> You think by fanatical wisdom and strength
> To extirpate the Martyr in his Grandson at length
> But the mighty Jehovah, the great God of Love
> Will protect and restore this his innocent Dove.[26]

The verse attacks the Hanoverians only to turn, in the end, to faith in divine protection for and restoration of the true heir. And, given its private form, the verse in fact was not intended to be read by the 'Rebellious Whigs' it excoriates.

Similarly, 'Britannias Speech' exclaimed: 'What shall a Cuckold thus possess our throne? / Invade our rights and hurl them headlong down?' The answer was a prayer to 'great Jove':

> Let not such Monsters in Britannia dwell
> Send home our native Prince, give him his right
> Whom thou hast made the Christian worlds delight
> Make him a happy and a glorious King
> Let him to Britain wealth and honour bring.[27]

James implicitly merges with Charles I, as the injunction to make him a 'happy and a glorious King' echoed the violated promises of an earlier parliament. Rhetorical violence – including the evocation of typological categories of good and evil – had an almost inverse proportion to the action urged. Not only did the verse in itself replace other action, it actually discouraged human initiative.

Given the striking passivity of the ideology linked with Charles as martyr king, it is perhaps not surprising that the image of Charles I had only a minor role in Jacobite verse on the Scottish rebellion of 1715, a serious affair in which the Earl of Mar raised Jacobite clans in the episcopal northeast for 'James III and VIII'. The 'Old Pretender' reached Scotland to join the uprising in late December 1715. Verses on the rebellion that did allude to the martyr king, Charles I – and they are few – show the difficulties of reconciling martyrdom with military might. Military uprisings were not easily made compatible with the image of the martyr.

One strategy, then, was to praise James as 'injur'd monarch' and avoid describing the battle altogether. Hence, 'To the King on his safe landing in Scotland' resolved the issue by first making James a 'glorious youth / With native goodness blest with native truth' and then evoking only the lineage, not the (non-)action, of the martyr:

> This day behold our blessed Martyrs breed
> For Heaven ordaind that Charles should Charles succeed
> O Heaven again shew mercy to our State
> Let James to James succeed with better fate.[28]

Description of imminent war was replaced by the innocuous 'breeding' of the line of martyrs.

Similarly, 'To the King on his landing in Scotland' evoked the famed Stuart mercy. Now, significantly, the verse (although remaining in manuscript) appealed to the entire nation:

> Arise Britannia! see around thy Head
> Young beams of hope and dawning glories thread
> In all thy charms thy Injured Monarch meet
> And throw thyself repenting at his feet
> Great though thy guilt has been, & deep thy stain
> Too well thou knowst pardon how to gain
> When you to Stuarts sued you never sued in vain.[29]

In neither of these verses does James actually fight. Rather, he simply arrives and is welcomed. Indeed, 'To the King on his landing' concludes by imagining the voluntary abdication of the usurper and ascent to the throne of the godlike James III: 'the God soon roused, and did himself restore / Resum'd his seat, and shone more awfull than before' (fo. 83).

English Jacobite verse on the '15 that urged military action did so through martial images of glory and shame:

> Bow England thy inglorious head in dust
> Shall Scotland rival thee in being just?
> Shall she proclaim thy injured monarch first?
> Shall her bold sons to doubtfull battles lead
> Shall foreign nations for his title bleed?
> And you not shame in the immortal deed?[30]

Repeatedly stressing the glory of battle, this verse describes James as 'injured monarch' but does not sanctify suffering and passivity. Rather, the English are urged to join the fight 'When James commands, and glory is the prize.' Only if the martyr king, so essential to legitimating the true heirs, is banished can James be portrayed as a fully martial figure. Martyrdom and military action did not cohere, and thus the only means by which the Stuarts could be restored conflicted with the powerful strand of martyrology in their own rhetoric of legitimation.

The eventual failure of the '15, however, and the return of James to France resurrected the language of martyrdom. In defeat, James could fully take on the aura of the martyr. 'On the Sight of his Majestys Picture' described a portrait of England's 'injur'd king':

> Behould unhappy James's Picture here,
> Whose Person 'tis that makes the Whiggs to fear
> His Loyal Subjects in another chance
> Tho' beaten lately still his Cause advance;
> And like the Palm Tree which the more opprest
> Still faster grows, because their cause is best.[31]

Alluding to *Eikon Basilike*, the verse removed James from the specifics of recent history and rewrote military and political loss as the sufferings of a martyr.

As with Charles I in earlier years, the trope of martyrdom transformed defeat into moral victory, shame into glory. The writer fully articulates this potent transformation:

> For to right Heirs Heaven has decreed it so,
> Their Glory must from their Misfortunes flow;
> He falls to Rise, his Losses are his Gain,
> For Pleasures are illustrated by Pain;
> His Enemies that think they pull him down,
> Exalt his Glory but eclipse their own.

Yet the poem also is an important example of what such divine-right ideology ultimately entailed: not action but patience, in the subject as in the exiled heir:

> Must James to Usurpation then give way,
> No, God forbid, Rebellion has no stay;
> God will in time the banish'd Heir bring home,
> Then rebels shall receive their cursed doom;
> But we, with Loyal Hearts will thank the Lord
> That does such Mercies to our Land afford.

Such verse, far from being a call to action, turned to divine action and initiative. Loyalty to the Stuarts was shown not in action but in loyal and thankful hearts. Indeed, such loyalty was expressed only privately, not to inspire action but to sustain belief.

A second manuscript poem offers a portrait of James in contrast to a recent painting of George I by Sir Godfrey Kneller. The language of martyrdom, glory and shame was in this text transferred to the 'injur'd canvass' of Sir Godfrey Kneller, who had disgraced his art and colours with an 'upstart German race'. Hence, the writer urged Kneller to make amends by painting one Stuart more: 'dare to display with art divine / The last of that unhappy line'. The verse-portrait fused Charles the martyr king with his grandson, James Francis Edward:

> In every feature, every line,
> Let the whole Royal Martyr shine.
> And let each lineament proclaim
> The noble stock from whence He came.[32]

The assimilation of Charles the martyr to his grandson and heir, James Francis Edward, transformed defeat into moral victory, exile into virtuous suffering, shame into glory. But it did not lead to, or even advocate, action. The same divine-right ideology that depicted the royal martyr shining godlike 'in every feature, every line' of James Francis Edward also undermined the rationale for action necessary to restore the exiled heir.

'Glorious in Thought': Charles Edward and the '45

We have seen that Charles the martyr king embodied 'strange contradictions' not only for the Williamites and Hanoverians but also for his own heirs. Such contradictions reappeared thirty years later, at the time of the last Jacobite uprising, in verse on Charles Edward Stuart, son of (still living) James Francis Edward and great-grandson of Charles I. In Scotland, however, the Jacobite appeal was broader and more public, and we turn for the first time to printed Jacobite verse. Printed texts at the time of the '45 uprising show a sustained attempt to merge the martyr and the warrior in the figure of Charles Edward. In the end the strategy was undermined by its own contradictions: although the blood of the martyr king continued to call for vengeance, his heir Charles Edward could not be both an 'inju'rd monarch' and the agent of revenge.

'Prince Charles, His Welcome to Scotland' initially described the Stuart heir in terms of martyrdom: 'Welcome to Scotia's Plains, dear injur'd Youth, / With thy great Sires were banish'd Love and Truth.' And Charles Edward was said to share in that characteristic Stuart trait of mercy: 'Space for Repentance Heaven affords to all, / And Charles, like Heaven, invites the Prodigal.' According to this poem, Britain had much for which to repent, and the blood of the martyr king cried out:

> Weep Britons! weep the Royal Martyr's Blood,
> For Vengeance, or Repentance calls aloud!
> True Penitents due Restitution make,
> And Heaven's appeas'd when Men their Crimes forsake:
> Fly then your Crimes, restore your injur'd Prince,
> And, by your Deeds, your Penitence evince;
> Kind Heaven that pities, will forgive your Fall,
> And late Posterity shall bless you all.[33]

The audience of the printed text broadens from the individual to the nation: 'weep Britons!' By focusing only on restoration, this verse avoided the conflict between the martyr and military action.

The cry of blood, it is worth noting, appeared in other polemical literature on the '45 uprising. 'The Advice of a Friend to the Army and People of Scotland', for instance, drew upon the martyr king:

> For my own Part, I am convinc'd in my Conscience, that as all the Miseries this Nation has felt for a Century past, (and God knows they are not a few) have flowed from our unnatural and base Treatment of the Royal family, from the Blood of the Royal Martyr which must always cry for Vengeance against us, till we do Justice to his Heir; so all the Happiness, Peace, and Security we can wish, or hope for, depends intirely, under God, upon the Restoration, Life, and Issue of our rightful sovereign Lord, King James.[34]

Through his very passivity and suffering, Charles the martyr king demanded action from Stuart loyalists. But the precise action to be taken was more problematic.

The strains of combining martial glory and martyrdom in the figure of Charles Edward were unavoidable in a long panegyric on the battle of Prestonpans, printed in Edinburgh in 1745. After hailing Charles Edward as 'Glorious Youth! The Wonder of the Age', the poem opened with the theme of Stuart mercy: 'Thou born to right three injur'd Nations Cause, / To strip Oppressors of oppressive Laws; / Like Heaven, thou comes with

Mercy in thy Eyes, / And Tears drop down when ev'n a Rebel dies.'[35]
Charles's foes seek to make him follow quite literally in the line of martyrdom:

> But say, when landed on a Native Shore,
> What Friends Thou found'st, what cou'd Foes do more?
> Friends faithless some, and some by far too slow,
> O'erwhelm'd thy Princely Heart with gen'rous Woe;
> Whiles Foes had destin'd thy devoted Head,
> Like Charles and Mary's on a Block to bleed. (4)

Yet the panegyric tried to encompass both martial glory and the mercy of
the martyr king: Charles was praised as a kind of timeless icon, but was
also set in action.

The poem hence lurches between the martyr and the warrior. The
Highland clansmen who have come to join their prince hail Charles
Edward as 'the righteous heir' in godlike, iconic terms: 'See, see that Face,
where all the Stewart shines! / Is bright Divinity in fairer Lines?' (8).
Charles evinces both the military might of his mother's line and the mercy
of the Stuarts:

> See mild good nature join'd with noble grace,
> Is't not the Stewart and Sobieska Race?
> Glorious Connection! Here the Warrior glows,
> There like his Great Fore-Fathers, Mercy flows;
> Mercy ill tim'd, ill plac'd, their only Crime,
> To trust too much, and trust it out of Time. (8)

Charles Edward's reply to the clansmen, 'I come to Conquer, or I come to
Die', only temporarily unites the tensions that reappear when he is
described as simultaneously fighting and urging mercy: 'These are my
Children, spare, ye Sons of War, / Tho Disobedient, yet my Children
spare' (16). In the end, the writer eschews the description of the battle altogether and opts for reiterating that Charles Edward's virtues, 'beyond a
mortal Height', are best left unexpressed.

The tension between military might and martyrdom in the figure of
Charles Edward might well have been transformed, as it had been with
James III, into unalloyed martyrdom after the failure of the '45: the disas-
trous decision of Charles's officers to turn back at Derby, the thwarted
French expedition, and the decisive defeat of the Jacobite army at
Culloden in April 1746 with its ensuing aftermath of brutal retribution.
Could Charles the martyr again be used to transform the failed Jacobite

Few know my Face, tho'all Men do my Fame;
Look ftrictly, & you'll quickly guefs my Name:
Through Deferts, Snows & Rain I made my Way,
My Life was daily rifqu'd to gain the Day !
Glorious in Thought ! but now my Hopes are gone;
Each Friend grows fhy,— & I'm at laft undone.

Peint par L. Tocqué.   *Et Gravé par J.G. Will en 1745.*

Sold by B. Cole, the Corner of Kings Head Court, near Fetter Lane Holborn.

Fig. 11.5 Engraving of Charles Edward Stuart, 'the Pretender', 1745.

cause? At least in the eyes of some, the answer was no. Charles I as Jacobite icon faded with the fading of the military threat. Divine-right ideology could not be sustained indefinitely in the face of military defeat and diplomatic failure.

Hence, in an engraving of 1745 (fig. 11.5), Charles Edward was simply a defeated Pretender, endowed with neither martial glory nor the glory of the suffering martyr.[36] The engraving shows Charles Edward clad in official uniform, with a distant, contemplative gaze. The verse below comments:

> Few know my Face, tho' all Men do my Fame;
> Look Strictly, & you'll quickly guess my Name:
> Through Deserts, Snows & Rain I made my Way,
> My Life was daily risqu'd to gain the Day!
> Glorious in Thought! but now my Hopes are gone;
> Each Friend grows shy – & I'm at last undone.

In comparison with the confident assertions of 'heavenly grace' in the portraiture of James Francis Edward, this engraving makes a much diminished claim – that the thoughts of Charles Edward had once been glorious. For all the action and efforts made by Charles Edward, his cause had been defeated, and he was 'at last undone'.

Yet for all its pessimism, the portrait in fact reaffirms the legitimacy of the Jacobite cause. Following the advice to 'Look Strictly, & you'll quickly guess my Name', we shall examine the engraving more closely. The arms and motto ('sequi finemque utere') below the figure give nothing away: they are not those of the Stuart family. Nor do the writing implements and books reveal the figure's lineage. But in the bottom left-hand corner, almost hidden from view, is a tiny portrait of a melancholy face with a distinctive beard and moustache. It is clearly the visage of the martyr king, Charles I.

Even in this engraving's pessimistic response to defeat, then, Charles the martyr king has only been moved to the margins, not erased altogether. In this engraving, Charles the martyr no longer provides mystical commentary that goes beyond the face value of the historical event. No longer an image of the divine expressed in the physical world, the image of Charles becomes merely narrative, even sentimental. Nonetheless, Charles the martyr king lives on – in the margins of the portrait, as in the margins of history – a pointed and poignant reminder of the failure of Jacobite hope and their final loss of glory.

Notes

I would like to thank Richard Sharp for his suggestions and inspiration in the early stages of this chapter, and Philip Jenkins and Don-John Dugas for their helpful comments on an earlier draft.

1 'Found on the Church Door at White Hall, January 30th 1696', Bodleian Library (hereafter Bod.), Rawlinson MS Poetry 169 fo. 9b.

2 The best essay on the thirtieth of January sermons remains Helen W. Randall, 'The Rise and Fall of a Martyrology: Sermons on Charles I', *Huntington Library Quarterly*, 10 (1947): 135–67. More sketchy, albeit useful, is Bryon S. Stewart, 'The Cult of the Royal Martyr', *Church History*, 38 (1969): 175–87. On the potential subversiveness of thirtieth of January sermons after 1688, see John Kenyon, *Revolution Principles: The Politics of Party, 1689–1720* (Cambridge University Press, 1977), 61–82. Tony Claydon explores Williamite uses of the anniversary in *William III and the Godly Revolution* (Cambridge University Press, 1996), 102–4. On the controversy in the 1690s over the authorship of *Eikon Basilike*, see Francis Madan, *A New Bibliography of the Eikon Basilike of King Charles the First*, new series 3 (Oxford Bibliographical Society Publications, 1949; Oxford University Press 1950), 126–63, and *Eikon Basilike*, ed. Philip Knachel (Ithaca, NY: Cornell University Press for the Folger Shakespeare Library, 1966).

3 The epithet 'Glorious' was contemporary with the events of 1688–9 and by the mid-eighteenth century was a widespread descriptor – with its attendant eulogistic bias. Only very recently have historians become sceptical of the 'Glorious Revolution' and the Whiggish historiography that it embodies. See Lois Schwoerer's commentary and citation of contemporary examples, 'Introduction', in *The Revolution of 1688–1689: Changing Perspectives*, ed. L. Schwoerer (Cambridge University Press, 1992), 2–3, and James R. Hertzler, 'Who Dubbed It "The Glorious Revolution?"', *Albion*, 19 (1987): 579–85.

4 Daniel Szechi, *The Jacobites: Britain and Europe, 1688–1788* (Manchester University Press, 1994) provides a useful introduction to Jacobitism. Provocative arguments for the conservatism of the 1688–9 revolution and the continuance of ideas of divine right and providence well into the eighteenth century are found in J. C. D. Clark, *English Society, 1688–1832: Ideology, Social Structure and Political Practice During the Ancien Régime* (Cambridge University Press, 1985), and Kenyon, *Revolution Principles*. Eveline Cruickshanks, *Political Untouchables: The Tories and the '45* (London: Duckworth, 1979) argues for widespread Jacobitism among the proscribed Tories after 1714; Linda Colley, *In Defiance of Oligarchy: The Tory Party, 1714–1760* (Cambridge University Press, 1982), in contrast, views the Hanoverian Tories as a loyal oppositionist party. Two collections of essays, *The Jacobite Challenge*, ed. Eveline Cruickshanks and Jeremy Black (Edinburgh: John Donald, 1988) and *Ideology and Conspiracy: Aspects of Jacobitism, 1689–1759*, ed. Eveline Cruickshanks (Edinburgh: John Donald, 1982), represent current views and issues. Studies of English Jacobitism have been complemented by work on Scottish and Welsh Jacobitism. See Bruce Lenman, *The Jacobite Risings in Britain, 1689–1746* (London: Methuen, 1980) and his *The Jacobite Clans of the Great Glen, 1650–1784* (London: Methuen, 1984); Murray Pittock, *The Invention of Scotland. The Stuart Myth and the Scottish Identity, 1638 to the Present* (London and New York: Routledge, 1991), and Philip Jenkins, 'Jacobites and Freemasons in Eighteenth-Century Wales', *Wales Historical Review*, 9.4 (1979): 391–406 and his *The Making of a Ruling Class: The Glamorgan Gentry, 1640–1790* (Cambridge University Press, 1983), especially chapter 6.

5 See Paul Kleber Monod's groundbreaking *Jacobitism and the English People, 1688–1788* (Cambridge University Press, 1989), especially chapter 2, and William Donaldson, *The Jacobite Song: Political Myth and National Identity* (Aberdeen University Press, 1988). In his important demonstration of the Jacobite appropriation of Aeneas/Augustus to counter the 'Augustan Age', Murray Pittock overstates the classicism of Jacobite verse and omits or understates biblical and sacred language, in particular, uses of Charles the martyr. See Pittock, *Poetry and Jacobite Politics in Eighteenth-Century Britain and Ireland* (Cambridge University Press, 1994). Richard Sharp reproduces a fascinating array of Jacobite portraits and engravings, although he does not deal with Charles the martyr, in *The Engraved Record of the Jacobite Movement* (Aldershot, VT: Scolar Press, 1996). An important essay on Jacobite martyrs more broadly is Daniel Szechi, 'The Jacobite Theatre of Death', in *The Jacobite Challenge*, ed. Cruickshanks and Black, 57–73.

6 On Charles the martyr in the 1650s and 1660s, see Lois Potter, *Secret Rites and Secret Writing: Royalist Literature, 1641–1660* (Cambridge University Press, 1989), chapter 5; and Laura Knoppers, *Historicizing Milton: Spectacle, Power, and Poetry in Restoration England* (Athens: University of Georgia Press, 1994), chapter 1. M. L. Donnelly's argument that the 'regicide decisively disrupted the royalist semiotics of hierarchy and power', underestimates, in my view, the recuperative power of royalist iconography. See his 'Caroline Royalist Panegyric and the Disintegration of a Symbolic Mode', in *'The Muses Common-Weale': Poetry and Politics in the Seventeenth Century*, ed. Claude Summers and Ted-Larry Pebworth (Columbia: University of Missouri Press, 1988), 163–76.

7 'A Collection of Loyal Poems Satyrs and Lampoons', Beinecke Library, Osborn Shelves b. 111, 1.

8 On *Eikon Basilike* and Anglican martyrdom, see Florence Sandler, 'Icon and Iconoclast', in *Achievements of the Left Hand: Essays on the Prose of John Milton*, ed. Michael Lieb and John Shawcross (Amherst: University of Massachusetts Press, 1974), 160–84.

9 'Loyal Poems', Beinecke, Osborn Shelves b. 111, 10.

10 Alexander B. Grosart, ed., *The Towneley MSS: English Jacobite Ballads, Songs, & Satires* (London: printed for private circulation, 1877), 23.

11 'The Anti-Curse September 1690', 'Loyal Poems', Beinecke, Osborn Shelves b. 111, 472.

12 See Tony Claydon, *William III and the Godly Revolution* (Cambridge University Press, 1996).

13 Bod., Rawl. MS Poet. 155, fos. 10–11.

14 'Loyal Poems', Beinecke, Osborn Shelves b. 111, 474–5.

15 See Monod, *Jacobitism and the English People*, 54–9.

16 'King James Speech', Bod., Rawl. MS Poet. 203, fo. 44v.

17 Milbourne's sermons were collected in *The Royal Martyr Lamented, in Fourteen Sermons, Preach'd on the Thirtieth January . . . By Luke Milbourne, Late Presbyter of the Church of England* (London, 1720). The charge of Jacobitism comes from C. Heywood, *High-Church Politicks; Or, The Abuse of the 30th of January Consider'd With Remarks on Mr Luke Milbourne's Observation of that Day* (London, 1710), 38.

18 Bod., Rawl. MS Poet. 181, fos. 73–4.

19 'The Royal Exchange', Bod., Rawl. MS Poet. 155, fo. 94.

20 Ibid., fo. 98.

21 Bod., Rawl. MS Poet. 203, fo. 22.

22 Bod., Rawl. MS Poet. 155, fos. 20–1.

23 Ibid., fo. 178.

24 Ibid., fos. 178–9.

25 'A Pindarique Ode on the 10th of June 1715', ibid., fos. 136–7.

26 Bod., Rawl. MS Poet. 203, fo. 48.

27 Ibid., fo. 47.

28 Ibid., fos. 81v–2.

29 Ibid., fo. 82.

30 Bod., Rawl. MS Poet. 181, fo. 60v.

31 Bod., Rawl. MS Poet. 207, fos. 62–3.

32 'A Copy of verse occasion[ed] by Mr Addison['s] Poems on the sight of King Georges Picture', Bod., Rawl. MS Poet. 203, fo. 88v.

33 'Prince Charles, His Welcome to Scotland' (Edinburgh, n.d.), 'Collection of Jacobite Tracts on the '45', Huntington Library.

34 'The Advice of a Friend to the Army and People of Scotland' (Edinburgh, n.d.), 20, 'Collection of Jacobite Tracts on the '45', Huntington Library.

35 'To His Royal Highness, Charles, Prince of Wales, &c. Regent of the Kingdoms of Scotland, England, France, and Ireland' (Edinburgh, 1745), 3, 'Collection of Jacobite Tracts on the '45', Huntington Library.

36 The engraving is cited (although not reproduced) in Sharp, *Engraved Record of the Jacobite Movement*, 118–19.

12

The royal image: an afterword

Kevin Sharpe

I

The title of this volume, *The Royal Image*, comes of course from the *Eikon Basilike*, the king's book. And the *Eikon Basilike* was Charles I's most enduring and most powerful legacy – to his own century and to history. As has been observed, the *Eikon Basilike* is not primarily concerned with events: its narratives are very much the king's own view of things and are allusive rather than specific. Nor is it, as Elizabeth Skerpan Wheeler points out, an account of deeds and actions; rather it brilliantly figures the king, as man and monarch; it literally characterizes him, or purports to open up his character. In two senses it is a text of representation: it represents Charles I to a wider public of readers, and it re-presents him in a new language (of intimacy and affect) and style. Through language, the interweaving of narrative and prayer, and the famous frontispiece of the king reaching for a crown of glory, the *Eikon Basilike* reconstituted images of the king into *the* image of the king as suffering martyr.[1]

Curiously, for all its importance in 1649 and for decades thereafter, historians (by which I mean here those writing within an academic department of history) have paid little attention to the *Eikon Basilike*. For sure they have, ever since the discovery of the Anglesey Memorandum, debated the authorship of the text.[2] Yet, perhaps not least because its authorship is in doubt, historians have not closely studied the *Eikon Basilike*, nor analysed it as a representation of the king, or as a text that continued to represent him to generations of subjects – whoever authored it. Here the explanation lies in what remains, regrettably, a large gulf between historians and critics. Traditionally, and with few exceptions, Roy Strong being the most important, historians have shown little interest in, and some discomfort with, the question of representation. Over the last twenty years literary scholars, in particular New Historicists, have sought to reread texts in their discursive moment and political context. Influenced greatly by the symbolic anthropology pioneered by Clifford Geertz, they have re-examined a number of texts as representations of, and interrogations of, the social and political structure of the Renaissance English state. Such critical approaches to literature have necessarily opened a broader interdisciplinary praxis, a study of the relationships of discursive and literary representation to other forms of signification – in image, festival and display. Indeed some of the most interesting work on visual and festive culture has been written by literary scholars. During this same period, however, historians of early modern England have shown little interest in these approaches and (when they have read them, sometimes before they have read them) have denounced New Historicist critics as anecdotal or unhistorical. Indeed the revisionist scholarship that has dominated sixteenth- and seventeenth-century historiography, and, for that matter, the anti-revisionist critique, have manifested a deep suspicion of literature, and more broadly of the concept of representation. To Conrad Russell, the 'reality' to be found in the archives, not the fictions displayed on the stage or canvas, is the material of history. And if the concept of 'representation' arouses the historian's scepticism, the concepts and problemizations of 'text' that have been a feature of much postmodern criticism excites undisguised hostility.[3] As David Norbrook put it, historians were unlikely to sympathize with a scholarship that depicted the court as a work of art and the prince himself as 'no more than an effect of discourse'.[4] Yet in the Renaissance state, and particularly in the reign of Charles I, the court and the king were very much works of art, and certainly after the publication of the *Eikon Basilike* Charles I had become, in large measure, an 'effect of discourse', indeed – as contemporaries were happy to use the word – a 'text'.[5] Even at court, the king was often a 'represented' as well as 'real' presence. In the Presence Chamber, the throne symbolized the king's actual presence in his absence; and in all the public rooms of state, be it in dining, going to chapel, receiving embassies or dancing in masques, the king executed elaborate and choreographed performances – performances which were as fundamentally acts of state as the sitting in Privy Council or the signing letters patent (which, of course, were themselves theatrical as well as political occasions). Beyond the court, for most the king was experienced only through representation: the studio copy of a painting, or an engraving; the sight of a statue, the reading or hearing of a royal proclamation, the exchange of coin stamped with the king's arms or face. After 1649, the deceased king could only be represented – be it through his own 'words', or his 'book', or his image on canvas or in stone, and through the observations and readings of contemporary and succeeding generations who perforce brought to those representations their own experiences and values. What the revisionist and post revisionist historians of the seventeenth century have lost sight of is that the histories of the representations of Charles I, of the royal image and text, are at the core of the history of the Civil War, Restoration and 1688 Revolution.

That the history of early modern political culture is being refigured by those outside the discipline of history is starkly manifest in our volume – in which the only historian contributes the endpiece.[6] Literary scholars and critics have not only been willing to explore the images and representations of authority, they have also richly brought to their investigations sensitivity to the issues of form and genre, the skills of close reading and rhetorical analysis, and the theorizing of both the production and reception of meaning through texts. As the contributors here are also quick to recognize, the historians' insistence on close and specific historicizing is also essential for an understanding of how such representations performed at a precise moment and shifted over time. Revisionist historians, whatever their failings, also complicated our view of the court, demonstrating that, rather than a monolith, it too was characterized by internal debates and differences and by a multiplicity of perspectives and refractions: that there was no one official position.[7] What we now need is to combine the skills of critics and historians in a full history of the relationships of courts and kings (and republics) to the images and representations of those courts and rulers over the period of the English Renaissance, from the accession of the Tudors to the Augustan age. In such a large and important enterprise, study of the image of Charles I, as prince and king, would deserve perhaps several volumes. What this collection has attempted is but a beginning: the identification of genres and moments through and in which the king's image performed polemically and politically – to shape a perception, a programme or a party, a narrative of political history.

II

As well as rightly drawing attention to the neglected subject of royal representation, our title *The Royal Image* shows how we too may be seduced or controlled by the force of that text. The *Eikon Basilike* subtly presents us with a particular view of the monarch and the reign, while concealing its partisanship. Whilst denying rhetoric and artfulness, it rhetorically constructs an account that, as Milton discovered, all but resists interpretation. Like Milton, we need to contest that control and to question each of the terms of our title that the king's book has bequeathed us. First, should we write of *The* king's image, or should we rather recognize that from the beginning there were a number of different representations of Charles I, and see that those were ever more multifaceted, altered and contested over time?[8] Secondly, to what extent is it appropriate to write of the *King's* image? Putting aside the issues of whether Charles I actually wrote the *Eikon Basilike*, to what extent did he personally fashion, control and disseminate the images of himself across a variety of genres of representation? And how far were those images images of 'the king', part of an established vocabulary and semiotics of royal representation, how far images personal and specific to Charles Stuart? Thirdly, what were the 'images' of Charles I? They were and are the paintings of Mytens and Van Dyck, the coins and medals, the volumes of prayers – material objects; but they are also the imaginings and memories of contemporaries who saw a masque or royal entry, heard or read a speech, or formed an impression – from text, engraving or common report. What all such questions point to is a more complex history of the production and reception of images of power than historians or critics often accommodate. David Loewenstein writes of the contemporary critic's recognition of 'the capacity of poetry and symbolic representation to sustain arbitrary regal power'; but, as his own and other chapters make clear, against the emphasis of too much New Historicist scholarship, neither such representations, nor poetry or art themselves, were subject to hegemonic regal power.[9] Even after only a century or so of print, there was a multiplicity of royal representations – chivalric warrior prince, godly reformer, Virgin queen, Rex Pacificus, heir of a new British empire – and therefore room for the subject to select, prioritize and play such representations against each other. In addition there were other images and texts that conveyed authority – the Bible, the classics, the common law – and which formed a symbolic and discursive context in which any specific act of representation was read. Inherited and remembered images, expectations and other representations all fashioned the production and consumption of the royal image.[10] And, as Joad Raymond has shown, by the 1620s the corantos and newsbooks proffered other representations and readings of events and implicitly of the royal actor himself.[11] As a connoisseur, John Peacock writes, Charles I was 'well qualified to plan and oversee the formulation of his own image'. And yet increasingly such formulations had to respond to other, sometimes unfavourable representations, to 'outface' other images that contested for support with the king's.[12]

The history of the image of Charles I, then, is the history of a complex interplay of texts and images, of expectations and memories of the exercise and experience of authority. It is also a history of change, of moments. Not only did different phases of the king's own life – as prince, monarch, husband, head of an army, prisoner, martyr – refigure the royal image. The success of representation, its capacity to garner support for the king's authority or actions, depended upon a conjunction of representation and circumstance. The Charles I who caused anxieties by what many regarded as arbitrary courses in the later 1620s emerged in the 1640s as the champion of the common law and subjects' rights; the king once suspected as popishly inclined was presented persistently after 1660 as the champion of the Church. As circumstance altered the hopes and fears of subjects, they reshaped how the image of the king was represented and imagined; and they determined how successfully it performed to enhance his or his successors' authority.

The chapters in this volume focus attention on a number of moments (the Ship Money Case, the regicide, the '45) and a variety of genres – masque, music, poetry, royal writing, coins, portrait. Some address radical contestation with the royal image and its rewriting in popular pamphlet and apocalyptic history. Together they form a series of case studies and also a series of points on a narrative arc of the history of the royal image. What I shall endeavour is some further reflection on the genres they explicate, and do not explicate, and a tracing of that historical arc they begin to plot. That Charles I is perhaps the most recognizable of all English monarchs undoubtedly owes much to the genius of Van Dyck. In a brilliant essay on one of the most famous paintings, Roy Strong showed long ago how Van Dyck was able to represent the king simultaneously as the Lord's anointed, as conquering emperor, chivalrous hero, master of his passions, elegant *cortegiano* and benign father of his people, ruling by love and example.[13] Sir Oliver Millar and others have cast light on the relationship of the images forged by Van Dyck to other secular and religious art that Charles I may have seen, and hence on their meaning to the royal sitter and other connoisseurs.[14] Yet there are many interesting historical questions about the paintings from which some recent art history, preoccupied with form and technique, has turned away. The extent to which, for

example, Van Dyck endeavoured to fashion stylistically a courtly community of shared tastes and representations from the contending factions and
personalities and different denominations at Whitehall awaits further
study. Though Van Dyck cleverly appropriated a variety of representations – the king as conqueror, as lover and as paterfamilias – he also
opened to observation and consideration the relations between them, and
the dialogues that ostensibly they seemed to silence. Is the 'private, lei-
sured world' depicted in Charles I *à la chasse* in 1635 compatible with that of
the martial victor, especially at a time when, after the death of Gustavus
Adolphus and the resurgence of militant Catholicism, there seemed to
some to be an urgent call to action?[15] Moreover, where we appreciate Van
Dyck's brilliance in combining a mystification of majesty with a realism in
depicting the king's humanity, was the observer also led to ponder the
relation between sacred and human, even encouraged by a less iconic representation to behold the very human contingencies of kingship? Too
often the paintings created by Van Dyck are discussed as images confined
to an elite court culture cut off from the country. John Peacock reminds us
of what was an industry of studio copies that disseminated the king's
image to a large number of noble and gentry houses, the practice of a
culture in which the painting was still as much venerated for its royal sitter
as for its talented artist: an emphasis on the subject of art that we need to
recapture if we are to comprehend how these works performed and were
viewed.[16]

Peacock, too, focuses helpfully on other visual genres in which the
image of the king was unquestionably more widely disseminated and read
by a different audience. All too little attention has been paid to the engravings of kings and courtiers that were becoming fashionable around the
end of the sixteenth century and to their woodcut illustrations in books.
There were plenty of engraved images of Charles I circulating in the 1620s
and 1630s (and later); as well as those based on Van Dycks, depictions of
the king in the tiltyard with the Earl of Dorset, or throwing down the
glove of challenge to the Scots, as he stood, in an engraving of 1638, in
armour, with helmet and baton.[17] Engravings are an important genre in
our understanding not only of aesthetic taste but of perceptions as well as
representations of authority. As Peacock shows, and the material traces of
many engravings manifest, engravers often borrowed the plates of earlier
images making minor changes to re-present the subject. As such, they
physically carried the traces of earlier and different significations as they
also reconstituted an image for a specific moment: a royal succession or

campaign. The engraving, too, often with an inscription, not only revived that combination of word and image that characterized much of Tudor royal painting, it could serve to determine or influence how an image was read.[18] Both the technology of print and inscription gave the engraved image the capacity to be adapted quickly for topical occasion. Together with its relatively cheap price, these made it a potentially very effective medium of royal representation, indeed of what we might risk (anachronistically) calling political propaganda. On the other hand, the engraving bears testimony to the role of subjects in constituting and, to some measure, controlling royal representation. Engravings, be they large collections like Henry Holland's *Brazili-logia: A Book of Kings*, or single sheets, were purchased by consumers with a desire for some symbol of the removed mystery of monarchy.[19] At the same time, once purchased, how they were arranged, displayed and viewed was the prerogative of the consumer whose coin had purchased him or her the property and the right. Tessa Watt has shown how woodcut images could be displayed alongside scurrilous ballads in books and on tavern walls.[20] Greater knowledge of the habits of collecting in seventeenth-century England would throw invaluable light on how the king's image performed, say, in the merchant household.

Engravings also (literally) graphically demonstrate the ways in which the royal image could be appropriated and contested. After the execution of his father, Charles II was quick to re-present himself in the image of Charles I, to stress a dynastic inheritance denied by the republic and to cash in on the cult of the martyr.[21] The R. White engraving of Charles I after Van Dyck, etched in 1685 with the inscription 'non eripenda', was presumably intended similarly to underpin the rights of James II, while, after the ruptures of 1688, Queen Anne carefully appropriated both the image of the Virgin Queen and the Stuart martyr.[22] Engraved images of Charles I in cartoon were also deployed to invalidate the claims of his enemies and to undermine the Rump. The Charles I who offered his hand to raise a fainting Ecclesia or came armed with his sword to protect the tree of religion from the ruffians and tub preachers who hacked at it undercut the godly rhetoric of the saints.[23] Significantly, there were no cartoons, even after 1649, denigrating the king's body.[24] Whether on account of a still powerful sense of the sanctity of the royal body, even in representation, or of a broader distrust of visuals, the parliamentarians and regicides neither censored nor countered the king's engraved image. As I have argued elsewhere, their decision or neglect was a damaging miscalculation. For the frontispiece to the *Eikon Basilike* and other engravings, it is not too much to argue, kept the memory and cause of monarchy alive.[25]

Engravings and portraits were, in the England of Charles I, still relatively new genres of representation. The coins and medals which John Peacock so helpfully studies were virtually timeless, and, despite early plans, Charles I introduced no new methods into mint production. Because of their similarity of form and process it is tempting to discuss medals and coins together, but generically they were fundamentally different. The medal was specific to a moment, pressed for an occasion, and distributed to selected and favoured recipients as a mark of participation. Coins, by contrast, were ubiquitous and circulated throughout a reign – and beyond, albeit different denominations current among different classes carried less or more elaborate images of the king and royal arms. Yet though medals had ancient origins, Charles I was evidently the first to issue them regularly from the time of his wedding; he evidently added those of his own minting to his collection of antique medals.[26] Here we witness a king constructing himself in history (a desire that would merit further reflection across the genres of royal representation) and quite clearly wishing to mark occasions by a token that was disseminated far beyond the coterie circles of Whitehall. John Peacock shows how the medals (and coins) borrowed images from Van Dyck's paintings and conceits from other genres: the Apollo and Diana representation, for example, from masque and Honthorst's canvas. Indeed such intertextual gestures go further. On the medal, for example, of Charles and Henrietta Maria with the inscription 'Iuncti Certius Pythonem', the serpent looks more like a dragon, and echoes Rubens's depiction of Charles I and St George. The serpent gestures to the dragon of rebellion that featured in Royalist cartoons against the Commonwealth.[27] Similarly, as Helen Farquar demonstrated, many Civil War badges and medals used emblems from the *Eikon Basilike*, and so the message of the king's book entered the battlefield.[28] Such study opens up, too, the neglected subject of escutcheons and banners, in particular the emblematic banners of Royalist infantry and horse. Colonel Pudsey and others, for instance, displayed the *bras armé* (also displayed on engravings) which Peacock attributes to Briot's borrowing from the Duke of Lorraine.[29] The appropriation by king and parliament of each other's images and motifs, especially for coin, helpfully extends historical discussion of the common languages in which the two sides pressed their case in pamphlet. Long before the *Eikon Basilike* rendered him as another Christ, Charles, on his coin, claimed Scripture as his aid against the enemy, 'Exurget Deus', and figured himself as Christ's chosen.[30] The importance of such coins can hardly be exaggerated. After the regicide, it took some time for the new regime to mint a new coin, and they never had enough bullion to replace royal coinage, especially those of small denomination. Cut off on the scaffold, the king's head circulated in the pockets of English men and women throughout the 1650s.[31]

In recent years court festival and masque have begun to receive the serious investigation that they were long denied. Though historians still tend to dismiss masques as a distraction from the arts of politics and government, most critics now discuss them rightly as acts of government in a political culture of magnificence and display. Peacock again helpfully adds to our understanding of the relationship of masque to other images of the king, confirming our sense that across the genres, the king himself was most likely the principal architect of his representation. But though, in its devising, production, staging and audience, 'the most controllable of cultural forms', masque was neither an unchanging nor entirely stable form of representation.[32] I have argued elsewhere, initially to a more hostile critical reception than of late, that the relationship of masque to antimasque was complex and licensed criticism as well as compliment.[33] Here Thomas Corns valuably points up the potential difficulties presented by the form at particular moments of uncertainty. From 1620, he argues, the earlier 'simplicity of representation' was complicated by the outbreak of the Thirty Years' War, and even masque began to resonate with the anxieties about a plurality of voices and visions.[34] Within the prince's circle itself, the masque images of fertile peace contrasted with a mounting rhetoric of war, as indeed they did with other representations of Charles as the martial prince, heir of Prince Henry.[35] We do not know how masques were 'read', either by those who viewed them at court or by those who saw the published text, but we discern not only that they confronted other discourse, news, and events; war entered on to their stage, complicating the masque's resolution of antimasque dialogue and dissent.[36]

Charles I has often been criticized for concentrating on court masque and neglecting the more public politics of festival in royal entry or procession which Queen Elizabeth had used to good effect.[37] Whilst it is true that the Stuart monarchy became less peripatetic, Charles I did participate in public festivals and entries – abroad and at home – the texts of which await study as representations of the prince and king. There were several accounts of the prince's reception in Spain, which were translated and publicly sold – for example 'at the Pied Bull near St Austin's Gate'. Here, for an audience beyond the confines of Whitehall, the language was fascinatingly reminiscent of masque: the prince, with his enamelled George shone, the reader was informed, 'as a sun amidst the stars'.[38] Along with all the detailed descriptions of the entertainments and Spanish court, the account focused on the prince who, though he rode his dapple greys 'curbed with no bit', yet, as if aware of his natural authority, 'they laid down all their natural and brutish fierceness'.[39] The French celebrations of the royal wedding received similar publicity in England, this time vended 'in Pope's Head alley, over against the sign of the horseshoe'. In the engraved frontispiece Cupid holds a crown between Charles and Henrietta Maria, announcing the 'blissful unitie' that would bring 'tottering Europe . . . all-admired protection'.[40] Again the language of masque scripts the account: all the king's subjects, it is said, 'as his pulses do beat according to the motion of his heart'.[41] The author went on indeed to present a character, a 'lovely portraiture' of Charles, the monarch in whom Mars and Venus contended, the 'rider and ruler of his affections'.[42] Accounts of the feasting at Dover where the king received his bride, and at Canterbury, praised the 'glory and grace now shining upon us from your High Majesties' as 'like the heavenly fire of Elias' sacrifice'.[43] On the way into London, 'both the king and queen stood publicly in the open barge, and not only discovered themselves to every honest and cheerful beholder but also with royal affability and grace distributed their favours'.[44] Evidently Charles I did not begin his reign neglecting self-representation in festival and procession. And though the plague prevented a coronation procession, he did not entirely neglect such rituals thereafter. The journey to Scotland for his coronation in 1633 became a long progress through England, ending with a state entry into London on his return.[45] Certainly in the late 1630s and 1640s Charles saw the importance of such occasions, and the accounts of his receptions at York in 1640, and his return to London in 1641, merit further study.[46] *England's Comfort and London's Joy*, for example, illustrated with woodcuts of the procession watched from windows 'embroidered with millions of people of all sorts', celebrated 'God's Great Lieutenant', as indeed another relation spoke of 'the return of the sun into our horizon'.[47] The echo of masque panegyric in accounts (albeit in some cases 'official' accounts) of popular processions or entries questions both assumptions about the unworldliness of masque and Joad Raymond's assertions about the inappropriate language of divine kingship in 1641.[48] Such receptions and texts powerfully and dramatically (the woodcuts make the entry to London look like a theatrical performance) presented the king to his people. Not surprisingly, as the realm divided in civil war, parliament was quick to make its own accounts of the king's entertainments, as at Chester for example, to 'prevent false copies', and to denigrate the cavaliers.[49]

Editions of masques and relations of festivals remind us that the image of the king was often a text. Elizabeth Skerpan Wheeler shows how, as well as its famous frontispiece, *The King's Image* published in 1649 rewrote Charles as a man of conscience and sensibility, as a character and figure of empathy. The early debate over the royal authorship sometimes obscures an important fact: the fact that, as Milton acknowledged, 'so advantageous to a book it is, only to be a Kings'.[50] It is noteworthy that Milton did not write 'this king's'. The *Eikon Basilike*, of course, drew much of its force from the circumstance of Charles I's death, but his other writings, and royal writing as a genre, deserve more discussion as the discursive context of the *Eikon Basilike* and as a form of royal representation more generally.[51] Long before 1649, Charles had put his name to and authorized, even if not always authored (the terms were used near synonymously in the early modern period), volumes of prayers and devotions. During the 1640s the prayers issued under his name and the collections of speeches delivered, at Oxford for example, proclaimed the king as defender of peace and Protestantism, as the warrior prince going out to fight the Lord's enemies.[52] Such self-representation in text was not new. Queen Elizabeth had published under her name and/or with her picture on a frontispiece several volumes of prayers, and James I had issued in 1616 a folio volume of his works, including commentaries on Scripture, and subsequently, exegeses of the gospel and the Lord's Prayer. The unusually loquacious James I regarded his writings as the living image of his kingship, and bequeathed them as his legacy to his son. What we need to appreciate is how all the king's words were a gift and a representation of his rule. Even royal words, of course, had, increasingly, to contend with and face reply from other pens. But we should not under estimate the force of royal writing with the populace, when Milton for one feared that once 'a King is said to be the Author, a name, then which there needs no more among the blockish vulgar, to make it wise, and excellent, and admir'd, nay to set it next the Bible'.[53]

The speeches and writings of Charles I continued to represent him after his death, not only in editions of his works but in (sometimes hostile) reports of his reign, trial and regicide. The 1650 edition of the *Reliquiae Sacrae Carolinae*, containing royal speeches, prayers and occasional papers, as well as the *Eikon*, bore an engraved frontispiece of the king, with a pen in his hand, depicted as a writer.[54] And throughout the 1650s, and after the Restoration, the writings of the martyr were cited and republished, often at critical moments, to repudiate the critics of authority.

Representations of the king in words was by no means limited to the king's own texts. In the case of poetry, we have the semi-official coronation odes and the celebratory volumes published by the universities to commemorate royal marriage, births and other celebratory occasions – many of which, in Hebrew and Greek, as well as Latin and English, remain unstudied.[55] As Raymond's chapter reminds us, there were, too, popular images of the king in squib and ballad, texts that reverberated back to the court leading James I to pen an answer to the 'railing rhymes' that offended him.[56] Historical and critical scholarship has largely ignored the verse panegyrics of the 1620s and 1630s that were not penned by canonical authors. Since many found their way into print and commonplace books (where they took their place alongside a variety of other texts), such neglect may be the loss of a rich opportunity to consider the reception as well as production of images of the king, and the relation (more complicated than that posited by Raymond and Cogswell) between 'elite' and 'popular' literature.[57] The study of Caroline plays, as allegorical representations of the king and his work, has only begun to be rescued from generations of critical contempt for a period of creative darkness that followed Shakespeare and Jonson, whilst depictions of Charles I on the stage (or in the text of a play) in the 1650s and after 1660 have not yet been catalogued, let alone studied.[58] The dramatic dialogue in civil war pamphlets – between, for example, the ghosts of Charles I and Cromwell – both drew on and influenced the state of theatre and the theatre of state.[59] As one commentator put it, so many plays were about kings and the ghost of Charles I joined the Harries and Edwards to 'teach the people' politics.[60]

Such plays lead us to another neglected genre pertinent to our study of the royal image: histories. As Annabel Patterson and others have established, different historical settings were common and often accepted ways of representing current political situations, and histories were often written as thinly veiled comment on the time – as Queen Elizabeth, famously identifying herself as Richard II, was quick to discern.[61] Charles I was no less quick or sensitive in objecting to parliamentary speeches that implicitly compared him to Tiberius.[62] Some histories made explicit the link between past and present. Robert Powell's *The Life of Alfred* (1634) was printed 'together with a parallel of our sovereign Lord King Charles', and

Powell, influenced by Wotton's panegyric on the king's return from Scotland, made clear that his purpose was to represent the king:

> It is most expedient that the lives of good and gracious princes being gods on earth should be set forth unto their people as *specula*, a supereminent watch tower whom their subjects might behold afar off and learn to obey their supreme power; and as *speculum*, a mirror wherein they might gaze on and strive to imitate their sovereign in virtue and goodness.[63]

Not all histories were as laudatory as that of the 'Constantine and Carolus Magnus of our age'. The histories of Edward II's reign that appeared around the time of the Duke of Buckingham's assassination implied less complimentary comparisons.[64] But whether panegyrical or critical, histories re-presented the image of the king directly and explicitly in the context of other royal representations, and so invited the comparisons that cast more, or less, favourable light on the incumbent of the throne. A history of historical writing from 1625 to the end of the seventeenth century – and beyond – will, when it is written, add a vital chapter to the history of the royal image.

After 1660 a new genre was mandated specifically to sustain the memory of Charles I and to re-present him to subjects, the sermons delivered on 30 January, the day of the regicide, many of which were published. These sermons shifted, were adjusted and even appropriated in changed circumstances and for different causes. They were subject to an interesting essay by Helen Randall over fifty years ago.[65] What both Lois Potter's and Laura Knoppers's chapters, along with other recent scholarship suggest, is that we need a full and extensive study of the sermons, provincial as well as metropolitan, and of how as occasion and text they help to shape denominational allegiance, party affiliation and the politics of memory. Remaining in the Prayer Book till 1859, the service for 30 January may even have helped form Victorian historical imaginations from which have descended so many of our own – though historians will dislike such a term about their discourse – representations of Charles. Our own unconscious memory, we might even venture, is itself a site of the royal image.

What all the types of writing I have briefly reviewed point to is a subject perhaps too little addressed in this volume: the role of language itself, of metaphor and tropes in representing the king and royal authority. Martin Dzelzainis does demonstrate how the term *tyranny* becomes redeployed by royalists against the parliamentarians, and how the language of 'necessity', criticized by the opponents of Ship Money, became an established discourse of a parliamentary executive that needed to fund the war. David Loewenstein continues the theme by showing how even 'regal tyranny' was applied by the Levellers against the republican regime, how the republic was attacked in the language deployed against Charles I.[66] Elizabeth Skerpan Wheeler argues persuasively for the *Eikon Basilike* signalling an important shift in language – a use of the language of affect to represent the king, a novel, arguably feminizing vocabulary that, she suggests, transformed and demystified royal representation.[67] What is curiously absent from these important critical observations is a larger engagement with the study of discursive shifts pioneered by John Pocock and Quentin Skinner. Skerpan Wheeler subjects the *Eikon Basilike* to close rhetorical analysis,[68] but what is perhaps of even greater interest is the way language was displayed over a variety of discourses, and how it was shared, appropriated and contested from the 1620s through civil war and, despite the illusion of unity, after Restoration. I have argued elsewhere that because the language of authority had for so long been royal, the republic was dogged by the absence of an alternative discourse of validation, such that the regime boasted of the 'Royal entertainment' given to its envoys in the United Provinces – another republic.[69] Throughout the 1640s and 1650s, metaphors of the sun, the head, the physician, metaphors and similes with royal valence, continued to be common and were freely applied to Oliver Cromwell, especially after he became Protector. As the author of *Catastrophe Magnatum* put it in 1652, 'All kings are represented by the sun', and to an extent the reverse was true: regal language made Cromwell a king, despite his refusal of a crown.[70] Language and metaphor did not resonate only with a generalized lexicon of kingship. Repetition and paraphrase of, allusion to, Charles I's own words, phrases and axioms alongside such similes and tropes all but made the language of authority his own. This discourse, and the republic's and Cromwell's struggle (for which Milton saw the need) to find a new, alternative verbal style, requires closer study – of speech and proclamation, panegyrical verse and sermon, pamphlet and political theory. Similarly, after 1660, we need to appreciate the ways in which, as well as endeavouring to reassert a royal control of discourse, the architects of Restoration appropriated the language of godly republicanism, and of commerce and interest, to reunite the realm. The 30 January sermons, not least on account of their long duration and formulaic properties, present an excellent example of how the representation of Charles I and monarchy shifted in language. By 1685 the treason that had so long been described as the ultimate sin of

rebellion against God was declaimed by Benjamin Woodruffe as a disturbance to 'civil commerce'.[71] A full analysis of the linguistic shifts in the
representation of the martyr king from 1649 would undoubtedly illumi-
nate and perhaps refine the discursive narrative plotted by Pocock from a
valorizing language of ius and grace to one of virtue and commerce.[72]

Painting, coin, medal, banner, masque, procession, verse, sermon,
history, metaphor: we might think such an exhaustive list of the media of
royal representation. However, our contributors touch on others to which
we must return. One, as Dzelzainis's chapter makes clear, is the state trial.
The legal court was an image of the king's justice and justice, as Royalist
cartoons remind us, was an emblem of majesty. Indeed, when he staged
the Ship Money Case and the trial of Prynne, Burton and Bastwick, King
Charles intended to advertise his justice and to justify his kingship. In
neither case were these trials a complete success. As with other genres of
representation, the form of the trial, the dialogue, the theatrical components, the festival (and the public gallery) did not admit of complete
control. Prynne and his brethren were seen as martyrs, and the division
among judges left, to some, the issue of Ship Money unresolved.[73] With
triumphant irony, Charles, of course, performed the same reversal at his
own trial, transmuting his 'judgement' into a vindication of his claims and
an invalidation of his accusers. As Lois Potter suggests, trials were more
complex representations of authority than cultural critics have allowed,
and the future trials of regicides further complicated, as they also prolonged, the memories of the king's own.[74] Where the trial focuses on the
king as custodian of the law, Corns reminds us of the importance of the
image of the king as head of the Church. Gardiner long ago made an
astute connection between Charles's liturgical preferences and his image
as king and Gyles Fleming, the author of *Magnificence Exemplified* (1634),
described the rebuilding of St Paul's Cathedral, with the west portico paid
for by the king, as a 'memorial' to Charles, and his piety and zeal.[75] During
his lifetime and after his death there were many of Charles's puritan subjects who sought to deny his image as a godly monarch, and this perhaps
was not least of the reasons why, in designing a tomb for Charles for
Westminster Abbey, Wren's plan resembled the engraved title page to
Basilika, Charles's collected works of 1662.[76] The king's image consisted as
much in his devotional practices, observed like masques, by visitors and
courtiers, and accounts of those practices, as in the more static representations on canvas or in stone.

This is why it is appropriate to view the court itself as an important image of the king. Charles I himself clearly saw it as 'a pattern' of his king-ship, and performed in Carew's masque in which reform of the court was the predominant theme.[77] In 1632 the Edinburgh preacher William Struther described the court of kings as 'an abridgement of their kingdom . . . and an image of the ruling of their estates'. 'People cannot always see the person of their kings,' he continued, 'but they may guess at their dis-position by manners of their court'.[78] And the manners of Charles's court impressed even some of his puritan enemies, who exhibited little sympa-thy for other facets – or representations – of his rule.[79]

Reference to the king's court and household brings me to the last image of Charles to which I wish to draw attention: that is the importance of the king's household stuff, not only jewels and regalia, but plates, tapestries, chairs, linens and even close-stools. As the late king's goods began to be studied, some surprising insights were gained into the material culture of majesty, Dr Lightbown writing, for instance, of the 'eroticism' of the gold-smiths' art in the reign of Charles I.[80] Royal regalia and household fittings were in large part inherited along with the palaces in which they were placed. Yet we know from the inventory of their sale that, as well as a new wardrobe, Charles I had beds, carpets, chairs, linens, as well as cutlery and plates made and stamped with CR.[81] The point here is the symbolic significance of such objects as items close to the sacred royal body. Charles, we know, stressed the sanctity of his royal person and the asso-ciated sacredness of objects with which he had come into contact.[82] One is then led to wonder in what ways those former royal objects signified after the regicide. How did Major Bass view the coronation robes passed to him, perhaps in lieu of debts owed? What did it mean to Rushworth or Major White to walk on a carpet stamped with the king's arms, or for Captain Joiner to sleep in beds or linen stamped CR?[83] Sold like Christ's cloak after Calvary, did such objects come to have, even for the king's enemies, something of the stature of relics, or did the dissemination of such quotidian items finally puncture the mystique of divine majesty? Holy mystery or domestic humanity? The circulation of the royal goods epitomizes the dualism of the king's two bodies and the ambiguities of all modes of royal representation.

Across all genres, as well as in its material artefacts, the image of the king, rather the imag*es* of the king, were labile and shifting, open to circumstances and variant readings, 'official' images (themselves multiple) contesting with other representations – during Charles's life and beyond the grave.

III

How, then, did the king's image perform? Did it succeed or fail? Historians have tended to ask such straightforward questions and to answer them as straightforwardly: 'not very well' and 'fail'. The questions as well as answers, however, need to be complicated. We need to consider what it means, and whether it is appropriate, to talk of 'success' or 'failure' of representations, and we need to historicize, over short and long periods of time, the question of performance. The image of Charles as prince made him a popular king; his marriage and military failure compromised that popularity. During the 1630s, when he most controlled his image and, when according to Corns, he got the symbolism right, he evidently evoked admiration in some and criticism, even fear, in others. Could any representation have overridden the tensions and differences over religion, foreign policy and factional disputes? In *Salmacida Spolia* we hear the masque struggling to unify the differences articulated within the court as well as beyond it, and to pacify the conflict that was looming.[84] In 1640 Charles did not persuade his propertied subjects to finance a war, nor ameliorate fears of popish conspiracy. But he still enjoyed a warm reception from the London crowds and persuaded men to fight and lay down their life for him. As far as his image with the people went, as Raymond puts it, 'Charles's reign began with a chorus decrying corruption, ill counsel and sodomy, and ended with a plainchant for a martyr.'[85]

What the *Eikon Basilike* succeeded in doing was overriding other representations of Charles, raising the king above the polemical fray and constructing an image that appealed to all classes of readers.[86] The *Eikon* responded to a tragic moment and the needs of subjects for such a response. It was a triumphant act of representation, but one that may have depended upon the real tragedy on the scaffold for its effect. Death ended not only the political choices for Charles, but the ambivalence of his – of all – representation. With the personal body of the king confined to the grave, the politic body, the image and memory could be iconicized, even to the extent of outfacing the image of Queen Elizabeth. After early attacks on the *Eikon* had failed, the only strategy for any political faction was to appropriate that image. After 1649, after 1660, after 1688 the struggles for power were in large part struggles to own the king's image. In the hands of those who criticized authority – be it Charles II's profligacy or James II's Catholicism – the image of Charles I became what the image of Elizabeth had been under the early Stuarts: an image that counselled, admonished and shamed. For those in power, Charles symbolized the duty of allegiance to divine kingship and the sin of resistance.

'The struggle of sovereignty', Tom Corns opines, 'is an unending one', and the struggle for the image of authority will always be part of it. And because authority and its representations descend to us marked with the traces of past images and memories, such struggles will always resonate into criticism and history. In 1650, the author of a verse that prefaced the *Reliquiae Sacrae Carolinae* lamented

> Unvalued Charles: thou art so hard a text,
> Writ in one age, not understood i' th' next.[87]

What he did not see, or might not have accepted, was that the king was not in one sense 'unvalued'; he was evaluated by readers. The 'text' of the king was not 'hard' in every sense but malleable, and rewritten, 're-understood', not only by different readers but by different ages.

Charles I has appeared and appears in the history books as an absolutist, a moderate ruler, a Machiavellian schemer and inept politician, a weak and malleable figure and a man of conviction and principle. It is people, Skerpan Wheeler tells us, as well as rulers who make kings.[88] And as well as kings, it is subjects, critics and historians who make the royal image.

Notes

1 See Lois Potter, *Secret Rites and Secret Writing: Royalist Literature, 1641–1660* (Cambridge University Press, 1989), 170–87; Steven Zwicker, *Lines of Authority: Politics and English Literary Culture* (Ithaca, NY: Cornell University Press, 1993), chapter 2; Thomas N. Corns, *Uncloistered Virtue: English Political Literature, 1640–1660* (Oxford: Clarendon Press, 1992), 80–91; Kevin Sharpe, 'The King's Writ: Royal Authors and Royal Authority in Early Modern England' in *Culture and Politics in Early Stuart England*, ed. Kevin Sharpe and Peter Lake (London: Macmillan, 1994), 136–8; Kevin Sharpe, 'Private Conscience and Public Duty in the Writings of Charles I', *Historical Journal*, 40 (1997): 643–65; Elizabeth Skerpan Wheeler, '*Eikon Basilike* and the Rhetoric of Self-Representation', above pp. 122–40.

2 See above p. 254.

3 For an elaboration of this argument see my *Reading Revolutions* (forthcoming), chapter 1, and Sharpe and Lake, *Culture and Politics*, introduction.

4 David Norbrook, 'The Life and Death of Renaissance Man', *Raritan*, 8.4 (1989): 89–110.

5 Charles I, *Reliquae Sacrae Carolinae* (The Hague [i.e. London], 1650), 353; below p. 305.

6 See Kevin Sharpe, 'Remapping Early Modern England', in Kevin Sharpe, *Remapping Early Modern England* (Cambridge University Press, 1999).

7 See for example, Kevin Sharpe, 'Faction at the Early Stuart Court', *History Today* (October 1983): 39–46; David Starkey, ed., *The English Court: From the Wars of the Roses to the Civil War* (London and New York: Longman, 1987), chapters 6 and 7.

8 For one, there were several variants of the *Eikon* and of the engraved frontispiece; see Skerpan Wheeler, '*Eikon Basilike* and the Rhetoric of Self-Representation', above pp. 132–4.

9 David Loewenstein, 'The King Among the Radicals', above p. 99. For a critique of New Historicism's excessive emphasis on hegemonic power, see D. Shuger, *Habits of Thought in the English Renaissance: Religion, Politics and the Dominant Culture* (Berkeley: University of California Press, 1990), 1–16; J. Dollimore and Alan Sinfield, eds., *Political Shakespeare* (Manchester University Press, 1985), introduction, 2–17.

10 On the importance of memories of Queen Elizabeth in seventeenth-century England, see C. V. Wedgwood, *Oliver Cromwell and the Elizabethan Inheritance* (London: Jonathan Cape, 1970); cf. below p. 304.

11 Joad Raymond, 'Popular Representations of Charles I', above pp. 47–50; see Richard Cust, 'News and Politics in Early Seventeenth Century England', *Past and Present*, 112 (1986): 63–90.

12 John Peacock, 'The Visual Image of Charles I', above p. 176. The consistency of representational themes over several genres reinforces the belief that Charles may have been responsible for formulating his own image.

13 Roy Strong, *Van Dyck: Charles I on Horseback* (London: Allen Lane, 1972).

14 Oliver Millar, *The Age of Charles I* (London: Tate Gallery, 1972); Millar, *Van Dyck in England* (London: National Portrait Gallery, 1982); *The Thirty-Seventh Volume of the Walpole Society, 1958–1960. Abraham Van Der Doort's Catalogue of the Collections of Charles I*, ed. Oliver Millar (Glasgow, 1960); Arthur. K. Wheelock and Susan J. Barnes, eds., *Anthony Van Dyck* (Washington: National Gallery of Art, 1990); Arthur MacGregor, ed., *The Late King's Goods* (London and Oxford: Alistair McAlpine and Oxford University Press, 1989).

15 David Howarth, *Images of Rule: Art and Politics in the English Renaissance, 1485–1649* (London: Macmillan, 1997), 134.

16 Peacock, 'Visual Image', above p. 228.

17 There is a magnificent collection of engravings in the Huntington Library's Richard Bull Granger collection. See vol. 6/13, 19. We await a study of engravings as representations of regality. For the market, see Alexander Globe, *Peter Stent, London Printseller, c. 1642–1665* (Vancouver: University of British Columbia Press, 1985).

18 See Margaret Aston, *The King's Bedpost: Reformation and Iconography in a Tudor Group Portrait* (Cambridge University Press, 1994), 1–5.

19 H. Holland, *Brazili-logia: A Book of Kings* (1618), a volume of engraved portraits, was evidently popular as it was reissued in 1630.

20 Tessa Watt, *Cheap Print and Popular Piety, 1550–1640* (Cambridge University Press, 1993), 193–217 *et passim*.

21 See Kevin Sharpe, '"An Image Doting Rabble": The Failure of Republican Culture in Seventeenth-Century England', in Kevin Sharpe and Steven Zwicker, eds., *Refiguring Revolutions: Aesthetics and Politics from the English Revolution to the Romantic Revolution* (Berkeley: University of California Press, 1998), 38–9.

22 Huntington Bull Granger, 6/8; 23/1; Queen Anne adopted Elizabeth's motto '*Semper eadem*' as her own and was painted in similar pose and costume.

23 Huntington Bull Granger, 6/25, 26; Sharpe, '"An Image Doting Rabble"', 39–41.

24 Huntington Bull Granger, 6/25, 30, 39. Thomas Corns confirms my own impression that the only engravings of regicide were Dutch or German.

25 Sharpe, '"An Image Doting Rabble"', 25–56.

26 Peacock, 'Visual Image, above pp. 187, 192.

27 The medal is engraved in Huntington, Bull Granger, 6/29; on Rubens's landscape with St George and the Dragon, see Kevin Sharpe, *The Personal Rule of Charles I* (New Haven: Yale University Press, 1992), 219–22; for the cartoon of the Commonwealth as a dragon, Huntington, Bull Granger, 10/26.

28 H. Farquhar, 'Portraits of the Stuarts on the Royalist Badges', *British Numismatic Journal* 2 (1906): 23–30.

29 Huntington, Bull Granger, 8/1; above p. 188.

30 'Coins of Charles I', engraved by Bull Granger 6/30.

31 See M. Seymour, 'Pro-Government Propaganda in Interregnum England, 1649–1660', Ph.D. thesis (Cambridge University, 1987), 120–4.

32 Quotation from Thomas Corns, 'Duke, Prince and King', above p. 6.

33 Kevin Sharpe, *Criticism and Compliment: The Politics of Literature in the England of Charles I* (Cambridge University Press, 1987). For a hostile review see M. Butler, 'Early Stuart Court Culture: Compliment or Criticism?', *Historical Journal*, 32 (1989): 425–35, and M. Butler, 'Reform or Reverence: The Politics of the Caroline Masque', in J. R. Mulryne and Margaret Shewring, eds., *Theatre and Government Under the Early Stuarts* (Cambridge University Press, 1993), 118–56. Butler, however, shifts his view considerably in 'Ben Jonson and the Limits of Courtly Panegyric', in Sharpe and Lake, *Culture and Politics*, 91–116.

34 Corns, 'Duke, Prince and King', above pp. 8–11.

35 See Butler, 'Ben Jonson', 99.

36 The masques *Chloridia* and *The Temple of Love* contain antimasques of news and libel. Whilst these are antimasques, they bring other oppositional discourses to the very stage of royal representation, a point that needs exploring further.

37 J. Richards, '"His Nowe Majestie" and the English Monarchy: The Kingship of Charles I Before 1640', *Past and Present*, 113 (1982): 70–96; R. Malcolm Smuts, 'Public Ceremony and Royal Charisma: The English Royal Entry in London, 1485–1642', in A. L. Beier, D. Cannadine and J. M. Rosenheim, eds., *The First Modern Society* (Cambridge University Press, 1989), 65–93.

38 [A. de Mendoza], *Two Royal Entertainments lately Given to the Most Illustrious Prince Charles . . . by . . . Philip the Fourth* (1623), quotation p. 7; *A Continuation of A Former Relation Concerning the Entertainment Given to the Prince* (1623).

39 *Two Royal Entertainments*, 27.

40 G. Marcellini, *Epithalium Gallo-Britannicum* (1625); the elaborate frontispiece with accompanying verse prefigures the theme of marriage in masque.

41 Ibid., 12.

42 Ibid., 97, 105.

43 *A True Discourse of All the Royal Passages, Triumphs and Ceremonies Observed at the Contract and Marriage of . . . Charles King of Great Britaine* (1625), after p. 29 (blank pagination) before renewed p. 30.

44 Ibid., 32.

45 For an itinerary of the progress to Scotland, see Bodleian Library, Rawlinson MS D49, and for a brief account, Sharpe, *Personal Rule*, 778–83.

46 York City Record Office, House Books, 35, 36; *Ovatio Carolina: The Triumph of King Charles* (1641); *England's Comfort and London's Joy* (1641).

47 *England's Comfort*, 2–3, [7]; *Ovatio Carolina*, 3.

48 Raymond, 'Popular Representations of Charles I', above p. 54.

49 *A True and Exact Relation of the King's Entertainment in the City of Chester* (1642), 5 et *passim*.

50 *Eikonoklastes*, in *Complete Prose Works of John Milton*, ed. Don M. Wolfe, 8 vols. (New Haven: Yale University Press, 1953–82), III, 339 (hereafter *CPW*).

51 See Sharpe, 'King's Writ'.

52 *A Form of Common Prayer* (1625, 1638); *A Form of Common Prayer Appointed by His Majesty* (Oxford, 1643); *A Collection of Prayers used in His Majesty's Chapel and His Armies* (1643); *Three Speeches Made by the King's Most Excellent Majesty* (1642); *Two Speeches Delivered by the King's Most Excellent Majesty at Oxford* (1642).

53 Milton, *Eikonoklastes*, *CPW*, III, 339. Sharpe, 'King's Writ', *passim*.

54 *Reliquiae Sacrae Carolinae* (1650). The title page carries the verse from 2 Kings 23:25: 'And like unto him there was no king before him that turned to the Lord with all his heart.' A poem adjoined to the engraving describes the work as 'but CHARLS contracted.'

55 See Ann Baynes Coiro, ' "A Ball of Strife": Caroline Poetry and Royal Marriage', above pp. 31, 39.

56 'King James His Verse Made Upon a Libel', in *The Poems of James VI of Scotland*, 2 vols., ed. J. Craigie (Edinburgh, 1955–8), II, 182–91.

57 See Thomas Cogswell, 'Underground Verse and the Transformation of Early Stuart Political Culture', in *Political Culture and Cultural Politics in Early Modern England*, ed. Susan D. Amussen and Mark A. Kishlansky (Manchester University Press, 1995), 277–300.

58 Martin Butler, *Theatre and Crisis, 1632–1642* (Cambridge University Press, 1984).

59 See, for example, *A Dialogue Betwixt the Ghosts of Charles I . . . and Oliver the late Usurping Protector* (1659).

60 *Prologue to His Majesty at the First Play Presented at the Cockpit in Whitehall* (1660).

61 Annabel Patterson, *Censorship and Interpretation: The Conditions of Writing and Reading in Early Modern England* (Madison: University of Wisconsin Press, 1984), *passim*.

62 Cambridge University Library, MS Dd 12 21 (Whitelocke's parliamentary diary) fos. 96–9; S. R. Gardiner, *History of England from the Accession of James I to the Outbreak of the Civil War, 1603–1642*, 10 vols. (London, 1883–4), VI, 107–8.

63 R. Powell, *The Life of Alfred . . . Together with a Parallel of our Sovereign Lord King Charles* (1634), epistle to the reader.

64 For example, F. Hubert, *The Deplorable Life and Death of Edward II* (1628).

65 H. W. Randall, 'The Rise and Fall of a Martyrology: Sermons on Charles I', *Huntington Library Quarterly*, 10 (1947): 135–67. I had originally intended to append my own study of the sermons to this chapter but was prevented by space. See my ' "So Hard a Text?" ': Charles I and the 30 January Sermons', forthcoming.

66 Martin Dzelzanis, ' "Incendiaries of the State": Charles I and Tyranny', above pp. 82–5; Loewenstein, 'King Among the Radicals', above pp. 97, 108–13.

67 Skerpan Wheeler, '*Eikon Basilike* and the Rhetoric of Self-Representation', above pp. 122–37 *passim*.

68 See Elizabeth Skerpan, *The Rhetoric of Politics in the English Revolution, 1642–1660* (Columbia: University of Missouri Press, 1992), chapter 5.

69 Sharpe, ' "An Image Doting Rabble" ', 29–30.

70 Ibid., 46–7; *Catastrophe Magnatum* (1652).

71 Benjamin Woodruffe, *A Sermon Preached January 30th 1685* (1685), 3.

72 J. G. A. Pocock, *The Machiavellian Moment: Florentine Political Thought and the Atlantic Republican Tradition* (Princeton University Press, 1975).

73 On Prynne, see Sharpe, *Personal Rule*, 750–65.

74 Lois Potter, 'The Royal Martyr in the Restoration', above pp. 242–4.

75 Corns, 'Duke, Prince and King', above p. 14; Gardiner, *History of England*, VII, 126–8, 159, chapter 69; G. Fleming, *Magnificence Exemplified and the Repair of St Paul's Exhorted Unto* (1634), 50.

76 Potter, 'Royal Martyr', above pp. 252–4.

77 P. Scot, *A Table Book for Princes* (1621) dedicated to Charles, urged him to make his court a pattern for virtue; on *Coelum Britannicum* see Sharpe, *Criticism and Compliment*, 233–42.

78 William Struther, *A Looking Glass for Princes and People* (1632), 70–2.

79 Lucy Hutchinson, *Memoirs of the Life of Colonel Hutchinson*, ed. James Sutherland (Oxford University Press, 1973), 46.

80 R. Lightbown, 'Charles I and the Art of the Goldsmith', in MacGregor, *The Late King's Goods*, 237 and 233–55 *passim*.

81 *The Forty-Third Volume of the Walpole Society, 1970–1972. The Inventories and Valuations of the King's Goods*, ed. Oliver Millar (Glasgow, 1972), e.g. 209, 254, 330, 334, 389.

82 Sharpe, *Personal Rule*, 217–19; and Sharpe, 'The Image of Virtue' in Starkey, ed., *The English Court*, 226–60.

83 Millar, ed., *Inventories*, 350, 354, 381.

84 Butler, 'Politics and Masque', especially 65–72.

85 Raymond, 'Popular Representations of Charles I', above p. 50.

86 The appeal to different classes questions prevailing dichotomies between elite and popular culture.

87 *Reliquiae Sacrae Carolinae; Or, The Works of that Great Monarch and Glorious Martyr King Charles I*, 353.

88 Skerpan Wheeler, '*Eikon Basilike* and the Rhetoric of Self-Representation', above p. 137.

Index

Achinstein, Sharon, 127
Act of Succession, 273
Adams, Simon, 147
Albemarle, Duke of, *see* Monk, George
Anglesey Memorandum, 124, 135, 254, 288
Anne of Denmark, 2, 27, 28, 29, 202
Anne, Queen of England and Scotland, 270,
    273, 294
Armada, 145, 148–9, 206
Arminianism, 14, 15
Arundel, Thomas Howard, Earl of, 221
Aspinwall, William, 114

Bacon, Sir Francis, 29, 128
Bakhtin, Mikhail, 42
Baldwin, Richard, 247
Bankes, Sir John, 80
Banqueting House at Whitehall, *see*
    Whitehall, Banqueting House
Barnard, John, 168
Basilika, see Charles I, *Basilika*
Bastwick, John, 302
Beaumont, Sir John, 18
Berkeley, Sir Robert, 81
Bernini, Giovanni Lorenzo, 216–17
Bing, Stephen, 164, 165, 166, 169
Boel, Cornelis, 204
Bond, John, 52
Book of Common Prayer, 14, 65, 130, 241, 247,
    300
Book of Sports, 63, 115
Boyne, Battle of the, 264
Bradshaw, John, 244
Bramston, Sir John, 81
Brandon, Richard, 60
Briot, Nicholas, 180–6, 188–93, 196, 204, 226

Bristol, 185, 196
Brownrigg, Ralph, Bishop of Exeter, 250
Buckingham, George Villiers, Duke of, 7–8,
    9–12, 15, 19, 27, 50, 53, 63, 102, 178,
    189
  death of, 15, 20, 37, 48, 55, 178, 300
  and Ile de Ré, 13, 15, 50–1, 102, 155
Burgess, Glenn, 13, 17
Burnet, Gilbert, 251
Burton, Henry, 302
Butler, James, *see* Ormond, Marquis of
Butler, Martin, 232
Butler, Samuel, 56

Cabinet Room at Whitehall, *see* Whitehall,
    Cabinet Room
Cadiz, 13, 15, 155
Campion, Thomas, 8
Canne, John, 106, 107
Canterbury, 297
Carew, Thomas, 17, 27, 37, 43, 151, 166, 214,
    230, 232, 303
Cartwright, William, 166
Cary, Lucius, *see* Falkland, Viscount
Cary, Mary, 106, 114–16
Catholicism, 8, 12, 14–15, 35, 57, 59, 98, 102,
    104, 143–53, 154–5, 206, 304
Chapel Royal, 167–8
Chapman, George, 8
Charing Cross, 74–5
Charles I, King of England and Scotland
  anti-Catholicism of, 14
  as Antichrist, 96, 105, 113–14
  Arminian tendencies of, 14, 15
  as art collector, 187, 209, 220
  Basilika, 242, 254, 256

relations with the Duke of Buckingham, 7–8, 9–10, 11–12, 13, 15, 37, 50–1, 53, 55, 63, 300
in captivity, 60–4
and Catholicism, 8, 12, 98, 102, 143–53, 154–5
and the Chapel Royal, 167–8
English coronation of, 15, 18, 19
Scottish coronation of, 15, 19, 52, 190, 193, 204, 297, 300
court of, 15–16, 98, 101, 152–3, 154, 171, 289, 293
depiction in *A Game at Chess*, 11–12
depiction on coins, 179–87
depiction on medals, 187–98
depiction in painting, 220–30, 241
depiction in the popular press, 47–66
depiction in prints, 199–209, 293–5
depiction by radical writers, 96–116
depiction in sculpture, 74, 178–9, 209–20
as Duke of York, 1–4, 202
Eikon Basilike, see Eikon Basilike
execution of, 64–6, 122, 198, 240–4, 247, 270–1
and the five members, 124–5
and the Forced Loan, 14, 100
and the war with France, 13, 15, 50–1, 155, 204
funeral of, 241
and the Order of the Garter, 43, 190, 195, 197, 216, 220, 231, 270
and Henrietta Maria, 13, 15, 19–21, 26–44, 59, 62, 147, 152–5, 168–71, 188–90, 198, 202, 209, 225–6, 295, 297
as Jacobite icon, 263–84
and the King's Cabinet, 22, 57–60, 98, 102–3
touching for the King's Evil, 53, 65–6
and Laud, 15, 55, 96, 145, 152, 215–16, 218
and masques, 1–6, 7, 8–10, 31, 98, 189, 212, 214–15, 225, 230–3, 296–7, 303, 304
and Milton, 35–8, 43, 64, 99, 127, 128, 141–57, 248–9, 254, 291
design for the monument to, 252–5, 302
as patron of the arts, 17, 101, 162–71, 176–233
as Prince of Wales, 4–15, 162–3, 166, 178, 180, 187, 200, 202, 206, 221, 222
and Ship Money, 77–85, 100, 300, 302
and Spain, 11, 13, 142, 147–51, 192, 221–2, 296–7
and the Spanish Match, 11–13, 15, 17, 50, 148
and Strafford, 51, 55
and the Thirty Years' War, 144, 146–51, 208
tilting, 7, 33, 293

Charles II, King of England and Scotland, 18, 177, 243, 244, 251–2, 254, 257, 294, 304
as Prince of Wales, 126, 131, 195
Chester, 298
Chichester, 216
Child, William, 168
Chiswell, Richard, 252
Clarendon, Earl of, *see* Hyde, Edward
Cleveland, John, 63
Clifton, Robin, 143
Cogswell, Thomas, 11, 299
Coke, Edward, 109
Commissions of Array, 81, 84
Cook, John, 64, 96–7, 98, 99–100, 102–5, 106, 111, 113
Coprario, John, 162, 163, 164, 165, 166
coronation odes, 17–18
Cowley, Abraham, 19
Cragge, John, 52–3
Crashaw, Richard, 28, 41–2
Crawford, Patricia, 87
Croke, Sir George, 81
Cromwell, Oliver, 88–9, 97, 103, 109–13, 241, 244, 301
Culloden, Battle of, 282
Culpepper, Sir John, 85
Cust, Richard, 14

Danby, Thomas Osborne, Earl of, 74
Daniel, Samuel, 2
Davenant, Sir William, 17, 19–20, 27, 232, 246, 304
Dering, Richard, 168
Devereux, Robert, *see* Essex, Earl of
Dieussart, François, 216–17
Digby, Sir Kenelm, 31
Diggers, 108–13
Dillingham, John, 63
divine right, 13, 98, 177, 183, 184, 202, 263, 264, 270
Dobson, Michael, 246–7
Donaldson, William, 264
Donne, John, 29, 30, 37, 43–4, 176–7, 179
Dover, 297
Dryden, John, 246, 249–50
Dugard, William, 132, 133
Duppa, Brian, 64
Dury, John, 150

Edgehill, Battle of, 64, 195
Edward II, King of England, 54, 300
Edward VI, King of England, 206

Eikon Aklastos, 128
Eikon Alethine, 127, 128
Eikon Basilike, 61, 62, 64–6, 122–37, 198, 241–2,
    257, 264, 266, 279, 288–9, 290–1, 295, 298,
    301, 302, 304
    and the Anglesey Memorandum, 254, 288
    and *Eikonoklastes*, 43, 64, 127, 128, 153–4, 157
    frontispiece, 123, 134, 295
    and Sir Philip Sidney's 'Pamela Prayer',
        128, 130, 132
    parodies of, 135
    Psalterium Carolinum, 134–5
Eikon E Piste, 127–8
Eliot, Sir John, 20
Elizabeth I, Queen of England, 2, 27, 29, 51,
    122, 148, 177, 178–9, 206, 296, 298, 299,
    304
Elizabeth, Queen of Bohemia, 2, 8, 28, 202
Elliott, John, 143
Elstrack, Renold, 200, 201
Essex, Robert Devereux, Earl of, 194–5
Evelyn, John, 177–8, 187–8, 198, 247

Faber, John, 270
Fairfax, Sir Thomas, Lord, 90
Falkland, Lucius Cary, Viscount, 85, 86
Farquar, Helen, 295
Feake, Christopher, 114
Felton, John, 50, 51
Ferrabosco, Alfonso, 162, 163, 164, 165, 166
Fiennes, William, *see* Saye and Sele, Viscount
Fifth Monarchists, 96, 107, 112, 113–16
Filmer, Sir Robert, 136
Finch, Sir John, 81
Fissel, Mark Charles, 75
Fleming, Giles, 302
Foucault, Michel, 240
Foxe, John, 130, 131, 136, 266
France, 11, 13, 15, 50–1, 102, 103, 155, 204
Frank, Joseph, 9
Frederick V, Elector Palatine, King of
    Bohemia, 8–9, 15, 28, 202

Gardiner, S. R., 78, 302
Garrett, Cynthia, 130
Garter, Order of the, 43, 190, 195, 197, 216,
    220, 231, 270
Gauden, John, 124, 135, 136, 254
Geertz, Clifford, 289
George I, King of England and Scotland,
    273–4, 280
Gerbier, Balthasar, 63

Gibbons, Orlando, 162, 163, 164, 165, 166
Gill, Alexander, 50, 145
Gittings, Clare, 241
Glorious Revolution, 247, 263
Goodwin, John, 89, 90, 104–7, 111
Grand Remonstrance, 53, 148
Grandi, Alessandro, 169
Greer, David, 167
Grotius, Hugo, 79–80, 91
Gunpowder Plot, 145, 155, 206
Gustavus Adolphus, King of Sweden, 149,
    151, 293

Hamilton, James Hamilton, Marquis of, 63,
    222, 228
Hampden, John, 78, 81, 82, 84–5, 124
Hampton, William, 240, 241, 242, 245
Hampton Court, 61, 63, 167, 186, 228
Hanoverian succession, 273–4
Harrison, Thomas, 89, 248–9
Hartlib, Samuel, 150
Hatton, Christopher, Baron, 165–6, 168–9
Heads of the Proposals, 87
Henri IV, King of France, 218, 225
Henrietta Maria, Queen of England and
    Scotland
    and Catholicism, 14, 19, 57, 59, 62, 147,
        152–3, 168–70
    depiction in masque, 4, 19, 37, 189
    depiction on medals, 188–90, 198, 295
    depiction in painting, 225–6, 227
    depiction in prints, 202, 209, 297
    and marriage with Charles I, 13, 15, 19–21,
        26–44, 59, 62, 152–5, 168, 188–90, 297
    and Milton, 35–8, 146, 152–3, 154–5
    Roman Catholic chapel at Somerset
        House, 168–70
Henry, Duke of Gloucester, 39
Henry, Prince of Wales, 1–7, 15, 162, 187, 202,
    204, 208, 215, 296
Henry VII, King of England, 2, 179, 212
Henry VIII, King of England, 28, 162, 206,
    243
Herbert, George, 62
Herrick, Robert, 27, 34–5, 37, 166
Hesilrige, Arthur, 124
Hilliard, Nicholas, 226
Hindmarsh, Joseph, 135
Hirst Castle, 61
Hobbes, Thomas, 85–6, 88–9
Holborne, Robert, 78, 79–80
Hole, William, 202

Holland, Henry Rich, Earl of, 216
Holland, Henry, 206–8, 294
Holland, Philemon, 206–7
Hollar, Wenceslas, 208–9, 210
Holles, Denzil, 124
Honthorst, Gerrit van, 189, 192, 295
Hoskins, John, 226
Howard, Thomas, *see* Arundel, Earl of
Howell, James, 151, 178
Hutchinson, Lucy, 16, 96, 101–2
Hutton, Sir Richard, 81
Hyde, Edward, Earl of Clarendon, 85, 86

Ile de Ré, 13, 15, 50–1, 102, 155, 204, 206
Innocent X, Pope, 208
Inns of Court, 8–9, 84, 163, 212
Ireland, 63, 97, 98, 100, 102–4, 143, 147, 155
Ireton, Henry, 88, 90, 91, 241, 244
Isle of Wight, 63, 64
Italy, 168–9, 220–1

Jacobite Uprising (1715), 264, 277–80
Jacobite Uprising (1745), 264, 280–4, 292
Jacobitism, 75, 263–84
James I and VI, King of England and
    Scotland, 3, 11, 16, 17, 18, 27, 145, 156, 176,
    180, 184, 218, 225, 241, 243
  and coinage, 180, 184
  and masque, 8–9, 10
  portraits of, 200–2, 203, 206
  writings of, 27, 298, 299
James II, King of England and Scotland, 256,
    257–8, 263, 265–70, 294, 304
Jane, Joseph, 128
Jeffreys, George, 165, 169
Jones, Inigo, 2, 17, 169, 180, 209, 212, 215, 217,
    218, 220, 230–2
Jonson, Ben, 2, 4–6, 9, 17, 20–1, 28, 29, 31–4, 37,
    43, 64, 151, 230, 232
Jordan, Thomas, 18
Juxon, William, 241

King, Henry, 244
Kings Cabinet Opened, The, 22, 57–60, 98, 102–3,
    154
King's Evil, 53, 65–6
King's Music, 162–71
King's Musicke, 134, 162–7
Knachel, Philip A., 124
Kneller, Sir Godfrey, 280
Knoppers, Laura Lunger, 249
Knott, John, 248

Lake, Peter, 143
Lanier, Nicholas, 34, 163
Laqueur, Thomas, 240, 243–4
La Rochelle, 13, 102, 155, 190, 204
Laud, William, 15, 55, 87, 88, 96, 145, 152, 167,
    169, 215–16, 218
Lawes, Henry, 4, 135, 166–7
Lawes, William, 4, 164–5
Le Sueur, Hubert, 74, 178, 209–20, 251
Levellers, 108–13
Lever, Christopher, 206
Lievens, Jan, 208–9
Lightbown, R., 303
Lilburne, John, 97, 108–10
Lilly, John, 165, 166
Lilly, William, 60, 63, 98, 102, 104
Lincoln's Inn, 8, 84
Lindley, David, 2
Littleton, Sir Edward, 80–1, 82, 186
Loewenstein, David, 129
London, 7, 12, 15, 53, 199, 208, 297, 304
Long Gallery at Whitehall, *see* Whitehall,
    Long Gallery
Long Parliament, *see* Parliament, Long
Louis XIII, King of France, 13, 102, 209
Lovelace, Richard, 27, 37, 39, 166
Ludlow, Edmund, 96, 102, 103, 105, 106, 107,
    111, 114, 247
Lupo, Thomas, 162, 164, 165, 166
Lyttleton, Sir Edward, *see* Littleton, Sir
    Edward

McKeon, Michael, 28–9
Madan, Francis Falconer, 122–3, 124
Madrid, 17, 50, 221
Maguire, Nancy, 244–5
Manchester, Edward Montagu, Earl of, 194
Mar, John, Earl of, 277
Marsh, John, 84
Marshall, Joshua, 74
Marshall, William, 123, 132, 134, 207–8
Marvell, Andrew, 28, 39–41, 98, 154, 157, 186,
    251
Mary, Queen of Scots, 43, 252, 273
Mary I, Queen of England, 206
Mary II, Queen of England and Scotland,
    247, 263
masques, 1–6, 7, 8–10, 31, 37, 98, 163–4, 170,
    189, 212, 214–15, 225, 230–3, 296–7, 303, 304
May, Thomas, 57
Mayne, Jasper, 47
Meade, Joseph, 150

medals, 187–98, 295
Mendle, Michael, 82
Mico, Richard, 165, 168
Middle Temple, 8
Middleton, Thomas, 11–12
Milbourne, Luke, 270
Millar, Sir Oliver, 292
Milton, John, 28, 96, 99, 103, 113–14, 141–57
  and Catholicism, 11
  and Henry Lawes, 166
  Defensio Secunda, 98
  Eikonoklastes, 43, 64, 103, 127–8, 135, 141,
    153–7, 248–9, 254, 291, 298
  'Elegia Quarta', 146
  Of Reformation, 147–9
  'On the Morning of Christ's Nativity',
    35–8
  Paradise Lost, 43
  Readie and Easie Way, 103
  Tenure of King's and Magistrates, 106,
    141–2
Monk, George, Duke of Albemarle, 252
Monod, Paul, 264
Montagu, Edward, *see* Manchester, Earl of
Monteverdi, Claudio, 169
Morley, George, 243
Morrill, John, 76, 88
Mountin, Gerrit, 202
Mytens, Daniel, 180, 192, 221–6, 227, 228,
  291

Naseby, Battle of, 57, 98, 248
Nedham, Marchamont, 57, 59, 60
Nero, 54
Newport, the treaty of, 91
Nineteen Propositions, 54, 85, 148, 150
Norbrook, David, 289
Northumberland, Algernon Percy, Earl of,
  58, 62, 228

Ollard, Richard, 257
Order of the Garter, *see* Garter, Order of the
Orgel, Stephen, 29
Ormond, James Butler, Marquis of, 208
Osborne, Thomas, *see* Danby, Earl of
Overbury, Sir Thomas, 243
Oxford, 104, 166, 171, 184–5, 215–16, 218

paintings, 220–30
Palomo, Dolores, 26
Parker, Geoffrey, 147
Parker, Henry, 57, 82–4

Parliament,
  Long, 52, 81, 91, 97, 113, 153
  Purged, *see* Rump
  Rump, 110, 111, 294
  Short, 81
Patterson, Annabel, 154, 299
Peacham, Henry, 210
Pepys, Samuel, 199, 242, 245, 246, 247, 257
Percy, Algernon, *see* Northumberland, Earl
  of
Perinchief, Richard, 135
Peter, Hugh, *see* Peters, Hugh
Peters, Hugh, 61, 90
Petowe, Henry, 17
Philip IV, King of Spain, 221
Pittock, Murray, 264
Playford, John, 162
Pocock, J. G. A., 257, 301, 302
Ponet, John, 89
Popish plot, 57–8, 142–4, 154–5, 252
Porter, Walter, 168
Portland, Earl of, *see* Weston, Sir Richard
Portsmouth, 178–9, 216, 232
Powell, Robert, 299–300
Presbyterians, 87, 89–90
prints, 199–209
Prestonpans, Battle of, 281
Price, John, 89, 90
Prideaux, Edmund, 110
Prynne, William, 302
Purcell, Henry, 163
Purged Parliament, *see* Parliament, Purged
Putney debates, 91
Pym, John, 82, 124

Queen's House at Greenwich, 222

Raleigh, Sir Walter, 177
Randall, Helen, 300
Rawlins, Thomas, 194, 196
Reeve, L. J., 75
Reitz, Heinrich, the younger, 199
Revett, John, *see* Rivett, John
Rich, Henry, *see* Holland, Earl of
Richard II, King of England, 54, 299
Richard III, King of England, 3, 54, 58
Richardson, Samuel, 89, 90
Rivett, John, 74, 220
Roehampton, 218, 220
Romano, Guilio, 228
Rous, John, 51, 151
Royal Exchange, 220

Royal Mint,
    Tower of London, 181, 182, 186
    Welsh branch, 183
    York, 183
Royston, Richard, 132, 135
Rubens, Peter Paul, 180, 222, 225, 231, 243
Rump Parliament, *see* Parliament, Rump
Rupert, Prince, 196
Russell, Conrad, 75, 289

Sacheverell, Henry, 270
Sadler, Anthony, 246
Sadler, John, 57
St James's Palace, 210, 212, 228
St John, Oliver, 78–9, 80
St Paul's Cathedral, 193, 220, 247, 302
Saye and Sele, William Fiennes, Viscount, 78, 82
Scot, Thomas, 248
Scotland, 15, 19, 52, 60, 63, 88, 100, 146, 147, 190, 192–3, 204, 277–82, 297, 300
scrofula, *see* King's Evil
sculpture, 209–20
Selden, John, 49, 77–8, 80, 84–5, 86, 141
Shadwell, Thomas, 246
Shakespeare, William, 246–7
Sharp, Richard, 264
Sharpe, Kevin, 6, 16, 96, 143, 232
Sherlock, William, 247
Ship Money, 77–85, 100, 300, 302
Shirley, James, 163, 212
Short Parliament, *see* Parliament, Short
Sidney, Sir Philip, 64, 128, 130
Simon, Thomas, 186
Skinner, Quentin, 301
Smith, John, 206
Somerset House, 168–70, 226, 228
Sommerville, J. P., 13
Southampton, Henry Wriothesley, Earl of, 221
Spain, 11, 13, 78, 142, 145, 147–51, 155, 178, 192, 221–2, 296–7
Spanish Match, 1, 11–13, 15, 17, 50, 148
Spenser, Edmund, 27, 43
Stanley, Thomas, 134
Staunton, Edmund, 87–8
Staves, Susan, 245
Stewart, J. Douglas, 254
Stone, Nicholas, 215
Strafford, Thomas Wentworth, Earl of, 51, 55, 216, 248
Stratford, 19

Strode, William, 124
Strong, Roy, 26, 288, 292
Struther, William, 303
Stuart, James Francis Edward, 270–80
Stuart, Charles Edward, 280–4
Stubbe, Henry, 106
Suckling, Sir John, 27, 166

Tate Gallery, 222
Tenth of June verses, 274–7
Thirtieth of January sermons, 240, 242, 244–8, 252, 263, 270
Thirty Years' War, 9, 144, 146–51, 208, 296
tilting, 7, 33, 293
Titian, 221, 228
Toland, John, 252
Townshend, Aurelian, 17, 151
Trevor-Roper, H. R., 124
Tuck, Richard, 86
Tyburn, 244

Underdown, David, 88
United Provinces, 148–51, 192, 301

Vallet, Adam, 163
Van Dalen, Cornelis, 204, 205
Van de Passe, Crispin, 200
Van de Passe, Willem, 200, 202, 204
Van der Doort, Abraham, 187, 193, 218
Van Dyck, Sir Anthony, 37, 176, 180, 186, 195, 199, 202, 209, 216, 221, 225–30, 231, 232, 291, 292–3, 295
Vane, Sir Henry, 106, 248
Van Leemput, Remee, 228
Van Voerst, Robert, 208–9, 226
Vaughan, Robert, 246
Vernon, Sir George, 81
Villiers, George, *see* Buckingham, Duke of
Vorsterman, Lucas, 208–9

Wales, 5–6, 88, 183
Waller, Edmund, 17, 20, 75, 166, 228, 251
Walwyn, William, 108
Watt, Tessa, 294
Wedgwood, C. V., 241
Weldon, Anthony, 243
Wentworth, Thomas, *see* Strafford, Earl of
Wentworth Woodhouse, 216
Westminster, 7, 222, 228, 241
Westminster Abbey, 15, 252, 302
Weston, Sir Richard, Earl of Portland, 74, 218
Westphalia, Peace of, 151

Wharton, Philip, Baron, 89, 228
Whigs, 268, 270, 275–7
Whitehall, 7, 8, 74, 98, 167, 176, 189, 212, 218,
    244, 251, 263
  Banqueting House, 2, 155, 163, 231
  Cabinet Room, 180, 187, 226
  Long Gallery, 228
William III, King of England and Scotland,
    247, 257, 263, 268–9
Wilson, John, 134–5
Winchester Cathedral, 218–19
Windsor, 88, 167, 241

Winstanley, Gerrard, 97, 108, 110–13
Wither, George, 96, 98–101, 104, 107
Wood, Anthony, 135
Woodington, John, 163, 164
Woodruffe, Benjamin, 302
Worcester, Battle of, 112
Wotton, Sir Henry, 19, 300
Wren, Sir Christopher, 74, 252–5, 302
Wriothesley, Henry, *see* Southampton, Earl of

York, 186, 297
Young, Thomas, 145–6